CORPORATE AND INSTITUTIONAL TRANSPARENCY FOR ECONOMIC GROWTH IN EUROPE

INTERNATIONAL BUSINESS AND MANAGEMENT

Series Editor: **Pervez N. Ghauri**

Published:

The Common Glue
Morosini

Non-Business Actors in a Business Network
Hadjikhani & Thilenius

European Union and the Race for Foreign Direct Investment in Europe
Oxelheim & Ghauri

Strategic Alliances in Eastern and Central Europe
Hyder & Abraha

Intellectual Property and Doing Business in China
Yang

Co-operative Strategies and Alliances
Contractor & Lorange

Relationships and Networks in International Markets
Gemünden, Ritter & Walter

International Business Negotiations
Ghauri & Usunier

Critical Perspectives on Internationalisation
Havila, Forsgren & Håkansson

Managing Cultural Differences
Morosini

Managing Networks in Transition Economics
Johanson

Network Dynamics in International Marketing
Naude & Turnbull

The Global Challenge for Multinational Enterprises
Buckley & Ghauri

Business Network Learning
Hakansson & Johanson

Managing International Business Ventures in China
Li

Other titles of interest:

International Trade in the 21st Century
Fatemi

Globalization, Trade and Foreign Direct Investment
Dunning

International Trade and the New Economic Order
Moncarz

Contemporary Issues in Commercial Policy
Kreinin

CORPORATE AND INSTITUTIONAL TRANSPARENCY FOR ECONOMIC GROWTH IN EUROPE

EDITED BY

LARS OXELHEIM
Lund University and the Research Institute of Industrial Economics (IUI), Sweden

United Kingdom – North America – Japan
India – Malaysia – China

Emerald Group Publishing Limited
Howard House, Wagon Lane, Bingley BD16 1WA, UK

Reprints and permission service
Contact: booksandseries@emeraldinsight.com

Printed and bound by CPI Group (UK) Ltd, Croydon, CR0 4YY

British Library Cataloguing in Publication Data
A catalogue record for this book is available from the British Library

ISBN: 978-0-08-044665-3
ISSN: 1876-066X (Series)

Contents

Contributors

Raj Aggarwal is the Firestone chair and professor of Finance at Kent State University, and he is a non-profit agency, and a corporate board member. Previously he has been the Mellen Chair at John Carroll and taught at Harvard, Hawaii, Michigan and South Carolina. He has authored over a dozen books and numerous papers, is a fellow of the Academy of International Business, has been ranked as the No. 1 international business professor by the *Journal of International Business Studies* (36#4), and also has been awarded a Fulbright Fellowship and university-wide Distinguished Scholar and Distinguished Faculty Awards. He is a chartered financial analyst (CFA).

Apanard (Penny) Angkinand is an assistant professor of Economics at the University of Illinois at Springfield. She received her PhD in economics from Claremont Graduate School in 2005 and was also a visiting scholar at Claremont Institute of Economic Policy Studies and the Freeman program in Asian Political Economy at the Claremont Colleges. Her current research projects include studying the effects of deposit insurance, bank regulation and crisis management policies on financial crises, and the relationship between the choice of exchange rate regimes and financial crises.

Söhnke M. Bartram is on the Finance faculty at Lancaster University Management School. His immediate research activities center around issues in international finance, corporate finance and financial markets, especially financial risk management. The US Federal Deposit Insurance Corporation, the PricewaterhouseCoopers Global Competency Centre, the Leverhulme Trust, the Institute for Quantitative Investment Research, Lancaster University, Lancaster University Management School, as well as the Maastricht Research School of Economics of Technology and Organizations granted financial support for his research activities in the area of international and corporate finance. In 2003, the Federation of European Securities Exchanges awarded the Joseph de la Vega Prize for his work on derivatives market microstructure. His work has been presented at conferences organized by the American Finance Association, the NBER and CEPR, and published among others in the *Journal of International Money and Finance, Journal of Emperical Finance, and European Finance Review.*

Iain Begg is a visiting professor at the European Institute, London School of Economics and Political Science. His main research work is on the political economy of European integration and he has directed a series of research projects on different facets of EU policy. This work includes studies of policy co-ordination under EMU, the EU budget and cohesion policy. He has published extensively on these topics and served as co-editor of the *Journal of Common Market Studies*, the leading academic journal focusing on the study of European integration, from 1998 to 2003.

Magnus Bild holds a PhD from Stockholm School of Economics. His research focuses on corporate takeovers and more specifically on their consequences for value creation. He is the founding and managing partner of Bild & Runsten, a Stockholm-based company specialized in financial training for executives and financial specialists.

Thomas L. Brewer is a professor at the McDonough School of Business, Georgetown University and an associate fellow at the Centre for European Policy Studies (CEPS) in Brussels. He specializes in issues associated with global warming/climate change, especially the political economy of the US responses to those issues and the nexus of international trade and climate change issues. His publications include several articles on those topics in the refereed journal, *Climate Policy*, and chapters in books published by Cambridge University Press and Elsevier. Professor Brewer has made presentations at conferences at the Royal Institute of International Affairs (Chatham House) in London, the CEPS in Brussels, the Economic and Social Research Institute (ESRI) in Tokyo, and the European Union, as well as Georgetown University, and other conferences for academic, business and government audiences. He is a former editor of the *Journal of International Business Studies*.

Jean-Pierre Casey is a research fellow at the Centre for European Policy Studies in Brussels. He is also directing the research program of the European Capital Markets Institute, a network for the production and dissemination of policy-oriented capital markets research. Jean-Pierre holds economics degrees from Georgetown University, the College of Europe in Bruges, Belgium and is currently involved in the research program at the Sorbonne. He has just completed a major study on European bond markets and his main field of interest includes the regulation and supervision of financial markets.

Andrew Delios (PhD, Richard Ivey School of Business) is an associate professor and head of the Department of Business Policy, NUS Business School, National University of Singapore. He is the author or co-author of more than 50 published journal articles, case studies and book chapters. His articles have appeared in journals such as the *Academy of Management Journal, Administrative Science Quarterly, Strategic Management Journal, Strategic Organization* and *Journal of International Business Studies.* He has authored five books including *International Business: An Asia-Pacific Perspective* (Pearson) and *Strategy for Success in Asia* (Wiley). He has written case studies and conducted research on companies in Canada, China, India, Italy, Hong Kong, Japan, Singapore and Vietnam. His research looks at foreign investment issues in emerging economies, particularly by Japanese multinationals, and the governance, strategy and performance of China's listed companies.

Jens Forssbæck is a researcher at the Institute of Economic Research, Lund University, and is affiliated to the Center for Law, Economics, and Financial Institutions (LEFIC) at Copenhagen Business School. His main research interests lie within the areas of international finance (particularly exchange rate economics and financial integration), and various micro- and macroeconomic aspects of financial markets and institutions. His publications in these areas include *Money Markets and Politics: A Study of European Financial Integration and Monetary Policy Options* (Cheltenham: Edward Elgar, 2003), and *On the link between exchange rate regimes, capital controls, and monetary policy autonomy in small European countries 1979–2000*, forthcoming in *The World Economy* (both with Lars Oxelheim).

Pervez N. Ghauri obtained his PhD from the Department of Business Studies, Uppsala University in Sweden where he also taught for some years. At present he is a professor of International Business at Manchester Business School, University of Manchester, UK. He has published more than 20 books and numerous journal articles on issues related to international business and marketing. He has worked as a consultant to UNCTAD, Airbus industries, Norwegian Export Council and the Ministry of Foreign Affairs in the Netherlands. He also holds an Honorary Doctor of Economics degree from Vaasa School of Management and Economics in Finland. Pervez Ghauri is the editor of *International Business Review.*

Philippe Gugler is a professor at the Department of Economic Policy, University of Fribourg, Switzerland, where he works on competition policy and competitiveness. He is a former director deputy of the Swiss competition authority. He is a guest professor at the University Institute of European Studies in Torino, Italy, at the World Trade Institute in Berne and at the International Institute of Management in Technology in Fribourg, Switzerland.

Amjad Hadjikhani is a professor of Marketing in the Department of Business studies at Uppsala University. He has published several books and numerous articles on international marketing, specifically on industrial and consumer marketing. His most recent book is *Non-Business Actors and Business Networks: The Case of International Firms in Interaction with Purchasers from Developing Countries* (Oxford: Elsevier, 2005) (with P. Thilenius).

Christina Håkanson is a researcher at the Department of Economics, Stockholm University. She is currently doing research in the fields of education, productivity and competition, and has recently finished an empirical assessment of productivity in different parts of the Swedish private sector. She contributed to the Swedish Government Official Report 2002:16 *Stabilisation Policy and the Monetary Union*, with a paper on employer-sponsored training in growth and stabilization policy perspectives (with Satu Johanson and Erik Mellander).

NyoNyo Aung Kyaw is an assistant professor of Finance at Iona College, New York. She earned her PhD in Finance from Kent State University in 2004, MA in Economics from Kent State University, MBA in International Business from Asian Institute of Technology (Bangkok) and a BBA in Finance from Assumption University. Her research interests include corporate finance, international corporate finance, capital structure and agency theory. She has published articles in the *International Review of Financial Analysis* and *Journal of Investing*.

Davide Lombardo is an economist at the International Monetary Fund (IMF). He obtained his PhD from Stanford, with a thesis on the effects of legal institutions on the workings of equity markets. His main interests are in the areas of public finance (including fiscal federalism and social security reform) and financial economics (corporate finance, banking, and law and finance).

Sarianna M. Lundan is an associate professor of International Business Strategy at the University of Maastricht. She received her doctorate from Rutgers University, and prior to her current appointment, she was a lecturer at the University of Reading. In addition to environmental issues, her current research is concerned with institutional factors in the relationship between FDI and growth, and the social returns to innovation in the pharmaceutical industry. She has published a number of research monographs and numerous articles in the area of international business.

Erik Mellander is acting director of the Institute for Labour Market Policy Evaluation (IFAU) in Uppsala, Sweden. He holds a PhD in economics from Uppsala University. His fields of research cover human capital issues, labor demand, production economics, and econometrics. The recent papers include *Human capital is the key to the IT productivity paradox*, IFAU WP 2004:13 (with G. Gunnarsson and E. Savvidou) and *Employer-sponsored training in stabilization and growth policy perspectives*, IFAU WP 2003:8 (with Christina Håkanson and Satu Johanson). He has also contributed to the Swedish government official reports on individual learning accounts and stabilization policy.

Ram Mudambi is an associate professor and Washburn research fellow in the Fox School of Business at Temple University, Philadelphia, USA. He holds a master's degree from the London School of Economics and a PhD from Cornell University. He has published over 50 peer-reviewed articles, including work in the *Strategic Management Journal and the Journal of International Business Studies*. He serves on the editorial boards of the *Journal of International Business Studies, the Asia Pacific Journal of Management* and the *Journal of International Management*. He is currently the book review editor of the *Journal of International Business Studies*. He has served as guest editor for the *International Business Review* and the *Journal of International Management.*

Pietro Navarra is a professor at the Institute of Economics and Finance, University of Messina. He holds a master's degree from the University of York and a PhD from the University of Buckingham. Pietro Navarra also serves as pro-rector of the University of Messina and as a research fellow at the London School of Economics, England. He has published over 25 peer-reviewed articles, including work in the *Journal of International Business Studies, Management International Review, Public Choice* and the *European Journal of Political Economy*, and has authored and edited several books.

Lars Oxelheim holds a chair in International Business and Finance at Lund University, Lund, and is an affiliate of the Research Institute of Industrial Economics (IUI), Stockholm and of the Fudan University, Shanghai. His current research focuses on the implications of macroeconomic disturbances for corporate performance and issues related to economic and financial integration. He has published some 25 books and numerous articles in the areas of international business and finance, corporate finance and corporate governance. Among his recent monographs are *Money Markets and Politics: A Study of European Financial Integration and Monetary Policy Options* (Cheltenham: Edward Elgar, 2003) (with Jens Forssbæck), *European Union and the Race for Foreign Direct*

Investment in Europe (Oxford: Elsevier, 2004) (co-edited/authored with Pervez Ghauri) and *Corporate Performance and the Exposure to Macroeconomic Fluctuations* (Stockholm: Norstedts Academic Publishers, 2005) (with Clas Wihlborg).

Marco Pagano is a professor of Economics at the University of Naples Federico II, research fellow of the Centre for Economic Policy Research, fellow of the European Economic Association and editor of the *Review of Finance.* Most of his work is in the area of financial economics, and specifically in market microstructure, banking, corporate finance, and law and finance. His publications have appeared in several journals, such as the *American Economic Review, Review of Economic Studies, Quarterly Journal of Economics, Journal of Finance, Review of Financial Studies, RAND Journal, Journal of the European Economic Association, European Economic Review* and *Economic Journal.*

Walter Schuster is Öhrlings Pricewaterhouse Coopers professor of Accounting and Auditing at the Stockholm School of Economics. He is a member of the Swedish Financial Accounting Standards Board and the International Accounting Standards Board/Financial Accounting Standards Board (US) joint working group on performance reporting. He is also a member of the Swedish Academy of Auditing. One of his special interests is group accounting. In this area he has published *Sweden — Group Accounts* (In D. Ordelheide, ed., *Transnational Accounting*, McMillan, 2nd ed., 2001) and *Group Accounting — an Analytical Approach* (Lund: Studentlitteratur, 2005).

Georg Stadtmann is an associate professor at the WHU – Otto Beisheim School of Management in Koblenz, Germany where he works at the Department of Economics. His main research interests lie within the areas of international finance. He has published in the field of market efficiency, central bank intervention, and expectation formation processes in financial markets. He is also a lecturer at the Leon Kozminski Academy of Entrepreneurship and Management in Warsaw (Poland).

Karin S. Thorburn is an associate professor of Finance and associate director of the Center for Corporate Governance at the Tuck School of Business at Dartmouth. She holds a bachelor's degree in Economics and a PhD in Financial Economics from the Stockholm School of Economics. Karin Thorburn's research focuses on takeovers, bankruptcy, corporate restructuring and corporate governance. Her work has been published in the top international academic finance journals, including *Journal of Financial Economics* and *Journal of Financial and Quantitative Analysis*. She is a member of the academic advisory council to the US Turnaround Management Association, research affiliate of the Center for Economic Policy Research (CEPR) in London, research associate of the European Corporate Governance Institute (ECGI) and associate editor of the *Journal of Corporate Finance*.

Clas Wihlborg is currently a visiting professor at the University of California, Riverside. He is a professor of Finance at the Copenhagen Business School (CBS) where he has been the director of the Center for Law, Economics and Financial Institutions at CBS (LEFIC) since 2002. Before taking up the position at CBS in 2000, he held positions at New York University and the University of Southern California in the US, and Gothenburg University in Sweden. He obtained his PhD in Economics in 1977 from Princeton University. His research and teaching activities have focused on international finance, corporate finance and financial institutions. He has published numerous articles in scientific journals and published a number of books, most recently *Corporate Performance and the Exposure to Macroeconomic Fluctuations* (Stockholm: Norstedts Academic Publishers, 2005) (with Lars Oxelheim). He is a member of the European Shadow Financial Regulatory Committee and the Royal Swedish Academy of Engineering Sciences (IVA).

Markus F. Wissmann is a researcher at the WHU – Otto Beisheim School of Management in Koblenz, Germany where conducts his work in the Group of Research in Industrial Dynamics (GRID). He studied business administration at the University in Essen (Germany) and University College Dublin (Ireland). He holds a master degree in business and worked in an international auditing company for several years. Recently, he finished his German tax consultant diploma. He is an expert in international Corporate Governance issues as well as German tax laws.

Preface

'Transparency' has become a catchword in the European growth debate. However, transparency as a concept is multidimensional as well as multifunctional. In the debate, the concept is used without much clarity about what dimension is used and what function it is supposed to play. Hence, the debate as such could be said to lack in transparency. Moreover, the long and winding road that supposedly binds together improved transparency in Europe and increased economic growth in the region has never been mapped out in a coherent way. The reason for this is simply the fact that the causal chain from transparency to growth needs to be discussed in a comprehensive, interdisciplinary way, incorporating different research areas and traditions — from accounting to economics and political science.

The interdisciplinary approach required for a proper analysis of the multifaceted concept of transparency makes most traditional scientific journals less well fitted as outlets for the results of such an analysis. This motivates why the results are here presented in the form of a book. The process behind the book was similar to that behind refereed journals. Following presentation of the main ideas of the project along the lines now appearing in Chapter 1, a number of research teams were invited to contribute and to address different aspects of transparency in a European economic growth perspective. First, drafts were delivered to a workshop held at Trolleholm Castle in the south of Sweden in February 2005. Each contribution was refereed by three referees; two of the other contributors to the book and by me, and then discussed at a seminar during the three-day meeting where the appointed referees acted as discussants. A second draft of each chapter was discussed at the annual European integration conference of the Swedish Network for European Studies in Economics and Business (SNEE) in Mölle in May 2005. Also on this occasion, each contribution had an appointed discussant. A third draft was then delivered to me by the end of August 2005 for final editing.

My greatest gratitude now goes to all those who have contributed different chapters and participated in the Trolleholm workshop and the Mölle conference. I am grateful for their efforts and their open and constructive attitudes in working with their own chapters, but also in reading and commenting on the other contributions.

I am also most thankful to SNEE for providing necessary support, particularly for the three-day workshop at Trolleholm. SNEE's support made it possible to bring together scholars from different countries and to develop this network of colleagues doing research on European transparency issues.

Finally, I want to express my thanks to Jens Forssbæck for valuable input and help with the editorial work and to Hannah Collett, Elsevier Oxford, for her very professional assistance in getting this project off the ground.

Lars Oxelheim

Outline of the book

The purpose of this book is to explore transparency in Europe in three main areas: in economic policy, in the corporate sector, and in the institutional and regulatory structures surrounding the markets. These three different areas are obviously not independent of each other—on the contrary there is a complex interplay between the three. What constitutes feasible or appropriate economic policies is dependent on both corporate behavior and the existing institutional framework. Business decisions rely both on present and likely future economic policies and on the incentives given by the institutions in place. Institutions and regulatory structures, finally, are products of the past and present policies and corporate structures.

The book addresses transparency as a condition for economic growth in general, with emphasis on the significance of transparency for finance and investment decisions. The underlying basic idea is that increased transparency increases the efficiency of resource allocation, thus raises the level of potential growth. In the context of European integration, increased transparency is possibly achieved by the dynamic of the integration process itself, but at the institutional and policy levels, it must be achieved by a combination of harmonization and policy competition and regulatory arbitrage. This line of reasoning implies a basic cost-of-capital framework of analysis, and a focus on the supply side of the economy, while relatively less attention will be paid in this book to the demand side (such as cross-national differences in consumer tastes and behavior). The focus on Europe is important because of the particular significance of transparency in the process of integration between different (national/regional) corporate and institutional structures.

The complex interaction between the three main levels of transparency (corporate, institutional and policy) and the cross-border dimension added through the focus on European integration gives rise to a multitude of possible concrete research questions, of which a single volume only can address a few. We here summarize the contributions to the present volume chapterwise.

In Chapter 1, a conceptual framework for the multidimensional analysis of transparency is outlined. Forssbæck and Oxelheim start out by summarizing findings about the link from savings over capital allocation and real investment to economic growth. They proceed to discuss the elements of transparency, nail down five important dimensions of this concept and determine the position of these dimensions of transparency in the chain between savings and growth. They go on to discuss consequences of deviation from 'optimal transparency' in terms of a risk premium charged by agents exposed to missing pieces of information. Hence, the working hypothesis for the book generated in this chapter is that the suboptimal transparency feeds into a risk premium that increases the cost of capital and ultimately has a negative effect on real investment and economic growth. The chapter provides an example to illustrate the causal chain: transparency $\Uparrow \rightarrow$ risk premium $\Downarrow \rightarrow$ cost of capital $\Downarrow \rightarrow$ real investment $\Uparrow \rightarrow$ economic growth $\Uparrow$.

Iain Begg focuses in Chapter 2 on a vital dimension of transparency intimately linked to economic policy: central bank transparency. He emphasizes that in the mid-2000s most central banks regard transparency as an important part of their toolkit for the conduct of monetary policy, because they recognize that what the central bank says, as well as what it does, can affect expectations and the transmission mechanism, with implications for the yield curve. The chapter explores the reasons for transparency and the different forms it takes in central banking, and how the use of communication can affect the cost of capital. It examines the approach to transparency of the European Central Bank and compares it with other central banks, then considers whether that approach is well conceived.

In Chapter 3 Philippe Gugler discusses the role of transparent competition policies. He analyzes the effect of transparency in competition policy enforcement upon the efficiency of firms. The first part discusses the role of transparency on the effectiveness of the competition agency as well as on the protection, the re-establishment and the promotion of competition. The second part examines this issue within the EU with respect to its new competition policy regime, which entered into force on May 1, 2004: the Regulation 1/2003 as well as the new EC merger control regulation (ECMR). The third part focuses on the international dimension of competition policy transparency, concentrating on multi-jurisdictional mergers.

Thomas Brewer and Sarianna Lundan, in Chapter 4, examine the impact of the EU's environmental policy on firms at three related levels: the supranational/regional level, the national level and the local level. At each policy level, they identify the sources of uncertainty, the available means to mitigate the uncertainty, and the role of corporate and regulatory transparency in meeting the policy goals, as well as in influencing the economic cost. They also distinguish between procedural and substantive transparency in connection with investment uncertainty that results from a lack of transparency. In an era that favors market-based implementation of regulations over command-and-control systems, the participation of large firms in the policy process is indispensable, and they stress that the issues of uncertainty and transparency are central to determining the firms' level of participation.

The lack of transparency in EU countries' education policies is the topic of Chapter 5. Erik Mellander and Christina Håkanson emphasize human capital as a crucial driver of economic growth. This makes transparency with respect to the EU human capital policy a vital issue. They distinguish between two aspects on policy transparency. The first concerns the *formulation* of the human capital policy, as expressed by the objectives regarding education and training that have been agreed upon within the Lisbon strategy. Here, transparency means that the policy is consistent and well defined. The second aspect concerns the *implementation* of this policy, by individual member states. Transparency with respect to implementation can differ substantially across states, due to the fact that the EU human capital policy is governed by the open method of coordination (OMC). In their empirical analysis, they first consider whether supplementing traditional "best-practice" objectives by objectives in the form of lower bounds on achievement can increase transparency. Secondly, they suggest a method for measuring transparency with respect to overall performance. To assess the practical importance of these two issues, they construct quantitative indicators for all of the objectives of the EU human capital policy. They find that for only one third of the 25 member states transparency is high with respect to overall performance. In contrast, for two-thirds of the member states, rankings will be very unstable. This sensitivity is due to uneven performance across targets. Moreover, they conclude that the use of lower bounds objectives has not had the desired effect. On the contrary, less transparency has resulted; due to the impossibility to impose sanctions on non-compliers under the OMC, the additional objectives have increased the room for maneuvering, instead of reducing it.

The design of the bankruptcy code determines the magnitude of different costs imposed on financially distressed firms and the transparency of the restructuring procedure to debt holders. In Chapter 6, Karin Thornburn analyzes how both these dimensions spill over to the cost of capital and further into investment in accordance with the causal chain outlined in Chapter 1. The costs include direct costs for formal proceedings, and inefficiencies caused by suboptimal allocation of assets and distorted investment incentives prior to filing. The chapter characterizes the bankruptcy regimes in the UK, France, Germany and Sweden. The creditor-friendly systems in the UK and Sweden have been warned to force asset sales at depressed prices and induce managers to delay filing while engaging in value-destroying risk-shifting activities. The French code, on the other hand, eliminates creditor influence over a reorganization procedure aimed at preserving employment opportunities. In Germany, firms have a three-month window to reorganize. Extant empirical evidence suggests that the Swedish auction system and the UK contract-based system have relatively low costs. The French and German systems, on the other hand, fail to successfully reorganize distressed firms and are much less transparent. This raises concerns with current reform efforts aimed at strengthening the reorganization provisions in European countries.

Since 2001 the regulatory framework for financial services has been fundamentally re-drawn at the EU level. In Chapter 7, Jean-Pierre Casey focuses on how one of the central pillars of economic governance, namely, transparency, can contribute to higher rates of economic growth in Europe by fostering better governance of the financial sector EU-wide and a smoother functioning of the internal market for financial services within the new regulatory structure. He emphasizes that transparency in the transposition of EU laws by national legislatures as well as in the exercise of discretion by national supervisory authorities in their oversight of banks, investment firms and insurance firms, is critical in a regulatory–supervisory framework as complicated, and relying so heavily on decentralized implementation and enforcement, as that of the EU. How transparent these processes are rendered will very likely affect the degree to which rules underpinning the internal market are uniform, and to what extent EU member states play by the rules.

The financial dimension is also the focus of Chapter 8. In this chapter, Apanard Angkinand and Clas Wihlborg focus on insolvency procedures and market discipline in European banking. They argue that market discipline in banking requires that explicit and implicit insurance schemes for financial sector firms are limited, and that the lack of insurance of important stakeholders is credible. This credibility cannot be achieved without transparent, predictable procedures for distress resolution for banks, including explicit rules for the liquidation of insolvent banks. They find that very few European countries have explicit procedures for dealing with problem banks. The propositions tested in Chapter 8 are that the credibility of non-insurance in European banking depends strongly on (1) the degree of coverage of deposit insurance schemes and (2) on the existence of enforceable rules that enhance the credibility of non-insurance of groups of stakeholders. The proxy used for credibility of non-insurance in Europe is the probability of banking crisis. Finding a U-shaped relation between the probability of banking crisis and the coverage of explicit deposit insurance they derive the degree of coverage that minimizes the probability of crisis in Western and Eastern Europe.

Recent research documents that better legal institutions are associated with broader equity markets. In Chapter 9, Davide Lombardo and Marco Pagano discuss how the legal system can affect the cost of capital for firms, and hence their real investment behavior. They ask if differences in institutions can explain cross-country differentials in expected returns? They present a model in which legal variables affect both the demand for, and the supply of, equity and show that if international markets are integrated, the correlation between institutional quality and equilibrium returns should be zero or negative. Empirically, they document instead a robust positive correlation. These findings are consistent with the joint hypothesis that equity markets are segmented and that the law affects equilibrium returns mainly via its effects on the supply of equity.

In Chapter 10, Magnus Bild and Walter Schuster discuss corporate transparency from an accounting perspective. They analyze the consequences for corporate transparency of the European adoption of International Financial Reporting Standards (IFRSs), considering the effects both in terms of an individual standard and in terms of the whole set of IFRSs. Looking at the standard on business combinations, they find no empirical evidence of reduced transparency. Analyzing the standard's effects on net income and relating these to the financial outcomes of takeovers, Bild and Schuster see a risk of negative consequences on resource allocation. Looking at the whole set of IFRSs, and considering the processes of preparation and use of accounting information, they argue that it is not clear that transparency will increase.

Chapter 11 investigates how the Sarbanes-Oxley Act (SOX) impacted corporate transparency in the statutory risk disclosure of European private issuers listed in the United States. Söhnke Bartram, Georg Stadtmann and Markus Wissmann examine in this chapter whether SOX is complementary to and consistent with the existing national standards that foreign issuers have to comply with in addition to SOX. Furthermore, they elaborate on the perceived cost and benefits of the Act for cross-listed companies. Since the introduction of SOX, a significant decrease in the share of foreign companies in new listings, as well as discussions by a substantial number of companies and lobbying institutions about the conditions for a delisting/deregistration, indicate a decline in the attractiveness of the US capital markets due to the new regulation. In support of this conjecture, results from a questionnaire-based survey suggest that the introduction of the SOX made the US financial market less attractive to currently cross-listed European companies as well as potential new European issuers.

Controlling for relevant firm, industry and national variables, Chapter 12 documents the impact of disclosure standards on corporate capital structures in 14 European countries. Raj Aggarwal and NyoNyo Aung Kyaw report in this chapter that transparency that reduces owner–manager agency costs, such as higher levels of accounting disclosures, better financial governance, audit intensity and enforcement of anti-insider trading laws, are all negatively associated with corporate debt levels. In contrast, transparency that helps creditors control operating risks (and wealth transfers from creditors to owners), such as disclosure timeliness, institutional trading and media coverage, are positively associated with corporate debt levels.

In Chapter 13, Amjad Hadjikhani and Pervez Ghauri focus on the link between transparency and the influence by particular economic interests over political decision-making. In particular they discuss transparency issues related to the interaction between multinational enterprises (MNEs) and the European Union (EU). Using network theory, the chapter develops a theoretical view and aims to augment knowledge on firms' political activities. This is done through studying lobbying activities of MNEs that are directed toward influencing decision-making in the EU. This has become connected to two fundamental variables, namely commitment and knowledge. The chapter divides the MNEs' networking activities into the two interconnected business and political markets. Firms' lobbying activities in the political market are introduced as an essential part, which subsidizes the business market and improves the firm's market position. The empirical part contains a study of these two types of activities of four Swedish MNEs in the EU market. The authors try to understand how these firms manage their political relationships with politicians in the EU and whether they are able to influence political decisions. The outcome of the analysis reveals that MNEs proactively try to influence these decisions before they are made in the European market.

Finally, in Chapter 14, Andrew Delios, Ram Mudambi and Pietro Navarra discuss corruption as a special dimension of lack of transparency. Prior research has pointed to both positive and negative influences of levels of corruption on levels of foreign direct investment (FDI) inflows. It has been argued that corruption can be an efficient response to a slow and cumbersome bureaucracy. On the other hand, corruption increases the uncertainty associated with an investment opportunity, which raises the cost of capital. The authors investigate this question in the context of FDI into Europe. They find that both aggregate world FDI inflows as well as subsidiary establishments by Japanese firms were not sensitive to the level of corruption in a European economy. Instead, the level of government effectiveness was the element of the institutional environment most closely tied to FDI inflows. Thus, the influence of corruption on FDI inflows needs to be considered in the broader context of a nation's institutions.

Chapter 1

Transparency, Capital Formation, and Economic Growth

Jens Forssbæck and Lars Oxelheim

1.1 Introduction

'Transparency' has become something of a buzzword in the economic-political debate in recent years. The reasons are manifold, but a series of 'big events' and broad trends have been instrumental in bringing the role of transparency in business, economics, and politics to the fore.

In the business world, a series of corporate scandals has spawned interest in and attention to corporate governance, conflicts of interest between different stakeholder groups in the firm, and the importance of corporate financial transparency. These events have manifested themselves, e.g., in the invocation of new corporate governance codes, disclosure rules for publicly traded firms, or similar regulation, in many countries — notably the Sarbanes-Oxley Act (SOX) in the US and the EU's Transparency Directive. In many ways, the starting signal was the series of financial crises in emerging market economies in the mid-1990s — not least the Asian financial crises in 1997–1998, which to many commentators were significantly consequences of opaque corporate structures, weak institutions, and resulting moral hazard problems (see, e.g., the Economist, 1998a, 2001a). More recent still was the unraveling, seemingly, of case after case of fraudulent mismanagement of large corporations both stateside and in continental Europe (Enron, Tyco, WorldCom, Parmalat, Ahold, etc.).

In the macroeconomic policy debate, a more or less universal trend toward more rule-based stabilization policies has incited a wide concern with the transparency of

Corporate and Institutional Transparency for Economic Growth in Europe

ISBN: 0-08-044665-5

economic policy, and of the institutions that execute it. The concern has been raised both from the point of view of the efficiency of policy, and from that of democratic accountability. In particular, the debate has been motivated by the increased prevalence, globally, of politically independent central banks, conducting monetary policy 'apolitically' in accordance with some pre-specified rule or target, and their increased inclination and need to effectively signal their policy stance through more or less elaborate communication strategies (see, e.g., the Economist, 1999, 2003; Dow, Klaes, & Montagnoli, 2005). However, the debate has also included fiscal policy rules (see Kopits & Symansky, 1998). Transparency has also been emphasized as a driver of growth in the EU's *Lisbon process* with its use of benchmarks.

In politics and regulatory affairs, more generally, increasingly internationalized economies have resulted in a correspondingly increased role of multilevel, supranational governance, which in turn, has put the search light on traditional inter-governmental decision processes based on the strict sovereignty of nation states, and raised calls for more transparency and accountability. Part of the criticism raised against multilateral bodies, such as the IMF and the WTO, also rests on such perceived lack of transparency and legitimacy of the decision processes—points which have resounded well beyond the crowds of Seattle, Genova, Göteborg, or Hong Kong (see, e.g., the Economist, 1998b). The same issues have been raised against the EU.

Another broad set of reasons for the increasing interest in transparency has to do with the transparency of the markets for goods and services, and two 'events' have triggered the interest: the emergence of 'the new economy,' the 'information society,' and of e-commerce toward the late 1990s, and the launch of stage 3 of the EMU in 1999. Both events were expected to do much the same thing: increase price transparency, thereby boosting competition and greatly enhancing the efficiency of exchange, both at the retail and at the intermediary levels (see, e.g., the Cecchini Report, 1988; the Economist, 1998c, 2001b, c, 2004).

It is not immediately clear from these various but related debates what exactly transparency means. It is something mostly good—that is clear—and has to do with openness, information (accessibility), communication, etc. The take on 'transparency' from the perspective of *economics research* similarly feeds on different, but related, sources and research traditions. Also within political science there is an interest in transparency—primarily from the point of view of democratic accountability (see, e.g., Keohane & Nye, 2000, 2001), but that is a perspective which we shall not pursue here; instead, the focus of interest will be the analysis of effects of transparency on economic growth.

The use of the word 'transparency' in economic research has gained momentum during the last two decades. It is tempting to relate this phenomenon to the spectacular development of information technologies in the same period. One way to illustrate the prominent role 'transparency' has received is to search for the word in the abstracts of the National Bureau of Economic Research (NBER) working papers (WPs). Such a search yields two main conclusions:

1) It is a recent thing to be interested in transparency. Out of the 32 papers featuring the word 'transparency' in the abstract, 23 were issued in 2000 or later (for the total number of WPs, the corresponding share is about 35%); 31 were written in 1995 or later; there is no observation before 1993 (whereas the very first NBER WP was issued in 1973).
2) The search confirms the diversity of 'takes' on transparency in the research. Out of the 54 observations on research area (several papers indicate more than one), 31% is in monetary economics, 24% in international finance, 15% in general macroeconomics and economic growth, 11% in corporate finance, and the remainder scattered between public economics, international trade, asset pricing, and labor economics.

Any theory that incorporates the idea of asymmetrically distributed information between different economic agents implicitly makes an assumption about transparency, and is potentially affected by altered assumptions about it. The concept of agency costs in firms seeking financing, the idea of the central bank signaling its intentions, the perceived need for checks and balances in politics in order to avoid corruption, etc. are all based on the notion that rational, self-interested individuals — when equipped with information that others do not have — will make economic decisions that result in inefficiencies, market failures, or at the very least outcomes that are *different* (and typically 'worse') as compared to the full-information Arrow–Debreu world.

The purpose of this chapter is to present a conceptual framework which attempts to unify the main 'takes' on transparency extant in the literature and their link through the economy's capital formation process, and thereby through the investment channel of economic growth. The conceptual framework identifies the main actors and their points of information exchange, and boils down to a cost of capital/exchange efficiency approach to 'transparency.' This perspective on transparency also allows a discussion of the costs and gains of transparency, thereby introducing the possibility of discussing the link between maximum efficiency and optimal transparency.

The chapter is organized in the following way. In Section 1.2, we review the literature and suggest a framework for analyzing the link between transparency and economic growth. In Section 1.3, we discuss transparency in an EU context, whereas in Section 1.4, we elaborate on the existence of 'optimal' transparency. An example of the link between transparency and economic growth is outlined in Section 1.5. Section 1.6 concludes the chapter.

1.2 Growth, Capital, and Transparency: Main Insights from the Literature and a Framework

This section begins with a short recap of main 'traditions' within the literature on economic growth. The review results in the conclusion that human and tangible capital accumulation, as the result of deliberate investment decisions, is a robust source of long-run economic growth, whether neoclassical, endogenous, or institutional views of growth are used. We go on to explore the role of transparency at different levels for investment activity. We incorporate such factors as corporate financial transparency, legal factors, and political risk into our conceptual framework.

1.2.1 Theories of Growth and Investment

Roughly, three main strands of literature on economic growth can be identified: the neoclassical; endogenous, or 'new growth' theory; and the institutional school. In terms of chronology, we might (still roughly) say that endogenous growth theory picks up where the neoclassical tradition leaves off, and the institutional view runs parallel to these two. It is not our purpose here to discuss these approaches to economic growth and their differences in any more detail than necessary to establish some common ground and to understand the role of investment for economic growth (for a very good overview of neoclassical and endogenous growth theory, see Mankiw, 1995; Matthews, 1986, similarly provides one for institutional economics as applied to economic growth). The conceptual framework we present in the following is essentially compatible with any of these approaches with the possible exception of the neoclassical assumption of exogenous technological change.

The neoclassical tradition is usually traced back to Solow (1956). The theory is built around a basic production function of capital and labor, and emphasizes the role of (physical) capital accumulation for long-run economic development. Its large impact depended on a combination of simplicity, richness of predictions, and the close correspondence of those predictions with actual growth patterns in the United States during a period of time.

The theory has some problems, however. First and foremost of these, perhaps—for the purpose at hand, but also from an epistemological and normative point of view—is its determinism. The economy approaches the steady state regardless of initial conditions and of economic activities; all interesting economic outcomes (such as the steady-state income level, capital accumulation rate, and growth rate) are ultimately exogenously determined; in particular, the sustainable growth rate of per capita income is determined only by the exogenously given rate of technological change; and so on. The questions of what drives growth and what we can do to stimulate growth are answered by a question mark and a 'nothing,' to put it harshly. Another problem is the model's 'out-of-sample' performance—i.e., its inability to reasonably predict or explain cross-sectional variations in, e.g., income levels or returns on capital, particularly differences between rich and poor countries.

Later versions of the neoclassical model (see, e.g., Lucas, 1988) largely come to terms with these empirical problems, significatively by expanding the definition of 'capital' to incorporate also human capital and 'capital accumulation' to include investments in human capital (schooling, on the job training, etc.). Endogenous, or 'new growth' theory, attributable primarily to Romer (1986, 1990), equally places much more emphasis than Solow-type models on the expansion of knowledge as a source of growth, but—more significantly still—drops the assumption of exogenous technological change (hence *endogenous* growth), and tones down the more 'fatalistic' features of the neoclassical model (in particular the idea of convergence toward the steady state). The upshot is that economic growth is driven primarily by technological improvements resulting from conscious investments in knowledge, that such investments do not exhibit diminishing returns, and that—as a consequence—the model is better able to explain persistence in income differences across countries and over time (because there is no 'automatic' incentive to transfer capital from rich to poor countries).

The role of institutions for long-run economic performance can easily be traced back to Joseph Schumpeter, and possibly further, but is in its modern incarnation often associated with North (1990), among others. The more precise role of institutions in the 'mechanics' of growth, however, is not entirely clear—largely because of the differing methodological traditions of this school of thought. In theory, the strongest argument for inferring institutions as a factor for economic growth is to say that institutions, while necessary for economic exchange in various forms, can exhibit varying degrees of efficiency. Less efficient institutions correspond to higher transaction costs, and so are a burden on the gains of exchange. Institutional improvements and innovations will then raise the efficiency of economic interaction between agents, and so increase growth. Matthews (1986) makes the rather compelling analogy of institutional change with technological change as sources of growth: transaction costs and production costs are two pieces of a pie—both inescapable realities of economic activity—and innovations that decrease either type of cost for a given level of output are innovations with potential to raise the growth rate. We may then work our way from new legislation down to organizational changes within individual firms as 'institutional' sources of growth.

While theory thus emphasizes the *dynamic* aspect of institutions, the empirical literature typically makes indirect inferences about the effects of institutional improvements through cross-sectional studies of the '*level*' of institutions and their association with average growth rates and/or income levels (with some success; see, e.g., Barro, 1991, 1997; Rodrik, Subramanian, & Trebbi, 2004). The most probable reason for this is the difficulty of operationalizing institutional *change*. The porous nature of the concept of institutions also presents problems when it comes to taking theory to the data. With regard to the role of institutions for economic growth we may then summarize with the conclusion that there seems to be a consensus that institutions do matter, but uncertainty about exactly which institutions matter, and how.

The three main approaches to economic growth are not entirely distinct; for example, as observed by Mankiw (1995), endogenous growth theory can in some ways be seen as a 'limiting case' of the basic neoclassical model; Solow characterizes his model as a 'tightrope' model of economic development whose general layout purposely ignores some certain well-known facts of life which can be interpreted as effects of institutions (for instance, labor market rigidities); all three approaches are to some extent historically conditioned; etc.

In more empirically or practically oriented applications, the three approaches often more or less mesh together. For instance, the World Economic Forum, in their Growth Competitiveness Index (see Blanke, Paua, & Sala-i-Martin, 2003), identify as the 'key underpinnings' of growth the following three factors: the stability of the macroeconomic environment, the quality of institutions, and improvements in technology, where the former two are subject to diminishing returns whereas the third is not, suggesting this latter factor as the key one for developed countries with stable macroeconomic policies and high-quality institutions, such as the (Western) European economies. There are, however, interactions between these key determinants of growth rather than strict additivity, according to this view.

The assumed interactivity between these factors, the assumed diminishing returns to improving 'institutions' (we will, from now on frequently talk of 'institutions' in a broad sense which encapsulates the macroeconomic policy environment), and the empirical complications with dynamic institutions, suggest to us that rather than viewing institutions as a fundamental source of economic growth, one might more appropriately—at least for the time being—keep viewing them as an exogenous factor. Institutions are the '*rules* of the game' (a turn of phrase frequently made use of by institutionalists, including North, 1990 and Frey, 1990) or else the organizational structure of the economy—from firms to governments and bureaucracies (definitions are from Frey, 1990)—and may be one factor influencing the outcome of economic activity, but ever so efficient institutions will not propel growth if there is no economic activity (i.e., if there is no 'game' under the rules).

If this premise is accepted, then the significant insight from this (admittedly overly cursory) review of the growth literature, is that the main engine of growth is technological change resulting from 'intentional actions taken by people who respond to market incentives' (Romer, 1990, p. 72)—in other words, growth is driven by rational (human and/or physical capital) investment decisions by private agents who are motivated by expected profits. The outcome of these decisions, as—indeed—the decisions themselves, may be influenced by the institutional environment in which they were made (Oxelheim, 1996), but the growth engine is a result of the investment activity as such. Below, we will conceptualize this issue in a simple framework.

1.2.2 Framework for Analyzing the Link between Transparency and Growth

Let us assume a production function of a basic and unspecified form, $Y = F(K, L)$, where Y denotes production, L labor, and K the stock of physical and human capital (including knowledge more generally). We can then write the rate of human and physical capital accumulation at a moment in time as $\dot{K}$. Suppose this rate is 'fundamentally' driven by the function G on a set of variables, X. The outcome of G on $\dot{K}$ is further influenced by the institutional environment (broadly construed, e.g., including the macroeconomic policy mix), described by H. The basic expression $\dot{K} = H(G(X))$ then describes the capital formation process.[1]

A simple way to characterize the *efficiency* of the capital formation process is to add to this function a random term, ε, let us say, with positive (structural over-investment), negative (structural under-investment) or zero mean, which describes what share of aggregate productive investment is *not* determined by rational economic decisions (i.e., aggregate deviation from the optimal level of investment given X). Its first and second moments can be interpreted as different measures of the (in)efficiency of the capital formation process. We have

$$\dot{K} = H(G(X) + \varepsilon) \tag{1.1}$$

i.e., institutions may influence capital formation efficiency as well, but not all such inefficiencies are attributable to institutions: underdeveloped capital markets, for

[1]If we believe that institutions have no essential effect, as in the 'hardline' neoclassical case, then H is trivial, for example, $H(\cdot) = 1 \times (\cdot)$; in other words, this unspecified mapping can harbor any theory of economic growth we might subscribe to.

instance — which can, in turn, be a consequence of poor institutions — may also have a detrimental effect on the efficiency of this process (as in, e.g., Wurgler, 2000; see further below).

From this simple basic framework, we get two main possible channels through which 'transparency' can affect productive investment $\dot{K}$, and thereby economic growth: at the level of institutions (again, we talk of 'institutions' in a broad sense here, including macroeconomic policies affecting business decisions), captured by H; and at the level where investment decisions are being made — which ultimately boils down to the level of corporations and the markets where they raise funding for their investment projects — captured by ε.

To make things a little more concrete, we refer to Figure 1.1. It describes the main steps of the mechanism through which income not consumed (i.e., savings) is channeled through the financial system to the investments that foment economic growth. It also identifies the main actors in this process and their points of information exchange, where arrows in the uppermost part of the figure signify the level at which corporate-level transparency enters the equation (through ε), arrows in the lower part of the figure signify the level at which the institutional level of transparency enters the equation (through H), and the arrow linking these two levels signifies the interaction between the corporate and institutional levels (the effect of H on ε).

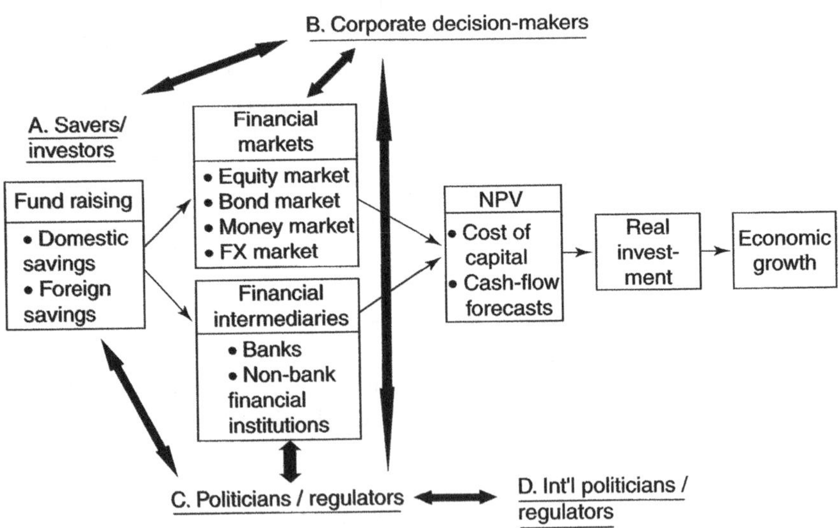

Figure 1.1: Transparency in the capital formation process.

1.2.3 Corporate- and Market-Level Transparency/Efficiency of Capital Allocation

There is reason to halt for a moment at the consideration of the role of the financial system, given the large recent literature[2] that has emerged linking economic growth to financial development. We might start at reflecting for a bit, as does Levine (1997), of why financial systems exist at all. Levine holds that the basic *raison d'être* of financial markets and institutions is to overcome otherwise unbearable transaction and information costs, and that in emerging to reduce such costs, 'financial systems serve one primary function: they facilitate the allocation of resources, across space and time, in an uncertain environment' (p. 691). Levine goes on to break down this primary function further and exploring its effect on growth through two main channels: capital accumulation and technological innovation.

Pagano (1993) similarly provides a motivation for the link between financial development and growth in the context of an endogenous growth model, attractive in its succinctness and simplicity. Here, financial development can have an (usually positive) effect on growth first through the saving rate,[3] second by more efficiently channeling savings to firms (a smaller fraction of savings is 'lost' on the way through the financial system to their ultimate destinations), and finally by raising capital allocation efficiency. This highlights steps 1–3 (seen as columns) of Figure 1.1. Each step and each aspect of transparency animated by it open up a multitude of research questions and sometimes a massive body of literature (such as transparency aspects of corporate governance or the role of information asymmetries in corporate finance topics more generally). Here we can only give some suggestive hints, and our purpose does not anyway extend beyond illustrating how many different aspects of transparency can be fitted into our unified framework.

In the first step, the propensity to save is potentially affected by a number of transparency-related issues, such as savers' confidence in the banking system (including banking regulation and supervision), and the ability of the financial system to channel savings onto productive investment that yields returns commensurate with savers' attitude toward risk.[4] The transparency of

[2]Early contributions to the study of the relationship between financial markets and the real side of the economy include Galbraith (1955), Temin (1976), Minsky (1982, 1986), Blanchard and Watson (1982), Shiller (1984), Oxelheim (1990), and Gertler, Hubbard, and Kashyap (1991). An early paper in the recent 'wave' is King and Levine (1993).

[3]This effect is ambiguous without further assumptions than those made in Pagano (1993).

[4]The saving ratio is of course also influenced by transparency issues related to legal institutions, macroeconomic policies, etc.

financial intermediaries here enter as a partial determinant of capital allocation and credit availability; but there is also a link to institutional/regulatory transparency through the importance of such transparency for the possibility of markets to discipline banks' risk behavior, and thereby for the efficient exertion of bank supervision.

This brings us to the second step, where the net fraction of savings absorbed by the financial system can be interpreted as a measure of efficiency of the financial system: any amount beyond payment for services rendered to savers are rents due to monopolistic market power or other market imperfections. Transparency here enters primarily through competition: How transparent is the pricing of financial services? How are buyers of financial services able to assess and compare the quality and price of financial services?

The third step relates to capital allocation efficiency—i.e., the mechanism through which economic growth is an effect of the increased productivity of capital. This step puts emphasis on the ability of the financial system to direct savings to the best investment projects, and in so doing stresses the function of the financial system as an arena for the sharing of information on available investment projects, but also on the information function in terms of *evaluation* of these projects. As an arena for information, (developed) financial systems thus help to alleviate problems of financing stemming from informational asymmetries, such as moral hazard and adverse selection. These functions are filled primarily by the pricing mechanism: the alleviation of information asymmetries reduces premiums on firms' cost of capital stemming from such asymmetries (agency costs, for instance); moreover, in efficient and transparent financial markets the information content impounded in the prices of various assets is high, which in turn facilitates efficient resource allocation.[5]

To the extent that financial development is associated with more *efficient* financial markets (in particular efficient pricing by virtue of a large *depth* of these markets), it is therefore also associated with higher growth rates, *ceteris paribus*. Financial development (in particular, with regards to the *width* of markets) also implies a higher ability to handle high-risk (and high-yield) projects, and, as a consequence, a higher ability to finance investment projects that represent large technological breakthroughs.

---

[5]The information—and thus the transparency—dimension of financial and credit market efficiency has been understood and researched for at least a quarter century; for instance, Grossman and Stiglitz (1980) showed that the equilibrium price in a market reveals most of the better-informed traders' information only if information is very inexpensive or precise, but that this is unlikely to occur; Stiglitz and Weiss (1981) showed that lenders' lack of information about borrowers can lead to credit rationing and thus inefficient capital allocation.

A large body of empirical literature has emerged during the last 10-year period or so, exploring primarily the capital allocation aspect of financial development over a number of overlapping and mutually non-exclusive mechanisms. A far from exhaustive sample is provided below to illustrate the above points. Most of these (as an illustration, perhaps, of the conceptual complexity and disarray in the area)—although they do not always directly test the transparency effect/information function of financial markets—use measures of corporate or financial market transparency (such as accounting standards), and sometimes also institutional transparency measures, directly or indirectly as indicators of financial development.

A benchmark result bearing on several of the factors/functions just mentioned is provided by Rajan and Zingales (1998), who test the hypothesis that industries more in need of external financing grow faster in countries with a higher degree of financial development on a large number of industries in 41 countries during the 1980s. They find this to be the case. With the auxiliary hypothesis that industries most in need of external financing (such as R&D-intensive industries) are also those with the greatest potential for faster technological progress, their result can also be interpreted along the lines that financial development leads to higher economic growth by facilitating technological progress. A related result comes from Svaleryd and Vlachos (2005), who treat financial development as a factor in the production of goods and services—an endowment. They show that, owing to the relative immobility of financial services, financial development is a source of comparative advantage and a robust determinant of the pattern of industrial specialization. In particular, they show that countries with well-developed financial systems tend to specialize in industries intensive in external finance.

Even clearer implications for our overarching theme of transparency, perhaps, can be derived from the notion that better-developed financial systems show higher ability to handle investments with a high degree of project uncertainty and/or a high share of difficult-to-evaluate intangible content. Huang and Xu (1999) theoretically derive a result that can be interpreted along these lines. Carlin and Mayer (2003) report empirical results on the associations between financial-system characteristics (including a proxy for information disclosure), industry growth, and investment activity for a sample of OECD countries over the 1970–1995 period, where the latter variable has been separated into fixed investment and R&D expenditure. Their results indicate a strong positive relationship between equity market development and transparency on the one hand, and industry growth and R&D expenditure on the other.

Results on the information value of efficient pricing in financial markets, and thereby of the significance of market and price transparency for economic growth, is provided by, e.g., Morck, Yeung, and Yu (2000) and Durnev, Li, Morck, and

Yeung (2004). They document that firm-specific equity return variation, and thus the information content of stock prices, is higher in financially more developed countries, and, conversely, that stock price 'synchronicity' (i.e., the tendency of stock prices to move together, regardless of firm-level fundamentals) is higher in less-developed countries. Moreover, stock price synchronicity is negatively associated with both output growth and productivity growth. Their results corroborate the hypothesis that the more efficient pricing associated with better-developed financial markets lead to more correct information being conveyed by prices set in the market. Consequently, the cost of capital is more precisely estimated in these markets, which means that investors and managers are better able to pick between good and bad investment projects. In addition, they add results regarding the effect of *institutional* transparency by showing that firm-specific return variation is positively associated with shareholder protection, and that synchronicity is negatively associated with institutional quality more generally, thereby providing results about the interaction between 'H' and 'ε,' with our previous terminology. The interaction is motivated by the need for institutional transparency for markets to work efficiently (and hence for prices to carry information). Wurgler (2000) similarly finds evidence of a positive association between capital allocation efficiency and firm-specific information in stock returns on the one hand, and institutional transparency (specifically, minority shareholder protection) on the other.

A more direct link between corporate transparency and economic growth (i.e., one that does not take the 'detour' over capital allocation efficiency) is explored by, e.g., Sadka (2004), who considers—and finds support for—the hypothesis that corporate transparency—specifically, the sharing of financial statements among competitors—increases the amount of useful knowledge in the public domain, which can be exploited to raise productivity in an entire industry, hence increasing growth.

The bulk of relevant literature here is of course that which studies the association between 'transparency' and various aspects of corporate financing without spelling out the link to growth or to financial development on the macro level. Much of the corporate governance literature fits in here. Most palpably, perhaps, the amount of agency costs arising from information asymmetries and conflicts of interest between investors and managers of firms is a determinant of the degree to which the cost of capital is streamlined around expected returns; the larger the agency premium and uncertainties related thereto, the more obscured is the relationship between actual financing costs and the expected marginal product of capital invested. The literature also contains a large number of contributions discussing possible remedies to this type of problem, including corporate strategies to bridge information asymmetries, such as various signaling strategies and 'bonding' (see, e.g., Oxelheim & Randøy, 2003). To the extent that these strategies are costly, however, lack of transparency still weighs on the financial system's capacity to allocate available capital with maximum efficiency.

Finally, a by now large literature studies the link between various measures of the quality of transparency/corporate governance/financial markets-related *institutions* and the degree of financial development. The widely quoted series of papers by La Porta, López-de-Silanes, Shleifer, and Vishny (for example, La Porta, López-de-Silanes, Shleifer, & Vishny, 1997) belongs to this category. Such measures of institutional quality relate to judicial efficiency and transparency, such as legal origin, protection of minority shareholder rights, creditor protection, etc., but also measures more directly related to corporate transparency, such as accounting standards. To the extent that such variables affect financial development they have the capacity to influence economic growth through this mechanism. However, to the extent that these measures express various aspects of the legal environment and the like, they most appropriately enter our conceptual framework at the level of *institutions* (through 'H')—the level to which we turn next.

1.2.4 Institutional Transparency/Laws, Regulations, and Policies

'Institutional transparency,' in our terminology, refers to any transparency aspect of political influence, laws, regulations, or even more informal institutions, such as 'culture' or 'traditions,' that affects firms' investment behavior—directly or indirectly through any of the mechanisms described in Section 1.2.3. Inevitably, we have already stumbled across a few of these factors, since (as noted previously) categorical consensus and consistency is not to be found in the literature. Particularly, empirical contributions frequently mingle variables measuring what we would refer to as 'corporate transparency' (such as accounting standards) with variables measuring anything from banking sector development to corruption perceptions on the right-hand side of their regressions, calling the whole thing 'institutions,' in complete disregard for our conceptual framework.

The role of institutional transparency, broadly defined, for investment (domestic and foreign), in terms of the rule of law, corruption, political risk, etc.—both the direct effect on investment activity of 'H,' and the effect through H's interaction with 'ε,' as exemplified in the previous section—is widely documented in the literature. Subsequent chapters in this volume address specific policy and regulatory areas (such as monetary policy, financial regulation, various legal variables, environmental and competition policy, etc.). In this section we shall focus on the conceptual definition of one specific manifestation of 'institutional transparency'—viz that of 'political risk'—in order to pave the way for the empirical example in Section 1.5 of this chapter.

Institutions, to the extent that they matter for growth (function *H* is positive and non-trivial) affect the transaction costs of economic activity. First, deviations from the maximum-efficiency policy or regulation (for instance, through insufficient monitoring of political agents, or political preferences) introduce a 'tax' on the exchange. In this regard, *all* theories of economic growth are compatible with public-choice-type ideas of the significance of institutional transparency. We may call this an 'efficiency effect' of the institutional environment. With a broader definition of 'transaction costs' to include also the dynamic influence of 'institutions' on agents' *expectations* of the outcomes of their economic transactions—in the present context, specifically the expected profits of their investment activities—we can add to the 'efficiency effect' an 'uncertainty effect,' which brings us closer to the concept we are looking for.

There are many obvious channels for governments, central bankers, and regulators to influence corporate profit expectations. In a financial context this influence is exerted primarily by way of market regulations, market operations, and taxation. Each of these devices has two dimensions: one *direct*, consisting of the actual size of a change in a tax rate, for instance, and the other *indirect*, consisting of a risk premium charged in compensation for the lack of transparency and the adjacent uncertainty about possible future changes (see Oxelheim, 1996).

Governments may reduce or eliminate some risk premiums by increasing transparency and by creating confidence in an absolute sense. However, at the same time the government may also increase risk premiums in other areas. By changing the rules of the markets they create a specific risk—a *political risk.* Whenever market rules are altered, companies perceive a change in the basis for their calculations of expected profit as well. Hence, if they are averse to risk they will claim a political risk premium.

A tentative definition of political risk as risk (from lack of transparency, ambiguity, or pure surprise) attaching to *changes in the market rules*, goes a long way toward capturing its essence, and is broadly consistent with the theory on how institutions primarily influence growth through a dynamic effect (see Section 1.2.1).

Studies[6] of corporate decision-making show that managers are greatly averse to political risk, and that such risk commands a price. If managers undertake an investment that is exposed to political risk, they will demand a premium in the form of a higher expected return. This incremental element in the return is the political risk premium.

---

[6]See Aharoni (1966), Basi (1963), Kobrin (1979), Kobrin et al. (1980), and Oxelheim (1984).

Political risk is not a clear-cut concept. It is often used synonymously with country risk, although it should rather be seen as a subset of that risk. Country risk encompasses all risks that an investor encounters in a country,[7] i.e., not only the risk of policy-induced changes but also the risk of strikes, riots, etc. Political risk thus constitutes that part of the risk, which is caused by politicians in the form of changes in the rules applying on that country's market. It comprises risks manifest at the company level as an involuntary loss of control over assets due to such things as expropriations, confiscations, etc., or as an increase in volatility in the expected returns due to, for instance, a tax change or a policy measure which sets the market forces out of action. Some political risks can be described as macro risks, since they affect all companies or investors in a country, while others are specific to an industry or a company.[8]

1.3 Transparency and European Integration

The focus in this volume on European integration clearly adds a dimension to the discussion about transparency. At the corporate level, it requires a specification of the way corporate transparency is affected by the internationalization of business activities. However, the integration across national borders of markets for goods and services is a global phenomenon, rather than specifically European. It is scarcely (any longer, at least) driven primarily by a politically conditioned integration project, which is motivated sometimes on political, sometimes on historical, and occasionally on economic grounds.[9]

Instead, the unique aspect of the EU project is its far-reaching consequences in terms of legislative activities, regulation, and the exertion of political power in a wide range of different areas in a multicountry setting. Consequently, it is primarily the institutional/regulatory/political aspect of transparency that is given another dimension by the focus on the EU. Several specific policy and regulatory areas are addressed in subsequent chapters of the book. In this section, we address a few of the more general issues contained in such a dimension.

Ever since the launch of the Single Market Programme, the European Union has strived to achieve a 'level playing field' for economic activity within the Union. In spite of obvious successes (e.g., trade policy — the EU speaks with one

---

[7]See, e.g., Leavy (1984).

[8]See, e.g., Kobrin (1982) and Oxelheim and Wihlborg (1987, 2005).

[9]The creation of the Coal and Steel Union, for instance, is usually referred to as a means to an end, rather than an end in itself; the single market, on the other hand, followed upon years of stagnation and 'Eurosclerosis', and might possibly be an example of a primarily economically motivated project.

voice *vis-à-vis* third countries — and, more ambiguously perhaps, competition policy), wide structural differences between member countries remain in areas of potentially crucial importance for achieving the overall objective of a single economic area. These differences can be found in economic policy (e.g., taxation), regulation and market institutions (e.g., labor markets), industrial structures, and corporate governance (e.g., ownership patterns and the relative importance of different financing sources). With the inclusion of ten new member states as of 2004, the heterogeneity of the EU's economic structures, and thus the significance of lack of transparency as an obstacle to integration, has increased exponentially.

Lack of transparency with regard to these structural differences suggests the existence of potentially high costs to bridging the gap between markets — a possible explanation for remaining segmentation and price differences. Partial remaining segmentation between national markets may amount to sub-optimal resource allocation and, ultimately, foregone opportunities in terms of economic growth[10] and dynamism of the integration project; and it stands contrary to the political aim of the project as such.

The policy debate in Europe often rests upon the implicit notion of 'the more harmonization the better' (also from an economic efficiency standpoint). However, in terms of regulatory and economic-political differences, the lack of complete harmonization within the union, in combination with the abolition of formal obstacles to integration, introduces the possibility of competition between regulatory and economic policies within the union. Such policy competition is in many ways a better way to achieve integration (as it minimizes the risk that rules and policies are applied that are sub-optimal or economically inefficient), but is at the same time potentially costly for individual countries in the short run, and politically unpopular (see Oxelheim & Ghauri, 2004). The choice between harmonization and competition introduces a conflict between 'static transparency' on the one hand, and 'dynamic transparency' and longer term institutional improvements on the other: a regulatory system can be transparent when harmonized in the sense that there is only one system of rules, and no ambiguity as to which rules apply; this however, does not mean that the rules as such are transparent or efficient. On the other hand, parallelism of several regulatory systems can be

---

[10]The extent to which integration has contributed to economic growth in Europe is on the whole unclear, as is the extent to which the EU can be considered 'integrated' in various aspects. It would seem, however, that in terms of the growth effects of integration, the EU project is often predicated on the idea that the growth implications of integration rests primarily, or even solely, in the scale economies of creating a bigger market, while mainstream 'new growth' theory emphasizes cross-border knowledge and technology transfer (see, e.g., Rivera-Batiz & Romer, 1991). Perhaps this idea of creating one big market also partially explains the preference for harmonization and coordination (not infrequently excessive) over policy and regulatory competition.

opaque, but the possibility for economic agents to shop around for the best regulation disciplines regulators, prevents them from frequently changing the rules (for the worse), and helps ensuring long-run efficiency.

As of the early 2000s, the EU's strategy with regard to the application of one or the other of these methods has been somewhat haphazard: applying harmonization where it is opportune or uncontroversial while leaving politically difficult areas aside; paying lip service to policy competition in some areas while suppressing it, or stressing its 'harmful' sides, in other instances.[11] Whether one strategy or the other is preferred, not just political inaptitude but lack of transparency with regard to what factors that segment markets to some extent puts a wet blanket on progress. Potential sources of such lack of transparency are things as diverse as language, culture and traditions, corporate interests (rents from price discrimination, etc.), the vested interests of special interest groups (such as labor unions), and the intrinsic inertia of complex structures (historical lock-in effects, or path dependence).

1.4 Optimal Transparency?

Is more transparency always better? We have spent a good part of this chapter arguing that increased transparency in various forms raises the efficiency of economic interaction—in particular that it raises the efficiency of resource allocation in the economy in a broad sense. For example, more transparent financial systems lead to cheaper and more efficient channeling of savings to their ultimate uses, more transparent firms reduce agency costs and moral hazard thus increasing the likelihood that the resources at the firm's disposal are put to the best possible use and the best investment projects chosen, more transparent institutions lead to lower transaction costs thus further lubricating the resource allocation process. Corporate governance or corruption scandals almost inevitably lead to calls for increased transparency as a remedy. Indeed, when one thinks of rent-seeking behavior within more or less opaque organizations (whether private firms or public bodies), it is easy to think of the matter as though there were a linear relationship between transparency and efficiency. For example, any extra bit of information released about a firm reduces the informational disadvantage of the firm's outsiders, and so reduces—presumably by about a proportional amount—agency costs and therefore also the inefficiency inherent in such costs.

[11]The 'haphazardness' of the strategies chosen of course also reflects what has been politically possible to achieve at the time a particular decision was taken, and perhaps also reflects the multiplicity of objectives that are possible to attach to the integration project (and which, of course, are subjectively weighted by decision makers), as mentioned above.

This section offers a few examples of research that addresses the question of transparency from somewhat different angles. The examples send a nuancing message about the blessings of increased transparency. They do so primarily by considering how the role of publicly available information might be a bit more complex than just informing interested parties about solid facts that matter to them in their economic decision-making. They might be thought of as caveats to the general message of this book that more transparency is better: it is, mostly, but not unconditionally.

A first example is given by Morris and Shin (2002) and by a number of related papers that study implications of the dual role of public information. The first of these roles is that of purveyor of knowledge about 'fundamentals' that will be of value for decisions under uncertainty simply by reducing uncertainty and increase efficiency of the decision. This is the role thought of when one calls for increased transparency as a remedy to corporate governance scandals. The second role of public information is that of a coordination device. When decisions are not taken in isolation, based on the best available information pure and simple, but are complementary to the decisions of others, then it may start paying off to try to anticipate, or imitate, the reactions of these other agents to public information announcements—that is, people start to pay attention not only to what they know, but what they think others might know. The basic conditions are that public information is imperfect, and that private information is asymmetrically distributed among agents.

Morris and Shin (2002) mostly use as example of this guessing game the central bank giving out public signals about its intentions regarding policy, to which financial markets attach 'too much' weight. Another example might be the release of information about the accounts of public firms through quarterly reports: financial analysts must not only analyze fundamentals in the reports, but must also attempt to second-guess the average reaction of other analysts to the release in order to cover their bets. Again, public information plays a double role here—both that of provider of knowledge about fundamentals, and that of something to rally around, something which—though in some sense orthogonal to available economically relevant information—may still have meaningful economic consequences and be optimal to take into consideration from the point of view of the individual decision maker.

How might this coordination role of public information be harmful, or lead to inefficient outcomes? In the example with central bank transparency, to the extent that central bank transparency might be an instrument to 'do good' by coordinating market participants' expectations, 'it also has the potential to do ill if expectations are coordinated away from fundamentals' (Morris & Shin, 2002, p. 1523). The argument resembles the one underpinning theories of, e.g., asset price bubbles by way of 'herding' behavior, or 'information cascades.' Such theories are presented by, e.g., Banerjee (1992) and Bikhchandani, et al. (1992) in the context of sequential games, where the basic premise, as in the case of Morris and Shin (2002) is imperfect public information and asymmetrically distributed private information among decision makers. Each decision maker acts rationally toward the possibility that someone else may have better private information, giving the result that everybody underweights the information on fundamentals available to him- or herself. The overall outcome is proved to be inefficient, and the basic reason is that the total body of available information is under-used. The role of *public* information, however, is less explicit in these models than in Morris and Shin (2002), and the implications for transparency therefore less precise.

In the case of asset pricing, the coordinating role of public information explains mispricing. Mispricing may lead to inefficient resource allocation, because the price signals do not convey accurate information and so are to some extent inadequate for making informed decisions (for example about what investment to place your savings in). Mispricing in financial markets, however, is only one of many possible consequences of the dual role of public information as conveyor of useful knowledge and behavioral coordination device. The list of potential inefficiencies arising from this problem seems too long to cover in the present text, and we may refer to Bikhchandani et al. (1992) for examples of implications in all sorts of situations.

Let us instead take a look at another way in which increased transparency can be detrimental, rather than beneficial, to growth. The work of Sadka (2004) was mentioned in Section 1.2.3, where it was said that corporate transparency can increase growth by allowing competing firms to share useful information, thus raising productivity in an entire industry. However, 'too much' transparency reduces incentives to undertake productive investment — for much the same reason — and so here, too, transparency can be excessive. The simple setup is as follows: among the population of competing firms using the same production technology, a firm has the opportunity to undertake an investment which improves its production process, thus creating a competitive advantage for itself. Assuming transparency is exogenous (presumably through imposed regulation), beyond a certain level of transparency, the competitive advantage will be revealed and the investing firm unable to exploit it. As a consequence, it will also not have the incentive to make the investment in the first place: productivity growth and therefore economic growth suffers.

The basic driver of this result is obviously a free-rider problem of a type similar to the one motivating protection of patents and other intellectual property rights. Indeed, some recent research (see, e.g., Kanwar & Evenson, 2003) has indicated that intellectual property rights protection does spur innovation, which is clearly an indirect economic-growth argument in favor of limiting transparency. Intuition suggests a relatively simple quadratic relationship between transparency and growth, which actually seems to be supported by Sadka's (2004) cross-sectional empirical evidence for 36 countries.

A third, and last, example of a situation where transparency is not unequivocally beneficial is provided by Geraats (2002). Here, private information is asymmetrically distributed between the authorities and the public. The holder of the private information is a public body (again, the primary application is monetary policy, but in principle, the result can be generalized), which takes policy action according to (or reveals a signal about) a variable of interest, x, whereas the private sector forms expectations about this variable. Geraats (2002) shows in a stylized setting that if the central bank is uncertain about x (one can think of the perfectly reasonable situation where the central bank is uncertain as to the exact structure of the economy), then being transparent about this uncertainty can be welfare-reducing by increasing the volatility of the private sector's expectations about x (of course depending on further assumptions about the effects of this volatility). In other words, the uncertainty of the authorities feed into the uncertainty of the public (which then feeds into the uncertainty of the authorities, and so on). Also on this basis, it seems, there may be a basis for restricting transparency. Other skeptical observers (e.g., Thornton, 2003) have questioned the non-satiety of central bank transparency on related, economic-efficiency grounds (see Chapter 2 of this volume).

In summation, this section has reviewed a few examples that modify the picture of transparency as something uniformly beneficial for the efficient working of the economy. In certain situations, depending on the precise structure and value of information, 'too much' transparency can generate mispricing, introduce free-rider problems, or cause inefficiencies in other ways. It can be noted, however, that the theoretical results giving rise to this conclusion, are generally relatively sensitive to the *exact* assumptions made. As an example, consider how Angeletos and Pavan (2004) or Hellwig (2005) reach almost the opposite results of Morris and Shin (2002), essentially just by making a few alterations in the assumption of how complementarity between agents' actions works.

1.5 The Link between Transparency, Political Risk, and Economic Growth—an Example

In this section we will provide an example on the link between institutional transparency (political risk) and economic growth. The example aims to illustrate the following causal chain: transparency $\Uparrow \Rightarrow$ political risk $\Downarrow \Rightarrow$ cost of capital $\Downarrow \Rightarrow$ investment $\Uparrow \Rightarrow$ economic growth $\Uparrow$. A key element in the transmission process is the cost of capital, and we shall focus on the relationship between political risk—as an indicator of lack of institutional transparency—and a key component in the cost of capital faced by firms, namely the general interest rate level in the economy, and its information content.

The general idea to be highlighted in the example is as follows: Part of the spread between the risk-free rates of interest of any one country and some representative benchmark country or countries, is explained by a difference in political risk premiums between the country in question and the benchmark. The political risk premium is time-varying and largely reflects (in)stability in the 'rules of the game' i.e., the propensity of policy-makers and regulators to alter the institutional framework for economic transactions within the jurisdiction. In other words, this premium is negatively correlated with institutional transparency. If we can somehow decompose the interest rate differential to reveal the size of the political risk premium (and if the benchmark is representative enough), then we can also tentatively quantify the opportunity cost of the lack of institutional transparency in terms of foregone GDP growth. In terms of the conceptual framework for analyzing the role of transparency for capital formation and economic growth, presented in Section 1.2 of the chapter, this cost represents an important aspect of the mapping of H on the capital formation process.

The empirical part of the example will be regional in scope and involves the four major Nordic countries — Denmark, Finland, Norway, and Sweden. There are several arguments for this choice. First of all, they are European. Second, they are all political economies, i.e., political-sector-dominated economies, which means that policy-makers in these countries are forced to offset domestic effects from shocks and disturbances in the world economy, mainly by changing the tax bases or the tax rates. Consequently, given our definition of political risk, we would expect companies in the Nordic countries to be exposed to high risks of this kind. The emergence of different policy regimes during the period of financial market transition can also be expected to reveal itself in political changes of varying frequency, which in turn affect the uncertainty of non-political actors about the stability of the market rules. Accordingly, we have good grounds to assume that the political risk fluctuates over time. A third argument in favor of using the Nordic region as our case region is comparability: the countries are similar in size and geographic position, and causes of segmentation such as *information barriers, transaction costs, home-country bias*, etc.[12] affect the countries in more or less the same way.

Furthermore, we have purposely chosen a period of study during which these countries — all high-tax welfare states with a traditionally fairly high portion of the economy under political control — underwent a transition process in terms of opening up for inward and outward foreign investment activity, and internal

[12]See Stonehill and Dullum (1981) for a further description.

deregulation of the financial systems. This process, however, by no means followed a straight path, and so we chose the period and the sample countries with the *ex ante* expectation that we would find both (a) political setbacks in the deregulation process generating political risk and (b) enough international interdependence of these countries that this risk be priced in international markets. The full sample period is 1974–1991 (with the demise of the Bretton Woods and the Smithsonian agreements representing the starting date).

The remainder of the example is structured as follows: In the next subsection follows a discussion of possible indicators of political risk as an expression for lack of policy transparency; be it ambiguity or missing information; or intentionally or not. The chosen indicators are thereafter applied to our sample countries in order to identify subperiods of high political risk during the sample period as a whole. In the subsequent subsection, we investigate the nominal sizes of the interest rate gap between our sample countries and the benchmark countries, after which these gaps are tentatively decomposed to reveal the sizes of the political risk premiums during periods of high political risk. The example is concluded by a brief subsection containing suggestive quantifications of the opportunity cost of these premiums in terms of foregone GDP growth.

1.5.1 Finding a Proxy for Political Risk

We are looking for a proxy of political risk that will enable us to estimate the size of the political risk *premium* contained in the domestic 'risk-free' interest rate level in the sample countries. Political risk premiums are often observed *directly* in the spread between the domestic and the Eurorate, with both rates having similar characteristics in all relevant aspects except jurisdiction.[13] Unfortunately, available time series of Eurocurrency rates for the Nordic currencies are not long enough to allow an interest rate comparison over the whole period under investigation. Thus, because the price of political risk is generally not directly observable for our sample countries, we will have to go about our business in a somewhat more cumbersome way.

The political risk premium is a form of compensation for the systematic component in political risk. The way to go is thus to find some sort of other proxy for this systematic component—the source of political risk—which can be assumed to strongly correlate with the actual risk premium, and then attempt an *indirect* estimation of this premium. Following the approach of Oxelheim (1996),

[13]See, e.g., Edwards (1984) for the use of the interest differential *vis-à-vis* LIBOR as the premium for country risk. Empirically, however, as is shown in Brewer (1983) for example, the determination of the premium is often more complex than this.

we can find two such sources: policy-makers' *need* to intervene and their *propensity* to intervene.

It has been found[14] that *relative indebtedness* is a good proxy for the first one of these sources, or components, of political risk. Indebtedness signals the *need* for interventions, since a high net foreign debt reduces the free scope for policy-making, thus making more likely the appearance of new taxes or similar measures affecting corporate returns on investment. Oxelheim (1996) reports that during the period 1977–1991, relative indebtedness represented an important reason for the gap between Nordic and foreign interest rates. We will here use indebtedness as a country's net foreign assets as a percentage of GDP.

For the second element of political risk—the *propensity* to intervene—we will use a proxy based on the past 'intervention record' of the politicians in a particular country. We have used the cumbersome but appealing way of describing this record by keeping an *ex post* calendarium of relevant policy changes. 'Relevant' refers here to policy measures whose effect is to increase uncertainty in a market. Consequently, we have removed from the calendarium all policy measures aimed at deregulation or at securing the financial infrastructure.[15]

Figures 1.2–1.5 show the 'propensity proxy' of political risk for each of the Nordic countries. To construct the proxy, all policy measures—fiscal and monetary—that appeared in the period 1974–1991 were screened, and the 'relevant' policy measures selected. Each day containing changes in the rules takes on the value of 1. It is assumed that investors or market participants have a 24-month memory: they base their view of the risk based on what has happened during the last 24 months. We further assume that memories fade away, which means that exponentially diminishing weights are attached to policy changes undertaken during

---

[14]See, e.g., Lessard (1983), Dooley and Isard (1986), and Oxelheim (1990) for the argument that a country's international relative indebtedness (as measured, e.g., as net foreign assets as a ratio of GDP) constitutes the fundamental source of the country risk for the country concerned, and that this source applies to LDCs as well as to industrial countries.

[15]The choice of policy measures to be included admittedly contains a subjective element. A related shortcoming concerns the importance of different policy changes, since we equate a 30% increase in capital gains tax, for instance, with a 1% increase in banks' investment obligations. Finally, it can effectively be argued that, rather than indicating future *propensity* to intervene, the measure can more appropriately be said to reflect the past *need* to intervene. In spite of these shortcomings, the measure *does* provide information about the authorities' propensity to intervene (if not in the future then historically—though it is true that propensity may be partially obscured by the necessity in the historical record), and for lack of a better alternative, we are content that this measure offers a satisfactory proxy of institutional transparency for the purpose at hand.

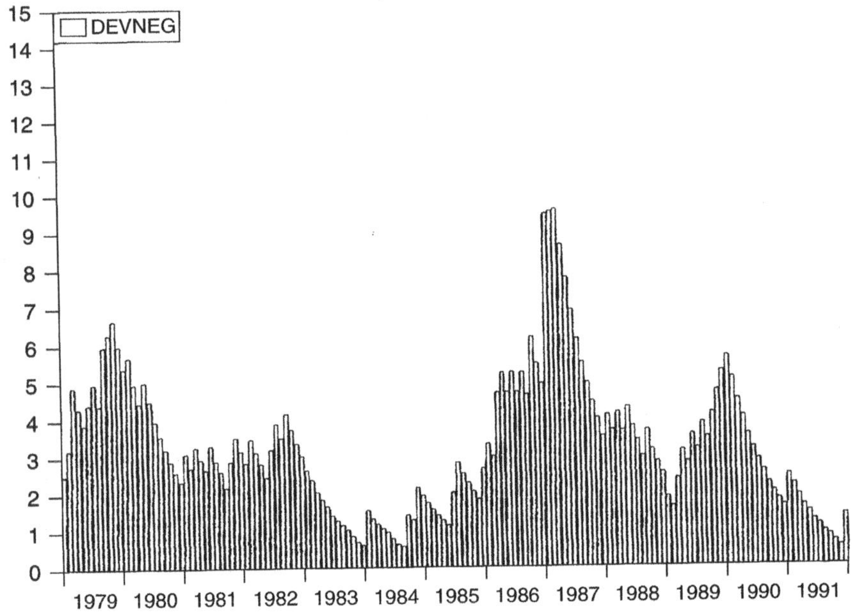

Figure 1.2: Political risk in Denmark. Number of days during the last 24 months when changes in the rules occurred, which increased uncertainty. Exponential weights.

the last 24 months.[16] We thus get a weighted moving average measure of political risk, based on policy-makers' *actual propensity* to intervene in the market.

From Figures 1.2–1.5 we can identify periods marked by a considerable propensity on the part of policy-makers to intervene and a need for transparency from the actors' side. In Denmark, such a period is seen at the time of the 'potato diet' in 1986–1987, in Finland at the beginning and end of the 1980s, in Norway at the time of the dramatic drop in the price of crude oil in 1986, and in Sweden on the occasions of the devaluations of the Swedish krona in 1981 and 1982.

We thus find clear indications that rules and policies in the Nordic countries were far from stable at intervals during our sample period. The political risk proxies used

[16]The number of days during the last month when changes in the rules occurred is allotted a weight equal to 1, while the number in the month before is allotted a weight of 0.9, then 0.9^2, 0.9^3, and so on. Thus, recollection of the number of changes 24 months ago is assumed to be weak, and is allotted a weight of $0.9^{24} = 0.08$.

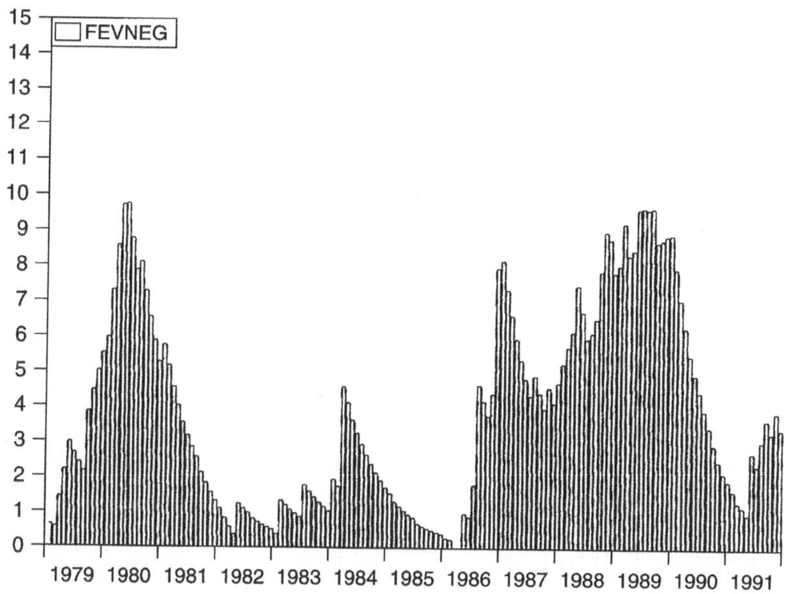

Figure 1.3: Political risk in Finland. Number of days during the last 24 months when changes in the rules occurred, which increased uncertainty. Exponential weights.

here strongly indicate that, given risk-averse actors, there are good grounds for assuming a non-negligible political risk premium charged for investing in these countries.

The two proxies for political risk identified in this example — that which indicates the need to intervene, and that which indicates the propensity to do so — can also be used in a combined form. If we establish a simple dichotomy between 'high' and 'low' values in the two variables, four possible combinations emerge, of which the case of a strong need to intervene and a high propensity to do so obviously represents the highest possible level of political risk. If instead, we assume a gradual increase in the variables as a relevant basis for risk, then the alternative of constructing a new total proxy by multiplying the necessity and the propensity variables should be considered.

If we adopt the threshold view and decide (discretionary), for example, that a need to intervene appears at an indebtedness in relation to the OECD average in excess of 25% (Oxelheim, 1996), as a high-risk signal, we can identify periods of high political risk in Denmark in 1979–1980, 1986–1987, and 1989–1990; in

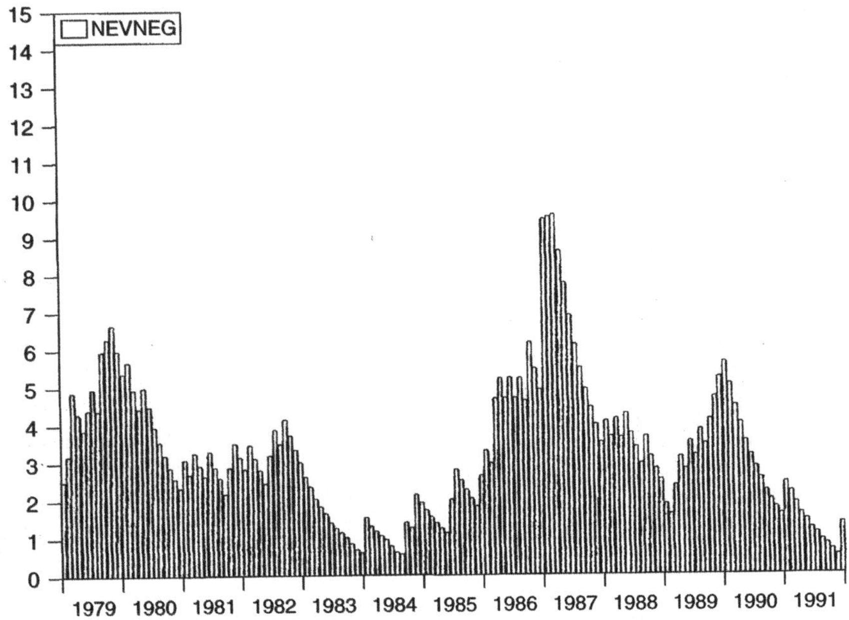

Figure 1.4: Political risk in Norway. Number of days during the last 24 months when changes in the rules occurred, which increased uncertainty. Exponential weights.

Finland in 1980–1981 and 1986–1990; in Norway in 1979–1980, 1987–1988, and 1990; and in Sweden in 1982–1983, and 1990.

If we establish a similar dichotomy in our proxy for the authorities' propensity to intervene, and assume that this propensity is important whenever more than 3 days (according to the fading-memory principle) during the last 24 months have witnessed a change in the market rules, then we can identify a substantial propensity in Denmark in 1979–1980, 1986–1987, and 1989–1990; in Finland in 1980–1981 and 1986–1990; in Norway in 1979–1980, 1986–1988, and 1990–1991; and in Sweden in 1979–1983 and 1990–1991.

When the two measures are combined we can identify periods of high political risk in terms of both a strong need *and* a high propensity to intervene. In this way we have identified the periods of high risk that we will later discuss in our example. The periods we will focus on as high-risk periods are 1986:2 to 1987:3 in Denmark; 1988:4 to 1990:2 in Finland; 1986:4 to 1988:2 in Norway; and 1990:1 to 1990:4 in Sweden.

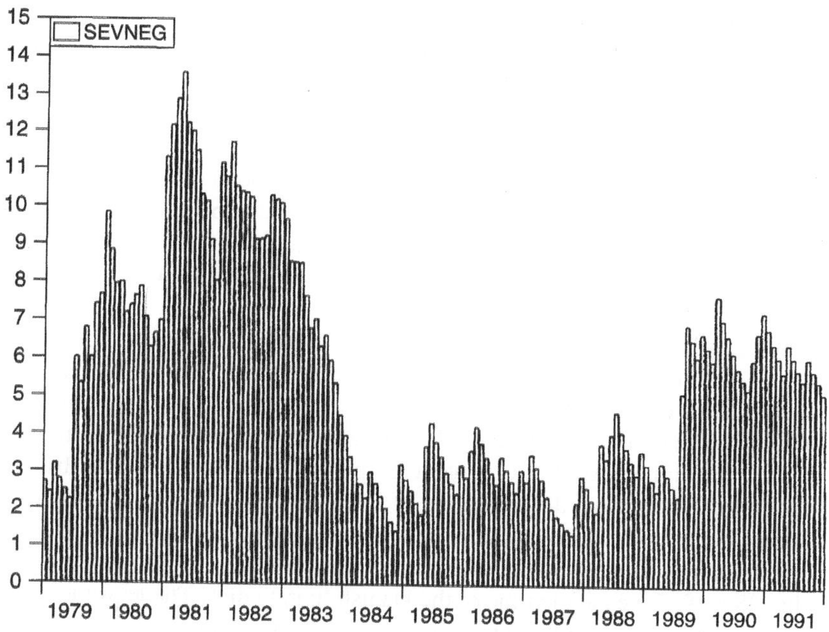

Figure 1.5: Political risk in Sweden. Number of days during the last 24 months when changes in the rules occurred, which increased uncertainty. Exponential weights.

1.5.2 International Interest Rate Differentials and the Size of the Political Risk Premium

So far in this example we have focused on the sources and the variations over time of political risk in our sample countries. Because we could not directly observe the price of political risk and the price of lack of institutional transparency (the actual risk premium) we constructed alternative proxies that we assume to be strongly co-varying with the actual premium charged. In order to find an estimate of the premium, we now turn to the analysis of interest rate differentials between our sample countries and the OECD rate (a weighted construct) as our representative international benchmark rate. We start by examining the nominal gaps between the domestic interest rates of our sample countries and our international benchmark rate, then proceed to an analysis of the elements contained in this gap in order to ultimately extract the approximate size of the political risk premium.

In the analysis, we use government bond rates as indicator of the risk-free rate relevant for cost of capital calculations and investment decisions. Which rate should be used as a representative international benchmark rate? For a long time the US rates exerted a strong influence on most domestic interest rates, but their impact were successively diminishing over the course of our study period. For the later part of the period in our example it has been found that bond rates were increasingly subject to the influence of a common factor that can be called the 'global bond rate.'[17] This can be described as a weighted average of the rates in the largest OECD countries. In our example we use the trade-weighted OECD rate as our benchmark government bond rate.

Figures 1.6–1.9 show that from 1982/1983 the Nordic government bond rates (apart from the Finnish) were more or less consistently higher than the OECD rate. The Danish rates exceeded the average OECD rate the entire period from 1974 onward. In the region as a whole the largest gaps are registered for Denmark, where they sometimes exceed 10 percentage points. However, the Danish gaps began to fall radically from the beginning of 1983, in a period when big issues of government bonds coincided with non-resident investors being allowed once again to invest in Danish krone-denominated government bonds. A large gap appeared again in 1986–1987, i.e., at the time of the Danish 'potato diet.' The gaps then successively diminished during the remainder of the sample period.

The spreads between the Finnish and OECD bond rates were among the smallest in the region during the period, but they are difficult to interpret because of preferential tax treatment of Finnish government bonds at the time. Nor can the Finnish rates be easily converted into a taxable equivalent, since for most of the period a marginal tax rate applied. Bearing all this in mind, it is found that except for a few years in the 1970s (1976–1978), the Finnish bond rates were more or less consistently below the global rates; occasionally, at the beginning of the 1980s, as much as four percentage points below. The size of the gap diminished from 1982 onward, and after August 1989 the Finnish government seized to issue tax-free bonds, but the Finnish rates did not pass the OECD rates until the early 1990s, when non-resident investors were again allowed to invest in Finnish markka-denominated government bonds and resident Finnish investors were allowed to invest in international bonds. Owing to the tax treatment of government bond we will in the case of Finland continue the discussion based on corporate bonds assuming that project and company risks are balanced.

The Norwegian rates were consistently below the global rates until the beginning of 1982. Thereafter they were above the global rate for the remainder of the period, with gaps sometimes exceeding six percentage points. The largest gaps of

[17]See, e.g., Oxelheim (1990).

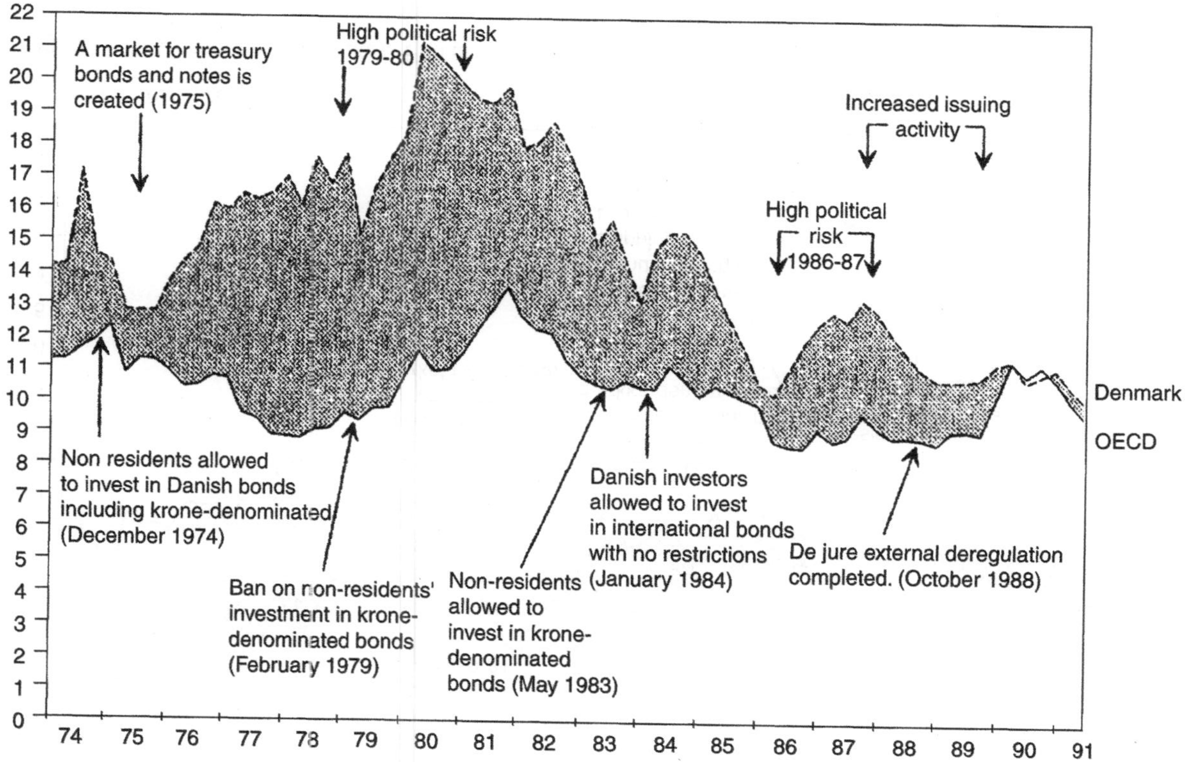

Figure 1.6: Government bond rates, Denmark as against OECD, 1974–June 1991. Percent per year, monthly data, end of period.

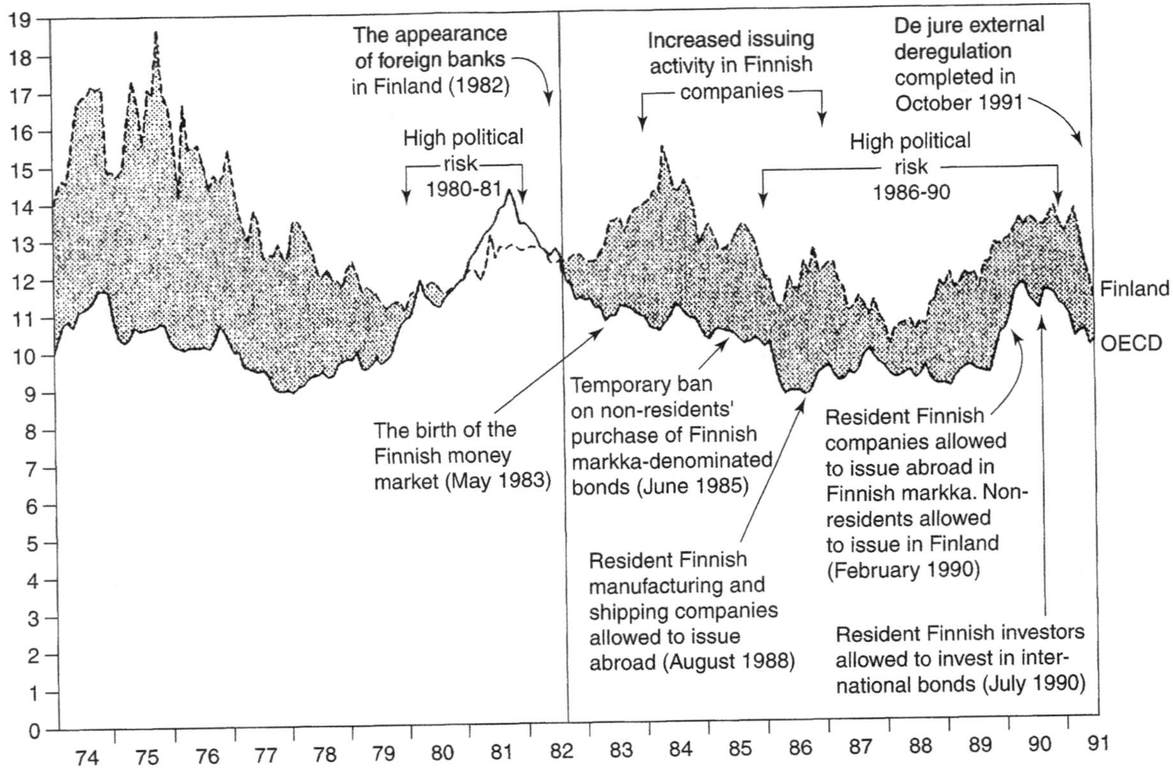

Figure 1.7: Corporate bond rates, Finland as against OECD, 1974–June 1991. Percent per year, monthly data, end of period.

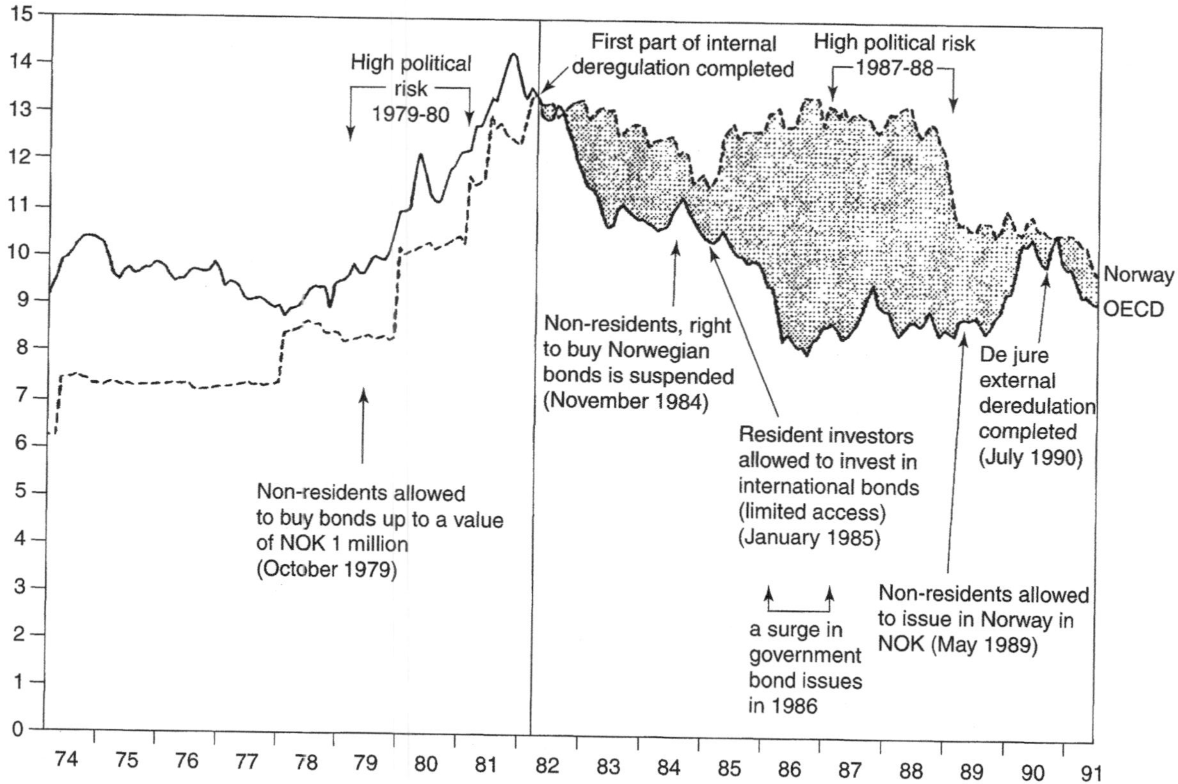

Figure 1.8: Government bond rates, Norway as against OECD, 1974–June 1991. Percent per year, monthly data, end of period.

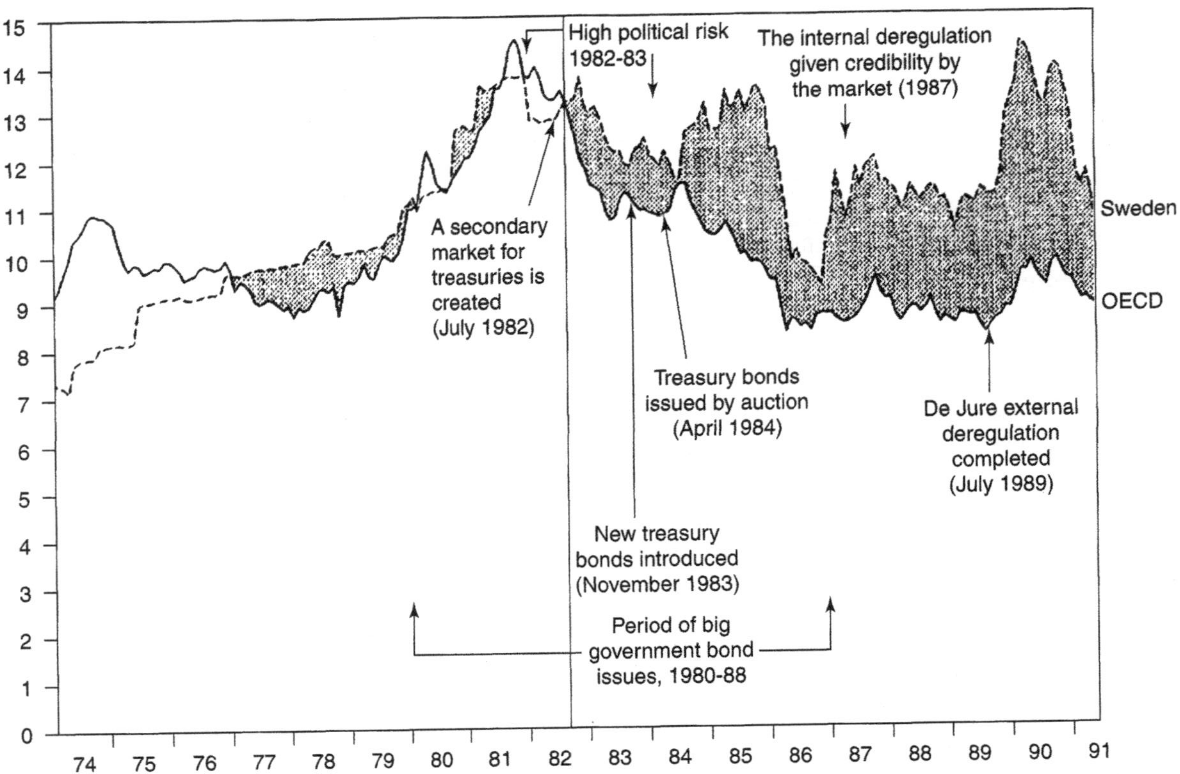

Figure 1.9: Government bond rates, Sweden as against OECD, 1974–June 1991. Percent per year, monthly data, end of period.

the 1980s occurred in 1986–1987, at the time of the dramatic drop in the price of crude oil and its aftermath, i.e., during a period of high political risk. The spread diminished considerably as of the completion of capital account liberalization.

The Swedish rates were well below the OECD rate in the mid-1970s. At the time of the introduction of the new exchange rate regime in August 1977, they began to overtake the OECD rate. However, large spreads did not appear until after the Swedish devaluation in the autumn of 1982. At the beginning of the 1990s the Swedish rates were sometimes five percentage points above the global rates.

Thus, in the case of the government bond rate we find that something happened in all the Nordic countries in the 1981–1982 period despite the fact that the Nordic capital controls were not abolished *de jure* until the end of the 1980s; Denmark in October 1988, Sweden in July 1989, Norway in July 1990, and Finland in October 1991. This reflects the importance of considering the *de facto* rather than *de jure* integration. A downturn in world interest rates occurred in 1981. The Danish rate followed but at a higher pace, diminishing the spread. In Finland, the gaps also decreased, but as a result of a more or less unchanged Finnish rate. The Norwegian and Swedish rates did not follow the downturn in the global rate in 1981–1983, resulting in increases in the spreads. To summarize, from late 1982, the Danish, Norwegian, and Swedish rates were consistently above the global rate, whereas the Finnish (tax-free) rates did not overtake the global rate until the beginning of the 1990s.

1.5.3 Decomposition of Interest Rate Differentials

We have found a gap between interest rates and will now attempt to identify and eliminate in a gradual process the different elements in this nominal interest rate gap.[18] Our aim is to isolate the incremental part of the interest rate that is due to lack of institutional transparency of different kinds; the political risk premium.

In exploring the gap between bond rates, we adopt a rate-of-return perspective and assume that the law of one price for interest rates holds. This can be studied in terms of the empirical validity of two of its expressions: the International Fisher Effect and the interest rate parity theorem.[19] The International Fisher

[18]For the case of Finland, we will, as mentioned, use the gap between corporate bond rates, since the tax exemption of Finnish government bond rates make these rates inappropriate for the analysis.

[19]It has become customary to regard the absence of deviations from interest rate parity as a sign of *perfect capital mobility*. Similarly, the absence of deviations from the International Fisher Effect is regarded as a sign of *perfect substitutability*.

Effect[20] expresses this law by taking the market's expectations regarding future exchange rate movements into consideration. However, to the extent that the matching of interest rates leaves some (idiosyncratic) risks unmatched, the investor in this framework is still regarded as being risk-neutral. It is thus assumed that different distributions of probability as regards exchange rate movements, do not generate any demand for a risk premium. The same applies to a premium for any increase in uncertainty associated with political changes, such as adjustments in taxes. In a risky environment with risk-averse actors, an extended International Fisher Effect is called for (Oxelheim, 1996; Forssbæck & Oxelheim, 2003).

Let us first address the role of 'expectations.' If an empirical test of the International Fisher Effect is to be satisfactorily underpinned, we must have information about the market's exchange rate expectations. If we do not have such information, we will have to make do (as is commonly done) with the actual (*ex post*) exchange rate movements and assume that rational expectations will cancel out systematic forecast errors over time. Still, the fact that we have no access to market expectations about exchange rate changes causes problems, since an analysis based on observed exchange rate movements instead of these expectations in fact includes an analysis of the two hypotheses on the right-hand side of Equation 1.2.

$$S_{t+n} - \mathrm{IFE}_t(n) = [S_{t+n} - S^*_{t+n}] + [S^*_{t+n} - \mathrm{IFE}_t(n)] \tag{1.2}$$

The deviation between the actual future spot rate (S_{t+n}) and the forecast from the International Fisher Effect [$\mathrm{IFE}_t(n)$] can thus be subdivided into a deviation between the actual future rate and market expectation (S^*_{t+n}) and a deviation between market expectation and the forecast [$\mathrm{IFE}_t(n)$].

The subdivision according to Equation 1.2 shows that conclusions based on *ex post* analysis can be difficult to interpret. For example, the market expectation may be correct, even though the actual exchange rate does not assume the relevant value. This situation can arise, within the boundaries of efficiency, if the transaction costs are so great that the financial transaction is not economically defensible. Yet another source of systematic deviation when it comes to empirical testing is to be found in the investors' risk-aversion and their demands for a risk premium to compensate for the exchange rate and political risks. Thus, any

[20]The International Fisher Effect, often also called Uncovered Interest Parity, dates back to the turn of the century, but what we could call the standard theory of the *international* pricing of financial securities did not really begin to evolve until the late 1960s and early 1970s. See, for example, Grubel (1968), Grubel and Fadner (1971), Levy and Sarnat (1970), Solnik (1973), Adler and Dumas (1975), and Grauer, Litzenberger, and Stehle (1976).

conclusions about the inefficiency of the market must also allow for an evaluation of these premiums.[21] The beliefs of market actors[22] and possible market inefficiencies also affect the outcome.

In order to capture the potential size of the risk premiums we first have to eliminate from the gaps the exchange rate expectations that prevailed at the time when the interest rate gap was created. There are two main ways of approaching it. One is to use *ex post* changes in the exchange rate. The other way is to assume that the market actors believe in purchasing power parity (PPP), i.e., their exchange rate expectation equals their expectation about the development of relative inflation.[23] Here we are trapped again, unless we add some further assumptions; for example, that we can use *ex post* observations also for the development of relative inflation (with the same argument as above), or that market actors form expectations about this development adaptively. Another PPP-based approach is to assume that market actors believe in the mean-reverting feature of the PPP process and that they always include the current deviation from parity as a complement to the forecasted exchange rate change as estimated from relative inflation.

In Table 1.1 we present four alternative proxies for the expected change in exchange rates. The elimination of these expected exchange rate changes as estimated by the proxies leaves us with a residual gap containing market inefficiency, and exchange rate and political risk premiums. The main systematic component of the former is the transaction cost. The literature suggests a maximum for this cost not exceeding 0.5 percentage points.[24] If we then assume that market inefficiency in excess of the transaction cost is negligible we are left with a spread containing the exchange rate and political risk premiums plus a transaction cost of 0.5 percentage points at most.

Table 1.1 shows alternative average sizes of this residual spread in the periods previously identified as high-risk periods, using different proxies for exchange

---

[21]Aliber (1974) suggests that the systematic difference between the interest differential and the observed exchange rate change must be analyzed in terms of two risks, an exchange risk and a political risk. Aliber concentrates on the information content in different rates of interest, and assumes that national interest rates, unlike Eurorates, contain premiums for political risks. Thus, by using the forward rate, Aliber felt able to distinguish the premium for exchange risk from the premium for political risk. He found the premium for both risks to be about the same size, and took the presence of risk premiums to mean that we can expect the interest differential to give a biased estimate of future exchange rate movements. Aliber demonstrates that the International Fisher Effect needs to be extended by the inclusion of terms for the premiums for exchange and political risks.

[22]See Oxelheim (1990).

[23]On the basis of an interview study, Oxelheim (1990) reports a strong belief in the PPP relationship among Swedish top managers.

[24]See, e.g., Oxelheim (1990) for an analysis of the transaction costs in the Swedish case as compared to some international observations.

Table 1.1: Quarterly data of average gaps in periods of high political risk.

		Denmark	Finland	Norway	Sweden
Period of high political risk		1986:2–1987:3	1988:4–1990:2	1986:4–1988:2	1990:1–1990:4
Average bond rate gap in the high-risk period		2.9	2.4	4.3	4.0
Average bond rate gap cleared from expected exchange rate changes	Bondgap — actual exchange rate change ($t+1$)	2.8	2.5	4.1	3.7
	Bondgap — relative inflation from previous year ($t-1$)	3.7	1.1	−3.8	1.5
	Bondgap — relative inflation for next year ($t+1$)	3.1	3.4	5.9	3.4
	Bondgap — (relative inflation for next year ($t+1$) + correction of accumulated deviation from PPP at time t)	−7.1	5.5	5.6	1.0

Note: Inflation is based on changes in producer price index.

rate expectations. In the table we find four proxies for exchange rate expectations for each country/period. We note that the two cases in which the market's exchange rate expectations are proxied by *ex post* developments give residual spreads of about the same size.

The table shows that the sum of the exchange and political risk premiums has been substantial during the periods identified as high-risk periods. For example, in the period (1986:2–1987:3) following the tax reform and the potato diet reform, the gap between the Danish and OECD bond rates contains risk premiums of about 2.3 percentage points (when a perfect foresight estimate is used for the expected exchange rate), after the elimination of a potential transaction cost of about 0.5 percentage points.

In Norway we found high political risk between mid-1986 and early-1988. In this period, the risk premiums amount to about 3.6 percentage points after the elimination of transaction costs when a perfect foresight estimate is used for the expected exchange rate. In Finland, the estimated risk premiums amounted to about 2 percentage points in 1988:4–1990:2, whereas in Sweden in 1990 they amounted to about 3.2 percentage points.

The next step is to split the risk premiums into its political and exchange rate parts. Figure 1.10 shows a possible proxy for the latter premium — the relative variability of inflation — for which it is assumed that a high value indicates a high exchange rate risk premium for investing in that particular market. Using this measure, it would appear as though, with the exception of Finland in 1986, exchange rate risk was low in the Nordic region during the period(s) considered.

1.5.4 Transparency, Political Risk, and Foregone Economic Growth

In our analysis of the gap between the Nordic domestic bond rates and the OECD benchmark rate we thus find indications that the premium for political risk during periods constituted a large part of the gap. To tie the whole thing together we might now go one step further and exemplify, tentatively, the order on which the cost — in terms of foregone GDP growth — of the sort of non-transparent policy-making that this political risk premium reflects ends up.

To illustrate the magnitude of foregone economic growth let us take the case of Denmark and the high political risk period following the 'potato diet cure' in Denmark in the mid-1980s. By combining the interest rate sensitivity of the Danish GDP we end up with an 'estimated' 1.2–1.5 percentage points lower growth rate in Danish GDP over the last years of the 1980s than would otherwise be obtained. In a similar way we can make an out-of-sample estimate using this line of arguing for Sweden. Contrary to Denmark and Norway, Sweden experienced increased political risk during the first half of the 1990s. The political risk was further fueled

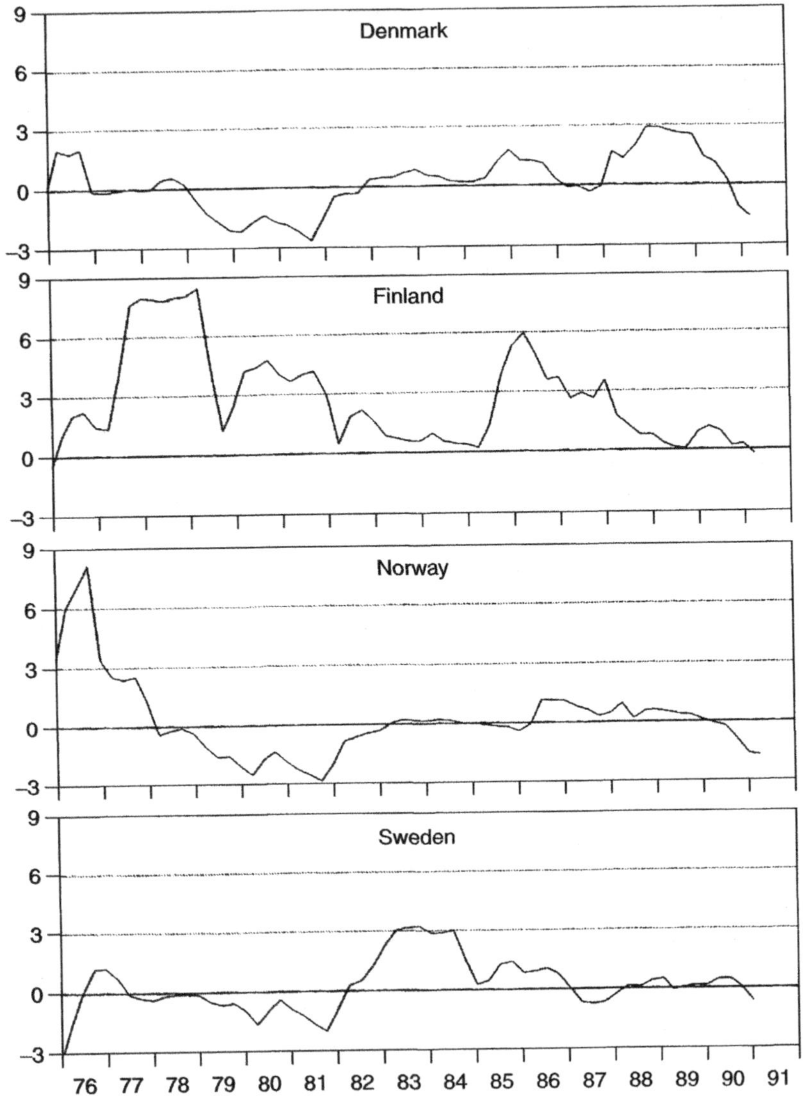

Figure 1.10: Relative variance in inflation as a measure of currency risk in the Nordic region. Quarterly data, end of period observations. Calculated as the difference between the variance in domestic inflation and the OECD inflation. The variances are based on annual inflation measured on monthly observations over the preceding 24 months.

by uncertainty about the rules of the game before and after the election in 1994. Using the same type of decomposition of the interest rate gap as above we argue that the political risk premium charged for investing in Sweden in 1995 was about 2.5 percentage points. Based on the interest rate sensitivity of the Swedish GDP (as estimated by the National Institute of Economic Research in December 1994), a risk premium of that size would cause a 1.5 percentage point lower GDP growth rate over 1996 and 1997 than would otherwise be obtained.

With this simple example we have illustrated how lack of transparency about policy-making feed into a political risk premium that incrementally increases the cost of capital, thus lowering investment and economic growth.

1.6 Conclusions

Transparency has become a keyword in the early 2000s. 'Lack of transparency' has been inferred as a retrospective explanation of a number of corporate scandals with both managers and politicians as targets for allegations. 'Transparency' has also received a prominent position in the European growth debate and played a very explicit role in the Lisbon process with benchmarking as a key pillar. And these are just two examples of areas where 'transparency' has received increased attention in recent years.

The aim of this chapter was to link transparency to economic growth. We have assumed this task by developing a framework for the analysis based on existing growth theory. In doing this we managed to sort out three different kinds of transparency. One of these is *institutional transparency* (H). Another is *corporate transparency* (ε). As a third category we suggested the interaction between H and ε. We then illustrated this link, for the case of institutional transparency, with an empirical example. Our causal chain is the following: An improved degree of transparency will lower uncertainty; reduced uncertainty will translate into a lower risk premium. This lower premium reduces the cost of capital by the same amount implying that—*ceteris paribus*—more investment projects will pass the needle's eye in terms of a positive net present value. The increased level of investment will then ultimately materialize in higher economic growth.

As stressed in the chapter, transparency is a multifaceted concept and typically situation-specific in character. A discussion of it requires a specification of area of application. One meaning of it may be useful in a policy context but show up as inadequate when a corporate transparency problem is addressed. A common denominator is uncertainty surrounding the exchange of information. Since the exchange means one sender of information and one (or many) receiver(s) of information it is easy to identify a multitude of sources of dissonance. The sender has his own objectives and expectations of the receiver's objective. In addition, there is also a source of problems in the information *content*. If it is to reflect an objective reality there is uncertainty about the sender's view on this reality (a kind of perception uncertainty). If the reality is to be estimated, then there is uncertainty about the estimate (estimation uncertainty). Moreover, there is also the sender's view on the receiver's objectives and demand for information influencing the information provided or signaled (uncertainty about the receiver). Then there is uncertainty about the information *per se*. Is it a matter of too little, too much, or too ambiguous information for the receiver to digest? Maybe the ambiguousness is of a creative kind? All the last-mentioned sources add to uncertainty about the content.

Considering the multidimensionality of the transparency concept and the important role of both the sender's and the receiver's expectations, it is easy to imagine all problems connected to quantitative studies on the link between transparency and economic growth. Nevertheless, we have made an effort to visualize the link in a simple example emphasizing institutional transparency. In the example we have pinpointed the different elements in the causal chain mentioned above. We have, however, made the assumption that the identified political risk premium—which we isolated in a step-by-step procedure—is entirely due to the lack of transparency, or more correctly, to a deviation from optimal transparency. This assumption conceals a number of issues that can be addressed in a more in-depth way in further studies; such issues include the way uncertainty is related to the deviation from optimal transparency, and how uncertainty is then transformed into risk.

In our example using data from four small, open, political-economy European countries, we identified a number of periods with high institutional uncertainty for which we extracted the political risk premium from the international interest rate differentials on government bonds. The size of the premiums are such that when multiplied with the aggregate interest rate sensitivity of economic growth of the country in question, the impression emerges that the foregone economic growth due to a lack of institutional transparency (or deviation from optimal transparency) may occasionally be very substantial. Because our measure—based on the uncertainty created by unstable and frequently changed policies—indicates substantial social costs, the argument that a reform is 'balanced' when it is financed (in a budgetary sense) appears simplistic, or downright incorrect: the argument ignores costs stemming from the uncertainty created and signaled by the policy change.

In the present chapter—aimed to be general in scope—we have been forced to paint with very broad brush strokes, and to attempt to encompass a wide range of areas of specialization. The remainder of the book will therefore be devoted to in-depth studies of different specific kinds of transparency. Hence, most of the combinations of 'H,' 'ε,' or '$H \Leftrightarrow \varepsilon$' will be addressed. Chapters 2–5 all emphasize institutional transparency (*H*). They focus on issues related to monetary policy, competition policy, environmental policy, and human capital policy, respectively. Chapters 6–9 also address institutional transparency, but with emphasis on the role of regulators and their opportunities to increase transparency about the cost of corporate exit—i.e., bankruptcy costs and the rules of the 'financial market game.' Chapters 8 and 9 link institutional transparency to corporate transparency ($H \Leftrightarrow \varepsilon$): Chapter 8 by combining bank insolvency procedures with market discipline, and Chapter 9 by linking legal determinants to the demand and supply of equity.

In Chapters 10–12, the main focus is on corporate transparency (ε) within a given institutional context. Chapter 10 discusses transparency effects of the new international financial reporting standards (IFRS), in effect in Europe as of January 2005, whereas in Chapter 11 the transparency effects of the SOX are discussed from a European perspective. Chapter 12 addresses the issue of how different types of disclosure and transparency are reflected in corporate capital structures. Finally, Chapters 13 and 14 return to the relation between institutional and corporate transparency, but now with a stronger role of companies ($H \Leftrightarrow \varepsilon$). Chapter 13 focuses on transparency issues related to the interaction between multinational enterprises (MNE) and the EU-level policy-making. Lobbying is here a key ingredient. Chapter 14, finally, addresses the lack of transparency in terms of the effect of corruption on inward foreign direct investment in Europe.

References

Adler, M., & Dumas, B. (1975). Optimal international acquisitions. *Journal of Finance, 30*, 1–20.

Aharoni, Y. (1966). *The foreign investment decision process*. Cambridge, MA: Harvard Business School.

Aliber, R. (1974). Attributes of national monies and the interdependence of national monetary policies. In: R. Aliber (Ed.), *National monetary policies and the international financial system* (pp. 111–126). Chicago: University of Chicago, Studies in Business and Society, Series 3.

Angeletos, G. -M., & Pavan, A. (2004). Transparency of information and coordination in economies with investment complementarities. *American Economic Review, 94*(2) (AEA Papers and Proceedings), 91–98.

Banerjee, A. V. (1992). A simple model of herd behavior. *Quarterly Journal of Economics, 107*(3), 797–817.

Barro, R. (1991). Economic growth in a cross-section of countries. *Quarterly Journal of Economics, 106*(2), 407–443.

Barro, R. (1997). *Determinants of economic growth: A cross-country empirical study*. Cambridge, MA: MIT Press.

Basi, I. (1963). *Determinants of United States private direct investment in foreign countries*. Kent State University, Kent, Ohio, USA.
Bikhchandani, S., Hirshleifer, D., & Welch, I. (1992). A theory of fads, fashion, custom, and cultural change as informational cascades. *Journal of Political Economy, 100*(5), 992–1026.
Blanchard, O. J., & Watson, M. W. (1982). Bubbles, rational expectations, and financial markets. In: P. Wachtel (Ed.), *Crises in the economic and financial structure*. Lexington, DC: Heath and Company.
Blanke, J., Paua, F., & Sala-i-Martin, X. (2003). *The growth competitiveness index: Analyzing key underpinnings of economic growth*. Global Competitiveness Report of the World Economic Forum.
Brewer, T. (1983). Political sources of risk in the international money market. *Journal of International Business Studies, 14*, 161–164.
Carlin, W., & Mayer, C. (2003). Finance, investment, and growth. *Journal of Financial Economics, 69*, 191–226.
Cecchini Report. (1988). *Cost of non-Europe*. Brussels: European Commission.
Dooley, M. P., & Isard, P. (1986). *Country preferences and exchange rate determination*. Washington, DC: IMF.
Dow, S., Klaes, M., & Montagnoli, A. (2005). Monetary policy by signal. Paper presented at the SUERF/Bank of Finland conference on open market operations and the financial markets, Helsinki, September 22–23, 2005. Forthcoming in D. Mayes, & J. Toporowski (Eds), *Open market operations and the financial markets*. London: Routledge.
Durnev, A., Li, K., Morck, R., & Yeung, B. (2004). Capital markets and capital allocation: Implications for economies in transition. *Economics of Transition, 12*(4), 593–634.
Economist. (1998a). The perils of global capital. Economist, April 11, pp. 52–55.
Economist. (1998b). Don't wait up. Economist, October 3, pp. 83–84.
Economist. (1998c). Euro brief: Faster forward. Economist, November 28, pp. 83–84.
Economist. (1999). The world economy: Coming in from the cold. Economist, September 25 (survey), pp. 35–38.
Economist. (2001a). In praise of rules. Economist, April 7, p. 3.
Economist. (2001b). The common good. Economist, December 1 (survey), p. 10.
Economist. (2001c). Borders and barriers. Economist, December 1 (survey), p. 18.
Economist. (2003). As clear as mud: Central banks. Economist, August 9, p. 64.
Economist. (2004). A perfect market. Economist, May 15 (survey), p. 4.
Edwards, S. (1984). LDC foreign borrowing and default risk: An empirical investigation 1976–1980. *American Economic Review, 74*, 726–734.
Forssbæck, J., & Oxelheim, L. (2003). *Money markets and politics — a study of European financial integration and monetary policy options*. Cheltenham: Edward Elgar.
Frey, B. S. (1990). Institutions matter: The comparative study of institutions. *European Economic Review, 34*, 443–449.
Galbraith, J. C. (1955). *The great crash*. New York: Houghton Mifflin.
Geraats, P. (2002). Central bank transparency. *Economic Journal, 112*, 532–565.

Gertler, M., Hubbard, R. G., & Kashyap, A. K. (1991). Interest rate spreads, credit constraints and investment fluctuations: An empirical investigation. In: R. Hubbard (Ed.), *Financial markets and financial crises* (pp. 11–31). Chicago: University of Chicago.

Grauer, F. L. A., Litzenberger, R. H., & Stehle, R. E. (1976). Sharing rules and equilibrium in an international capital market under uncertainty. *Journal of Financial Economics, 3*, 233–256.

Grossman, S. J., & Stiglitz, J. E. (1980). On the impossibility of informationally efficient markets. *American Economic Review, 70*(3), 393–408.

Grubel, H. G. (1968). International diversified portfolios: Welfare gains and capital flows. *American Economic Review*, (December), *58*(5), 1299–1314.

Grubel, H. G., & Fadner, K. (1971). The interdependence of international equity markets. *Journal of Finance*, (March), *26*(1), 89–94.

Hellwig, C. (2005). *Heterogenous information and the welfare effects of public information disclosures*. Working Paper, October, UCLA.

Huang, H., & Xu, C. (1999). Institutions, innovations, and growth. *American Economic Review, 89*(2), 438–443.

Kanwar, S., & Evenson, R. (2003). Does intellectual property protection spur technological change? *Oxford Economic Papers, 55*(2), 235–264.

Keohane, R. O., & Nye Jr., J. S. (2000). Globalization: What's new? What's not? (And so what?). *Foreign Policy, 118*, 104–120.

Keohane, R. O., & Nye Jr., J. S. (2001). *Between centralization and fragmentation: The club model of multilateral cooperation and problems of democratic legitimacy*. Research Working Paper 01-004, John F. Kennedy School of Government, Harvard University.

King, R. G., & Levine, R. (1993). Finance and growth: Schumpeter might be right. *Quarterly Journal of Economics, 108*(3), 717–737.

Kobrin, S. (1979). Political risk: A review and reconsideration. *Journal of International Business Studies, 10*, 67–80.

Kobrin, S. (1982). *Managing political risk assessment: Strategic response to environmental change*. Berkeley: University of California Press.

Kobrin, S., Basek, J., Blank, S., La Palombara, J. (1980). The assessment and evaluation of noneconomic environments by American firms: A preliminary report. *Journal of International Business Studies, 11*, 32–47.

Kopits, G., & Symansky, S. (1998). *Fiscal policy rules*. Occasional Paper no 162, Washington, DC: IMF.

La Porta, R., López-de-Silanes, F., Shleifer, A., & Vishny, R. W. (1997). Legal determinants of external finance. *Journal of Finance, 52*(3), 1131–1150.

Leavy, B. (1984). Assessing country risks for foreign investment decisions. *Long Range Planning, 17*(3), 141–150.

Lessard, D. R. (1983). Comments on Buiter. In: R. Hawkins, R. Lewich, & C. Wihlborg (Eds), *Research in international business and finance*. JAI Press, Greenwich, Conn.

Levine, R. (1997). Financial development and economic growth: Views and agenda. *Journal of Economic Literature, 35*(2), 688–726.

Levy, H., & Sarnat, M. (1970). International diversification of investment portfolios. *American Economic Review*, *60*, 668–675.

Lucas Jr., R. E. (1988). On the mechanics of economic development. *Journal of Monetary Economics*, 22, 3–42.

Matthews, R. C. O. (1986). The economics of institutions and the sources of growth. *Economic Journal*, *96*(384), 903–918.

Mankiw, N. G. (1995). The growth of nations. *Brookings Papers on Economic Activity*, *1995*(1), 275–326.

Minsky, H. P. (1982). *Can 'it' happen again?: Essay on instability and finance*. Armonk: M. E. Sharpe.

Minsky, H. P. (1986). *Stabilizing an unstable economy*. New Haven: Yale University Press.

Morck, R., Yeung, B., & Yu, W. (2000). The information content of stock markets: Why do emerging markets have synchronous stock price movements? *Journal of Financial Economics*, *58*, 215–260.

Morris, S., & Shin, H. S. (2002). Social value of public information. *American Economic Review*, *92*(5), 1521–1534.

North, D. C. (1990). *Institutions, institutional change and economic performance*. Cambridge: Cambridge University Press.

Oxelheim, L. (1984). *Exchange risk management in the modern company—a total approach*. Stockholm: Scandinavian Institute for Foreign Exchange Research.

Oxelheim, L. (1990). *International financial integration*. Heidelberg: Springer.

Oxelheim, L. (1996). *Financial markets in transition—globalization, investment and economic growth*. London: Routledge and International Thomson Press.

Oxelheim, L., & Ghauri, P. (2004). *European Union and the race for foreign direct investment in Europe*. Oxford: Elsevier.

Oxelheim, L., & Randøy, T. (2003). The impact of foreign board members on firm value. *Journal of Banking and Finance*, *27*(12), 2369–2392.

Oxelheim, L., & Wihlborg, C. (1987). *Macroeconomic uncertainty—international risks and opportunities for the corporation*. Chichester: Wiley.

Oxelheim, L., & Wihlborg, C. (2005). *Corporate performance and the exposure to macroeconomic fluctuations*. Stockholm: Norstedts Academic Publishers.

Pagano, M. (1993). Financial markets and growth—an overview. *European Economic Review*, *37*, 613–622.

Rajan, R., & Zingales, L. (1998). Financial dependence and growth. *American Economic Review*, *88*(3), 559–586.

Rivera-Batiz, L. A., & Romer, P. M. (1991). Economic integration and endogenous growth. *Quarterly Journal of Economics*, *106*(2), 531–555.

Rodrik, D., Subramanian, A., & Trebbi, F. (2004). Institutions rule: The primacy of institutions over geography and integration in economic development. *Journal of Economic Growth*, *9*, 131–165.

Romer, P. M. (1986). Increasing returns and long-run growth. *Journal of Political Economy*, *94*(5), 1002–1037.

Romer, P. M. (1990). Endogenous technological change. *Journal of Political Economy*, *98*(5, pt. 2), S71–S102.

Sadka, G. (2004). *Financial reporting, growth, and productivity: Theory and international evidence*. Working Paper, Columbia Business School.

Shiller, R. J. (1984). *Stock prices and social dynamics*. Brookings Papers on Economic Activity, pp. 457–498.

Solnik, B. (1973). *European capital markets. Towards a general theory of international investment*. Lexington: Lexington Books.

Solow, R. M. (1956). A contribution to the theory of economic growth. *Quarterly Journal of Economics*, *70*(1), 65–94.

Stiglitz, J. E., & Weiss, A. (1981). Credit rationing in markets with imperfect information. *American Economic Review*, *71*(3), 393–410.

Stonehill, A., & Dullum, K. (1981). *Internationalizing the cost of capital*. Chichester: Wiley.

Svaleryd, H., & Vlachos, J. (2005). Financial markets, the pattern of industrial specialization and comparative advantage: Evidence from OECD countries. *European Economic Review*, *49*, 113–144.

Temin, P. (1976). *Did monetary forces cause the great depression*. Cambridge: MIT Press.

Thornton, D. (2003). Monetary policy transparency: Transparent about what? *The Manchester School*, *71*(5), 478–497.

Wurgler, J. (2000). Financial markets and the allocation of capital. *Journal of Financial Economics*, *58*, 187–214.

Chapter 2

Economic Policy and Institutional Transparency: The ECB[1]

Iain Begg

2.1 Introduction

The world of central banking has changed considerably in recent years for all sorts of reasons (Blinder, 2004) and in the process, considerably more attention has been paid to how central banks (CBs) communicate with the financial markets, other policy-makers and the public at large. Much recent research has sought to explore the different dimensions of CB transparency and the strategies by which CB communication with other actors is achieved. The more the market knows about the approach, aims and likely tactics of the monetary authorities, the greater is the probability that market practitioners will make soundly based choices and be able to limit uncertainty. As a result and to the extent that mistaken interpretations are avoided, the cost of capital ought to be kept down.

Yet, part of the art of the CB is to wield its power to surprise financial markets in order to alter behaviour, a power that may, on occasion, lead to mis-pricing of financial instruments. A balance therefore has to be struck between the elements of certainty and surprise. In resolving this tension, any CB has to pay particular attention to its communication strategy and to consider where to set limits on how much it reveals about its approach and thinking. Many authors (see Winkler,

[1]The research on which this paper draws is part of the Integrated Project 'New Modes of Governance' (www.eu-newgov.org), financially supported by the European Union (EU) under the 6th Framework programme (Contract No CIT1-CT-2004-506392). The customary caveats apply.

Corporate and Institutional Transparency for Economic Growth in Europe

ISBN: 0-08-044665-5

2002; Issing, 2005) have stressed that transparency and volume of information are far from equivalent, and there are also debates about what should be disclosed and when.

As a comparative newcomer, the European Central Bank (ECB) has had simultaneously (and rapidly) to establish its credibility in assuring price stability and to fulfil its role in EU economic governance, while also being sensitive to the demands of financial markets. Certain early communication blunders plainly caused misunderstandings and some dismay, even if the overall verdict on the ECB is generally positive (see, for example, Allsopp & Artis, 2003; and, from an operational perspective, Bartolini & Prati, 2003). However, the more important questions are whether, on the one hand, the institutional structures allow an appropriate level of transparency, and on the other, whether the ECB is able to easily adapt its practices to reflect changing circumstances.

The aim of this chapter is to assess the role of the ECB in signalling its intentions to other economic agents and thus in shaping the environment in which savers and borrowers function. In terms of the overall aims of this book, CB transparency can be regarded as a key element and in this sense it can be regarded as a horizontal facet of transparency insofar as it affects both sides of the capital formation process. The chapter adopts a normative approach to the assessment of ECB transparency, focusing on whether the current approach is optimal in how it affects the risk premia. It starts by discussing the changes in central banking practice, then goes on to explore the notion of transparency as applied to CBs and how it bears on the conduct of monetary policy. Section 2.4 explains and documents the ECB approach to transparency and how it compares with other CBs, then Section 2.5 examines some of the key debates about transparency and what they might imply for the ECB and the capital formation process. Concluding comments complete the chapter.

2.2 The Changing Face of CBs

Central banks have been transformed in the last 20 years and in the process they have had radically to rethink their approaches to transparency (Fry et al., 2000). Two decades ago, it was part of the approach of CBs to be distant and opaque (Mishkin, 2004). Part of the reason was that CBs had to work hard to keep themselves at arms length from political pressures. An intellectual rationale for this stance could be identified in terms of the necessity for a long-term focus on price stability, rather than the short-term priorities of political leaders; hence, Rogoff's (1985) idea of the conservative central banker, itself stemming from the time inconsistency literature (Kydland & Prescott, 1977).

The changes that have taken place in central banking are partly rooted in developments in macroeconomic theory, but also reflect underlying change in markets, on the one hand, and in the process of holding policy-makers to account, on the other. Blinder and Wyplosz (2004) identify four mains trends that have characterised the recent evolution of CBs. These are

- Granting of independence to CBs, with the aim of shielding them from political influence. Blinder and Wyplosz note that the development of the time inconsistency literature gave a momentum to this trend and they also suggest that the empirical evidence shows that there have been clear gains in stability as a result, without apparent loss of output. There is not, however, a single model of CB independence and other contributors (see the survey by Berger, de Haan, & Eijffinger, 2001) have highlighted the various differences in types of independence that can be observed.
- A shift towards inflation targeting is the second major trend, although Blinder and Wyplosz point out that the three largest CBs (the Federal Reserve, the Bank of Japan and the European Central Bank) do not formally target inflation.
- Third, there has been a widespread shift towards monetary policy committees, rather than having the decision vested in a single individual, be it the head of the CB or the finance minister. In this respect, other CBs have adopted the long-standing practice of the Bundesbank and the Federal Reserve.
- The fourth trend is towards greater transparency, which Blinder and Wyplosz argue is part of a wider political shift towards holding policy-makers to account[2] and providing access to information, as well as a presumption that it is economically desirable for information to be made available unless there is a compelling reason to withhold it.

Blinder and Wyplosz also note that these four trends are inter-related: 'Central bank independence calls for accountability and also seems to have tilted the playing field in the direction of decision-making by committee. Accountability, in turn, would seem to require a higher degree of transparency. And transparency, of course, is one of the most visible hallmarks of inflation targeting.' In particular, they argue that the links between the third and fourth trends are critical and that, in any CB communication strategy, it is important to identify both how CB information is distributed and for there to be effective channels through which the CB receives information. This will involve a variety of methods of communication, rather than a single approach aimed at all 'stakeholders'.

[2]They note that the Fed open-market committee (FOMC) has embraced greater transparency in recent years, even though its statutes are unchanged and it consequently faced no obligation to behave differently.

A fifth trend that could be added to this list is that in a financially integrated global economy, the decisions of the most powerful CBs are at the heart of global economic stability. What the Fed or the ECB decide has ramifications not just for their respective economies, but also for other countries. In parallel, the CBs have become more dominant actors in shaping economic policy. In part, too, what is expected of CBs has changed as a result of the growing sophistication, liquidity and centrality of financial markets in modern economies. The proliferation of different sorts of financial instruments and the power of financial markets means that CBs have to work with, rather than dictate to, these actors. At the same time, predicting what the CB will do has important repercussions for the cost of capital and for capital formation, and has become an industry in itself. Their credibility, too, has become ever more crucial in supporting this enhanced role in economic governance, shifting the balance away from active fiscal policy, and part of this is how the policy is presented. What CBs say now has as much impact as what they do—memorably captured in the title of an article by Guthrie and Wright (2000) as 'open ***mouth*** operations' [emphasis added].

The move to boost communication has not only been widely followed among CBs, but is also now seen as a critical part of the central bankers' toolkit. Despite marked differences in statutes, mandates and settings, the shift to higher visibility and the use of well-researched arguments to explain and justify decisions is pervasive. It also represents a sea change in approach from the Olympian reserve of the central bankers of yester-year that has been reinforced by changing organisation within CBs. Research, these days, is at the heart of what CBs do, not only because it provides the basis for decisions, but also because its dissemination is an important means of communication.

Goodfriend (2005), commenting on the Fed, makes the following connections:

> The return to fully explicit interest rate policy in 1994 initiated greater use of communications in support of monetary policy actions. The enhanced visibility of interest rate policy actions increased the public's appetite for transparency and encouraged even more Fed communication with markets. The train of events worked like this: Announcing the federal funds rate targets enabled the federal funds rate futures market to mature. That, in turn, made the path of expected future interest rate policy actions more visible to the public. Market participants and the public began to debate Fed concerns and intentions for future interest rates more openly. By measuring the distance between market expectations and its internal intentions for the future funds rate, the Fed could judge the effectiveness of its communications about monetary policy and how

they might be adjusted to achieve a desired effect. The "conversation" between markets and the Fed became particularly important in 2003, when the federal funds rate was 1 percent and the Fed wished to lower the yield curve to fight the deflation risk by steering expected future interest rates lower with language that signaled its intention to be patient in raising interest rates.

2.3 The Meaning of Transparency as Applied to CBs

There is no single definition of what constitutes CB transparency. Recognising that what is at issue is access to information, Geraats (2002, p. 533) defines CB transparency as 'the absence of asymmetric information between monetary policy makers and other economic agents', a definition that does not necessarily mean that the greater the volume of information published, the more transparency there is. From an operational perspective, a simple definition of transparency is provided by the ECB on its website. 'Transparency means that the CB provides the general public and the markets with all relevant information on its strategy, assessments and policy decisions as well as its procedures in an open, clear and timely manner.' In short, the aim is to explain what it does and why it does it, though the use of the word 'relevant' is intriguing. Geraats (2002, p. 533) while acknowledging that greater transparency should reduce uncertainty, goes on to say that 'transparency may affect the incentives that policy makers face to manipulate private sector beliefs through signalling'. She also highlights an apparent paradox, which is that some theoretical arguments against transparency stress its effects on uncertainty, yet reduced uncertainty—which ought to reduce the cost of capital—is seen by policy-makers as one of the main benefits of a more transparent system.

While the meaning of the term might appear to be self-evident, there are arguably two very different facets of transparency with regard to CBs. First, if it is correct that the *quid pro quo* of conferring independence on a CB is that it should then be subject to more intensive accountability, then how it is achieved matters. This can be seen as a political bargain in which the CB, as the agent for conducting monetary policy, has to be able to demonstrate to governments and citizens alike that it has conducted its affairs in a manner consistent with the mandate. As Issing (2004, p. 12) explains, 'this requires transparency in all areas relevant to the fulfilment of its mandate and a willingness to convey to the public, in a systematic and consistent way, all information relevant to its decision-making.'

The second dimension of transparency concerns communication with economic actors so as to ensure that whatever monetary policy is followed is effective. It has little to do with accountability in the sense of democratic oversight, but is about economic efficiency: the use of the policy instrument (the interest rate) can be as precisely calibrated as possible and any variability in the effects of policy change is kept to a minimum. Issing (2004, p. 12) observes that 'it should contribute to the anchoring of inflation expectations and minimise false expectations on the part of financial markets and the wider public regarding policy responses.' By doing so, the CB gains credibility and can also achieve a better trade-off between price stability and growth in the real economy (Levin et al., 2004). A measure of success in this latter regard is whether the CB is able to achieve the desired performance; in this context, it is the rather different concept of 'output legitimacy' as espoused by political scientists such as Scharpf (1999) that is relevant in judging the CB. ECB President Jean-Claude Trichet[3] emphasises that 'successful central bank communication supports predictability and correct price formation in financial markets, contributes to efficient allocation of funds and reduces uncertainty about future interest rates'. He describes a vision of effective communication that conveys clarity about monetary policy, but recognises that it is impossible for a CB (because of uncertainty about economic circumstances and changes in the economy, as well as inevitable risks) to preannounce to the market precisely its future monetary policy decisions. Arguably, therefore, the test of good communication is that the markets will, on the basis of the same information, arrive at broadly similar conclusions.

The second need for transparency does not necessarily call for the same strategy or forms of communication as the first, especially where the market expects the information to be sufficiently detailed to allow adequate understanding of what is intended. Where it is technical information about the assumptions underlying the conduct of monetary policy, the implicit policy model or the data and forecasts used, it is a fine judgement how much to reveal. Moreover, the CB has to communicate its approach to the public rather than letting markets assume that they can work out—rightly or wrongly—what the strategy is (Woodford, 2005). By contrast, for political accountability purposes, it can actually be confusing, if not misleading if there is too much detail. Issing (2005, p. 12) explains the dilemma thus: 'there is clearly a need to strike a balance between, on the one hand, being clear enough to be properly understood by the general public and, on the other, providing information which is sufficiently comprehensive to do justice to the uncertainties and complexity of the decision-making process.' Part of this is that the CB should not deliberately mislead the market in trying to steer expectations, nor should it be a slave to them: a tricky balancing act. Blinder (2004) makes the point emphatically that the long-term perspective sought from the CB, as well as

[3]In a speech to the International Club of Frankfurt Economic Journalists on 24 January 2005, Frankfurt am Main.

independence, can be compromised by taking a lead from the market just as surely as by being instructed by politicians. Yet, the financial markets are the means by which monetary policy is transmitted and, for this reason, have to be courted.

Bernanke (2004, p. 3) suggests that the 'value of more-open communication is that it clarifies the CB's views and intentions, thereby increasing the likelihood that financial-market participants' rate expectations will be similar to those of the policymakers themselves—or, if views differ, ensuring at least that the difference can not be attributed to the policymakers' failure to communicate their outlook, objectives, and strategy to the public and the markets'. He also observes (Bernanke, 2004, p. 3) that 'without guidance from the central bank, market participants can do no better than form expectations based on the average past behavior of monetary policymakers, a strategy that may be adequate under some or even most circumstances but may be seriously misguided in others'. Timing is also crucial, especially the distinction between short-term communication needed to explain decisions and the medium- to long-term obligation to demonstrate consistency and, by implication, predictability (Issing, 2005).

An important question that arises from this debate is whether there are real conflicts between the accountability and efficiency rationales for transparency and, if so, how to separate the two dimensions. Although supporters of open government might find his views somewhat extreme, Thornton (2003, p. 480) argues forcefully that policy efficacy should be the sole test of whether transparency is worthwhile and that it should never be an end in itself. He asserts that 'when it comes to policy effectiveness and democratic accountability, economists' preferences are—i.e. they should be—lexicographic. The principle of democratic accountability enters the decision-making process only if actions taken to increase transparency do not impinge on the effectiveness of policy'.

2.3.1 The Economic Motivations for Transparency

From the cost of capital perspective central to this volume (see introductory chapter by Forssbaeck and Oxelheim), it is not unreasonable to focus on the economic efficiency dimension. Concentrating on the economic case, especially since much of the recent interest in the subject concerns its role in the transmission of monetary policy, it is evident that there is a degree of consensus in the recent literature on the principal motivations for transparency (Bernanke, 2004; Blinder, 2004; Howells & Biefang-Frisancho, 2005; Poole, 2005; Issing, 2004, 2005; Woodford, 2005). These are to

- assure the predictability of interest rate decisions.
- anchor longer-term expectations of what the CB will do and, most importantly, its views on inflation. In addition to shaping expectations, Jansen and de Haan

(2004) suggest that an important motivation is to reduce noise, thereby improving predictability.
- signal to market participants what the future course of policy decisions will be, thereby bridging the gap between what short-term interest rates mean and the economic significance of long-term interest rates, which affect spending and investment decisions.

There are several attributes that will be conducive to effective transparency and communication and which could be regarded as desiderata for a modern CB (Blinder, 2004). They include

- How clear the messages being conveyed are.
- Openness to public scrutiny in relation to nature of deliberations, decisions and possibly the way votes go and the models or forecasts that inform them.
- Substantive content that means that what the CB reveals provides other stakeholders with information that enables them to make informed judgements. This could embrace a range of themes (Woodford, 2005; Poole, 2005), such as the economic analysis that informs decisions, explanation of decisions, exposition of the underlying 'model' or rules that govern policy and presentation of views (or biases) on economic prospects and how they will affect future policy decisions.

A conceptual framework for appraising the economic dimension of transparency, reproduced here as Figure 2.1, is put forward by Eijffinger and Geraats (2005), echoing previous papers by the latter of those authors.[4] They, identify five different facets of economic transparency[5] which, they argue, represent different stages in the policy process for which choices can be made about what, or how much, to reveal. For each element in the chart, a variety of transparency questions will arise and these will have both direct and indirect effects on the costs of capital. Thus, if a CB is willing to be open about operational errors (the fourth box in the second row of the chart), it seems to be more likely that it will have a reduced inflation bias that will send signals about the trade-off between price and output stability. Transparent procedures can send messages about the likely next move of the CB, especially if minutes or a voting record show whether decisions of the arguments behind them show unanimity or divided viewpoints (Goodhart, 2005; Reinhart, 2005).

It is not, however, easy to judge optimal transparency. On the whole, analysis and explanation are readily accepted as being necessary elements of CB communication, but there is greater controversy over the extent to which CBs should be

[4] A similar approach is to distinguish between transparency in goals, instruments and implementation (Carpenter, 2004).

[5] Although they list a political dimension, it is in the sense of openness about the strategic aim, rather than the link to accountability as discussed above.

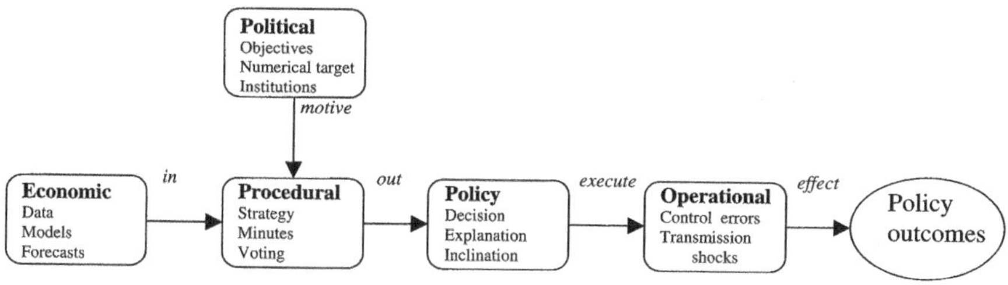

Figure 2.1: The dimensions of transparency in monetary policy (from Eijffinger & Geraats, 2005).

explicit in expounding their forward thinking. There will also be differences among 'consumers/users' of CB communication as well as over time in what is most significant in assessing risk. The implication is that the relationship between the particular configuration of CB transparency and the cost of capital will not necessarily be a stable one. What these and other contributions reveal is that although, there is much common ground in the things about which CBs should be transparent, translating these analyses into policy prescriptions is never easy.

2.3.2 *Transparency and the Transmission Mechanism*

Although some of the answers may seem obvious, given the rationales just discussed, why should transparency matter? A crucial reason is that despite the prominence accorded by market practitioners to the short-term interest rate set by the monetary policy authorities (FED- and ECB-watching and so on), the interest rates which matter for decision-making by private agents only imperfectly follow the lead given by the CB. If the slope of the yield curve is in doubt, the impact of monetary policy decisions (i.e. short-term interest rate changes) will be less easily predictable. This could increase uncertainty, but may also mean that the impact of the policy rate varies depending on the circumstances. Do long rates lead or follow short rates? Monetary transmission occurs principally via the demand for loans, but may be affected by the willingness of lenders to provide them (a credit channel). Monetary transmission channels also include the exchange rate and asset prices, and an effect on expectations of all these variables.

While firm empirical evidence is scant (for early work, see Angeloni & Ehrmann, 2003), the impact of CB communication on the yield curve, on market expectations and on the overall level of interest rates can be quite pronounced. Eusepi (2005, p. 22) finds 'that a sufficient degree of transparency by central banks make the optimal policy rule robust to expectational mistakes, even in the plausible case where the economic agents face other sources of uncertainty about the economic environment'. In an exercise in which they examine the effects of actual interest rate-setting decisions and the statements that accompany the decisions, Bernanke, Reinhart, and Sack (2004) find that the latter have the greater impact on financial market responses. Communication explains two-thirds of the variance, compared with only an eighth of the variance being explained by the decision itself. The significance of transparency for the cost of capital is not easily measured, though the available evidence suggests that well-orchestrated transparency can allow CBs to have lower, and possibly less volatile short-run (i.e. policy) rates. The impact on the long-run nominal interest rate may be up to 50 basis point (Geraats & Eijffinger, 2004), which must be regarded as significant. Transparency can also induce commercial banks to change interest rates quicker in response to monetary policy decisions, yet can diminish volatility. Thus, in Australia, a change in the CB rate translates more quickly into retail rates, with the long-run adjustment time halving to nine months, and increased transparency has reduced the volatility of bank lending rates (Morkel-Kingsbury & Allen, 2005).

However, communication cannot be a substitute for good policy decisions. Thornton (2003, p. 50) argues that credibility has to be earned by results and that consistency is critical to earning credibility, even if the CB does not fully explain its approach: 'a CB that consistently delivers low and stable inflation will have credibility even if it does not publicly announce a specific target'. Good communication has to complement track record, implying that they are not ready substitutes (Issing, 2005), but CBs need to take care to explain the limits of their powers and mandate so as not to engender unrealistic expectations. In comments that manifestly apply to the ECB, Issing stresses the need for a new institution to be clear in its communication for a variety of reasons.

The effects of monetary policy on expectations and the influence thereon of CB communication consequently hold the key to monetary policy effectiveness. The implication is that CBs, which are less transparent will struggle to stabilise expectations, with mis-interpretation of the output gap likely. These points about the impact of transparency are summed up in Figure 2.2, which identifies two main channels affecting the cost of capital, namely what CBs do and what they say. However, it is also important to note that an increasing role is played by market expectations, which simultaneously shape, and are shaped by, both CB decisions and statements.

2.4 Transparency of the ECB's Monetary Policy

Like all other CBs, the ECB has thought carefully about transparency and has adopted procedures that it considers to be appropriate. On its website it states that

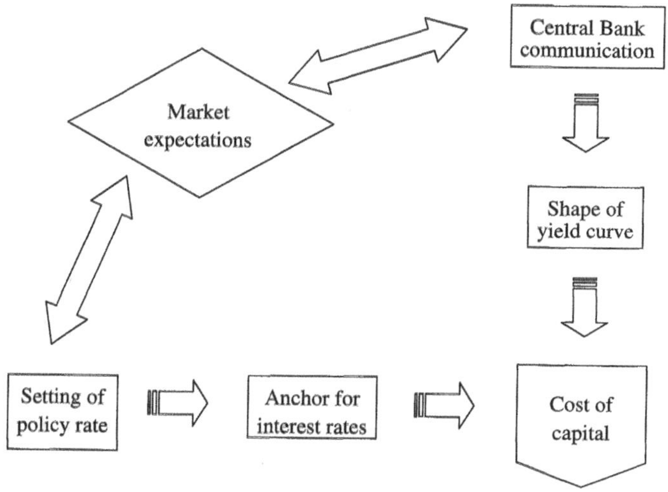

Figure 2.2: Central Bank influences on the cost of capital.

'today, most CBs, including the ECB, consider transparency as crucial. This is true especially for their monetary policy framework. The ECB gives a high priority to communicating effectively with the public.' Credibility, self-discipline and predictability are highlighted as aims. The ECB argues, further, that transparency imposes a vital discipline on the CB because it provides the means for effective scrutiny of its actions, while predictability is about having in place a system that will progressively build up in the public mind an understanding of how the CB can be expected to respond. The underlying logic is that 'if market agents can broadly anticipate policy responses, this allows a rapid implementation of changes in monetary policy into financial variables. This in turn can shorten the process by which monetary policy is transmitted into investment and consumption decisions. It can accelerate any necessary economic adjustments and potentially enhance the effectiveness of monetary policy.' It is, thus, evident that the ECB takes transparency seriously and is aware of its potential to affect the cost of capital.

2.4.1 The Approach to Transparency of the ECB

There are many components to the ECB's strategy towards transparency and communication, several of which reflect practices adopted by other CBs. These can be summarised as follows:

- Its target and monetary policy strategy have been clearly explained.
- Voting procedures and other aspects of decisions making have been made public, although decisions have, up to now, been reported to be taken by consensus.
- However, it does not reveal voting records (irrelevant anyway, so long as decision-making by consensus prevails), nor does it publish minutes of meetings — indeed, the first President of the ECB (Duisenberg) frequently voiced his opposition to such publication.
- The ECB holds a 'real-time' press conference immediately after Governing Council meetings at which the decision is presented and the reasons for it explained. Journalists also have the opportunity to question the President or other members of the Executive Board (EB) present.
- It publishes its forecasts, although it did not do so at first, but presents them as the work of staff, rather than being a firm institutional view.
- The six EB members give frequent speeches on different aspects of ECB policy and make these speeches freely available via the website, and the national CB Governors also make frequent speeches.
- Unlike the Fed (since 2003), the ECB does not try to signal a bias (for example towards tightening) in its likely future decisions.
- The European Parliament is consulted about the appointment of EB members though it does not have a formal power of veto.
- Accountability procedures, such as appearances before the Economic and Monetary Affairs Committee of the European Parliament, appear to be meticulously respected, and there is also a considerable visibility of the ECB before national parliaments.
- In addition, EB members participate in the EU's macroeconomic dialogue, a forum in which the social partners as well as national finance ministry representatives discuss policy orientations. Board members also sit on the (powerful) *Economic and Financial Committee* along with Finance Ministry representatives from Member States.

2.4.2 The ECB Compared

Eijffinger and Geraats (2005) make a valiant attempt to quantify the overall transparency of different CBs by building up scores for each of the components shown in Figure 2.1, above. They find that the most transparent CBs are the Reserve Bank of New Zealand and the Bank of England, while the ECB and the Federal Reserve are similarly ranked. In their methodology, the ECB falls down on procedural transparency because it does not publish minutes or votes. It is, however, more transparent than the Fed in respect of the political dimensions and some aspects of 'operational'. The research also shows that the ECB had become more transparent by 2002 than it had been at the outset, notably through the decision to start publishing forecasts.

The institutional context of the ECB is unique in that it has no direct counterpart in the form of a powerful finance ministry that both sets fiscal policy and can 'bargain' on the macroeconomic policy mix. Some critics, such as Boyer (1999) regard this as a flaw in the architecture and argue for the establishment of a *gouvernement économique* as a counter-weight, the implication being that without it, the balance of power in macroeconomic policy-making is too uneven in favour of an unelected agent. Although it is always important to recall that the ECB is still a young institution and to recognise that an initial need to establish credibility was a high priority, it has been criticised in the literature for inadequate transparency. Buiter (1999), for example, has argued for publication of minutes and voting records, while de Haan and Eijffinger (2000) have suggested that the ECB (in common with other continental CBs prior to 1999, may have been too prone to hiding its strategy from the markets. It may be that the monetary policy strategy itself bears on transparency. This strategy comprises two pillars (Issing et al., 2001), the first being that the ECB sets a reference value for the growth of broad money, while the second pillar comprises scrutiny of a broader range of indicators. Svensson (2004) has been a consistent critic of this approach, and others have suggested that the ECB is behind the state of the art in not explicitly adopting an inflation-targeting approach and there are suggestions that it is the inflation targeting CBs, which have been most innovative (Woodford, 2005), especially in their approach to communication.

Yet the ECB does seem to fulfil expectations in relation to accountability. Research by Lepper and Sterne (2002) shows that the extent of ECB appearances before Parliament and the commitment of its president and senior board members to attend is in line with practice elsewhere. They note that the US Congress holds fewer meetings on monetary policy than its EU counterpart. Moreover, the practice that has evolved has been for the CB President to report on its monetary policy and whether its aims have been achieved, something that has not become established in a majority of other contexts, including the US. It can also be argued that the press conference has been a key innovation (Trichet, 2005). Evidence that the communications strategy is working is that interest rate spreads in the euro area have narrowed, signalling low expectations of future inflation. In addition, a range of other indicators of stability can be cited in support of the contention that ECB decisions are as predictable as comparable CBs (Issing, 2005).

2.4.3 The ECB's Transparency Record

Why then is the ECB criticised? Certainly, in its early years, it was prone to the occasional communications gaffe and there may in addition have been a sense in which the markets were probing it for vulnerabilities in a way that could have increased the risk premium. It is also true that the reluctance to divulge minutes and voting records has been seen as a less complete form of transparency than elsewhere, though decisions by consensus mute this point. However, there is weight in the ECB defence that this was a justified reticence in a new, multinational institution that had to assert its independence from political interference and therefore had to safeguard its NCB governors from the sort of domestic pressures that might arise. Transcripts of FOMC meetings, after all, are only published five years later. It is also germane that parts of the ECB approach to transparency, such as the press conference at the end of GC meetings, go beyond what others CBs do. As the Economist once put it: 'the ECB's mistake, perhaps, has been not to call its press statement "minutes", and not to call its monthly bulletin an "inflation report"' (Economist, 27 September 1999).

Jansen and de Haan (2004) conduct an interesting study of ECB communication in which they try both to quantify it and to appraise its evolution. They conclude that in some respects the ECB has improved its communication, becoming more consistent and clearer on its stance towards the external value of the euro. They also draw attention to the important role played by national CBs, in particular the Bundesbank, though their statements are more prone to being contradictory statements, especially about topics other than the inflation rate. Heinemann and Ullrich (2005) conduct a similar exercise based on identification of key phrases in ECB press conferences in which they concentrate on how ECB communications bear on the expected evolution of monetary policy. Although they find that ECB statements provide a good guide for markets, they assert that these cannot fully substitute for harder research based on analysis of relevant variables.

Ehrmann and Fratzscher (2005) also investigate ECB communication in comparative context and arrive at three distinct models:

- The FOMC makes decisions collegially, but allows more individuality in communication.
- The Bank of England Monetary Policy Committee (MPC) members vote individually, but pursue more collegial communication strategies.
- The ECB is collegial both in communication and voting.

They conclude that the communications emanating from the ECB accord most closely with future decisions. This, they argue, means that the ECB becomes highly predictable, whereas for the FOMC, the markets have to decide which members of the FOMC are the most credible, and the task is most difficult for the Bank of England. The empirical finding is, nevertheless, that although the approaches of the FOMC and the ECB Governing Council are distinctive, they both provide a high level of predictability.

2.5 Issues for Debate

Transparency has made great strides in central banking in barely a decade and has fundamentally altered the inter-play between monetary policy and the capital formation process. Yet, as Bernanke, Reinhart, and Sack, (2004) observe, while it is evident that the shift towards transparency has had a marked effect in making CBs more predictable, there is a limit to how far they can go in making binding commitments or adhering strictly to policy rules. More generally, a crucial question is whether the communication mix, especially of the ECB, is correct. If not, how could the ECB improve on what it currently does? Poole (2005, p. 4) articulates the challenge succinctly: 'the ultimate test is whether disclosure yields better policy outcomes.' Blinder (2005, p. 10) makes a fascinating observation: 'Suffice it to say that while the Federal Reserve has often hesitated over specific incremental increases in disclosure, and while it has sometimes warned of adverse consequences from greater transparency, virtually none of these adverse consequences have ever come to pass, and the Fed has never regretted its step-by-step movements toward greater openness'.

2.5.1 Communication about What?

Communication comprises a range of mechanisms that can go beyond simply explaining CB decisions and also involves behavioural adaptation. For example, Bernanke et al. (2004) show that when Greenspan emphasised that the FOMC would give more weight to payroll data than other labour market measures, market expectations started to change. They show that a change in CB statements in August 2003 led subsequently to a statistically significant increase in the reaction of the markets to a 'surprise' in payroll data: specifically, a positive surprise of 100,000 jobs resulted in an 11 basis point rise in Treasury bond yields compared with 4 basis points beforehand. The inference to draw is that by signalling what might influence future decisions on the federal fund rates, the FOMC is able to steer the market's expectations and thus increase predictability. In the absence of such a steer, the markets might anticipate less well and therefore be obliged to increase the risk premium.

By the same token, the evidence adduced by Bernanke et al. suggests that market expectations can be led away from factors to which the CB pays less attention. What matters most in assessing market expectations is whether markets believe that any change in short-term rates will persist, more than whether they will change, and there is also evidence that what is communicated makes a difference. Chortareas, Stasavage, and Sterne, (2002) examine a key facet of transparency, which is the publication of forecasts. They find that increased transparency in the form of publication of more information on the forecasts is associated with lower inflation irrespective of whether the monetary regime is an inflation targeting one or one in which control of money is the rule. Thus the provision of the information is clearly adding to the markets' capacity to price correctly.

An interesting comment made by Reinhart (2005, p. 2) is that 'more information is usually better. But when policy is made by a committee, that information has to explain the consensus view, identify relevant differences of opinion, and be structured in a way that does not impede the Committee's deliberations or ability to reach a consensus.' The implication is that signalling of short-term intentions is tricky because it can be seen as a promise which, if broken—even for the good reason that circumstances have changed—undermines confidence in the CB. The trick is, therefore, to communicate any signal as being conditional, but the obvious risk is that capital market actors will be more susceptible to confusion, with the implication for the cost of capital that risk premia would increase. Moreover, CBs should do more to make explicit the extent of their commitment to output as opposed to price stabilisation. For the ECB, this may be especially challenging, given that its mandate gives primacy to price stability. Yet if there is an implicit and entrenched criticism—whether warranted or not—of the ECB it is that it pays too little regard to output and employment (Bibow, 2005; Mishkin, 2004).

Any forward-looking statements have to be about balances of risks and thus conditional on events that might alter the assessment of policy priorities. It may also be subject to a re-calibration of the risks based not on any major change, but simply on the accumulation of small packets of information. A critical question is how to deal with prospective turning points. When a tightening or loosening cycle begins, it is generally easy to impart the correct signals to the markets, but as the point at which a step-change or even a reversal approaches, conveying the right signal becomes harder and, potentially, confusing. There may be dissent within a monetary policy committee about future directions as well as the immediate interest rate decision. As a result, what to reveal about the deliberations and the basis for a decision (votes, balance of opinion or whatever) may not be as easy as it sounds (Poole, 2005).

2.5.2 *How much Transparency?*

Judging the optimal degree of CB transparency is not easy, because there is often a disjunction between the need to know and the need to understand (Issing, 1999) and part of the challenge is to achieve a balance between clear communication of strategic aims and the retention of a capacity for tactical surprise (de Haan & Eijffinger, 2000). Some CBs may have gone too far in forgoing the latter with the result that they confuse, rather than enlighten the markets. In transmission, it is arguably the probability that a policy shift will persist that is influential in the capital markets: if they do not believe a short-term rate will persist, it will not be transmitted. An underlying argument in relation to the cost of capital is whether a deviation from 'optimal' transparency will increase risk premia.

There are several aspect of transparency that remain open to debate and for which it is by no means obvious that increased openness will help to lower the cost of capital (or, indeed, have another positive impact). In relation to the forecasting of the inflation rate, Mishkin (2004) shows that there are, in fact, considerable complications in arriving at a decision. Because any forecast is necessarily conditional, publication of the forecast also implies announcement of the conditions that are being used. If the forecast relies on market expectations, the argument can become circular: the CB is then relying on market expectations of what the CB will do. But it is far from easy for the CB to divine its own policy path. On this issue, therefore, Mishkin (2004, p. 13) concludes that 'except in exceptional deflationary circumstances like the one Japan has experienced, announcement of a policy-rate path does not have much to recommend it.' Yet it must be consider a moot point whether publishing the forecast will mislead and thus have costs as well as benefits, or whether instead the market can learn to interpret what the CB publishes. In principle, the expectation would be that a learning-by-doing process would be engaged that should ultimately enable more precise pricing of financial instruments.

Should the CB explain its objective function and thus, reveal what account it takes of the real economy? Here much of the argumentation put forward in Section 2.2 suggests that it should. However, Mishkin (2004) suggests that a potential problem is that it will be difficult to understand for the general public, in contrast to a simple inflation target, and may be counter-productive if it results in confusing signals. But given sophisticated market analysis, it is not obvious why this should be problematic.

Some aspects of what is described in Figure 2.1 as procedural transparency also raise doubts. Gersbach and Hahn (2004), for example, find that publication of voting records is by no means welfare enhancing, especially if some members of the decision-making body are less competent than others or are swayed by the need to be re-elected. Winkler (2002), similarly, casts doubt on the value of too much transparency if the risk is that it confuses rather than informs. On this issue, Issing (1999) has argued that given the composition of the ECB Governing Council in which national CB governors are numerically dominant, a risk is that too much publicly available information on the positions they take may undermine their ability truly to be independent of domestic pressures in their decision-making.

Analysis of transcripts of the FOMC shows that increased transparency can have the effect of reducing the freedom of committee members to express discordant views. After 1993, members of the FOMC knew that their points of view would be made public through the publication of transcripts. Noting that the usual pattern was for Fed Chairman Greenspan to give his view first, and at some length, then to solicit other opinions, Meade and Stasavage (2004, p. 29) show that 'Fed policymakers appear to have responded to the decision to publish meeting transcripts by voicing less dissent with Greenspan's policy proposals for the short-term interest rate'. Insofar as dissent is regarded as creative or desirable in allowing options to be more fully explored, the implication is that transparency can have a negative impact on the quality of decision-making.

Thus, while some types of transparency, in some circumstances, may do harm rather than good, the circumstances in which transparency would have an adverse effect on the cost of capital are not obvious. Even so, how much transparency there should be and whether CBs have the mix right remains an open question (Hughes, Hallett, & Viegi, 2003).

2.5.3 The Way Forward for the ECB

The ECB has, plainly, put in place comprehensive transparency mechanisms. Assessed on both the political and economic dimensions of transparency, the ECB can be regarded as being in line with current practice among leading CBs. Its procedures do, however, differ in detail compared with some other CBs, giving rise to criticisms, but it is probably fair to say that issues such as the non-publication of individual voting records are of a second order of importance compared with the big questions of whether the ECB communicates enough information for markets to understand its strategy or voters to be persuaded that it is acting in accordance with its mandate. From the perspective of this volume as a whole, the key question is whether the ECB could do more, by amending its approach to transparency, to improve the efficiency of its monetary policy in such a way as to lower the cost of capital.

The gradual increase in transparency revealed by the empirical work of Eijffinger and Geraats (2005) suggests that the ECB is alert to the need to review its approach. However, there are two main areas in which it might develop its approach to transparency. The first is explanation of decisions and of the balance of opinion. Though there are, as Glöckler (2005) argues, constitutional constraints that cannot wholly be overlooked, it seems that despite not publishing minutes or announcing a policy bias, the markets are able to 'read' the ECB sufficiently well. But does this go far enough? Although the press conference provides immediate, relevant information, it could be regarded as flawed, especially as any verbal responses to question do not quite have the endorsement of the full Governing Council. By contrast, edited minutes, though they take longer to surface, have been approved by all members. To remedy this, Goodhart (2005) has recommended a 24-hour delay in a press conference and considers that minutes would help the ECB to present its case more clearly, as well as signalling a policy bias. There is, probably, scope in this regard for reform that would enhance predictability and be favourable in terms of the cost of capital.

The second area for rethinking is in what the ECB reveals about the links between its forecasts and its projected policy path, though there are obvious pitfalls. In particular, in any modelling exercise, providing a forecast interest rate more than a few time periods out is subject to a widening range of probabilities and, especially with a committee decision, the possible outcomes become too divergent. Nevertheless, the issue is whether some guidance of the sort practiced by the Fed can help to lower variability in rates. Reinhart (2005) cites evidence that eurodollar future rates have fallen since August 2003, possibly reflecting the announcement of a policy bias, but he also points out that so too have euro rates, despite no announcement. This illustrates the distinction between what Reinhart calls news about the 'policy factor'—that is the setting of the repo rate—and the 'path factor', by which he means information on the likely future setting of the policy rate. Nevertheless, given that it seems to have worked in the US, a shift in this direction may well help to lower risk premia.

2.6 Concluding Comments

Transparency has become a vital part of the central banking toolkit and CBs everywhere have chosen to adopt a far more open approach to the provision of information to the markets, on the one hand, and subjecting themselves to scrutiny, on the other. In part, this trend has been driven by statutory changes, with procedures for holding CBs to account introduced as the direct counterpart of the granting of independence in the conduct of monetary policy. Much of the motivation for greater transparency is, though, the result of a rethinking of how to conduct monetary policy. Rather than using surprise to discipline markets, the current philosophy is that it is understanding of the strategy and the predictability of response that underpins good policy. Behind these changes there is plainly a concern to ensure efficient pricing in the capital market.

There is a growing body of evidence that CB transparency matters for the cost of capital, so that it is an issue that needs to be taken into account in appraising the ECB approach and considering how it might evolve. For example, Bernanke et al. (2004, p. 50) conclude that 'overall, the evidence suggests that FOMC statements have importantly shaped the policy expectations of investors, particularly over the past five years. Indeed, yield-curve movements around FOMC decisions cannot be adequately described by the unexpected component of policy decisions, but are instead influenced to a greater extent by a second factor, which appears to be associated with surprises in the policy statements'. Reinhart (2005, p. 13) sums up the salience for capital formation: 'central bank talk about the future and contingency plans is not an attempt to manipulate markets but rather an effort to ensure more accurate pricing in financial markets. In essence, it is a reflection of the properties that investment decisions depend on the distribution of possible policy outcomes well into the future and that the central bank may well have an information advantage in knowing about its likely future action'.

Does the ECB perform well? The evidence suggests that the markets do not regard the ECB as idiosyncratic in its behaviour and that even if some might have liked to see a more activist response to the stagnation of the EU economy, the ECB has not acted out of character at any point. The ECB has a well-explained goal but is less clear about how it intends to reach it and in signalling its future stance, in contrast to the FED which does signal a bias, but is more cagey about its goals. In these respects, the ECB is circumscribed in its ability to signal via minutes, votes or a policy statement. As the ECB matures (and it is, after all, only just beyond its infancy), it may be that it will elect to adopt somewhat different forms of transparency, such as providing explicit minutes or publishing voting records.

Is all this enough for the ECB to be adjudged as having an optimal degree of transparency from the perspective of the cost of capital? Trichet (2005), admittedly not an unbiased observer, claims that academic studies suggest that the ECB achieves a high degree of predictability, though a critic might suggest that may have something to do with the relative infrequency with which it changes rates. The evidence on spreads and on volatility indicates that the ECB's transparency has become better with encouraging results for risk premia. However, other CBs now place greater reliance on signalling a policy bias and in so doing are able to impart an important signal to financial markets, suggesting that this is a direction the ECB would be advised to take. An overall assessment of ECB transparency would, nevertheless, be 'so far, so good' though with the caveat that it cannot stand still.

References

Allsopp, C. J., & Artis, M. J. (2003). The Assessment EMU, Four Years On. *Oxford Review of Economic Policy*, *19*(1), 1–29.

Angeloni, I., & Ehrmann, M. (2003). Monetary transmission in the euro area: Early evidence. *Economic Policy*, *37*, 470–501.

Bartolini, L., & Prati, A. (2003). The execution of monetary policy: A tale of two central banks. *Economic Policy, 37*, 436–467.

Berger, H., de Haan, J., & Eijffinger, S. (2001). Central bank independence: An update of theory and evidence. *Journal of Economic Surveys, 15*, 3–40.

Bernanke, B. (2004). Central bank talk and monetary policy. Remarks at the Japan Society Corporate Luncheon, New York, 7 October 2004.

Bernanke, B. S., Reinhart, V. R., & Sack, B. P. (2004). Monetary policy alternatives at the zero bound. *Brookings Papers on Economic Activity, 2*, 1–100.

Bibow, J. (2005). *Refocusing the ECB on output stabilization and growth through inflation targeting?* The Levy Economics Institute Working Paper no. 425.

Blinder, A. (2004). *Central banking goes modern.* Princeton, NJ: Princeton University Press.

Blinder, A. (2005). What have we learned since October 1979? *Federal Reserve Bank of Saint Louis Review, 87*, 283–286.

Blinder, A., & Wyplosz, C. (2004). Central bank talk: Committee structure and communication policy. Prepared for the session on "Central Bank Communication" at the ASSA meetings, Philadelphia, January 9, 2005.

Boyer, R. (sous la présidence), (1999). *Le gouvernement économique de la zone euro* Paris: La documentation française.

Buiter, W. (1999). Alice in Euroland. *Journal of Common Market Studies, 37*, 181–210.

Carpenter, S. B. (2004). Transparency and monetary policy: What does the academic literature tell policymakers? Mimeo. Federal Reserve.

Chortareas, G., Stasavage, D., & Sterne, G. (2002). Does it pay to be transparent? International evidence from central bank forecasts. *Federal Reserve Bank of Saint Louis Review, 84*, 99–117.

De Haan, J., & Eijffinger, S. C. W. (2000). The democratic accountability of the European Central Bank: A comment on two fairy-tales. *Journal of Common Market Studies, 38*, 393–407.

Ehrmann, M., & Fratzscher, M. (2005). *Communication and decision-making by central bank committees: Different strategies, same effectiveness?* ECB Working Paper Series no. 488. Frankfurt: ECB.

Eijffinger, S. C. W., & Geraats, P. M. (2005). *How transparent are central banks?* Cambridge Working Papers in Economics no. 0411.

Eusepi, S. (2005). *Central bank transparency under model uncertainty.* Federal Reserve Bank of New York Staff Report no. 199.

Fry, M., Julius, D., Mahadeva, L., Roger, S., & Sterne, G. (2000). Key issues in the choice of monetary policy framework. In: L. Mahadeva, & G. Sterne (Eds), *Monetary frameworks in a global context.* London: Routledge.

Geraats, P. M. (2002). Central bank transparency. *Economic Journal, 112*, F532–F565.

Geraats, P. M., & Eijjfinger, S. C. W. (2004). *Does central bank transparency reduce interest rates?* Working paper, Universities of Cambridge and Tilburg.

Gersbach, H., & Hahn, V. (2004). Should the Individual Voting Records of Central Bankers be Published?' http://ssrn.com/abstract=238949

Glöckler, G. (2005). Why more is not always "better": Information availability and central bank transparency. In: L. Tsoukalis (Ed.), *Governance and legitimacy in EMU*. Florence: European University Institute.

Goodfriend, M. (2005). The monetary policy debate since October 1979: Lessons for theory and practice. *Federal Reserve Bank of Saint Louis Review*, *87*, 243–262.

Goodhart, C. (2005). An open letter to the President of the ECB. In: L. Tsoukalis (Ed.), *Governance and legitimacy in EMU*. Florence: European University Institute.

Guthrie, G., & Wright, J. (2000). Open mouth operations. *Journal of Monetary Economics*, *46*, 489–516.

Heinemann, F., & Ullrich, K. (2005). Does it pay to watch central bankers' lips? The information content of ECB wording' prepared for the National Bank of Poland Conference *Central Bank Transparency and Communication: Implications for Monetary Policy*, Warsaw, 2–3 June.

Howells, P., & Biefang-Frisancho, I. (2005). *Central bank transparency: A market indicator.* University of the West of England Economics Discussion Paper Series no. 03/05.

Hughes Hallett, A., & Viegi, N. (2003). Imperfect transparency and the strategic use of information: An ever present temptation for central bankers'. *The Manchester School*, *71*, 498–520.

Issing, O. (1999). The Eurosystem: Transparent and accountable or 'Willem in Euroland' *Journal of Common Market Studies*, *37*, 503–520.

Issing, O. (2004). *The Euro — the first five years*. Mais Lecture, Cass Business School, London, 12 May, 2005, at <www.cass.city.ac.uk/media/stories/story_53_45816_35515.html>

Issing, O. (2005). Communication, transparency, accountability: Monetary policy in the twenty first century. *Federal Reserve Bank of Saint Louis Review*, *87*, 65–83.

Issing, O., Gaspar, V., Angeloni, I., & Tristani, O. (2001). *Monetary Policy in the Euro Area*. Cambridge: Cambridge University Press.

Jansen, D. J., & de Haan, J. (2004). *Look who's talking: ECB communications during the first years of EMU*. CESifo Working Paper no. 1263.

Kydland, F., & Prescott, E. (1977). Rules rather than discretion: The inconsistency of optimal plans. *Journal of Political Economy*, *85*, 473–492.

Lepper, J., & Sterne, G. (2002). Parliamentary scrutiny of central banks in the United Kingdom and overseas. *Bank of England Quarterly Bulletin*(Autumn issue), *42*(3), 274–284.

Levin, A., Natalucci, F. M., & Piger, J. M. (2004). The Macroeconomic Effects of Inflation Targeting. *Federal Reserve Bank of St. Louis Review*, *86*(4), 51–80.

Meade, E. E., & Stasavage, D. (2004). *Publicity of debate and the incentive to dissent: Evidence from the US Federal Reserve*. Mimeo. London School of Economics and Political Science.

Mishkin, F. S. (2004). *Can central bank transparency go too far?* NBER Working Paper no. 10829.

Morkel-Kingsbury, N. J., & Allen, D. E. (2005). Central bank transparency and bank lending rates: Australian evidence. Paper presented at the Financial Management Association European Meeting, June 8–11, 2005, Siena.

Poole, W. (2005). FOMC transparency. *Federal Reserve Bank of Saint Louis Review, 87*, 1–9.

Reinhart, V. (2005). A colleague central banker watching the ECB. Paper presented at a conference on the ECB and its watchers VII at the Center for Financial Studies in Frankfurt, June 3rd.

Rogoff, K. (1985). The optimal degree of commitment to an intermediate target. *Quarterly Journal of Economics, 100*, 1169–1189.

Scharpf, F. W. (1999). *Governing in Europe: Effective and democratic*. Oxford: Oxford University Press.

Svensson, L. (2004). How should the Eurosystem reform its monetary strategy?' Briefing paper for the Economic and Monetary Affairs Committee of the European Parliament, available at http://www.princeton.edu/~svensson/index.html#401bru

Thornton, D. L. (2003). Monetary policy transparency: Transparent about what? *The Manchester School, 71*, 478–497.

Trichet, J.-C. (2005). Communication, transparency and the ECB's monetary policy. Speech at the New Year's reception of the International Club of Frankfurt Economic Journalists on 24 January 2005, Frankfurt am Main.

Winkler, B. (2002). Which kind of transparency? On the need for effective communication in monetary policy making. *Ifo Studies, 48*, 401–427.

Woodford, M. (2005). Central bank communication and policy effectiveness. Paper prepared for the Conference on inflation targeting: Implementation, communication and effectiveness, June 10–12, Sveriges Riksbank, Stockholm.

Chapter 3

Transparency in Competition Policy

Philippe Gugler

3.1 Introduction

Competitive markets maximise efficiency and therefore promote economic growth (Motta, 2004). However, real markets are not perfect, in general, due to market failures such as externalities, natural monopolies and other structures laid down by economies of scale, public goods and anticompetitive behaviours. One of the most important sources of externalities is the lack of transparency, such as asymmetric information. Economic theory has explored market failures resulting from asymmetric information, such as moral hazard[1] and adverse selection[2] (Akerlof, 1970). Lack of information causes economic inefficiencies and thus impedes economic growth. Facing a lack of information, investors and savers will seek higher risk premiums. Thus, from a microeconomics point of view, uncertainties will have a negative impact on a firm's competitiveness and long-term sustainable profits. This will increase the cost of capital and thereby lead to a decrease in investments (Oxelheim, 1996). The theory of economic growth as well as empirical studies have clearly shown that any decrease of investment leads to lower economic growth.

Investors are facing two major information asymmetries. The first one vis-à-vis corporate decision makers and the second vis-à-vis governmental institutions.

[1]Moral hazard describes the tendency of a person who is imperfectly monitored to engage in dishonest or undesirable behaviour.

[2]Adverse selection is a problem that arises in markets where the seller knows more about the attributes of the goods being sold than the buyer does.

Corporate and Institutional Transparency for Economic Growth in Europe

ISBN: 0-08-044665-5

They both lack transparency, which will create uncertainties and adversely affect investors in terms *inter alia* of higher risk premium. Oxelheim (1996) determined that these developments will lead, in many cases, to a decrease in investments. In this chapter, we will focus on one of the sources of lack of transparency developed by Oxelheim and elaborated on in Chapter 1: the institutional level. We will address a particularly interesting topic regarding institutional issues: transparency of competition policy enforcement.

This chapter comprises three parts. The first part deals with the general issue of transparency in competition policy enforcement. It analyses the impact of transparency on the main components of an effective competition policy: the effectiveness of the competition agency tasks, the protection of competition, the re-establishment of competition and the promotion of competition. The second part analyses the situation within the European Union (EU) according to the new competition policy regime which entered into force on 1 May 2004: the Regulation 1/2003 as well as the new European Commision (EC) merger control regulation (ECMR). This second part identifies the way in which this new regime enhances or reduces transparency in competition policy enforcement. The third part focuses on the international dimension of competition policy transparency, concentrating on multijurisdictional mergers. The lack of a unique international body dealing with those international mergers is discussed according to its negative effects on firms' efficiency due to the uncertainties regarding the different national procedures for merger control.

3.2 Transparency and Competition Policy

Competition is the motor of static and dynamic economic efficiency (Motta, 2004). Theoretically, the role of competition for competitiveness and economic growth has been well developed by numerous scholars (Porter, 1990, 2001; Nicoletti & Scarpetta, 2003; Ahn & Hemmings, 2000). Studies dedicated to the effects of competition in the EU indicate the same positive links between competition and economic performance (Gjersem, 2004; Blanke & Lopez-Claros, 2004, p. 2).

Competition law bans anticompetitive behaviour of firms (cartels and monopolisation of markets) and in some cases of government practices such as state aids. In many jurisdictions, competition law bans mergers and acquisitions, which would eliminate competition or reduce it significantly. We will focus on competition laws regarding firms' behaviour and will not address competition policies addressing states practices. Competition laws are enforced in most countries by independent competition agencies. The role of a competition law and thus of a competition agency may be divided into three main goals: first to protect competition (to prevent the occurrence of any anticompetitive behaviour), second to re-establish competition (to detect and prohibit any anticompetitive behaviour restricting or eliminating competition in order to re-establish competition in the affected markets) and third to promote and expand competition (by fostering, at the microeconomic level, firms efficiencies and by influencing any regulations which may unduly impede competition).

As far as competition policy is concerned, a substantial information asymmetry occurs between firms and competition agencies.

- On the one hand, the competition agencies' main problem is to identify firms' anticompetitive behaviours such as cartels. Conspiracy is hard to detect.
- On the other, firms may suffer from a lack of transparency regarding *inter alia* the criteria used to judge cases, the procedures' mechanisms, the evidence gathered by authorities, the duration and the length of their inquiries, the type and the magnitute of sanctions and of remedies requested. Another source of lack of transparency in competition policy enforcement arises if several competition agencies deal with the same case when firms are doing business in various countries. The more law enforcers involved, the more likely are diverging interpretations of the substantive legal rules, thereby reducing the predictability of the outcome of a proceeding (Pirrung, 2004, p. 89; Evenett, 2002; Jenny, 2002).

The importance of transparency in competition policy enforcement has been recognised for many years (Grimes, 2003, p. 944; Jorde, 1987, p. 594). The objective of improving the transparency of competition agency enforcement has been taken into account by recent reforms of competition laws in several jurisdictions, including the EU.

Transparency of competition agency enforcement has direct as well as indirect effects on the effectiveness of competition policy and thus on the competitiveness and growth within the jurisdiction concerned (Stiglitz, 2002). First, transparency improves the effectiveness of competition agency activities. Second, through effective competition law enforcement, transparency influences the effectiveness of the three above-mentioned goals of competition law, e.g. the protection, the re-establishment and finally the promotion and strengthening of competition. These three components are highly dependent upon the effectiveness of the competition agency activity, which acts as a fourth force (Figure 3.1).

While considering the overall effects of these four components of economic efficiency, we may argue that transparency of competition law enforcement may have two effects on the economic performance of firms doing business in a particular jurisdiction.

First, transparency induces a *horizontal influence* on industry performance considered as a whole. Indeed, by strengthening the role of promotion, protection

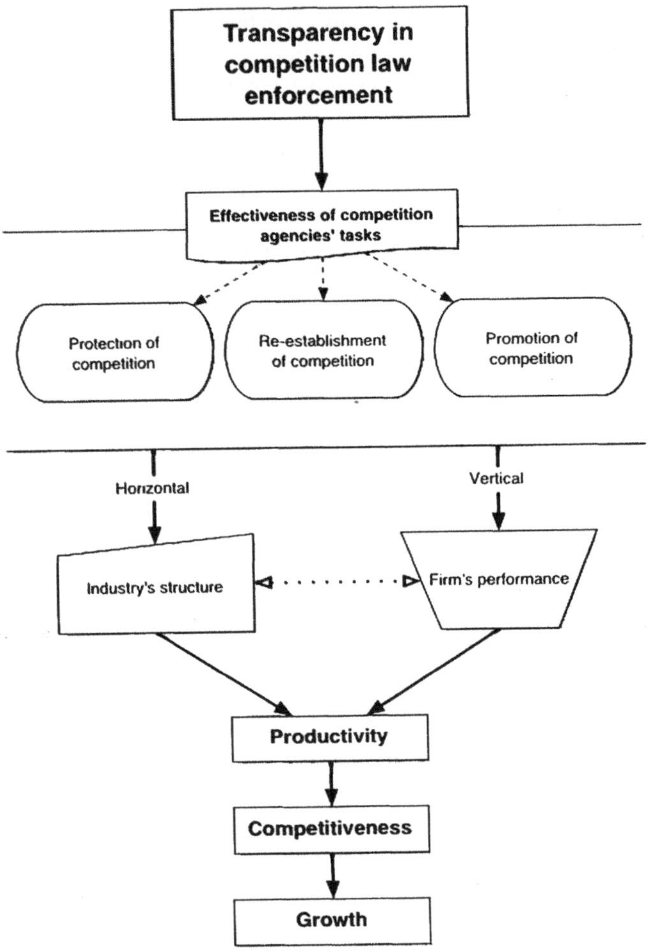

Figure 3.1: Transparency in competition law enforcement.

and re-establishment of competition, transparency of competition agency enforcement promotes static and dynamic efficiency of all firms competing within a specific industry. Thus, these horizontal effects apply to firms under competition agencies' investigations as well as to the other firms competing in the same market.

Second, transparency, by reducing information asymmetry for any firm investigated by competition authorities, leads to a *vertical effect* which may influence this firm's performance within a specific industry (e.g. by lowering risk premiums, transparency reduces risk costs and pushes towards more efficient investments).

This distinction is very important in order to understand both effects of transparency in competition law enforcement on firms' performance and therefore on economic growth.

Thus, as illustrated in Figure 3.1, the horizontal and vertical forces — enhanced or reduced by the level of transparency of competition agency enforcement — influence the economic foundation of a firm's economic performances (i.e. industry structure and the relative position of each firm within the industry considered) by influencing the effectiveness of competition agencies' tasks as well as the protection, re-establishment and promotion of competition.

3.2.1 Effectiveness of the Competition Agency Activities

Transparency regarding competition agencies' activities and methods is one of the most important institutional challenges faced by competition agencies to perform their tasks effectively. By performing competition agencies' tasks effectively we mean not only that their duties are accomplished rationally but also that they do not create negative externalities for the economy.

If it is not possible for firms to correctly predict how competition enforcers will evaluate a particular behaviour or project, they must bear additional risk. The costs of these risks take several forms including higher risk premiums. In other words, transparency of competition policy enforcement prevents undue costs for enterprises by reducing uncertainty (Wils, 1999, p. 145).

3.2.2 Protection of Competition

Transparency enhances knowledge of and compliance with the law. Transparency regarding an agency decision increases understanding of the agency's policy and will likely increase voluntary compliance with that policy. There are different approaches to law enforcement. Two extreme types of law enforcement are mentioned in the literature (Versluis, 2002, pp. 3–4): the advisory form and the sanctioning form. The advisory form is based on information exchange: the authority and the firm try together to find a solution through negotiations, consultation and persuasion. The sanctioning form is often referred to as the legalistic form: the authority applies the rules mechanically and exacts punishment if the regulated parties do not comply with that law. The more lenient styles are based on prevention, which relies on transparency through information exchange between firms and authority.

3.2.3 Re-establishment of Competition

Transparency of specific antitrust procedures, such as leniency programmes,[3] is necessary to eliminating cartels by encouraging firms to disclose their collusive activities. Leniency programmes have had unprecedented success in terms of identifying and eliminating domestic and international cartels. A critical component to this success is the ability to obtain the cooperation of some companies and individuals against their fellow cartel members (Spratling, 1999, p. 1). This cooperation from offenders has been dependent upon the antitrust agency's readiness to provide transparency throughout the anticartel enforcement programme. For example, in the US the enforcement programme is based on the following principles:

- An effective anticartel enforcement programme depends on cooperation from at least some of those who have engaged in the cartel activity.
- Prospective cooperative parties come forward to disclose the cartel in direct proportion to the predictability and certainty of their treatment following co-operation.
- Therefore, prospective cooperating firms need to know the rules, how prosecutorial will be exercised in applying the rules, and that they will be treated fairly and equitably.

An anticartel enforcement programme maximises the incentives for cooperation from cartel members if it provides for transparency in its enforcement programme and equitable treatment of offenders.

3.2.4 Promotion and Expansion of Competition

Transparency may prevent pro-competitive behaviours and deals may be abandoned by firms fearing negative decisions of a competition agency. Thus, transparency may promote productive efficiency and dynamic efficiency. By inducing more effective markets, transparency reduces firms' costs, such as premium costs. This has a direct effect on the economic performances of the firms. By reducing premium costs, transparency promotes more efficient investments and strategic operations for instance enhancing the firms' competitiveness.

---

[3]Leniency programmes are based on confidential information given by a member of a cartel. In exchange, the firm will get immunity. This information will help the competition agency to get evidences of the law infringement.

3.2.5 Transparency Drawbacks

While transparency has important positive effects on competition enforcement's effectiveness, it is nevertheless important that in some cases competition agencies do not disclose all information. Indeed, transparency may also induce negative externalities. As stated by Grimes, "If transparency is excessive, misplaced, or poorly implemented, it can do more harm than good" (Grimes, 2003, p. 948). In a pre-decision phase, secrecy may be crucial to get enough evidence for example as far as leniency programmes are concerned.

Even post-decision disclosure, however, may have serious drawbacks such as the burden of preparing for public disclosure; the risk that confidential business information would be disclosed or that the threat of disclosure would make it more difficult for the agency to obtain voluntary submission of information; the risk that disclosure of past competition agency decisions may unreasonably constrain the agency in making future enforcement decisions, and the risk that more disclosure will politicise enforcement decisions and increase burdens of staff (Grimes, 2003, p. 948; Baer, 1996, p. 9).

3.3 Transparency of Competition Policy Enforcement within the EU

Firms doing business within the EU must comply with EC competition law as well as with the national member state's competition laws. Several sources leading to a lack of transparency may occur at the national jurisdiction stages as well as at the Community level. It would be beyond the scope of the chapter and the goal of this book to analyse the situation in each member state. Thus, we will concentrate on the overall issue in light of "radical changes" of competition policy as applied within the EU since 1 May 2004. The enlargement of the EU from 15 to 25 Member States on 1 May 2004 was accompanied by several important changes such as the modernisation of EC competition law (Regulation 1/2003) and amendments to the ECMR.

The analysis of these new developments shows that Regulation 1/2003 as well as the ECRM influence the information asymmetry affecting firms and competition agencies. A global assessment of the effects of the new development in EU competition policy on efficiency and growth cannot be declared without taking into account the transparency issues affecting firms as well as competition agencies. While sticking to our main subject, e.g. information asymmetry affecting firms, we will also consider effects of information asymmetry affecting competition agencies in order to have a comprehensive picture of the effects of the new competition policy developments on European growth.

Disclosure of information regarding competition policy enforcement seems to be quite developed within the EU compared to the situation in the U.S. (Grimes, 2003, pp. 956–959). *Ceteris paribus*, we could argue that firms doing business in the EU register fewer negative externalities due to uncertainties created by competition law enforcement than firms doing business in many other countries such as the U.S.

3.3.1 New Regime of Regulation 1/2003

The new Regulation 1/2003—which entered into force on 1 May 2004—modifies the rules governing the enforcement of Articles 81 and 82 of the EC Treaty.[4] The new regime creates a shift from a highly centralised system of application to a decentralised regime involving a greater role for national competition agencies (NCAs) and national courts in the enforcement of EC competition law, and a greater reliance on self-assessment by firms.

The previous regime set out in Regulation 17/62 has been replaced by new procedures, in Regulation 1/2003. The new Regulation marks an important shift away from the previous enforcement system in three key aspects whose effects on transparency will be analysed.

3.3.1.1 Suppression of the notification system The notification procedures for individual exemptions as requested by firms under Article 81(3) have been abandoned.[5] According to many experts, this new development creates a loss of legal certainty for enterprises (Pirrung, 2004, p. 87; Holmes, 2000, p. 59; Gustafsson, 2000, p. 173; Paulweber, 2000, p. 41). This negative vertical effect for firms will be accompanied by a negative horizontal effect for the whole industry as well as for other industries. Indeed, the new system induces a loss of information, which was universally provided through a publication of the notified restrictive practices (Pirrung, 2004, p. 101).

However, some specific provisions have been foreseen in order to mitigate this transparency problem. Existing block exemption regulations remain valid and new ones can be issued. Furthermore, Article 10 of Regulation 1/2003 empowers the Commission to issue a positive decision that a restrictive practice does not

[4]Article 81 forbids cartels, whereas Article 82 forbids abuses of dominant position.

[5]Under a notification system, a restrictive practice that fell under Article 81(1) EC was void pursuant to Article 81(2) unless it was properly notified to the Commission and the Commission decided that it satisfied the condition of Article 81(3) and could therefore be exempted.

constitute an infringement. These provisions seem to temper the horizontal and vertical effects due to a lack of transparency issued by the new regulation.

3.3.1.2 Decentralisation Under the previous regime (Regulation 17/62), the enforcement of Article 81 EC was allocated in a hybrid way. Whereas the NCAs and national courts were empowered to apply Articles 81(1) and (2) EC, only the Commission was entitled to apply Article 81(3) and to issue an exemption decision.[6] The direct applicability of Article 81(3) by NCAs and courts under the new Regulation 1/2003 will therefore lead to a switch from *de facto* centralised law enforcement to more decentralised law enforcement. In the new enforcement system, the enforcement of Articles 81 and 82 will be completely shared by the Commission and the NCAs.

As far as transparency is concerned, two major issues have been raised. First, the identification of the level of enforcement (the Commission or the NCAs) and second the coherence regarding the enforcement of Articles 81 and 82 by the EC and the NCAs.

The case allocation mechanism raises some concerns regarding the predictability of which competition agency will be in charge of a particular case. The case allocation principle introduced by the new Regulation is as follows. As indicated by the Director of DG Competition, the case allocation criteria are merely indicative criteria for the division of work between the network members (Lowe, 2003, p. 3). The criteria can be summarised as follows: first, cases should be dealt with by an authority who is well placed to restore competition in the market. It follows that a single national competition authority is usually well placed to deal with agreements or practices that substantially affect competition mainly within its jurisdiction. However, "single action of a national competition authority may also be appropriate regarding infringements of wider scope where the action of a single national competition authority is sufficient to bring the entire infringement to an end" (Lowe, 2003, p. 3). Second, where an agreement or practice has substantial effects on competition in several territories and the action of one authority would not be sufficient to stop this infringement or to sanction it adequately, parallel action by two or three member state's competition authorities may be appropriate in order to ensure effective deterrence. Such parallel action should involve close coordination between the authorities concerned in order to avoid an inconsistent outcome. However, regarding the differences between the competition authorities of the 25 member states, we may doubt that this mechanism will work, at least in the short term. Third, where an infringement has effects in more

[6]Article 81(3) states exemptions to the cartels' prohibition.

than three member states, the Commission will be frequently considered to be the best placed to deal with the case (Lowe, 2003, p. 3). Here again, there is a large *marge de manoeuvre* to determine which authority will deal with the case. As indicated by the Director General of DG Competition, "(. . .) within the modernised enforcement system, each authority is free to decide for itself whether it wants to deal with a given case or not, based on its own enforcement priorities" (Lowe, 2003, p. 4). The downside of this relaxed approach is that parties will not know whether the Commission will later decide to view their actions as falling outside the safe harbour exemptions of Article 81. This lack of predictability reduces the transparency of the entire system.

This new enforcement of Articles 81 and 82 EC will only lead to an increased effectiveness of the enforcement of competition rules, if all enforcers apply the rules in a coherent way. Transparency among the Commission and the national authorities on the one hand, and among the national authorities on the other will be crucial.

Another point of concern is the decentralised application of Article 81(3) by courts and NCAs leads to the risk of "forum shopping" (Geradin, 2002, p. 24). Decentralisation creates a risk that different authorities may not apply Article 81 in a coherent way. This means that firms or private litigants will choose the NCA or court that they deem to be most favourable to their interests (Pirrung, 2004, p. 87). This may be negative for the competition protection mechanism.

The flexible approach introduced by the decentralisation of competition law enforcement could certainly improve the ability of competition authorities to get more information given that the most appropriate authority will be in charge of the case. This enhanced horizontal effect due to a higher transparency seems to be opposed by a negative vertical effect for firms at least in the short term. In the long term, this negative vertical effect could become a positive one: once the firm learns whom to deal with, they gain a proximity advantage (with the authority), which enhances transparency, that they did not have before with the old regulation and the centralised system. This statement is true concerning the protection and the promotion of competition but also concerning the re-establishment of competition: the application of a leniency programme is much easier when informer and authority have a close relationship (in terms of proximity and trust).

3.3.1.3 The European competition network In order to enhance coherent competition regime enforcement within the EU, the new European Competition Network (ECN) has been created. The ECN bears the difficult task of providing an effective forum of cooperation and disclosure of information among competition authorities. This will improve the information process between the NCA and the EC and should also improve the efficiency of their activities while enhancing their results as far as protection, re-establishment and promotion of competition are concerned. These improvements should have positive horizontal effects on the industries. The exchanges of information among the NCAs and with the EC should also improve the coherence of the individual competition agencies' actions and therefore should induce a positive effect at the vertical level.

3.3.1.4 Effects of new Regulation 1/2003 on transparency To sum up, the new Regulation 1/2003 seems to provide a global positive effect on transparency at the horizontal level, whereas at the vertical level, firms seem to encounter a lack of transparency. Thus, the new system would lead, as often stated by the EC competition commissionaire, to a more efficient and transparent system but for the activities of the NCA and of the EC. In turn, there should be an increased level of economic efficiency and thus higher growth within the EU. On the other hand, the new system does not seem to have the same positive effects at the firm level (vertical dimension). The new system has some negative consequences for firms as far as transparency of competition law enforcement is concerned (Figure 3.2). The firms will face higher costs under the new regime (legal exception system rather than *ex ante* notification system) due to an increased need for external advice. The new system is likely to increase the risk premium of firms. The reduced legal certainty will also lead to risk costs, which stem from suboptimal decisions made by risk-averse decision makers (Pirrung, 2004, p. 106). These costs will finally have to be borne by society at large.

Effects of the new regulation 1/2003 on transparency of EC competition law enforcement	**Horizontal level** (enhancement of competition in specific industries: efficiency of the industry)	**Vertical level** (efficiency of firms in a specific industry)
Suppression of the notification system	↓	↓
Decentralisation	↑	↑↓
ECN	↑	↑
Global effect*	↑	=

↓ = decrease of transparency
↑ = increase of transparency
* The global effect is a weighted average of each criterion.

Figure 3.2: Regulation 1/2003.

Several provisions in Regulation 1/2003 can reduce this problem but cannot eliminate it entirely. Nonetheless, the time perspective has to be put in parallel with our analysis as we stated in the section concerning the decentralisation: at long terms some lack of transparency, created by the imposition of the new regulation, may be improved or may even disappear over a longer period of time.

3.3.2 New Regime of Merger Control

When the EC began its formal review of the ECMR in December 2001, it could not have anticipated the criticism levelled against it by the Court of First Instance of the European Communities in its judgments of June and October 2002, which overturned its decisions to prohibit the Airtour/First Choice, Schneider/Legrand and Tetra Laval/Sidel mergers. These, together with the prohibition of the General Electric/Honeywell merger led businesses. The EU merger process had become tougher and less certain. Member States also critised the EU procedures in some cases such as Volvo/Scania (Sweden) and Schneider/Legrand mergers (France).

Within this climate of criticism, the new ECMR was adopted in November 2003 and entered into force on May 2004. The key changes include

- a new substantive test based on the notion of a significant impediment to effective competition which is likely to apply to a wider array of mergers;
- a more flexible timetable for merger review, in particular for remedy negotiations; and
- a reinforced "one-stop-shop" concept in which the parties may play a role.

3.3.2.1 Substantive test The new ECMR introduces a new test to assess whether a merger should be declared incompatible with the common market. According to Article 2(2) of the new ECMR, concentration, which would significantly impede effective competition in the common market, or a substantial part of it, in particular as a result of the creation or strengthening of a dominant position, shall be declared incompatible with the common market. This new test, called the "substantive" test replaced the old test called the "dominance test". The new system gives a larger *marge de manoeuvre* to the Commission. However, this positive horizontal effect seems to be counterbalanced by a negative one due to the uncertainties created by the decentralisation of activities at the member state level. However, some member states will continue to apply the old test (dominance test) even if the EC and some other member states will apply the new substantive test. This may create inconsistencies, which will have both negative horizontal and vertical effects.

To sum up, the new test seems to create both negative and positive effects at the horizontal level as well as at the vertical level.

3.3.2.2 Flexible timetable To provide both the Commission and the parties with enough time to develop and assess additional important evidence, carry out a market test and collect relevant information, the new ECMR provides for longer periods for both phase I (preliminary review) and phase II (in-depth review). Phase I is now 25 working days long instead of one month and phase II is 90 working days long rather than four months. Phase I can be further extended to 35 working days and phase II can be further extended to 105 working days in some cases. Additionally, where requested by the parties or with their consent, 20 working days can be added to a phase II review. This new practice should allow the competition agencies to get more information regarding a specific case and therefore enhance their efficiency. This should induce a positive horizontal effect. The parties are no longer as pressed for time as in the past nor subject to an inflexible time frame. However, this new mechanism will create more uncertainty for firms, particularly those whose merger is at the same time under the jurisdiction of non-EU competition agencies. It will be more difficult to coordinate the timing of a final decision owing to the fact that the timetable within the EU is more flexible. These new uncertainties created by this procedural changes should induce more negative vertical effects than positive ones.

3.3.2.3 Reinforced "one-stop shop" The ECMR is based on the "one-stop-shop" principle, which means that a particular merger is only reviewed by one competition authority within the EU being either the EC or a national member state's competition agency. Thus, Community and domestic legislation regarding merger control have no overlapping scope. One of the objectives of the new ECMR was to put in place a more rational corrective mechanism of case allocation between the Commission and Member States based on subsidiarity for cases that would be dealt with more effiency by another authority that allocated jurisdiction on the basis of the turnover thresholds. Theoretically, the new system intends that the authority or authorities best placed to assess the impact on competition of a merger should be responsible with such a case (Lowe, 2003, p. 6). The new system should enhance the effiency of the competition authorities (positive horizontal effects). It should also induce positive horizontal effects due to this allocation of competences based on the best-placed position to assess a given merger.

However, these positive effects are tempered by some concerns regarding inconstancies in merger reviews. One of the major concerns is how to preserve consistency in applying equivalent standards of assessment whereas each member state has its own legal provisions regarding merger control. The new system does not solve this problem while also creating some uncertainty regarding the competition authority, which will finally review the case. As recognised by the Director General of DG Competition "However, it cannot be excluded that situations of disagreements or uncertainty would need to be resolved on a consensual basis by the members of the network" (Lowe, 2003, p. 8). These uncertainties will likely increase transaction costs at the expense of firms.

3.3.2.4 Effects of the new ECMR on transparency The new ECMR should lead to improved horizontal effects as the new mechanisms put in place should enhance transparency as well as the effectiveness of the competition authorities. From a vertical point of view, the results are less clear (Figure 3.3). In the short term, uncertainties related to the new mechanisms put in place could counterbalance some of the positive effects due to the enhancement of transparency particularly owing to the new structure of DG Competition and the reinforced "one-stop shop". However, in the medium and longer terms, these uncertainties should be reduced depending on the effectiveness *inter alia* of the collaboration within DG Competition and between DG Competition and NCAs.

Effects of the new ECMR of transparency of EC competition law enforcement	**Horizontal level** (enhancement of competition in specific industries: efficiency of the industry)	**Vertical level** (efficiency of firms in a specific industry)
Substantive test	↑↓	↓
Flexible time table	↑	↓
Reinforced "one stop shop"	↑	↑
New structure of DG competition	↑	↑
Global effect*	↑	=

↓ = decrease of transparency
↑ = increase of transparency
* The global effect is a weighted average of each criterion.

Figure 3.3: New ECMR.

3.4 Transparency in Multijurisdictional Merger Enforcement in the Global Economy

3.4.1 The Multijurisdictional Issue

Firms are doing business in a global economy but they do not live in a global state (Melamed, 1998a). For firms located within the EU, once the challenge to comply with EC competition laws as well as with member states' competition laws has been completed, they also have to consider other national competition laws, depending upon the foreign markets where they are doing business. Most competition laws are based on the "effect principle" which means that a national competition law applies to all effects influencing domestic markets even though they may concern firms located outside its jurisdiction. It is therefore very difficult for a firm doing business in several countries to deal with multiple competition laws and agencies. The problem is particularly acute in merger cases. The EC recognised in 2005 "that the continued growth in internationalisation of business activities, and the increasing number of jurisdictions which have adopted merger laws, correspondingly increase the number of mergers that are subject to review under merger laws in more than one jurisdiction" and that "reviews of transnational mergers can impose substantial cost on competition authorities and merging parties, and that it is important to address these costs without limiting the effectiveness of national merger laws" (OECD, 2005). We will therefore concentrate on merger issues.

Sometimes, markets remain national due to market's specificities and regulations but merging firms nevertheless may have assets or sales in various jurisdictions and compete in a substantial number of national markets. And even when merging parties' assets are located only in a single domestic market, their business activities may affect markets in many countries, since the parties' customers, suppliers and potential competitors may be located around the globe. The significant increase in the number of jurisdictions that have adopted merger review regimes makes it increasingly likely that international mergers and acquisitions will be reviewed by multiple competition authorities. Therefore, many different national competition authorities may investigate the same transaction.

3.4.2 Transparency Problems Raised in Multijurisdictional Merger Cases

The fact that we do not live in a global state is not just a legal formality. It is of tremendous importance because it implicates issues of procedures and efficiency in antitrust enforcement and, more important, because different states may have different views and policies as to what kinds of substantive competition rules and enforcement policies are in their interests. We register more than 100 national or regional antitrust regimes, with roughly 70 of those requiring a pre-merger notification. As stated by Charles A. James (2002), Assistant Attorney General, "But the assertion of overlapping antitrust jurisdiction by multiple sovereigns has the potential to harm the very competitive values that antitrust is meant to protect".

Such differences, especially when coupled with the significant extraterritorial reach of many merger control laws, present challenges for merging parties as well as for reviewing competition agencies. There are three basics risks posed by multi-jurisdictional merger reviews.

First, there is a risk that the cost, complexity and uncertainty of having to comply with numerous different merger regimes, with different information requirements and different time schedules, will kill some efficiency-enhancing international deals and cause others not to be attempted. For the merging parties, these challenges include *inter alia* higher uncertainty regarding the ultimate legality of the proposed transaction; the necessity for interacting and negotiating with multiple reviewing authorities; the possibility of inconsistent and perhaps conflicting rulings; and the potential for overly burdensome remedies. These challenges increase transaction costs for merging companies and, in the worst-case scenario, may result in the abandonment of pro-competitive transactions (ICPAC, 2000, pp. 41–43).

Second, there is a risk that different reviews may yield different results. Different results may be obvious where the relevant economic facts (e.g. affected markets) are different in different jurisdictions. However, concerns arise when these differences arise from differing legal standards or analytical processes. Inconsistent assessments of transactions, different timing of review procedures or application of conflicting remedies by diverse enforcement authorities, could impose substantial costs on businesses and on the markets that they serve.

For example, in multinational mergers, firms are subject to different timetables and different procedures of various reviewing competition agencies. However, the problems are deeper than that

> They reflect at their core the fact that different countries have different substantive views about what constitutes sound competition policy. They might, of course, all be right about that; it might be that what is sound competition policy for one country is not—at least in some respects—sound competition policy for another country. But, regardless of what any one country thinks is sound competition policy for itself or for others, the fact is that there are differences. The critical question, therefore, is how to ameliorate those differences over time, and how to deal with

> the differences when and to the extent they exist (Melamed, 1998b, p. 8).

Finally, there is a significant risk that economic nationalism will prevail in antitrust merger enforcement in some jurisdictions, with the accompanying politicisation of enforcement. For example, in some countries, even within the EU, such as France, the decision regarding the approval or the rejection of a merger depends upon the Minister of Industry and Finance.

As stated by James (2002, p. 3),

> The potential economic consequences of antitrust law meaning one thing in one jurisdiction and something quite different in another are enormous. And if the public and the international business community find that merger decisions around the world are being based, not on sound, consumer-welfare-based, economic theory, but on the basis of local interest buttressed by dubious economic and social theories unencumbered by economic evidence, then public support for sound antitrust enforcement necessarily will falter, and the global economy will suffer.

These three risks are highly related to a lack of transparency and uncertainty and may incur tremendous costs for firms not only in terms of expenses but also in terms of lack of competitiveness due to the difficulty of dealing with this multijurisdictional issue. Given the greater uncertainty observed in multijurisdictional mergers, contracting parties suffer *inter alia* from higher risk premiums due to the uncertainty regarding whether or not and when their merger will be authorised or challenged. In some cases it would result in the withdrawal of mergers or acquisition projects.

3.4.3 Developments Under Way in Order to Improve Transparency Problems in Multijurisdictional Merger Cases

The GE/Honeywell debate (where a proposed merger was cleared by the U.S. antitrust authorities but blocked by the EC) has made an important contribution to convergence in merger review. This case has demonstrated some fundamental, doctrinal disagreements over the economic purposes and scope of antitrust enforcement. This case has reinforced, for antitrust officials on both sides of the Atlantic, the value of close consultation on cases. Some convergence has also been reached due *inter alia* to the new merger regulation adopted by the EC in 2004. The concerns raised by multijurisdictional merger review can be significantly reduced by transparent, cooperative and efficient merger review procedures.

Divergent outcomes will remain as long as underlying substantive differences in merger control laws exist and multiple agencies continue to review a single transaction. However, these problems may be significantly reduced by facilitating, where possible, harmonisation and convergence of substantive standards and approaches to merger review. As far as harmonisation of procedures is concerned, several international fora such as the OECD, the International Competition Network (ICN) and official institutions such as ICPAC have proposed recommendations or are in the process of formulating recommendations (OECD, 2005; ICPAC, 2000; ICN, 2004). Cooperation agreements among antitrust authorities may also be a way to address this issue. Both ways improve transparency of competition policy enforcement in multijurisdictional merger cases and therefore reduce costs for enterprises and avoid unnecessary loss of competitiveness.

3.5 Conclusions

Transparency of competition policy enforcement sustains static and dynamic efficiency of market mechanisms. Increased efficiency fosters productivity, competitiveness and economic growth. We stated that the role of competition policy is to protect, re-establish and promote competition. The importance of transparency has been demonstrated on these three levels: Transparency may act as a deterrent of anticompetitive behaviour helping firms to comply with competition law. In cases where firms purposely bridge the law, transparency of procedures, such as in leniency programmes, helps competition agencies to detect anticompetitive behaviours such as cartels. Transparency may prevent the withdrawal of efficient practices due to a lack of information upon the decision process of antitrust agencies. Transparency pushes towards more efficient investment by reducing risk costs and lowering risk premiums.

The revised antitrust and merger control regulations substantially enlarge the powers of national authorities and national courts to enforce EU competition law. First, the full predictability of distribution of competence to deal with a specific case between the Commission and national competition authorities in enforcing the new merger control and antitrust regulations remains unattained. It is not clear how cases will be allocated in practice between the national competition authorities and the Commission or how they will interrelate with parallel proceedings in national courts. A case may be allocated to one NCA, several NCAs acting in parallel or to the Commission, depending on factors such as the number of territories affected, the need to gather evidence in several countries, and the remedies sought.

Second, there is a risk of incoherent decisions being issued by each of the competition authorities in the 25 member states. The EU comprises countries with disparate cultures, resources and views towards economic competition policy, and many of the national competition authorities and courts are inexperienced in the fields of antitrust and merger control issues. Using economic tools, we considered two levels of effects (as developed in the first section) on transparency of the new Regulation 1/2003: on a horizontal level (efficiency of the industry) and on a vertical level (efficiency of firms in a specific industry). We concluded that the new Regulation 1/2003 has a global positive effect on transparency on the horizontal level whereas a lack of transparency seems to have appeared on the vertical level at least in the short term. As a matter of fact, the creation of a formal network (the ECN) that links EU competition officials with NCA competition officials is the only point in the new Regulation which enhances transparency in both levels by cooperating and sharing expertise to reduce the risk of inconsistent enforcement. This result regarding vertical effects may change over time depending on the consistencies of future decisions. The uncertainties and a lack of transparency could reflect a first phase and could disappear in a second phase.

The new ECMR should result in positive horizontal effects since the new mechanisms put in place should enhance transparency as well as the effectiveness of the competition authorities. From a vertical point of view, the results are more contrasted. In the short term, uncertainties related to the new mechanisms put in place could counterbalance some of the positive effects arising from improved transparency particularly due to the new structure of the DG Competition and the reinforced "one-stop shop". However, in the medium and longer terms, these uncertainties should be reduced depending on the effectiveness *inter alia* of the collaboration within the DG Competition and between the DG Competition and the national competition agencies. The EU Commission should consider this problem as soon as possible in order to avoid any uncertainties due to the new Regulation 1/2003 and the new ECMR. Elaboration of guidelines as well as information regarding the first cases reviewed under the new framework would contribute to reduce uncertainties and costs due to any lack of uncertainties, in particular regarding which authority will be in charge of cases. Further cooperation at the multilateral level in the field of merger control would also contribute to reduce uncertainties arising in multijurisdictional mergers.

As stated by Melamed (1998a), firms are doing business in a global economy but they do not live in a global state. This was the subject of the third section. It is important not to impede pro-competitive, efficiency-enhancing multijurisdictional mergers due to the complexity and uncertainty of having to comply with sometimes more than 20 different merger regimes. This assumption leads us to two important key processes: harmonisation and cooperation. These are the two main directions of development under way to improve transparency. But a lack of transparency still remains, especially in cooperation process. That is why the business community has recommended the development of a framework to improve cooperation.

To conclude on this theme, every drawback considered, *ceteris paribus*, transparency still remains one of the most important key assumption to promote, re-establish and protect competitive market mechanisms: Lower risk premiums foster lower risk costs which lead to an efficient investment process and promote economic growth and static and dynamic efficiency fosters productivity and competitiveness leading, as a consequence, to growth.

Acknowledgement

The author is grateful to Mr. Jérôme Daellenbach, research fellow at the University of Fribourg/Switzerland for his research assistance and his considerable help.

References

Ahn, S., & Hemmings, P. (2000). *Policy influences on economic growth in OECD countries: An evaluation of the evidence*. OECD, Economic Department Working Paper no. 246.

Akerlof, G. A. (1970). The market for "lemons": Quality uncertainty and market mechanism. *Quarterly Journal of Economics, 84*, 488–500.

Baer, W. J. (1996). The dollars and sense of antitrust enforcement. Paper presented before the antitrust section of the New York State Bar Association, January 25, New York.

Blanke, J., & Lopez-Claros, A. (2004). The Lisbon Review 2004: An assessment of policies and reforms in Europe. World Economic Forum, Geneva.

Evenett, S. J. (2002). *Private international cartels: Evidence and enforcement experience from 1990's*. Mimeo, World Trade Institute, Berne.

Geradin, D. (2002). Competition between rules and rules of competition: A legal and economic analysis of the proposed modernization of the enforcement of EC competition law. *Columbia Journal of European Law, 9*, 1–28.

Gjersem, C. (2004). *Policies bearing on product market competition and growth in Europe*. OECD, Economic Department Working Paper no. 378.

Grimes, W. S. (2003). Transparency in federal antitrust enforcement. *Buffalo Law Review, 51*(4), 937–993.

Gustafsson, M. (2000). Some legal implications facing the realisation of the commission white paper on modernisation of EC antitrust procedure and the role of national courts in a post-white paper era. *Legal Issues of Economic Integration, 27*(2), 159–184.

Holmes, K. (2000). The EC white paper on modernisation. *Journal of World Competition 23*(3), 51–79.

ICN (International Competition Network). (2004). *Competition advocacy in regulated sectors: Examples of success*. Paper presented at the 2004 Annual Conference (April), Seoul.

ICPAC (International Competition Policy Advisory Committee). (2000). *Final report on international competition issues*. Washington: US Department of Justice Antitrust Division.

James, C. A. (2002). Antitrust in the early 21st century: Speech by assistant Attorney General James. Paper presented at the seminar sponsored by the EC Directorate General for Competition and the U.S. mission to the European Union in Brussels.

Jenny, F. (2002). International cooperation on competition: Myth, reality and perspectives. Paper presented at the University of Minnesota Law School conference on global antitrust law and policy.

Jorde, T. M. (1987). Coping with the merger guidelines and the government's "fix-it-first" approach: A modest appeal for more information. *32nd Antitrust Bulletin*, *32*, 579–594.

Lowe, P. (2003). Implication of the recent reforms in the antitrust enforcement in Europe for National Competition Authorities. Paper addressed at the Italian competition/consumers day, Rome.

Melamed, D. (1998a). International antitrust in an age of international deregulation. *George Mason Law Review*, *6*, 437–438.

Melamed, D. (1998b). Antitrust enforcement in a global economy. Paper addressed at the 25th annual conference on international antitrust law and policy, New York.

Motta, M. (2004). *Competition policy*. Cambridge: Cambridge University Press.

Nicoletti, G., & Scarpetta, S. (2003). *Regulation, productivity and growth: OECD evidence*. OECD, Economic Department Working Paper no. 347.

OECD. (2005). Recommendation of the council on merger review. Competition law and policy, Paris.

Oxelheim, L. (1996). *Financial markets in transition—globalization, investment and economic growth*. London: Routledge and International Thomson Press.

Paulweber, M. (2000). The end of a success story? The European Commission's white paper on the modernisation of the European Commission Law. *Journal of World Competition*, *23*(3), 3–48.

Pirrung, M. (2004). EU enlargement towards cartel paradise?. *Erasmus Law and Economics Review*, *82*(18), 77–109.

Porter, M. (1990). *The competitive advantage of nations*. New York: The Free Press.

Porter, M. (2001). Competition and antitrust: Towards a productivity-based approach to evaluating mergers and joint ventures. Paper based on a presentation to the American Bar Association, Washington, DC.

Spratling, G. R. (1999). Transparency in enforcement maximizes cooperation from antitrust offenders. Paper presented at the 26th annual conference on international antitrust law & policy, Fordham University, New York.

Stiglitz, J. E. (2002). Competition and competitiveness in a new economy. In: H. Handler, & C. Burger (Eds), *Competition and competitiveness in a new economy*. Vienna: Austrian Ministry for Economic Affairs and Labour, Economic Policy Center.

Versluis, E. (2002). *The enforcement of EU directives*. Utrecht University, Germany.

Wils, W. (1999). Notification, clearance and exemption in E.C. competition law: An economic analysis. *European Law Review*, *24*(2), 139–156.

Chapter 4

Environmental Policy and Institutional Transparency in Europe[1]

Thomas L. Brewer and Sarianna M. Lundan

4.1 Introduction

Firms operating in the European Union (EU), whether domestic or foreign, face uncertainty arising from changes in environmental policy on three levels: the supranational level, the national level and the local level. On the supranational level, together with all other OECD countries, but in contrast to firms in the US and Australia, firms in Europe face uncertainty resulting from the implementation of the Kyoto Protocol, and specifically related to the development of the EU Emission Trading Scheme (ETS), which came into effect in the beginning of 2005. On the national level, firms operating in Europe face differences in the level of environmental protection and monitoring between the EU-15 and the 10 new accession countries that joined in 2004. On the local level, whether at their headquarters or operating subsidiaries, firms face increasing demands from global civil society towards transparency and accountability on environmental and social issues.

The three levels of policy making are not strictly separate, as national-level transparency affects the credibility of EU-wide policies, for example, and the classification is used primarily to distinguish between environmental policy issues that are by their nature either global, regional or country specific. The effective

[1]Portions of this chapter were presented as papers at the annual meeting of the European International Business Academy in Llubljana, Slovenia, in December 2004.

Corporate and Institutional Transparency for Economic Growth in Europe

ISBN: 0-08-044665-5

rules under which firms operate in any given country are a complex mixture of domestic regulation, which is often influenced by regulation in other countries, the firms' internal standards, which can also be influenced by regulatory standards abroad, as well as the prevailing market standards, which are influenced by the activities of non-governmental organizations (NGOs), and which in turn can also be influenced by prevailing standards abroad (Lundan, 2004).

This chapter will examine the simultaneous impact the three levels of environmental policy making have on firms operating in Europe. We will seek to identify the sources of uncertainty at each policy level, the available means to mitigate the risk, and the role of corporate and regulatory transparency in achieving an efficient outcome, both in terms of the stated policy goals as well as in terms of the economic cost. We will also attempt to distinguish between procedural and substantive transparency in our analysis.

We begin by briefly examining the environmental concerns at the local level, and specifically the firm's interaction with stakeholders or the firm-civil society nexus. By posing threats to firm reputation, NGOs have gained a prominent role alongside regulation in affecting corporate environmental strategy. Since the value destruction following a media attack can be substantial, firms are increasingly aware of the need to manage the long-term environmental liability of the firm, and consequently their vulnerability to such attacks. Issues of transparency arise when investors want to assess the environmental risks associated with a firm, and the emergence of social rating agencies as well as the publication of social and environmental reports by the firms themselves are measures to reduce the information asymmetry in the marketplace. (In terms of the framework introduced in Chapter 1, this corresponds to information asymmetries between A. Savers/investors and B. Corporate decision-makers.)

The primary regulatory issues on the national/regional level are credibility and consistency. Information asymmetries, and consequently a lack of transparency, exist between national governments and EU regulators on one hand, and between national governments and corporate decision-makers on the other hand, concerning the true degree of compliance and the effectiveness of environmental monitoring across the EU-25. (In terms of the framework introduced in Chapter 1, this corresponds to information asymmetries between B. Corporate decision-makers and C. Politicians/regulators.) The expectation is that divergence in the environmental standards between countries in the EU will continue for the foreseeable future. During the period of transition, when the new member countries are supposed to act on the commitments of the *acquis communautaire*, regulatory credibility and transparency are essential not only to achieve the stated policy objectives, but to secure corporate participation as well. We argue that this is of particular importance, since without the input of (foreign) investors, the likelihood of meeting the costs of compliance of the environmental *acquis* in Central and Eastern Europe (CEE) are low.

The final section of this chapter will address the supranational level of regulation, and discuss in detail the evolving regime for climate change regulation in Europe. At this level, information asymmetries arise between national governments and the EU in new areas of environmental policy, where directives are used to establish new areas of common policy across borders.[2] Examples include the Commission's proposal for a new policy on Chemicals Registration, Evaluation, Authorisation and Restriction (REACH), which is currently being considered by the Parliament, and the introduction of the ETS. As we will discuss, the ETS introduces two types of uncertainty; the uncertainty related to policy credibility and transparency at the community level, and the uncertainty related to the functioning of the newly created market for carbon credits, both of which are partly dependent on developments outside of the EU. (In terms of the overall framework of this book, this corresponds to information asymmetries between B. Corporate decision-makers, C. Politicians/regulators and D. International politicians/regulators.)

We conclude this chapter by summarizing our findings on the interconnections between environmental issues and transparency at different policy levels. In an era that favours market-led regulation over command-and-control, the participation of large firms in the policy process is indispensable, and the issues of uncertainty and transparency are central to determining their level of participation. We find that while more transparency concerning environmental measurement, compliance and enforcement is likely to be essential to encourage private investment, in evolving areas of policy, such as climate change, there are some potential tradeoffs between transparency and policy effectiveness.

4.2 Local Standards and Civil Society Activism

Since the EU adopted the Århus convention in 2001, there has been an institutional mechanism in Europe for individuals and NGOs to get information on a wide range of environmental concerns.[3] The convention is intended to improve

---

[2]Not all areas of environmental policy are harmonized at the EU level. Directives establish common standards, which are adopted into national law, but for other areas of policy, mutual recognition across member states applies.

[3]The convention has so far been ratified by eight EU countries, and in 2003 the European Commission adopted a package of legislative proposals to bring Community legislation in line with the convention. See also the Proposal for Regulation applying the Århus Convention to EU institutions, COM (2003) 622.

transparency by enabling individuals to obtain information on environmental matters, to involve stakeholders in decision-making and to offer ways for affected groups to seek legal resolution to environmental conflicts. The convention also provides for horizontal accountability, which means that an NGO anywhere in the EU can enquire about the activities carried out by public or private entities anywhere else in the EU.[4]

There is already a great deal of anecdotal evidence on the growing influence of NGOs on corporate decision-making, and research is also beginning to look at the role of civil society in broader terms. Some civil society groups are strictly local, while many are not, and the largest NGOs are organized globally to match their corporate targets (Teegen, Doh, & Vachani, 2004). In some instances, it is possible, that by collaborating with NGO a firm can distinguish its product from those of competitors and to increase or defend its market share, or derive a price premium (Rondinelli & London, 2003). However, such possible benefits aside, NGOs introduce significant risks, particularly to firms dealing in consumer markets, where a large part of the market value of firms is made up of intangibles including the brand name and reputation of the firm. These assets have been cultivated over time at great expense to the firm, while the destruction of market value due to adverse publicity is immediate. Although the probability of such an attack is relatively less, firms will differ in the number of potential areas of liability they entail, and consequently markets should value firms with more areas of potential liability at a discount.

Throughout this chapter, we define transparency as the nature and availability of relevant information that can have an impact on the value of the firm. Furthermore, we make a distinction according to whether the transparency is procedural or substantive. Procedural transparency concerns the extent to which information is made available on timely and non-discriminatory basis. Substantive transparency pertains to the content of the information, i.e. whether the information is sufficient, reliable and precise.

In terms of both procedural and substantive transparency, NGOs (in comparison to most regulators) are not very transparent. Indeed, while NGOs contribute to making diverse viewpoints heard, institutionally they are unelected and generally unaccountable for their actions (Jordan & van Tuijl, 2000; Robertson, 2000). NGOs typically accuse firms (or supranational institutions, like the WTO) of a lack of transparency concerning their environmental performance and decision-making processes, but the NGOs themselves give out few concrete indications of what level of performance they would consider acceptable. The uncertainty related

[4]World Resources Institute: Environmental accountability beyond the nation state: The implications of the Århus convention, April 2000.

to target setting and standards of acceptable performance is detrimental to environmental investment, and like corruption, risks imposing a random tax on firms (see Chapter 14).

To mitigate the problem of information asymmetry and missing standards in the marketplace, self-regulation by firms, sometimes coupled with third-party verification, has become increasingly popular. The publication of corporate environmental or social reports, describing the firms' self-selected performance benchmarks, has grown significantly, partly due to regulation, and partly due to firms' own initiative (Christmann & Taylor, 2002; Kolk, 2005). Complementary to this is the growth in accreditation and rating schemes, such as GRI[5] and DJSI that serve the needs of the socially responsible investment community. Instead of either excluding specific sectors (such as tobacco) or only including certain sectors (such as renewable energy), socially responsible funds that want a diverse portfolio increasingly use best-in-class indices like the Dow Jones Sustainability World Index (DJSI World),[6] which contains the top 10% in terms of sustainability, in each industry group, chosen from the 2500 biggest firms in the Dow Jones Global Index. While such efforts have improved the procedural transparency of both the firms and the rating agencies themselves, problems remain regarding substantive transparency, since firms continue to be the gatekeepers of much firm-specific environmental information.[7]

4.3 National Standards and Divergence within the EU

Instead of pursuing regulatory harmonization, the EU follows a (market-led) process of gradual convergence, with domestic and community measures complementing each other under the principle of subsidiarity (cf. Ziegler, 1996). Owing to mutual recognition, the leading countries in Northern Europe have not had to compromise on their level of environmental protection, and if anything, so far the EU-15 have gradually gravitated towards a tighter environmental regime. Indeed, Neumayer (2001) presents evidence to suggest that while environmental quality in the EU-15 has improved as a consequence of EU policies, it has not converged among the member countries. The situation within the enlarged EU is

---

[5]The Global Reporting Initiative (GRI) develops sustainability reporting guidelines to establish common standards in corporate social reporting.

[6]The DJSI currently has more than 50 outstanding licences to investment funds, with accumulated assets under management of over €3 billion.

[7]The Toxics Release Inventory in the United States provides plant-level information, while the EU's proposed REACH policy would require firms to track the safety and use of a wide range of chemicals.

not a North–South scenario, since all member countries have committed to achieving the same standards under the *acquis communautaire*. Nonetheless, considerable uncertainty relates to the ability and willingness of the governments to live up to their commitments under difficult economic conditions.[8]

4.3.1 Environmental Challenges in CEE

The countries of CEE that joined the EU in 2004 face substantial costs of compliance arising from European environmental regulations. Funding from the EU will only cover a fraction of these costs, and the likeliest source of investment in new 'greener' technologies is foreign direct investment (FDI). While FDI can contribute to an upgrading (rather than a downgrading) of environmental standards in the accession countries, this process is vulnerable to problems of adverse selection, which can lead to the creation of a market for lemons (Akerlof, 1970) in terms of investor quality. Specifically, the existing literature on multinational enterprises (MNEs) and environmental investment suggest that firms are sensitive to the institutional quality in the host location in terms of the predictability, consistency and enforcement of environmental regulations (Lundan, 2004). Institutional failure in these key areas is likely to remove the incentive for high-quality investors to enter the market, leading either to little investment, or to a market populated with 'dirty lemons'.

Within the past 10 years, the EU has brought into effect important directives regarding the quality of drinking water (98/83/EC), urban wastewater treatment (91/271/EEC), the use of landfills (99/31/EC), the incineration of municipal waste (89/369/EEC) and hazardous waste (94/67/EC) as well as the quality of ambient air (96/62/EC and 99/30/EC). Although municipal utilities are the major investors within the water and waste management sectors, industrial companies also face investments in wastewater treatment systems and waste disposal, as well as in instrumentation to enable continuous air and water quality monitoring. Additionally, the Integrated Pollution Prevention and Control (IPPC) directive (96/61/EC) necessitates investment in new cleaner processes using best available techniques (BAT), that are prescribed for the pollution intensive industries, including pulp and paper, iron and steel, ferrous and non-ferrous metals, tanning and refineries.[9] While some older directives date back as far as 1975, most of the environmental directives have been passed in the past decade, and along with the system of mutual recognition of additional environmental

---

[8]This is true of many areas of EU-level policy, such as competition policy (see Chapter 3 in this volume).

[9]European Commission: The challenge of environmental financing in the candidate countries, Annex 1, COM (2001) 304.

regulation, these directives establish the basic level of environmental protection across the EU.

All accession agreements impose 'nationhood costs' of integration in terms of the extent and pace of institutional reform (Gray & Lundan, 1994). A part of the process of the accession countries entering, the EU has been a requirement for the applicant countries to show that they have complied with the *acquis communautaire*. As part of their membership negotiations, the new member countries have agreed on individual deadlines to reach full compliance with the EU environmental directives. In some cases the deadlines extend as far as the year 2015, but for all the new member countries, significant areas of compliance have to be established as early as in the period 2004–2008. Overall, the current estimates are, that it will cost the 10 new member countries in the order of €80–110 billion to comply with the environmental rules, which would require investments amounting to 2–3% of GDP annually.[10] The most investment is required in the treatment of wastewater and sludge to comply with the wastewater directive, and in facilities for waste storage and disposal to comply with the waste and landfill directives. According to World Bank estimates from 1999 to 2000, the countries facing the largest environmental investments are Poland, the Czech Republic and Hungary. The same three countries also exhibit a high share of inward FDI stock to GDP, and a high share of foreign MNE affiliates' output in manufacturing exports.

While the process of privatization involved brownfield investment, recent manufacturing investment is more likely to have been in the form of greenfield investments, which offers the possibility of technology transfer and higher environmental standards. Estrin, Hughes, and Todd (1997) estimate that the initial foreign investment undertaken a decade ago served to improve local environmental standards, and helped to compensate for the lack of investment and proper maintenance under the communist regime. However, owing to the extent of pollution under the old regime, and in the aftermath of privatization, brownfield sites have become virtually untouchable for foreign investors, who see potential environmental liability as a major deterrent, even if governments have been willing to grant them amnesty from past pollution (see Auer, Reuveny, & Adler, 2001).

4.3.2 Regulatory Transparency, Uncertainty and Investment

Within the EU, environmental standards are likely to continue to diverge, and while great improvements can be expected in the new member countries, somewhat different standards are likely to prevail even after the prescribed period of adjustment.

[10]European Commission: The challenge of environmental financing in the candidate countries, Annex 2, COM (2001) 304.

The expectation based on existing literature is that the tightening of environmental standards itself will have little impact on investment flows. Foreign investment is not attracted by lax regulation, and if anything, improved environmental conditions will make it more attractive for leading multinationals to invest in these countries. By transferring technology, MNEs may contribute to the upgrading of standards, although it is likely that the best firms are attracted to locations that have already made considerable strides in safeguarding the environment (Lundan, 2004).

We have argued elsewhere that there is in fact a simultaneous race to the top and to the bottom to attract foreign investment within the EU (Lundan, 2003b). The race to the top is the race to attract clean investment, and in this context, the compliance mechanisms of the Kyoto Protocol, as well as the EU environmental directives which form a part of the *acquis*, are the key in providing an incentive for technologically advanced firms to invest in clean technologies in the new member countries. The race to the top should be most evident for manufacturing investment aimed at export generation, since the scrutiny faced by large MNEs in their home markets increasingly extends throughout the value chain. The race to the bottom would involve continuing dirty production and/or 'environmental dumping'. However, in this case foreign investment is less likely to play a decisive role, since any 'environmental dumping' is most likely to be carried out by domestic firms or small multinationals selling to local markets with inadequate resources to invest in environmental protection.

The institutional costs of accession are likely to be substantial, since transparency and credibility in the measurement and enforcement of environmental standards is needed to ensure that the problem of adverse selection and the attraction of investors that are 'dirty lemons' does not occur. Within the EU-25, the negotiated timetables should ensure a sufficient level of procedural transparency. However, major concerns remain concerning the substantive transparency of national governments concerning the level of monitoring and enforcement of environmental regulations. The importance of institutional infrastructure is beginning to be recognized in the literature as a major determinant of FDI in developing and transition economies (Bevan & Estrin, 2004; Henisz, 2000; Lundan, 2003a; Meyer, 2001; Phelps, MacKinnon, Stone, & Braidford, 2003), and the development of credible and predictable environmental regulation and enforcement is a specific example of this effect.

4.4 Supranational Level and Uncertainties Related to Climate Change Policy

In this section of the chapter, we analyse the issues of transparency and uncertainty associated with the EU ETS. Like the preceding sections of the chapter, we include analyses at more than one institutional level. In particular, we focus on the multilateral level, represented by the Kyoto Protocol on climate change as well as the EU regional level and national member level. In addition, we consider bi-lateral international relations with the US and other countries.[11]

Throughout the past development, current implementation and future planning of the ETS, issues of transparency have been—and will continue to be—central concerns. Such issues are concerns for EU and member state officials, for industry executives and for NGOs and interested segments of the public. We will illustrate a wide range of ETS transparency issues and place those issues in the context of the broader concerns about their effects on investment decisions.

4.4.1 EU Kyoto Commitments and the Development of the ETS

In the 1997 Kyoto agreement, which came into effect on 16 February 2005, the EU-15 along with the 10 accession countries agreed to an 8% reduction in greenhouse gas (GHG) emissions to be achieved during the period from 2008 to 2012, using 1990 as the base year.[12] While most of the EU-15 are likely to exceed their targets,[13] all the accession countries (with the exception of Slovenia) were on track in 2001 (the latest year data are available) for meeting their Kyoto targets. Furthermore, several accession countries, such as Latvia, Estonia, the Czech Republic and Slovakia, far exceed the required reductions in GHGs, which opens up the possibility that these countries will become the sellers in a future market for tradable emissions permits.[14] The EU scheme is an installation-based system, where each large emitter is issued its own allocation of allowances. These allowances can be freely traded within the EU-25. In July 2003, the European Commission proposed a new Directive to allow the linking of carbon trading from Joint Implementation (JI) and Clean Development Mechanism (CDM) projects under the Kyoto Protocol to the EU emissions trading scheme.[15]

[11]Another set of uncertainties about the multilateral climate regime revolves around interactions between the provisions of the Protocol, its implementation by an international secretariat, and the national policies and measures that individual governments adopt, on the one hand, and the rules and procedures of the World Trade Organization (WTO) on the other. See Brewer (2003) and Brewer (2004) for details.

[12]In the United States the state and local governments have been actively filling a perceived void in national-level policy-making, and a complex array of regimes at several levels has begun to develop.

[13]European Environment Agency: Greenhouse gas emission trends and projections in Europe 2003, No. 36 2003.

[14]The EU-15 have their own established targets and a burden-sharing agreement under the Kyoto Protocol, so the excess credit of the new accession countries is not automatically counted against this target.

[15]Proposal for a Directive of the European Parliament and of the Council amending the Directive establishing a scheme for GHG emission allowance trading within the Community, in respect of the Kyoto Protocol's project mechanisms, COM (2003) 403.

The entry into operation of the ETS on 1 January 2005 was a landmark event in the history of the European integration process. It was also the result of a process of regulatory innovation that has overcome extraordinary political and technical challenges. Its development extended over many years and included extensive involvement of the Parliament and Council as well as the Commission, and of course member states, industry and environmental NGOs. Analysts in think tanks, consultancies and universities were also involved throughout the long development process.

Although the origins of the ETS can be traced back to the early 1990s, it was during 2003 and 2004 that it achieved formally approved status and began to gain tangible form as the National Action Plans (NAPs) of the member states were developed and approved. From the beginning of 2005, the scheme entered into a period of implementation. However, the first phase from 2005 through 2007 is only a preliminary phase, with further major regulatory issues yet to be resolved before the beginning of the second phase, 2008–2012, which coincides with the first commitment period of the Kyoto Protocol. The development of the ETS is therefore an on-going, long-term process of regulatory innovation.

The industry sectors which are explicitly included in the ETS in Phase I are electric power and other energy sectors; ferrous metals; cement, glass and ceramics; and pulp, paper and cardboard. Approximately, 12,000 individual installations in these sectors have received European Union allowances (EUAs). They are expected to produce approximately 46% of the EU's carbon dioxide emissions in 2008–2012. The specific issues that firms face depend in part on the *country of location* of their facilities, as each member government has its own National Allocation Plan (NAP) to achieve its national emission targets within the context of the EU 'bubble'. There are both commonalities and distinctive elements in the national plans, as discussed in detail in a subsequent section of the chapter. The specific regulatory issues that firms face also depend in part on their *industry sector*; again, there are both commonalities and distinctive features across industries in the specific types of regulatory issues they face. Regardless of variations across countries and industries, however, as the ETS has been under development and as it enters into force, regulatory uncertainties are among the most significant issues encountering firms; for regulatory uncertainties have already been among the important determinants of prices and expectations about prices in carbon market transactions.

Several categories of literature are relevant to the analysis we present here; we will briefly mention some of the essential contributions. The book by Schneider, Rosencranz, and Niles (2002) is a wide-ranging collection of studies, including introductions to the science, economics and politics of climate change; it also has chapters on more specialized topics concerning agriculture, forestry and energy. Michaelowa and Koch (2001) give a useful, extensive glossary of terms that are commonly used in climate change parlance, particularly in the context of the UN Framework Convention on Climate Change (FCCC) and Kyoto Protocol. An analysis of the evolution of the world's pluralistic climate regime, with an emphasis on regional approaches, is presented in Egenhofer, Fujiwara, Kernohan, Brewer, and van Schaik (2004). The highlights of a conference sponsored by the Aspen Institute and Pew Center for Global Climate Change on institutional frameworks for mandatory GHG reductions are summarized in the Global Environmental Change Report (2004).

4.4.2 The Development of Carbon Markets

The EU ETS is not the first or only market in the world for trading carbon dioxide and other GHG emissions. There have been domestic national carbon markets operating in Denmark and the UK, and there are national and sub-national carbon markets, as well as international carbon markets, already functioning or in the process of being created in many parts of the world.[16] Although this chapter focuses on the EU ETS, it also includes information about the institutional contexts of other markets. As in several other areas of policy, such as the multijurisdictional issues relating to competition policy in the case of cross-border mergers (Gugler, in this volume), the ETS scheme and its implications for firms cannot be fully understood without an understanding of the relationship of the ETS to the other elements of the world climate regime.

While many of the conceptual and empirical issues are generic and thus pertain to all carbon markets, others are specific to the EU.[17] The emerging world regime is highly fragmented; the relationships among its components are complex and will continue to change for many years. The components of the world regime can be conveniently considered in terms of their 'levels'—i.e. multilateral, regional, bi-lateral, national and sub-national. At the *multilateral* level, the UN FCCC and its Kyoto Protocol are the specific manifestations of international arrangements.

---

[16]For reviews of recent developments in the carbon markets, see especially the annual reports on the *State and Trends of the Carbon Market* by the Prototype Carbon Fund of the World Bank (2001, 2002, 2003). An overview of institutional arrangements in the carbon markets is provided by de Coninck and van der Linden (2003). Also see the data base on institutional arrangements and other information on the website of the International Emissions Trading Association (IETA) at www.ieta.org.

[17]The book by Kopp and Thatcher (2000) is a collection of papers, most of which are focused on emissions trading, particularly in the context of Kyoto Protocol institutional arrangements. The International Energy Agency (2001) reports the results of simulation studies of international GHG emissions trading and assesses features of trading systems. Buzengeiger, Betz, and Bode (2001) discuss issues and alternatives in the design of emissions trading systems—both national and international.

At the *national* level, it is useful to distinguish among the governments that have ratified the Kyoto Protocol, on the one hand, and the others (Australia and the US) which have not. It is also useful to distinguish between those national governments that are participants in the EU ETS, and those which are not. EU members are included in the Kyoto Protocol EU 'bubble', but also have individual NAPs within the context of the EU ETS.

At the *international regional* level, in addition to the EU ETS, there is a voluntary, non-governmental arrangement—namely the Chicago Climate Exchange (CCX)—which is based in the United States and includes participants from Canada, Mexico and Brazil. There was briefly some consideration of the possibility of a regional arrangement in the context of the Commission on Environmental Cooperation (CEC) which includes the NAFTA governments of Canada, Mexico and the US. However, the prospects for such an arrangement have apparently been diminished by US government opposition. There is a trans-national regional agreement among a group of US states and Canadian provinces.

There is also a *sub-national regional* arrangement within the US that includes some of the same states as the above trans-national arrangement, plus other states in the north-eastern section of the country. Also, at the sub-national level, New South Wales in Australia has begun to develop an emissions trading regime, and Victoria has indicated that it may do so as well.

4.4.3 EU ETS Institutional Framework

The start-up of operations of the ETS on 1 January 2005 followed several years of development through actions by the institutions of the EU and on the basis of the NAPs of the member states. A combination of community-level and national-level polices is integral to the functioning of the ETS. At the community level, there are a series of landmark events in the creation of the ETS, and they can be traced back to the early 1990s:[18]

1991—The Commission issued the first community strategy to limit carbon dioxide emissions and improve energy efficiency.

1997—The Commission signed the Kyoto Protocol of the FCCC.

2000—The Commission launched the European Climate Change Programme, which included the outlines of an emissions trading scheme.

---

[18]This chronology is not intended to be an exhaustive list of regulatory events, but rather an overview of the evolution of the ETS with selected highlights to indicate landmark events. It was drawn from commentaries and documents at http://europa.eu.net/comm/enviroment/climat/htm, downloaded on 13 May 2004.

2002—The EU ratified the Kyoto Protocol.

2003—The Parliament and Council adopted a *directive* establishing the ETS, later amended to include projects.

2003—The Commission issued *guidelines* for ETS NAPs.

2004—The Commission established *guidelines* for monitoring and reporting GHG emissions.

The Scheme applies mandatory caps for the annual emissions of carbon dioxide at approximately 15,000 installations in the 25 members of the EU. (Cyprus and Malta are not included in the ETS at the outset, though they were expected to develop NAPs along with the other members during 2004.) In addition, four non-EU countries may be included, but their plans were not yet clear in late 2004. Norway is likely to be included, perhaps in 2005. Iceland and Liechtenstein can also, but may decide not to do so. Switzerland may also be included, but on the basis of a bi-lateral agreement. Firms with installations that exceed their caps have to pay a fine of €40 per ton for 2005–2007, and €100 starting in 2008 and also make up the shortfall in subsequent years; or they have to buy carbon allowances (EAUs) from firms with installations whose emissions are below their caps. A carbon market is thereby created.

During the elaboration of the specific rules and procedures in the run-up to its formal operational start on 1 January 2005, the development of NAPs was the object of much interest—and the source of much regulatory uncertainty. The Commission established a series of guidelines and deadlines for the submission, revision and approval process for the NAPs during 2004. The national-level coverage of emissions and installations that had been reviewed by the Commission as of early July 2004 include eight members' NAPs that had been unconditionally or conditionally approved at that time. The relative importance of Germany and the UK in terms of both emissions and installations is evident. In Germany, there were 2419 installations to be covered by caps, and 1078 in the UK. At the other extreme, there were 98 in Slovenia (which was the only one among the 10 new members to have submitted its NAP for review at that time).

The carbon market in Europe is constantly evolving, and a number of sources exist monitoring its development. For analyses of the ETS, there are numerous studies and reports sponsored by the Centre for European Policy Studies (CEPS), such as Egenhofer and Mullins (2000), Egenhofer and Legge (2002) and Egenhofer and Fujiwara (2004) (also see Haites & Mullins, 2004). The website of the EU contains links to the key documents of the Commission, Parliament and Council, as well as news updates and other materials; see especially the home page of its climate change unit at www.europa.eu.int/comm/environment/climat/home. A presentation by Dessain (2004) on the implications of the EU ETS for business includes information about the directly affected sectors, especially the electricity sector. A study by Gummer and Moreland (2000) sponsored by the Pew Center reviews the emissions trading policies and other elements of the climate policies of five member governments as well as the EU.[19]

Additionally, two publications contain a large number of short but useful case studies and discussions of institutional arrangements and other policy developments. One is published by IETA, the International Emissions Trading Association (2003), and the other by Responding to Climate Change (2003); both are annual publications. Other publications reflecting the status and prospects for the ETS include Environmental Finance (2004), Hobley and Hawkes (2003) and Nicholls (2004). More generally, www.climate.biz, offers resources for firms that are looking for information about climate issues and alternatives for responding to them.

4.4.4 *Regulatory Uncertainties and Prices*

Two closely related questions about the effects of regulatory uncertainty can be explored in a preliminary way with the price data available to date. It should be emphasized that this is a preliminary exploration. The analysis here does not offer robust tests of hypotheses, but rather anecdotal and *ad hoc* examinations of the limited evidence that is available. The presentation should nevertheless demonstrate that this is a promising area for further, more systematic econometric testing and modelling exercises.

(1) How does the clarification of regulations affect EAU *price levels*?
(2) How does regulatory uncertainty affect EAU *bid-offer spreads*?

Of course, as the ETS and other carbon markets become increasingly active and generate much more data in the next few years, it will be possible to apply more advanced methodological techniques to much larger data sets. Until then, the data of Figure 4.1 and Table 4.1 provide sufficient grounds for early observations. Figure 4.1 traces the weekly closing prices of a 2005 vintage EAU over the period from July 2003 until early August 2005.

[19]There are also several indispensable periodical and electronic resources for monitoring developments in the EU ETS (individual items from them are cited in the sections below). The monthly publication, Environmental Finance and its companion newsletter, Carbon Finance, published by Fulton in London, are both excellent for keeping up with developments. The electronic newsletter Carbon Market Europe, produced by Point Carbon in Norway, is also indispensable. Another useful monthly is Global Environmental Change Report, which is published by Aspen publishers in the US. The electronic newsletter, Climate-l, contains frequent updates on a wide range of matters concerning climate change, including developments in the EU.

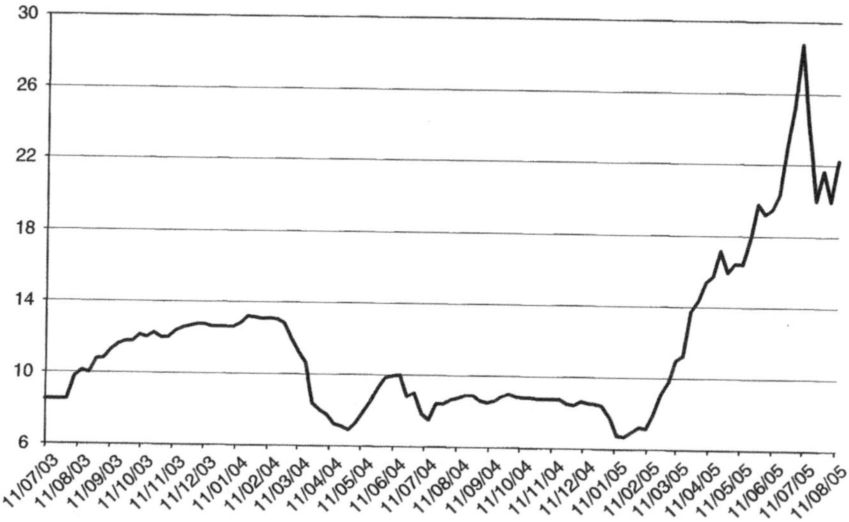

Figure 4.1: Prices for 2005 EU allowances, July 2003–August 2005 (€ per metric tonne of carbon dioxide). *Source*: *Carbon Market Europe*, 12 August 2005. Used with permission.

Four periods are evident in Figure 4.1 in terms of the direction of change. During the 10-month period from early May 2003 (not shown) until late February 2004, there was a rather steady climb resulting in a doubling of the price from less than €6 to more than €13. It was during this period that decisions by the EU institutions clarified many aspects of the ETS regulations. In the second period, March and April of 2004, there was a rather precipitous drop of about €5 in eight weeks. In this period, there were apprehensions about whether the Commission and national governments would be able to make the ETS operational in a timely manner and whether the specific emission limits within industry sectors and at the installation level would be sufficient for it to achieve its objectives. In the third period, early May to mid-June, there was a rather steep rise of €3 in 6 weeks—from about €7 to about €10. During this time, several member governments finally submitted their NAPs and it became clear that the Commission would be making some key decisions and announcing them within a matter of a couple of months or so.

This brings us to the fourth period, during which the focal event was the announcement by the Commission on 7 July of its decisions about NAPs. Only Germany, among the member governments, had published a proposed NAP and submitted it to the Commission by the 31 March 2004 deadline. However, by

Box 4.1: The Commission's decisions on members' national allocation plans on 7 July 2004.

Approved (unconditionally):

Denmark
Ireland
Netherlands
Slovenia
Sweden

Partially rejected (conditionally approved):

Austria—Problem: ex-post allocation adjustment, i.e. redistribution of allowances during 2005–2007 trading period

Germany—Problem: ex-post allocation adjustment, i.e. redistribution of allowances during 2005–2007 trading period

UK—Problem: lack of information on new entrants and installations on Gibraltar

Infringement proceedings launched for late submission:

Greece
Italy

Pending Further Action:

All others

Source: *Carbon Market Europe*, 7 July 2004.

7 July the Commission had enough submissions to make public its decisions on eight of them. This was widely viewed as a particularly significant regulatory event because it was the first public indication of the combination of firmness and flexibility with which the Commission would oversee the NAP review process. For a summary of the Commission's decisions announced on 7 July 2004 (see Box 4.1). For an encapsulated narrative of the market events of 7 July (see Box 4.2).

The data in Table 4.1 make it possible to observe the behaviour of the market around the time of the 7 July Commission announcement of its decisions on NAPs. The data in the table include the levels and changes in the bid and offer prices, and the levels and changes in the spread between the bid and offer prices. As for *prices*, after rising steadily throughout May and into mid-June, the mid-point

Box 4.2: A day in the life of the EUA.

EU ETS price drops following EC NAP announcement.

Following the announcement of the European Commission's verdict of the first eight NAPs today [7 July 2004], the price in the EU ETS market dropped significantly. The spread has widened, while the bid level is down €0.60 cents from this morning.

The market started out today with bids around the €8.50/tonne level and offers around €8.80/tonne. Rumours flew around all morning that the Commission's response to the NAPs would not be of the strict kind, and 20 minutes before the EC press conference, a trade went through at €8.55/tonne. However, after the market saw the press material from the Commission, noticing that the total cap of the German and UK NAPs in particular had not been reduced, the reaction was a drop in prices.

Before the midday press conference was even over, bids were down at €7.90/tonne, offers at €8.35. "It seems like most market participants interpret the EC ruling as not on the strict side", broker John Molloy at TFS commented. "The market reacted bearishly, continuing the downward trend of the past few days", added Paddy Shord at GFI. "The general tone of the announcement was not greeted with massive surprise".

Source: Point Carbon (2004). EUA prices. Carbon Market, Europe, 5, 1. Used with permission.

of the bid and offer prices began to decrease in anticipation of the 7 July announcement. On the 7th, it declined by 0.52, and on the 8th by another 0.43. It had thus declined about €2 over the approximately one-month period from 10 June to 8 July. However, this was neither particularly large in absolute size nor particularly negative in terms of the decline, relative to the experience of the previous 12 months. As for *spreads*, although they increased slightly on the 7th, they declined the next day, and in any case the changes were relatively small compared with those during the previous month. In sum, there was a notable price decline in anticipation of the 7 July announcement and in its immediate aftermath, but the spreads did not markedly change.[20]

[20]The sporadic trading in the carbon market during the preliminary period before the official start of the ETS is likely to have contributed to the volatility in prices and the size of the spreads.

Table 4.1: EAU prices June–July 2004 before and after Commission decisions on NAPs on 7 July 2004.

	3 June	10 June	17 June	24 June	1 July	7 July am	7 July pm	8 July
Offer	9.60	10.50	10.30	8.80	9.10	8.80	8.35	7.85
Bid	9.50	9.40	9.70	8.70	8.80	8.50	7.90	7.55
Spread	0.10	1.10	0.60	0.10	0.30	0.30	0.45	0.30
Change in spread	na	+1.00	−0.50	−0.50	+0.20	0.00	+0.15	−0.15
Mid-point	9.55	9.95	10.00	8.75	8.95	8.65	8.13	7.70
Change in Mid-point	na	+0.40	−0.25	−0.95	+0.20	−0.30	−0.52	−0.43

Note: € per metric tonne of carbon dioxide, close except 7 July am.
Source: Computed by the author from *Carbon Market Europe*, issues of 4 June, 11 June, 18 June, 25 June, 2 July and 9 July 2004.

After the initial version of this chapter was written during the summer of 2004, there was a period of relative stability in prices, then period of sustained and dramatic increases, followed by moderate declines. The substantial increases in the price of carbon allowances — from less than €10 to nearly €30 during the first six months of 2005 — was presumed to be a result of the increasing oil prices during that period, which in turn led to greater use of coal for generating electricity, and thus expectations of higher future emissions.

4.4.5 Regulatory and Market Uncertainty

Regulatory uncertainties are evident along three dimensions of the EU ETS, and other climate change regulatory regimes as well — i.e. country, industry and level (multilateral, regional, national, sub-national). Further, these three dimensions interact to produce distinctive regulatory uncertainty profiles for each combination of level–country–industry.

Over the 20-month period for which there were data as of January 2005, the price movements of EAUs were broadly consistent with what would be expected on the basis of the clarification of the regulatory environment. As for bid-offer spreads, they shifted generally in accord with variability over time in regulatory uncertainties.[21] It should be noted, however, that disentangling the effects of variability over time in uncertainty versus the nature of the clarifications of the regulations is a central analytic challenge. During early July 2004, as the Commission made public its decisions about eight of the NAPs, it was *simultaneously* reducing some elements of uncertainty about its regulations and specifying the projected levels of emission reductions that it would find acceptable.

Whatever the future course of the EU ETS, it will no doubt provide much 'fodder' for further research. For instance, the effects of regulatory uncertainty on the *volume* of transactions could be determined, at least in principle, in addition to the effects on prices and spreads. Additional data collection towards this end should be a high priority for further research. In terms of theory development, the regulatory capture model — and specific hypotheses derived from it — could be applied to the evolution of the ETS regulations. Because of the importance of the ETS as an early and significant GHG regulatory regime, it will surely be a subject worthy of the serious attention of scholars, no matter what their particular theoretical, methodological and topical interests may be.

[21]During a cold spell in Europe in February 2005, the carbon market reacted according to expectations when prices rose promptly from about €6.70 to €9 per ton (Financial Times, 25 February 2005, p. 3).

Table 4.2: Environmental policy, uncertainty and institutional transparency in the EU.

Policy level	Source of uncertainty	Possible effect on firms	Measures to reduce uncertainty
Local/national	NGO activity	Loss of corporate value Lack of investment Increasing costs	Corporate social reporting Rating schemes (e.g. DJSI, GRI)
National (among member states)	Regulatory enforcement	Lack of investment	Regulatory transparency and consistency
Regional/supranational (between the EU and member states)	New areas of regulation	Increasing costs Lack of investment	Regulatory transparency and consistency
	Development of ETS carbon market	Unknown cost of using the market	n.a.

4.5 Conclusions

This chapter has reviewed different kinds of uncertainty related to EU environmental policy at three levels (local, national/regional and supranational). Not surprisingly, our general finding is that the impact of a lack of transparency on all three levels is to reduce the possibilities for firms to respond to the challenges in an efficient manner. However, the specific impact on firm behaviour depends on the kind of uncertainty, and the available means to mitigate uncertainty by increasing transparency. We have summarized our findings in Table 4.2.

At the local and national levels, uncertainty about NGO demands and expected standards of performance push firms towards self-regulation and participation in third-party rating schemes. Regulatory inconsistency (uncertainty related to expected performance) generally discourages environmental investment, while uncertainty related to enforcement raises the possibility of the emergence of a market for lemons, which firms with extensive environmental investments would prefer to avoid. This is particularly the case concerning the financing of the environmental *acquis* in CEE, and the ability of the accession countries to attract foreign investors to share some of the costs.

At the supranational level, the issue of climate change will be an important test for the EU of both regulatory consistency and implementation. On one hand, firms are looking for signs from the Commission that the US staying out of the Kyoto Protocol (and China and India not being required to make reductions) will not change the Commission's policy objectives. On the other hand, firms operating under the NAPs will follow the development of the carbon market to decide whether to invest or to trade for their share of the allocation. Although one can imagine a time when the carbon market will contain all the necessary information to make such decisions, for the foreseeable future, the Commission's perceived commitment to its policy on climate change, as well as the likelihood of the imposition of the planned penalties, will pay an important role in determining the price levels in the EU carbon market.

These carbon prices and the associated uncertainties affect the cost of capital and therefore the prospects for economic growth, especially in the most carbon dependent economic sectors.

Acknowledgements

We are indebted to panel participants for their comments on the papers. In addition, Tom Brewer is indebted to Christian Egenhofer of the Centre for European Policy Studies (CEPS) in Brussels for his extensive comments on a draft of the conference paper. Sarianna Lundan is indebted to Minna Kanerva for research assistance.

References

Akerlof, G. A. (1970). The market for 'lemons': Quality uncertainty and the market mechanism. *Quarterly Journal of Economics, 84*(3), 488–500.

Auer, M., Reuveny, R., & Adler, L. (2001). Environmental liability and foreign direct investment in Central and Eastern Europe. *Journal of Environment and Development, 10*(1), 30–35.

Bevan, A. A., & Estrin, S. (2004). The determinants of foreign direct investment into European transition economies. *Journal of Comparative Economics, 32*, 775–787.

Brewer, T. L. (2003). The trade regime and the climate regime: Institutional evolution and adaptation. *Climate Policy, 3*(4), 329–341.

Brewer, T. L. (2004). The WTO and the Kyoto Protocol: Interaction issues. *Climate Policy, 4*(1), 3–12.

Buzengeiger, S., Betz, R., & Bode, S. (2001). *Making GHG emissions trading work—Crucial issues in designing national and international emissions trading systems.* HWWA Discussion Paper 154. Hamburg Institute of International Economics, Hamburg.

Christmann, P., & Taylor, G. (2002). Globalization and the environment: Strategies for international voluntary environmental initiatives. *Academy of Management Executive, 16*(3), 121–135.

de Coninck, H. C., & van der Linden, N. H. (2003). *An overview of carbon transactions.* ECN-C-03-022.

Dessain, V. (2004). Implications and opportunities for European business in a carbon constrained economy. Europe Research Center, Harvard Business School, Paris (Powerpoint presentation).

Egenhofer, C., & Fujiwara, N. (2004). *Completion of the EU emissions trading scheme in the emerging global climate regime.* CEPS Task Force Report no. 49. Centre for European Policy Studies, Brussels.

Egenhofer, C., Fujiwara, N., Kernohan, D., Brewer, T. L., & van Schaik, L. (2004). *The future of the international climate change regime: The contribution of "regional approaches" towards an international climate change agreement.* Final Report for the International Forum for Environmental Issues. Economic and Social Research Institute, Government of Japan, Tokyo, March.

Egenhofer, C., & Legge, T. (2002). *Greenhouse gas emissions trading in Europe: Conditions for environmental credibility and economic efficiency.* Report of the CEPS Task Force on Emissions Trading and the New EU Climate Change Policy. CEPS Task Force Report no. 43. Centre for European Policy Studies, Brussels.

Egenhofer, C., & Mullins, F. (2000). *The role of emissions trading in EU climate policy: Priority issues.* Report of a CEPS Working Party. Centre for European Policy Studies, Brussels.

Environmental Finance. (2004). EU emissions trading: Success or stillborn? *Environmental Finance, 5* (June), 22–23.

Estrin, S., Hughes, K., & Todd, S. (Eds). (1997). *Foreign direct investment in Central and Eastern Europe: Multinationals in transition.* London: Pinter.

Global Environmental Change Report. (2004). Climate change policy dialogue: Framework for mandatory reductions. *Global Environmental Change Report, 12* (June), 11–12.

Gray, H. P., & Lundan, S. M. (1994). Nationhood, the GATT ideal and a workable international trading system. *Banca Nazionale del Lavoro Quarterly Review, 188*(March), 99–114.

Gummer, J., & Moreland, R. (2000). *The European Union and global climate change: A review of five national programmes.* Washington, DC: Pew Center on Global Climate Change.

Haites, E., & Mullins, F. (2004). *Greenhouse gas emission trading: The linkages between domestic systems.* Paris: International Energy Agency.

Henisz, W. J. (2000). The institutional environment for multinational investment. *Journal of Law, Economics & Organization, 16*(2), 334–364.

Hobley, A., & Hawkes, P. (2003). The EU emission allowance trading scheme: A prototype for global GHG emissions allowance trading? *Environmental Finance, 4* (May), 1–4.

International Emissions Trading Association. (2003). *Greenhouse gas market, 2003: Emerging but fragmented.* Geneva: IETA.

International Energy Agency. (2001). *International emission trading: From concept to reality.* Paris: IEA.

Jordan, L., & van Tuijl, P. (2000). Political responsibility in transnational NGO advocacy. *World Development, 28*(12), 2051–2065.

Kolk, A. (2005). Environmental reporting by MNEs from the Triad: Convergence or divergence? *Management International Review, 15*(Special issue no.1), 145–166.

Kopp, R. J., & Thatcher, J. B. (2000). *The Weathervane guide to climate policy: An RFF reader.* Washington, DC: Resources for the Future.

Lundan, S. M. (2003a). Institutions, exclusivity and foreign investment. In: H. P. Gray (Ed.), *Extending the eclectic paradigm in international business* (pp. 93–106). Cheltenham: Edward Elgar.

Lundan, S. M. (2003b). The role of environmental issues in the competition for inward investment within Europe. In: L. Oxelheim, & P. Ghauri (Eds), *European Union and the race for foreign direct investment in Europe* (pp. 101–122). Oxford: Elsevier.

Lundan, S. M. (2004). Multinationals, environment and global competition: A conceptual framework. In: S. M. Lundan (Ed.), *Multinationals, environment and global competition* (pp. 1–22). Oxford: JAI (Elsevier).

Meyer, K. E. (2001). Institutions, transaction costs, and entry mode choice in Eastern Europe. *Journal of International Business Studies, 32*(2), 357–367.

Michaelowa, A., & Koch, T. (2001). *Glossary of international climate policy terms.* HWWA Report 208. Hamburg Institute of International Economics, Hamburg.

Neumayer, E. (2001). Improvement without convergence: Pressure on the environment in European Union Countries. *Journal of Common Market Studies, 39*(5), 927–937.

Nicholls, M. (2004). Taking tough decisions on emissions. *Environmental Finance Supplement, 5* (April), VIII–XI.

Phelps, N. A., MacKinnon, D., Stone, I., & Braidford, P. (2003). Embedding the multinationals? Institutions and the development of overseas manufacturing affiliates in Wales and North East England. *Regional Studies*, *37*(1), 27–40.

Responding to Climate Change. (2003). *Responding to climate change, 2003*. Cambridge: Entico Corporation.

Robertson, D. (2000). Civil society and the WTO. *World Economy*, *23*(9), 1119–1134.

Rondinelli, D. A., & London, T. (2003). How corporations and environmental groups cooperate: Assessing cross-sector alliances and collaborations. *Academy of Management Executive*, *17*(1), 61–76.

Schneider, S. H., Rosencranz, A., & Niles, J. O. (2002). *Climate change policy*. Washington, DC: Island Press.

Teegen, H., Doh, J. P., & Vachani, S. (2004). The importance of nongovernmental organizations (NGOs) in global governance and value creation: An international business research agenda. *Journal of International Business Studies*, *35*(6), 463–483.

World Bank, Carbon Development Fund. (2001). *State and trends of the carbon market, 2001*. Washington, DC: World Bank.

World Bank, Carbon Development Fund. (2002). *State and trends of the carbon market, 2002*. Washington, DC: World Bank.

World Bank, Carbon Development Fund. (2003). *State and trends of the carbon market, 2003*. Washington, DC: World Bank.

Ziegler, A. R. (1996). *Trade and environmental law in the European Community*. Oxford: Clarendon Press.

Chapter 5

Transparency in Human Capital Policy: A Prerequisite for European Economic Growth

Erik Mellander and Christina Håkanson

5.1 Introduction

Human capital is one of the most important drivers of economic growth, arguably *the* most important. This makes transparency with respect to policies governing human capital formation in the EU a crucial issue. It is useful to distinguish between two aspects on policy transparency in this context. The first concerns the *formulation* of EU human capital policy, as expressed by the objectives regarding education and training that have been agreed upon within the context of the Lisbon strategy. Here, transparency means that the policy is consistent and well defined. The second aspect concerns the *implementation* of this policy, by individual member states. In countries that perform well on (almost) all objectives, or perform poorly throughout, policy implementation can be said to be characterized by high transparency. By contrast, in member states where the achievements vary greatly between different objectives implementation transparency can be said to be low.

Transparency in this latter sense can differ substantially across member states, owing to the fact that the EU human capital policy is implemented by means of the open method of coordination (OMC). Unlike the other main method for decision making in the EU, the Community method, which operates through legislation, agreements reached by means of the OMC are not legally binding. Accordingly, member states failing to comply with them cannot be sanctioned.

Corporate and Institutional Transparency for Economic Growth in Europe

ISBN: 0-08-044665-5

Differences in transparency can thus arise because some countries may choose to (partly) deviate from the objectives agreed upon, while others may choose to comply. Moreover, there can be large differences in implementation also among complying countries. The reason is that under the OMC, only the political objectives are formulated at the EU level; the choice of measures to achieve these objectives is left to the individual member states.

Our analysis on the transparency of the EU human capital policy is both theoretical and empirical. In the theoretical analysis we consider two issues. The first is whether supplementing traditional "best-practice" objectives by objectives in the form of lower bounds on achievement can increase transparency. Second, we discuss possibilities and means for assessments of overall performance. Both of these two issues relate to transparency with respect to policy formulation as well as policy implementation.

In the empirical analysis we suggest quantitative indicators for all the objectives of the EU human capital policy. Using the latest available data, we report the achievements of all the member states on each of the objectives. We also carry out empirical analyses corresponding to our theoretical discussions.

The chapter unfolds as follows. In the next section we discuss the relation between the transparency of the EU human capital policy and European economic growth. Section 5.3 deals with various aspects of the OMC that are relevant with respect to policy transparency. In particular, we consider the fact that policies formed by means of the OMC are, by nature, more vague and imprecise than policies decided upon by means of the Community method. Sections 5.4 and 5.5 contain the theoretical discussions. In Section 5.6, we provide a listing of the objectives of the EU human capital policy and present the associated quantitative indicators. Sections 5.7 and 5.8 report the results of empirical analyses and concluding comments are provided in Section 5.9.

5.2 Transparency in Human Capital Policy and Economic Growth

We first consider the positive relation between human capital and economic growth implied by endogenous growth theory. We then discuss how transparency in human capital policy can increase human capital accumulation by reducing uncertainty. Finally, we consider how human capital investments also contribute to growth indirectly, through capital-skill complementarity and skill-biases in technical and organizational change.

According to endogenous growth theory, human capital can increase the individual's capacity to generate innovations, thereby increasing the rate of technological change and economic growth (see Romer, 1990). Furthermore, there are externalities in human capital; through workplace interaction the benefits of education and training extend to non-participating individuals, improving their productive capacity, too (see Nelson & Phelps, 1966; Lucas, 1988).[1]

A well-functioning policy for education and training is thus crucial for European growth. This is especially so as most countries in Europe cannot compete with other continents in terms of wage costs, implying that their competitive edge must lie in a highly qualified workforce.

The more transparent human capital policies are, the less uncertainty will there be about the conditions governing society's human capital accumulation. Less uncertainty will attract more students and suppliers of education and training. For firms and investors, less uncertainty about the access to high-skilled labor will be translated into lower (political) risk premia in capital costs. The resulting decrease in the cost of capital will spur investments in general, i.e. in human capital and in fixed capital alike, both of which will lead to a higher rate of growth.

Besides having a direct effect on growth, investments in human capital will also have indirect effects. As noted by Griliches (1969), high-skilled labor and fixed capital are complements, implying that an increase in human capital will increase fixed capital investments, and vice versa.

Moreover, human capital investments will also have positive effects on growth through skilled-biased technical change and skill-biased organizational change (see Berman & Griliches, 1994; Caroli & Van Reenen, 2001). The idea underlying both of these notions of skill-biases is that high-skilled labor is more capable of exploiting, and adapting to, changes which can increase efficiency in production and, hence, productivity and economic growth.

5.3 Transparency Aspects of the Open Method of Coordination

The OMC constitutes a middle-of-the-road alternative to the Community method, which implies full harmonization across countries, on the one hand, and complete member state sovereignty, on the other. As argued in Chapter 7 in this volume, on regulation of financial services, when social preferences and market structures are as heterogeneous as in the EU, a mixture of coordination and member state self-reliance may well be more efficient than full harmonization.[2]

---

[1]Overviews of the theoretical and empirical literatures on the relation between education and growth can be found in Aghion and Howitt (1998, Chapter 10) and Krueger and Lindahl (2001), respectively.

[2]See Chapter 7 in this volume. Coopetition is the author's term for a balance of cooperation and competition.

In particular, as noted by Collignon et al. (2005), a key feature of the OMC is its flexibility: it means drawing up "guidelines" that each member state is to translate into specific action plans, in accordance with its own particular situation.[3] While this flexibility in many instances will be an advantage, it will necessarily lead to lower transparency with respect to policy implementation, compared to when the Community method is employed. This is especially true because countries cannot be forced to follow the guidelines. Accordingly, in addition to trying to carry out a given policy guideline by possibly different means, countries may differ with respect to which policies they implement, and when they implement them.

The most important instruments to address these problems and the resulting lack of transparency are peer reviews and benchmarking, both of which rely on indicators signaling the progress of individual EU member states toward achieving the objectives agreed upon. At the most general level, the European Commission each year prepares a report about how the member states are contributing to making the EU the "most competitive and dynamic knowledge-based economy in the world". By necessity, these reports cannot contain in-depth analyses of all of the different objectives making up the Lisbon strategy. Instead, they provide broad assessments and sometimes focus on specific issues. Nevertheless, the Commission's report identifies leaders and laggards among the member states. Peer pressure and the sharing of information about successful strategies, when the reports are reviewed at the spring meetings of the European Council, is supposed to help the countries lagging behind to catch up with the others.

However, the peer pressure system has not lived up to expectations. Member states are often reluctant to carry out the tasks of "naming, shaming and blaming", especially the two latter ones. Members that criticize other countries for slow progress within one policy field always run the risk of being criticized in return, with respect to another policy area; as it is hard to improve performance relative to all of the large number of different targets involved in the Lisbon strategy this risk is quite substantial. Also, while peer pressure often is an effective tool for corporate governance, it might be less well suited in a non-hierarchal, European context (Sisson, Arrowsmith, & Marginson, 2003).

Recently, ways have been suggested to improve upon, and complement, the peer review system. These suggestions are all related to the issue of transparency. Kok (2004) propose that each member state should formulate a national action program setting out how it is going to reach the Lisbon targets and, moreover, put a high-level member of government in charge of the day-to-day implementation

---

[3]A general discussion of the OMC is beyond the scope of this chapter but can be found in, e.g., De La Porte and Pochet (2002), Borrás and Jacobsson (2004), and Zeitlin, Philippe, and Magnusson (2005).

of this program.[4] In addition, Kok (2004) and, likewise, Collignon et al. (2005) stress the need for more information to, and more active involvement from, the social partners and other stakeholders, including non-governmental organizations.

Another suggestion put forward to increase transparency is to reduce the number of targets. Kok argued that the present large number of targets for the Lisbon strategy

> ". . . makes it very likely that every country will be ranked as best on one indicator or another. This makes the instrument ineffective. Member states are not challenged to improve their record. Simplification is vital. The establishment by the European Council of a more limited framework of 14 targets and indicators offers the opportunity to improve the working of the instrument of peer pressure." (Kok 2004, p. 43)

While this suggestion concerns the Lisbon strategy as a whole, a similar argument could be made with respect to the field of human capital policy; as will be seen in Section 5.6 of this chapter, the EU human capital policy involves 18 objectives, which is a large number, too.

We do agree that the number of performance indicators has grown excessively large and that a reduction might benefit transparency. However, we do not believe that a reduction will by itself lead to increased efficiency. Indeed, our view is that a cut-down as drastic as the one proposed can lead to *decreased* efficiency and *less* transparency. The reason is that the remaining indicators may become too few to provide meaningful information.

For example, the Kok proposal implies that human capital policy performance should be gauged by one single indicator, namely the educational attainment of 20–24 year olds. Clearly, if this is the only indicator measured, a high rating on it can be achieved at the expense of poor performance with respect to other important human capital dimensions. That would obviously not be in line with the idea of across-the-board improvements that underlies the Lisbon process.

Of course, trading off different objectives against another is possible also when several indicators are applied. The difference is that in the latter case the trade-off can be recorded. This information can contribute to increased transparency and it is also necessary if one wants to enable corrective measures.

---

[4]In the context of education and training policies, a further complication arises from the fact that several member states' decisions are partly formed at the sub-national level, making the follow-up of policy implementation a task not only for the central government but for regional and local bodies as well.

To limit the scope for trade-offs across policy objectives, the ministers of education in the EU member states decided in the year 2002 that in addition to agreeing on objectives in the sense of targets — aiming at maximum or "best-practice" performance — the member states should also agree to reach at least certain reference levels. The latter should ascertain minimum levels of performance ("floors"), thereby limiting the possibilities to trade-off different objectives against another.[5]

The next section contains a theoretical discussion of targets and reference levels. Our conclusion is that while reference levels increase transparency with respect to policy formulation, they *decrease* transparency with respect to implementation, by increasing the scope for manipulative behavior. The reason is that the OMC cannot punish violations of the reference levels, just like it cannot impose sanctions on countries failing to comply with the targets agreed upon. For this reason, the introduction of reference levels will in practice merely add to the possible trade-offs: in addition to trade-offs between different targets there will be possibilities for trade-offs between different reference levels and between targets and reference levels. In the empirical analysis we show that this is not just a theoretical point; it does matter in practice.

These discouraging findings give rise to the question whether it is possible, at all, to control the behavior of individual member states and to increase transparency, given that the objectives formulated under the OMC are not legally binding? One possibility, which we briefly consider in the next section, is to use the carrot instead of the stick.

In general, however, attempts to increase transparency should be based on two key observations. First, the interdependence between different objectives should be taken into account. Second, there is a need for a single, scalar measure of overall performance. Hitherto, benchmarking assessments have concerned individual objectives, one at a time. For a given country, rankings regarding different objectives may well point in opposite directions, leaving politicians, firms, investors and people in general without a clear message about where the country is heading.

We propose to account for the two key observations by the construction of overall performance indexes, i.e. weighted averages of the performance with respect to individual objectives. The problem, then, is to choose the appropriate weights. We consider this problem in Section 5.5.

---

[5]See COM (2002) 629 final. In that communication the term "benchmark" is used to denote what we call reference levels. The reason why we do not adopt the Commission's terminology is that the verb benchmarking often refers to comparisons of country performance also with respect to what we call target indicators, which might create confusion.

5.4 What to Aim For? The Relationship between Targets and Reference Levels

Figure 5.1 illustrates the formulation of objectives in the form of targets and reference levels. To simplify, we have assumed only two objectives. The solid curve indicates the maximum attainable combinations of the two objectives, when their respective shares vary between zero and one. The broken lines represent the reference levels, which may be interpreted as lower limits — "floors" — with respect to the performance on the two objectives.

For any given combination of the two objectives — for any ray through the origin — performance increases along the ray and is maximized when it hits the solid curve. If there are no special requirements regarding the proportions in which the two objectives are to be combined, all points along the curve are "optimal". In other words, no distinction is made between Point A (which gives priority to Target 1) and Point C (where the main emphasis is on Target 2).

The reference levels are satisfied at any point on or above the two broken constraint lines — the shaded area in the diagram. Point B satisfies the reference levels for both objective 1 and objective 2. Point A satisfies the reference level for objective 1, but not for objective 2. Like Point B, Point C satisfies both reference

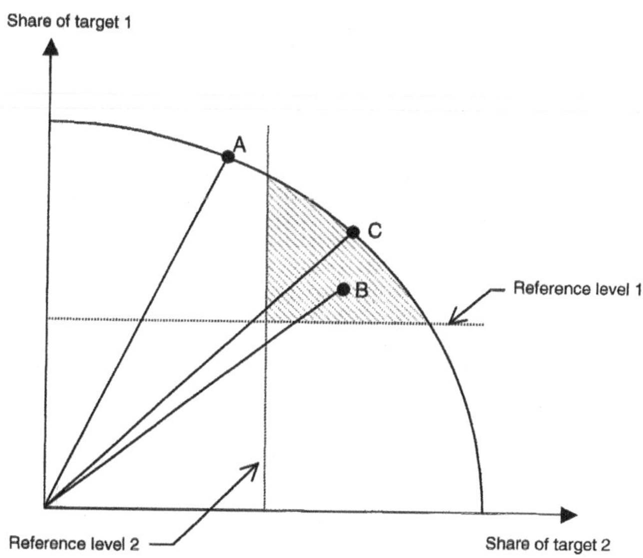

Figure 5.1: The relationship between targets and reference levels.

levels, but in contrast to B it simultaneously constitutes an optimal point with respect to target performance. Points with this characteristic are located on the portion of the solid line at the edge of the shaded area.

As noted in Section 5.3, the idea behind the introduction of reference levels is to ascertain a minimum level of performance. This increases transparency with respect to policy formulation; in addition to stating the ultimate policy goals, the politicians explicitly state what they consider to be lowest level of acceptable performance.

However, transparency in policy implementation is most likely to be reduced. The reason is that the reference levels are not enforceable, under the OMC. Accordingly, they will not act as constraints in the implementation of the policy. Instead, they will increase the scope for maneuvering on the part of the member states; states that find it difficult to achieve the targets can choose to focus on reference levels. And just as there is a trade-off between the performance with respect to different targets, there will be a trade-off between the extent to which different reference levels are satisfied.

As long as there is no way of telling how satisfaction of reference levels relates to performance in terms of target achievements, both have to be assessed. From Figure 5.1 it is clear that such parallel assessments can yield quite different results. With respect to target performance, Point A will be unambiguously preferred to Point B, while precisely the opposite conclusion will be reached if priority is given to compliance with reference levels.

In conclusion, the positive effect reference levels have on transparency with respect to policy formulation is more than outweighed by their negative effect on transparency with respect to implementation. Economic incentives to meet the policy objectives, as proposed by Collignon et al. (2005), might alleviate the problem. It should be recognized, however, that rewarding compliers is a second-best solution — sanctions on non-compliers being the first-best solution — and that any use of the scarce EU funds can only be motivated in the absence of better alternative uses.

5.5 How to Weight the Various Objectives? The Aggregation Problem

The issue of aggregation is of paramount importance for transparency with respect to policy formulation. Had the relative importance of the different objectives of the human capital policy been specified, it would have been a simple task to compute an index of overall performance.

Table 5.1: Illustration of how the choice of weights can affect cross-country comparisons of overall performance.

	Country A	**Country B**
Indicator values		
Indicator 1	0.9	0.5
Indicator 2	0.3	0.6
Indicator 3	0.6	0.7
Aggregation with weights		
1/3, 1/3, 1/3	0.60	0.60
0.1, 0.5, 0.4	0.48	0.63
0.4, 0.4, 0.2	0.60	0.58

In the absence of relative valuations it is hard to justify that a particular objective should receive a greater weight than some other objective. This leads to the conclusion that all objectives should be weighted equally.

But equal weights can also be discarded. If it is impossible to say what weight should be attached to a given objective, how can any weight between zero and one be preferred to any other weight in the same interval? Accordingly, a human capital policy which merely amounts to the specification of a multitude of objectives does not provide for transparency—without a rule for how the objectives should be aggregated any weighting system can be defended, implying that the policy as a whole is not well defined.[6]

These considerations also have negative implications for transparency with respect to implementation. Table 5.1 provides a simple example.

We assume that we want to compare the overall performance of two countries, A and B. For simplicity, we consider three objectives only. The performance indicators for these three objectives take on values between zero and one. On an objective-by-objective basis it is hard to distinguish between the two countries. While A performs really well with respect to objective 1 it also performs quite poorly with respect to objective 2. Country B, on the other hand, does not perform particularly well on any objective, but not particularly poor, either. In this situation it is natural to look for a measure of overall performance.

[6]It should be pointed out that this does not mean that a *given* (fixed) weighting scheme is a necessary requirement for transparency—a *rule* for aggregation might encompass different weighting systems. Indeed, the procedure that we discuss below specifies a way of *choosing* the weights, not the weights themselves.

If the three indicators are equally weighted, the result (average performance) says that A and B have performed equally well. However, if we instead use the weights 0.1, 0.5 and 0.4, we conclude that country B has performed better than country A. Finally, if weights 0.4, 0.4 and 0.2 are applied, country A will have the highest overall performance index. In other words: three different weighting systems and three different results.

As this simple example shows, the stability of country rankings can be tested by applying different sets of weights. Hoffman (2005) has recently proposed an appealing way to do so. His approach involves determining weights by means of random draws from a statistical distribution. A large number of draws and, hence, sets of weights, are generated. The stability of each country's ranking over these weighting schemes is then investigated. We will apply this procedure in Section 5.8 of this chapter.

5.6 The Objectives of the EU Educational Policy and Indicators for these Objectives

In this section, we describe the objectives of the EU educational policy. We first consider the targets and then the reference levels. Finally, as part of the discussion about transparency with respect to policy formulation, we consider the issue of consistency among the various objectives.

Based on three strategic goals, 13 targets have been specified.[7] For each of these we have specified a quantitative indicator. About half of our indicators (6 out of 13) are in line with the suggestions about indicators put forward by the Council of the European Union.[8] For those which are not, there is a comment motivating why we have deviated from the Council's suggestions.

In the listing below the 13 targets are denoted by two digits; the first digit indicates the strategic goal and the second digit denotes a specific target, within the framework of that strategic goal. Following the targets we describe the reference level (the "floors").

With respect to the indicators, we have used the latest available information. Still, some of our indicators refer to the very first years of the 21st century, due to lags in the publication of official statistics. Scores on the target indicators and the reference level measures are provided in Appendix 5.A.2. With respect to the target indicators information is provided also on scores for non-EU countries.

---

[7]Cf. the Council of the European Union document 5828/2, EDUC 17, from 2002.

[8]Cf., again, the Council of the European Union document 5828/2, EDUC 17. It should be noted that in 2005 no decision had been taken to put into use the indicators suggested by the Council.

5.6.1 Strategic Goals and Specific Targets

1 ***Improving the quality and effectiveness of education and training systems in the EU***

1.1 *Improving education and training for teachers and trainers*
Indicator: The proportion (%) of teachers participating in skills training programs other than information and communications technology (ICT) programs, in 2000/2001.

1.2 *Developing skills for the knowledge society*
Indicator: Average score on math test for 15 year olds in the Programme for International Student Assessment (PISA) in 2003 (Mean student score in the OECD countries normalized to 500).

1.3 *Ensuring universal access to ICT for everyone*
Indicator: The proportion (%) of upper secondary school pupils attending a school offering e-mail access for teachers and pupils in the year 2000.

1.4 *Increasing recruitment to scientific and technical studies*
Indicator: The change (%-age points) between 2000 and 2002 in the proportion of graduates in higher education programs with a duration of at least three years, who have studied science, technology or mathematics.

1.5 *Making the best use of resources*
Indicator: The proportion of students (%) participating in higher education programs with a duration of at least three years, who in the year 2000 received their degrees within the time stipulated.
Comment: The indicator proposed by the European Council is "increased investments per capita in human resources". In our view, this indicator measures the volume of resources utilized rather than how they are put to use. Our indicator measures whether resources are efficiently allocated in the sense that the education system produces graduates to the extent planned. So defined, the efficiency depends partly on how effectively the admissions system selects suitable students, and partly on how effective the actual education program is.

2 ***Facilitating the access of all to education and training systems***

2.1 *Open learning environment*
Indicator: The proportion (%) of the population aged 25–64 who participated in education and training during a specific four-week period during 2003.

2.2 *Making learning more attractive*
Indicator: Earnings of individuals with at least three years of university education, compared to earnings of those with upper secondary education, in the age range 25–64, in 2003, measured in percentage.

Comment: The European Council proposed to measure participation in education or the proportion of people with a low level of education. We believe, however, that these indicators measure consequences of the attractiveness of learning rather than the attractiveness of learning itself. Our indicator provides a rough idea of the financial incentives for education (at the university level) which we consider to be an important aspect of the attractiveness of learning.

2.3 *Supporting active citizenship, equal opportunities and social cohesion*
Indicator: Differences in literacy among 15-year-olds across schools according to the PISA study conducted in 2000. Measured as the total variation between schools, expressed as a percentage of the total variation within the country. (The lesser the variation, the better.)
Comment: The Council's recommendation is to measure the proportion of young people with a low level of education. In our view, the relation between this indicator and the objective stated is very weak. Our indicator emphasizes the "equal opportunities" aspect and measures whether literacy among 15-year-olds is dependent upon the particular school they attended.

3 *Opening up education and training systems to the wider world*

3.1 *Strengthening the links with working life, research and society at large*
Indicator: The number of years that a 15-year-old could expect to be unemployed or out of the labor force, excluding periods of studies, up to the age of 29, in 2001. (The lower the number of years, the better.)
Comment: We have not followed the Council's suggestion to measure the number of students participating in "sandwich" training schemes, since we believe that this indicator focuses too much on links with working life only. Our indicator measures the degree of "inactivity", and hence covers links with both working life and society as a whole.

3.2 *Developing the spirit of enterprise*
Indicator: The number of persons per 100 in the age range 18–64 who established businesses in 2002–2003.
Comment: We have been unable to follow the Council's proposals to measure the proportion of entrepreneurs in the knowledge-intensive sectors of the economy, or the proportion of educational establishments that provide guidance in the establishment of businesses. The reason is that the data required are not available. We have therefore been forced to use an indicator which we do not consider to be fully satisfactory—partly because it measures the consequences of an entrepreneurial spirit rather than attempts to develop such a spirit, and partly because it is sensitive to institutional differences between countries.

3.3 *Improving foreign language learning*
Indicator: The average number of foreign languages per pupil in upper secondary schools in 2003.

3.4 *Increasing mobility and exchange*
Indicator: The proportion of university students with foreign citizenship in 2002, relative to the 1998 proportion (%).
Comment: The Council proposed to measure either the proportion of the home country's students studying abroad, the proportion of foreign teachers in home-country education programs, or the proportion of foreign students in the home country. All these indicators reflect levels rather than changes, as envisaged in the objective. In addition, the first indicator probably is heavily dependent upon the economic status of the home country. We have therefore selected the final indicator, but expressed it in terms of a change, in line with formulation of the objective.

3.5 *Strengthening the European cooperation*
Indicator: The share (%) of eligible voters participating in elections for the European Parliament in 2004.
Comment: In our view, the proposal of the European Council to measure the proportion of students studying in other countries and/or receiving degrees which are common for several European countries reflects an unduly narrow view of the reinforcement of European cooperation. We have instead chosen an indicator expressing the general interest in European cooperation.

5.6.2 Reference Levels[9]

R1 *Early school leavers*

> "By 2010, Member States should at least halve the rate of early school leavers compared to the rate recorded in the year 2000, in order to achieve an EU-average rate of 10% or less." (COM, 2002, 629, final)

Measure: The proportion, in percent, of persons aged 18–24 in 2002 who fulfilled the following two conditions: (i) had an education not exceeding compulsory schooling; (ii) had not received any form of education or training during the four weeks prior to the interview, divided by 10. (The smaller, the better.)

[9]We have disregarded one of the reference levels proposed initially, namely investments in education and training. The reason is that compared to the other reference levels, this one is too general to be informative.

Comments: Unfortunately, data are not available on changes in the proportion of school leavers, relative to the year 2000. Therefore the proportion itself is used, normalized by the required EU average rate of 10 percent.

R2 *Graduates in science and technology*

> "By 2010, Member States should have increased the number of graduates in mathematics, science and technology by at least 15%, compared to the year 2000, and reduced the gender imbalance among the graduates." (COM, 2002, 629, final)

Measure: The percentage change in the number of graduates with at least three-year university education in mathematics, science and technology between 2000 and 2002, divided by 3. Moreover, a dummy indicator is used to show whether the female share of graduates has increased between the years 2000 and 2002.
Comments: The division by 3 is motivated on the ground that an increase by 15 percentage points over 10 years corresponds to an increase of 3 percentage points over a two-year period.[10]

R3 *Upper secondary education attainment*

> "By 2010, Member States should ensure that the EU average percentage of 25–64 years olds with at least upper secondary education reaches 85% or more." (COM, 2002, 629, final)

Measure: The proportion of 22-year-olds who have at least completed an upper secondary school education in 2002, relative to 85 percent.

R4 *Key competencies*

> "By 2010, the percentage of low-achieving 15 year olds in reading literacy should have decreased by at least 20% in the EU, compared to the year 2000." (COM, 2002, 629, final)

[10]In a follow-up report published jointly by the Council of the European Union and the European Commission in 2004, in the *Official Journal of the European Communities* (2004), a measure of the proportion of students in higher education studying mathematics, science and technology is employed. This measure is not used here since it neither provides information about the number of graduates nor about the change in this number.

Measure: Inadequate literacy is defined as having not higher than level 1 in the PISA study. Data are for the years 2000 and 2003. The change in the share of low achieving between 2003 and 2000, relative to the share in 2000, has been divided by 3 × ((1/5)/10), where 1/5th is the required 20 percent change over the whole period 2000–2010, the corresponding average yearly change is ((1/5)/10) and the multiplication by 3 is to account for the fact that the data cover a three-year period.[11] (The more negative, the better.)

R5 *Lifelong learning—adult participation in education and training*

> "By 2010, the EU-average level of participation in lifelong learning should be at least 15% of the adult working age population (25–64 year olds) and in no country should it be lower than 10%." (COM, 2002, 629, final)

Measure: The proportion of interviewees in the Eurostat labor-force surveys who participated in education or training at some time during the four weeks that preceded the labor-force survey in 2003, divided by 10 percent.

5.6.3 Consistency among Targets and Reference Levels

An examination of the targets and reference levels does not reveal any obvious inconsistencies. However, not surprisingly, a tension can be noted between efforts made to ascertain widespread general competencies (for example, Target 2.3 and Reference Levels 1, 3 and 4), on the one hand, and to promote specialized knowledge (cf. Target 1.4 and Reference Level 2), on the other.

It can also be noted that as there are only five reference levels there is not a one-to-one correspondence between targets and reference levels, in contrast to the stylized picture in Figure 5.1. Only for two of the targets are there directly corresponding reference levels—Reference Level 2 corresponds directly to Target 1.4, and Reference Level 5 corresponds directly to Target 2.1. With respect to the other targets, the links to the reference levels are weaker, or non-existent. However, this does not change the relation between the targets and the reference levels from a conceptual point of view. And it does not, by itself, imply an inconsistency.

In general, the risk of inconsistencies will increase with the number of objectives specified. Given that the present number is quite high, attempts to cut down on objectives should be welcomed while addition of new ones should have to be very carefully motivated.

---

[11]In the follow-up report published in 2004, cf. note 10, a measure based on the share of low-achieving 15-year-olds in the year 2000 was used.

5.7 Monitoring Targets and Reference Levels in Practice

In this section, we make an empirical assessment of how the parallel occurrence of objectives in the form of targets and reference levels affect transparency with respect to policy implementation.

As the targets are designed to make the European education and training systems world leading, performance must be measured relative to the best country in the world. In practice, this will mean that we compare with the best country for which we have data for the indicator in question. For the sake of simplicity, we have also normalized the values of the indicators to ensure that they always lie between zero and one. For most indicators, this means that, the normalized value is the country's actual value divided by the score for the best country. However, with respect to the Targets 2.3 and 3.1, for which "less is better", the original numbers have been inverted before the normalization. Finally, the indicator for Target 1.4 assumes negative values for some countries. To ascertain indicator values in the [0,1] interval, a positive number has first been added to all of the original values, ensuring that the country with the lowest score gets a new value just above zero. The new values are then normalized. This procedure maintains the relative positions among the countries.

Diagrams showing the rankings of the EU member states with respect to each of the 13 targets are provided in Appendix 5.A.2 and information is also given about non-EU countries that have indicator values, which are at least as high as the indicator value of the last-ranking of the EU member states. Moreover, instructions are provided for retrieving the original, non-normalized indicator values.

Which countries are world leaders with respect to the 13 targets? In other words, what countries have normalized indicators equal to one? As indicated in Table 5.2, only two countries are world leaders with respect to more than one target. Of these one belongs to the EU, namely Sweden, while the other, Iceland, does not. The table also indicates that countries outside the EU are recorded for maximum target performance for 6 of the 13 targets.

One curiosity is the appearance of Uganda in Table 5.2. Uganda is the best performing country with respect to the target "developing an entrepreneurial spirit", measured by the percentage of persons in the age range 18–64 who started business operations in 2002–2003. Here we have an (extreme) example of a problem which occurs in connection with some indicators, namely dependence on institutional factors. The fact that there is a high degree of entrepreneurship in Uganda may simply be attributed to an economy and a labor market, which are so undeveloped that, for many people, setting up a business is the only way to obtain employment.

In Figure 5.2, we have condensed the indicators for the 13 targets into a single aggregate indicator, namely the simple (unweighted) average of the scores for the country's target indicators. Only countries which have scores for at least half of the

Table 5.2: "Best-practice" countries with respect to the 13 targets, i.e. countries whose normalized target indicators are equal to one.

Country	**Number of normalized target indicators = 1**	**Targets**
Iceland	2	2.3, 3.1
Sweden	2	1.1, 2.1
Belgium	1	3.5
Denmark	1	1.3
Hong Kong	1	1.2
Hungary	1	2.2
Japan	1	1.5
Netherlands	1	3.3
New Zealand	1	3.4
Slovak Republic	1	1.4
Uganda	1	3.2

Note: Countries with the same number of target indicators equal to one have been placed in alphabetical order.

targets have been included in the diagram. This is to prevent the outcomes on individual indicators to unduly affect the value of the aggregate (average) indicator.

Obviously, the average score will be less sensitive to the scores for specific indicators the larger the number of indicators for which there are values. The fact that the three Nordic countries, Sweden, Finland and Denmark, which have the highest scores in Figure 5.2, have values for at least 11 target indicators suggests that the results for these countries are relatively stable, at least when all indicators are weighted equally.

Another reason why aggregated indicators encompassing many indicators should be regarded as more reliable is that countries with values for only a few indicators may have (partially) confined themselves to reporting indicators on which they perform well. There is no way of determining whether this is in fact the case, but the possibility cannot be excluded.

The rankings are very even for most of the countries in Figure 5.2. There is only a difference of 0.05 points, for example, between the UK in seventh place and Italy in place thirteen. This suggests that the choice of weights may be important. We return to this issue in the next section.

We now consider country performance in terms of reference levels. Like the target indicators, the reference level measures have been normalized. However, unlike

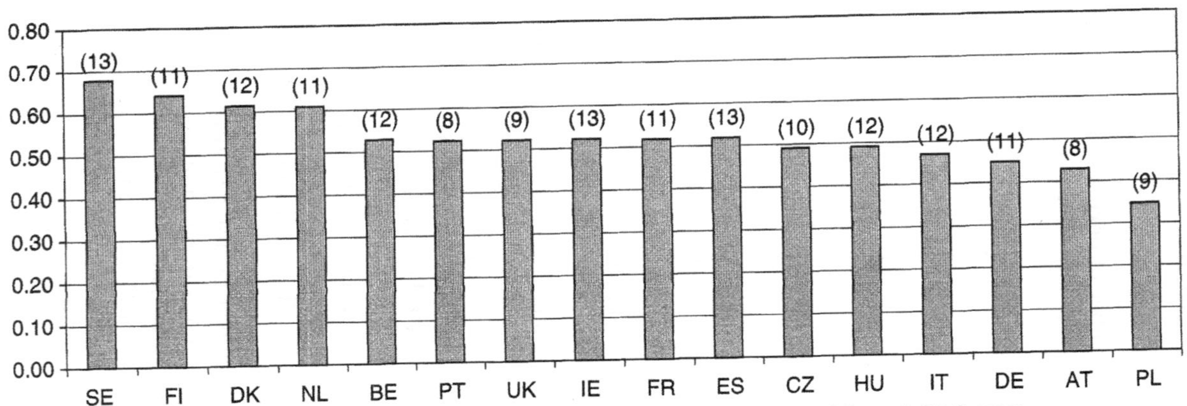

Note 1: Country codes (see Appendix 5.A.1): AT=Austria, BE=Belgium, CY=Cyprus, CZ=Czech Republic, DK=Denmark, DE=Germany, EE=Estonia, ES=Spain, FI=Finland, FR=France, GR=Greece, HU=Hungary, IE=Ireland, IT=Italy, LT=Lithuania, LU=Luxembourg, LV=Latvia, MT=Malta, NL=Netherlands, PL=Poland, PT=Portugal, SE=Sweden, SI=Slovenia, SK=Slovak Republic, UK=United Kingdom.

Note 2: Only countries with data on at least 7 of the 13 target indicators are included in the figure.

Figure 5.2: Overall performance using equal weights, i.e. the arithmetic average (average of the scores on the target indicators).

the normalized target indicators, the normalized reference level measures are not confined to the interval [0,1]. Instead, the reference level measures are only normalized such that they equal 1 if they exactly fulfill the reference level requirement. Diagrams showing the rankings of the EU member states on the five reference level measures are provided in Appendix 5.A.2. In connection to the diagrams, instructions are provided on how to retrieve the non-normalized measures.

In Figure 5.3, we have ranked the EU member states with respect to their performance in terms of the number of reference level requirements satisfied. As discussed in connection with Figure 5.1, the most important consideration is whether the country is operating above the "floor" indicated by the reference level. The distance to the floor is of secondary interest. Figure 5.3 takes these considerations into account. Countries have been primarily ranked in accordance with the number of reference level requirements satisfied. Secondly, countries satisfying an equal number of reference level requirements have been ranked in accordance with the (unweighted) average of the reference level measures.

Similar to Figure 5.2, only countries which have values for at least half the reference level requirements (three or more) have been included. This criterion is met by all 25 EU countries, with the exception of Malta. There is no bar for six of the countries in Figure 5.3; however, these six countries failed to live up to any of the five reference level requirements.

It may be noted that no country had managed to comply with all five of the reference level requirements at the beginning of the 21st century; Finland was the only country to meet four of the requirements.

In some respects, the rankings in Figure 5.3 agree well with the rankings in Figure 5.2. For example, the two Nordic countries Finland and Sweden have high rankings, just as in Figure 5.2. Likewise, Germany and Italy are a long way down the scale in both Figures. For these four countries, it makes no difference whether performance is measured in terms of targets or in terms of reference levels.

But there are also striking differences between Figures 5.2 and 5.3. The Slovak Republic and Slovenia, which do not appear in Figure 5.2 at all, rank 3 and 4, respectively, in Figure 5.3. Further, in Figure 5.2 Austria and Poland were ranked 15 and 16, respectively, whereas they ranked 9 and 2, respectively, in Figure 5.3. These countries thus illustrate the point made in Section 5.4 that states which perform badly with respect to the targets are likely to try to show progress by instead concentrating on satisfying the reference levels.

Somewhat surprisingly, there are also a few countries that receive a considerably lower ranking in Figure 5.3 than in Figure 5.2. Two examples are the Netherlands and Belgium. This is possible only because there is no one-to-one correspondence between targets and reference levels; the Netherlands and Belgium have scored relatively well on the targets which do not have a directly corresponding reference level.

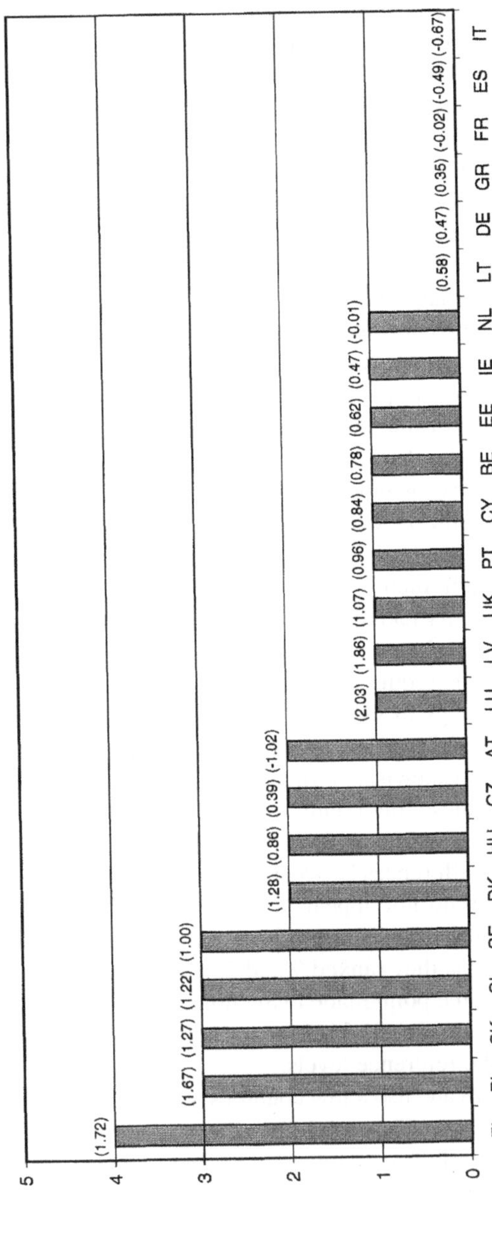

Note 1: For country codes, cf. Note 1 in Figure 2.
Note 2: Countries with data on at least 3 of the 5 reference level requirements are included in the diagram. This condition is met by all EU countries but Malta.
Note 3: Countries for which there are no bars have not satisfied any of the reference level requirements.
Note 4: Countries that have satisfied equally many reference level requirements are ranked in terms of their average values on the reference level measures.

Figure 5.3: Performance in terms of number of satisfied reference levels (in parenthesis: average values on the reference level measures).

To summarize, for several member states, the addition of objectives in terms of reference levels ("floors") to the original target objectives has led to decreased transparency with respect to policy implementation. Prominent examples are Poland, Austria, the Slovak Republic, Slovenia, the Netherlands and Belgium, which score very differently depending upon whether average performance is expressed in terms of targets or reference levels. Roughly speaking, about a third of the 25 member states exhibit low transparency with respect to the aspect on policy implementation considered here.

5.8 Sensitivity of Country Rankings to the Choice of Weights for Individual Target Indicators

With respect to overall performance, transparency in terms of policy implementation depends upon how sensitive aggregate performance measures are to the choice of weights for individual target indicators. Transparency is high if sensitivity is low, and vice versa. To be able to categorize the member states accordingly, we examine how the ranking of overall country performance is affected when we depart from the equal weighting used in Figure 5.2. To focus on the *variation* in the aggregated indicators resulting from different choices of weights, we select the weights such that in expectation they coincide with the equal weights employed in Figure 5.2.

The procedure used is one of repeated sampling. For a given sample, the weights are determined by draws from a uniform distribution, defined on the [0,1] interval. The number of draws is equal to the number of performance indicators. To qualify as weights, the values drawn are normalized by the sum of all the values obtained. The number of repetitions is 10,000. The resulting sets of weights are used to conduct 10,000 country rankings. For a detailed description of the procedure see Hoffmann (2005).

In the process, we have to take into account that the countries differ with respect to number of performance indicators for which there are scores. In the case of Portugal, for example, which has scores for eight target indicators (cf. Figure 5.2), we make use only of the first eight of the 13 randomly selected values.

For each country, we calculate the probability that it will receive a ranking of 1, 2, 3, . . ., 16.[12] Listing all these probabilities would drown the reader in numbers, however. Instead, we merely provide the probabilities of achieving a ranking of 1–4, 5–12 and 13–16, respectively (see Figure 5.4). Obviously, these probabilities must sum to 100 percent. Accordingly, each country has a bar on the chart ranging

[12]The countries analyzed are the same as the ones in Figure 5.2.

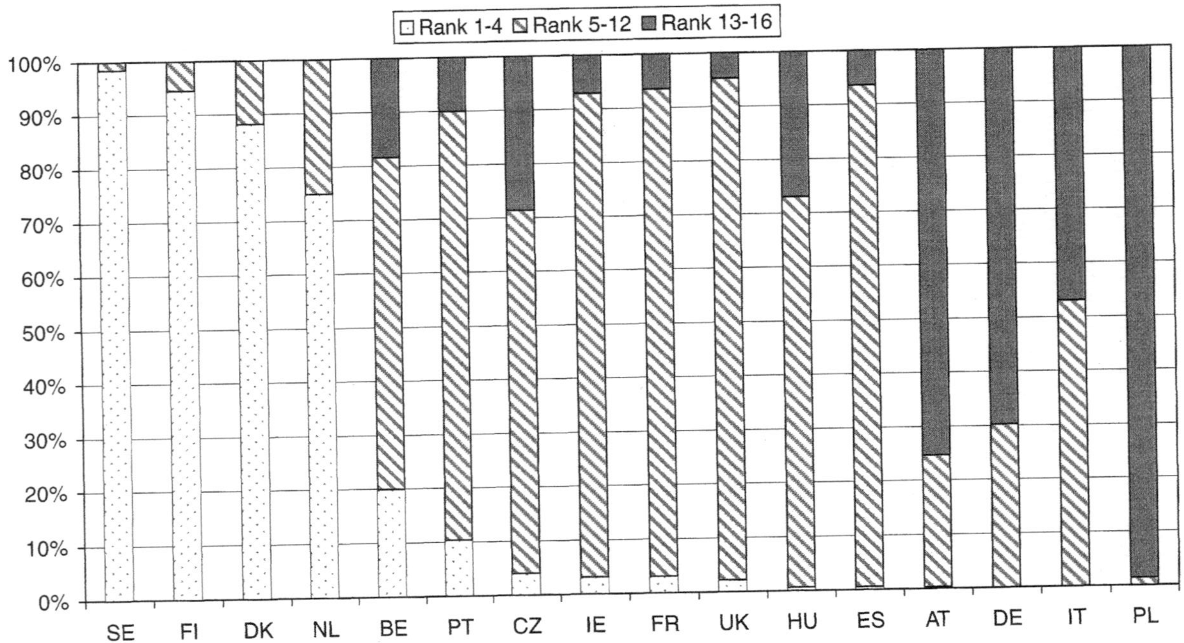

Note 1: For country codes, cf. Note 1 in Figure 2.
Note 2: The countries are ordered according to their probabilities of receiving a 1–4 ranking.

Figure 5.4: Probabilities of different ranking order categories with respect to overall performances when target indicators are aggregated using random weights.

from 0 to 100 percent. The countries differ, however, with respect to how the bars are partitioned into areas corresponding to the three categories of rankings.

In the figure, the countries are ordered according to their probabilities of receiving a 1–4 ranking. Sweden has a 98.4 percent probability of winding up in this category. The next country is Finland, for which the corresponding probability equals 94.5 percent. Poland and Italy have the lowest probability (0) of being placed in the 1–4 ranking category.

The ranking of a country will be sensitive to the choice of weights—implying low transparency with respect to policy implementation—if the country performs unevenly, i.e. scores very high on some targets and does quite poorly on others. Such a pattern is consistent with a trading-off behavior, where large efforts in some fields are made at the expense of low activity in other areas. Clear examples in Figure 5.4 are Belgium, Portugal and the Czech Republic.

We now turn to countries whose rankings are stable. If we define the ranking to be insensitive to the choice of weights—implying high transparency with respect to policy implementation—when the probability is at least 90 percent that its ranking will fall in one of the three categories in Figure 5.4, we find high transparency in six countries. Sweden (SE) and Finland (FI) both have probabilities exceeding 90 percent of being placed in the 1–4 category, while for the UK, Spain (ES) and France (FR) the probabilities are over 90 percent of belonging to the 5–12 category. Finally, the probability of a ranking in the 13–16 category is more than 90 percent for Poland (PL).

While the 90 percent definition seems rather natural it is, of course, arbitrary. And the cut-off value chosen does matter for the result. For instance, using instead 85 percent as the cut-off value we get two additional countries with high transparency with respect to policy implementation, Denmark and Ireland. And if the cut-off is set to 95 percent only Sweden and Poland will be characterized as highly transparent.

However, given that the appropriate cut-off lies somewhere between 85 and 95 percent we may conclude that regarding overall performance only 2–8 of the 25 member states can be characterized as being highly transparent with respect to policy implementation. Consequently, in a large majority of the member states, between 17 and 23 countries, transparency is low regarding overall performance.

5.9 Conclusions

Obviously, human capital policy transparency at the member state level is not independent of transparency at the EU level. Presumably, a completely transparent EU human capital policy is not feasible. Within the context of the Open

Method of Coordination (OMC) it may not even be desirable; as noted in Section 5.3 the OMC intends to provide guidelines rather than elaborated action plans. Under these circumstances it is not surprising that for only one third of the 25 member states transparency is high with respect to overall performance. What this means is that when countries are ranked according to a weighted average of their performances on the 13 different policy targets, the rankings of one third of the countries will not be much affected by the choice of weights. For instance, Sweden and Finland will almost always be ranked among the top four countries irrespective of how the weighted average is constructed and Poland will consistently belong to the bottom four. In contrast, for two third of the member states rankings will be very sensitive to the weights chosen. This sensitivity is due to uneven performance across targets—when large (small) weights are attached to the country's high-score targets and small (large) weights assigned to its low-score targets the country will be ranked highly (lowly).

This lack of transparency makes it important that sensitivity analyses are conducted on a regular basis. The method we have proposed for this purpose is easy to apply. Preferably, the computations could be carried out annually, by the Commission. In line with the suggestion put forward by Kok (2004), a high-level government official should be responsible for commenting on the results and, if need be, initiate corrective actions. Both the Commission's assessment and the member state's response to it should be made public and subject to debate, so as to involve pressure groups outside government. In particular, information should be duly disseminated to firms and investors. Reduced uncertainty about the political intentions can thereby have a moderating effect on the political risk premium and, hence, capital costs.

We have examined one strategy that has been tried to increase transparency, namely to complement the original target objectives with objectives in the form of lower bounds on performance, reference levels. This strategy has not had the desired effect. The reference levels have led to *less* transparency with respect to policy implementation, because of the impossibility to impose sanctions on non-compliers that is an inherent property of the OMC. Several of the countries that have had difficulties to achieve the targets have instead been content with trying to show progress by satisfying some of the reference levels. That is to say, reference levels have been substituted for targets.

We conclude that unless a way can be found by means of which a high rate of compliance can be achieved, the reference levels might as well be abandoned. The idea of Collignon et al. (2005) to use positive economic incentives rather than sanctions might be worthwhile trying. However, such an attempt should be preceded by a careful investigation of whether the required EU funds could not be better spent for other purposes.

Most important of all, however, is that actions be taken as soon as possible. If the Lisbon vision is to become more than just a vision it is imperative that the rate of change during the second half of the process be much higher than during the first half. This will be possible only by providing political conditions that are stable and transparent enough to spur the increased investments in human capital and physical capital that will ascertain a high rate of European economic growth.

References

Aghion, P., & Howitt, P. (1998). *Endogenous growth theory*. Cambridge: MIT Press.

Berman, E. J., Bound, J., & Griliches, Z. (1994). Changes in demand for skilled labor within US manufacturing: Evidence from the annual survey of manufactures. *Quarterly Journal of Economics, 109*, 367–397.

Borrás, S., & Jacobsson, K. (2004). The open method of coordination and the new governance patterns in the EU. *Journal of European Public Policy, 11*, 185–208.

Caroli, E., & Van Reenen, J. (2001). Skill-biased organizational change? Evidence from a panel of British and French establishments. *Quarterly Journal of Economics, 116*, 1449–1492.

Collignon, S., Dehousse, R., Gabolde, J., Jouen, M., Pochet, P., Salais, R., Sprenger, R. -U., & de Sousa, H. Z. (2005). *The Lisbon strategy and the open method of coordination*. Policy Paper no. 12, Notre Europe Etude & Recherches. http://www.notre-europe.asso.fr/IMG/pdf/Policypaper12.pdf.

COM. (2002). 629, final. *Communication from the commission: European benchmarks in education and training: Follow-up to the Lisbon European Council*. http://europa.eu.int/eur-lex/en/com/cnc/2002/com2002_0629en01.pdf.

Council of the European Union. (2002). *Document 5828/2, EDUC 17: Detailed programme on the follow-up of the objectives of education and training systems in Europe*. http://register.consilium.eu.int/pdf/en/02/st05/05828en2.pdf.

De La Porte, C., & Pochet, P. (Eds). (2002). *Building social Europe through the open method of coordination*. Brussels: PIE Peter Lang.

Eurostat Labour Force Surveys.

Griliches, Z. (1969). Capital-skill complementarity. *Review of Economics and Statistics, 51*(4), 465–468.

Hoffmann, A. (2005). *Micro-policies for growth and productivity—synthesis and benchmarking user guide*. OECD, Directorate for Science, Technology and Industry. http://www.oecd.org/document/2/0,2340,en_2649_34555_34941890_1_1_1_1,00.html.

Kok, W. (2004). *Facing the challenge—The Lisbon strategy for growth and employment*. Report from the High Level Group. Luxembourg: The Office for Official Publications of the European Communities.

Krueger, A., & Lindahl, M. (2001). Education for growth: Why and for whom? *Journal of Economic Literature, 39*, 1101–1136.

Lucas, R. (1988). On the mechanisms of development planning. *Journal of Monetary Economics*, *22*, 3–42.

Nelson, R. R., & Phelps, E. S. (1966). Investment in humans, technological diffusion, and economic growth. *American Economic Review*, *56*, 69–75.

Official Journal of the European Union. (2004). Note 2004/C 104/01. *Education & Training 2010: The success of the Lisbon strategy hinges upon urgent reforms*. Joint interim report of the Council of the European Union and the European Commission on the implementation of the detailed work programme on the follow-up of the objectives of education and training systems in Europe. http://europa.eu.int/eur-lex/pri/en/oj/dat/2004/c_104/c_10420040430en00010019.pdf

Romer, P. (1990). Endogenous technical change. *Journal of Political Economy*, *98*, 71–102.

Sisson, K., Arrowsmith, J., & Marginson, P. (2003). All benchmarkers now? Benchmarking and the 'Europeanisation' of industrial relations. *Industrial Relations Journal*, *34*, 15–31.

Zeitlin, J., Philippe, P., & Magnusson, L. (2005). *The open method of coordination in action: The European employment and social inclusion strategies*. Brussels: PIE Peter Lang.

Appendix 5.A.1

In the diagrams, the countries are denoted by country codes. The ISO 3166 Country codes (www.theodora.com/country_digraphs.html) are listed here for all countries that show up in at least one diagram in the text or in Appendix 5.A.2; 52 countries altogether. The left column contains the country codes, in alphabetical order, while the right column is ordered by country names. The EU member states are written in boldface.

By country codes		By country names	
AR	Argentina	Argentina	AR
AT	**Austria**	Australia	AU
AU	Australia	**Austria**	**AT**
BE	**Belgium**	**Belgium**	**BE**
BG	Bulgaria	Brazil	BR
BR	Brazil	Bulgaria	BG
CA	Canada	Canada	CA
CH	Switzerland	Chile	CL
CL	Chile	China	CN
CN	China	Croatia	HR

(Continued)

Appendix 5.A.1: (*Continued*).

By country codes		By country names	
CY	**Cyprus**	**Cyprus**	**CY**
CZ	**Czech Republic**	**Czech Republic**	**CZ**
DE	**Germany**	**Denmark**	**DK**
DK	**Denmark**	**Estonia**	**FR**
EE	**Estonia**	**Finland**	**FI**
ES	**Spain**	**France**	**FR**
FI	**Finland**	**Germany**	**DE**
FR	**France**	**Greece**	GR
GR	**Greece**	Hong Kong	HK
HK	Hong Kong	**Hungary**	**HU**
HR	Croatia (Hrvatska)	Iceland	IS
HU	**Hungary**	India	IN
IE	**Ireland**	**Ireland**	**IE**
IL	Israel	Israel	IL
IN	India	**Italy**	**IT**
IS	Iceland	Japan	JP
IT	**Italy**	Korea	KR
JP	Japan	**Latvia**	**LV**
KR	Korea	Lichtenstein	LI
LI	Lichtenstein	**Lithuania**	**LT**
LT	**Lithuania**	**Luxembourg**	**LU**
LU	**Luxembourg**	**Malta**	**MT**
LV	**Latvia**	Mexico	MX
MT	**Malta**	**Netherlands**	**NL**
MX	Mexico	New Zealand	NZ
NL	**Netherlands**	Norway	NO
NO	Norway	**Poland**	**PL**
NZ	New Zealand	**Portugal**	**PT**
PL	**Poland**	Russia	RU
PT	**Portugal**	**Slovakia**	**SK**
RU	Russia	**Slovenia**	**SI**
SE	**Sweden**	South Africa	ZA
SI	**Slovenia**	**Spain**	**ES**
SK	**Slovakia**	**Sweden**	**SE**
TH	Thailand	Switzerland	CH
TR	Turkey	Taiwan	TW
TW	Taiwan	Thailand	TH
UG	Uganda	Turkey	TR
UK	**United Kingdom**	Uganda	UG

(*Continued*)

Appendix 5.A.1: (*Continued*).

By country codes		**By country names**	
US	USA	**United Kingdom**	**UK**
VE	Venezuela	USA	US
ZA	South Africa	Venezuela	VE

Appendix 5.A.2

The first part of this appendix contains figures showing country performance on each one of the 13 Targets 1.1–3.5. The scores of EU countries for which there are data are ordered according to magnitude. The EU countries for which no data are available are listed in the diagrams without bars. These countries are ordered alphabetically, in terms of country codes. While only scores of EU-countries are provided in the diagrams, below the diagrams scores are listed for non-EU countries that have scored at least as high as the EU-country with the lowest (positive) score.

The second part of the appendix shows the performance of the EU-countries on each one of the five reference level objectives. Unlike the target indicators, the reference level measures are not normalized to lie between 0 and 1. Instead, they are normalized such that values of 1 or above means that the reference level criterion is satisfied. EU countries for which there are no data are listed in the diagram without bars, ordered alphabetically by country codes.

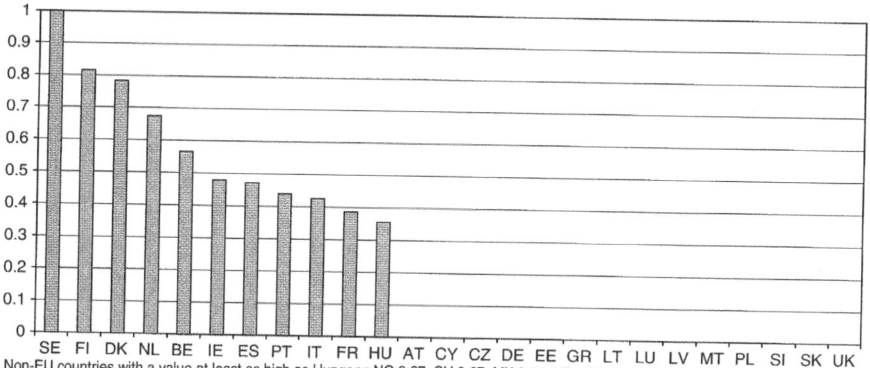

Non-EU countries with a value at least as high as Hungary: NO 0.67, CH 0.67, MX 0.54, KR 0.39. For country codes, see Appendix 5.A.1.
To obtain non-normalized indicators: multiply by 84.3.
Number of countries with available data: 15.

Source: *OECD Education at a glance 2003, table D4.3.*

Target 1.1: Improving education and training for teachers and trainers.

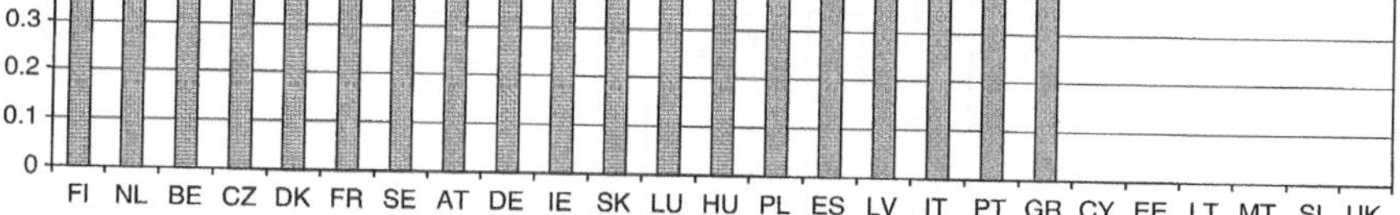

Non-EU countries with a value at least as high as Greece: HK 1, KR 0.99, LI 0.97, JP 0.97, CA 0.97, CH 0.96, CN 0.96, AU 0.95 NZ 0.95 IS 0.94, NO 0.90, US 0.88, RU 0.85. For country codes, see Appendix 5.A.1.
To obtain non-normalized indicators: multiply by 550.

Source: OECD "Learning for tomorrow's world, first results from PISA 2003", table 2.5 C.

Target 1.2: Developing skills for the knowledge society.

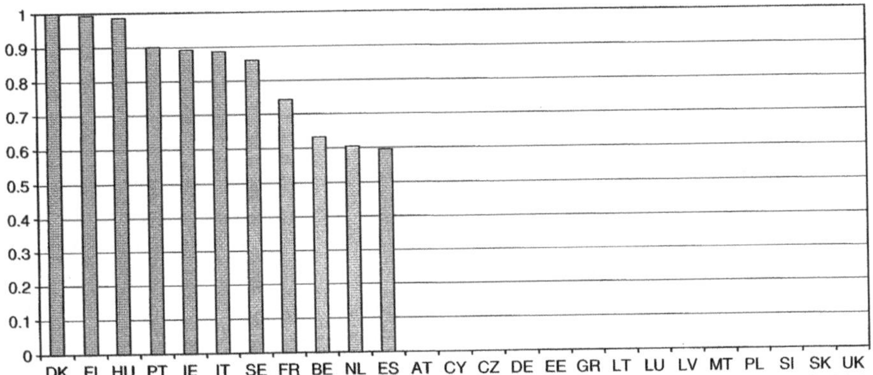

Non-EU countries with a value at least as high as Spain: KR 0.93, NO 0.91, CH 0.90. For country codes, see Appendix 5.A.1.
To obtain non-normalized indicators: multiply by 98.6.
Number of countries with available data: 15.

Source: OECD Education at a glance 2003, table D 3.1.

Target 1.3: Ensuring universal access to ICT for everyone.

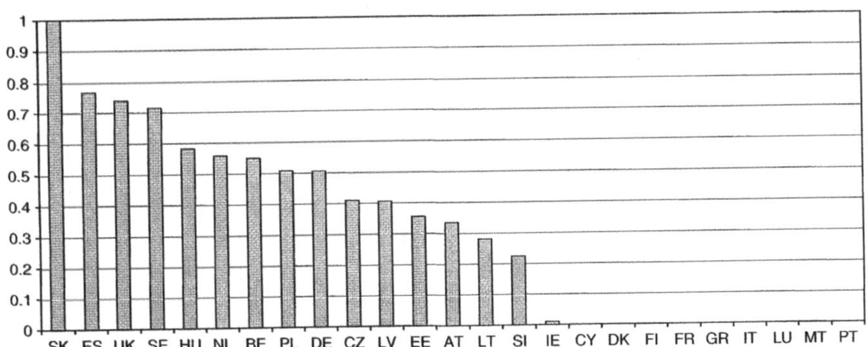

Non-EU countries with a value at least as high as Ireland: IS 0.70, JP 0.58, US 0.57, NO 0.46, TR 0.36. For country codes, see Appendix 5.A.1.
To obtain non-normalized indicators: multiply by 9.9 and subtract 5.4.
Number of countries with available data: 21.

Source: Eurostat database, www.europa.eu.int.

Target 1.4: Increasing recruitment to scientific and technical studies.

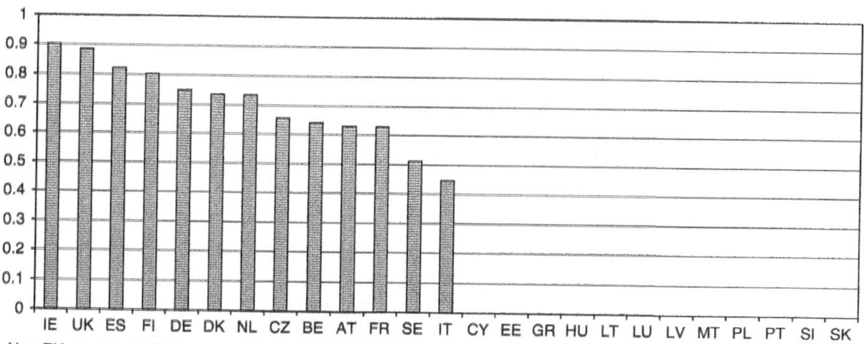

Non-EU countries with a value at least as high as Italy: JP 1, TR 0.94, KR 0.84, IS 0.78, IL 0.74, MX 0.74, AU 0.74, US 0.70. For country codes, see Appendix 5.A.1.
To obtain non-normalized indicators: multiply by 93.8.
Number of countries with available data: 21.

Source: OECD Education at a glance 2004, table A 3.2.

Target 1.5: Making the best use of resources.

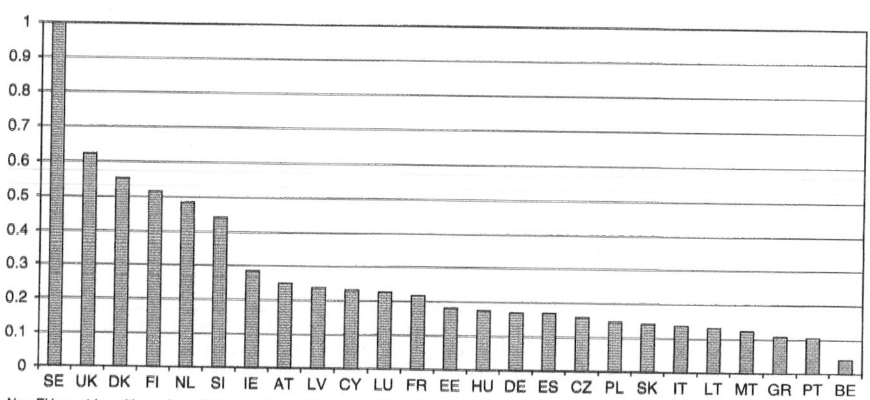

Non-EU countries with a value at least as high as Belgium: CH 0.73, IS 0.70, NO 0.62, AU 0.22, BG 0.04. For country codes, see Appendix 5.A.1.
To obtain non-normalized indicators: multiply by 34.2.
Number of countries with available data: 31.

Source: Eurostat Labour Force Survey, www.europa.eu.int.

Target 2.1: Open learning environment.

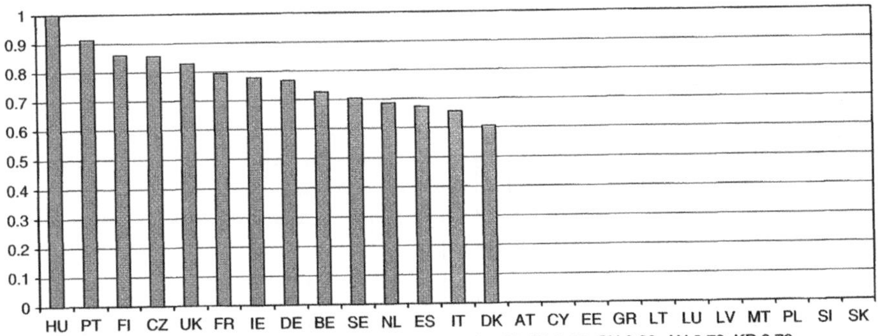

Non-EU countries with a value at least as high as Denmark: US 0.93, CA 0.84, CH 0.80, AU 0.70, KR 0.70, NO 0.64, NZ 0.63. For country codes, see Appendix 5.A.1.

To obtain non-normalized indicators: multiply by 210.1.

Number of countries with available data: 21.

Source: OECD Education at a glance 2004, table A11.1a.

Target 2.2: Making learning more attractive.

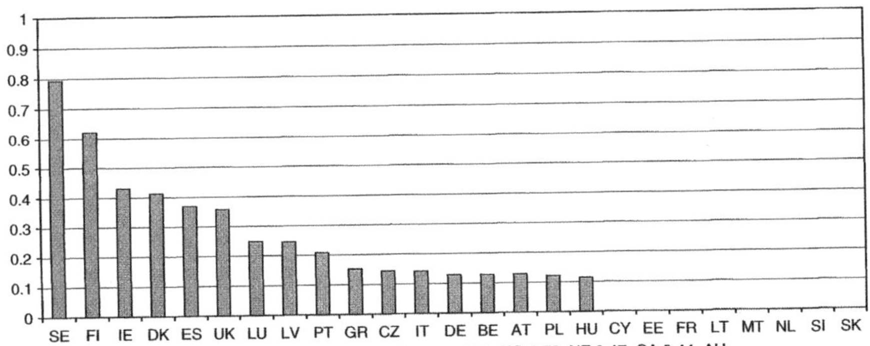

Non-EU countries with a value at least as high as Hungary: IS 1, NO 0.70, NZ 0.47, CA 0.44, AU 0.41, US 0.26, RU 0.21, KR 0.20, BR 0.18, CH 0.18, LI 0.17, JP 0.17, MX 0.14. For country codes, see Appendix 5.A.1.

To obtain non-normalized indicators: take the inverse and multiply by 7.7

Source: OECD Education at a glance 2003, table A7.1.

Target 2.3: Supporting active citizenship, equal opportunities and social cohesion.

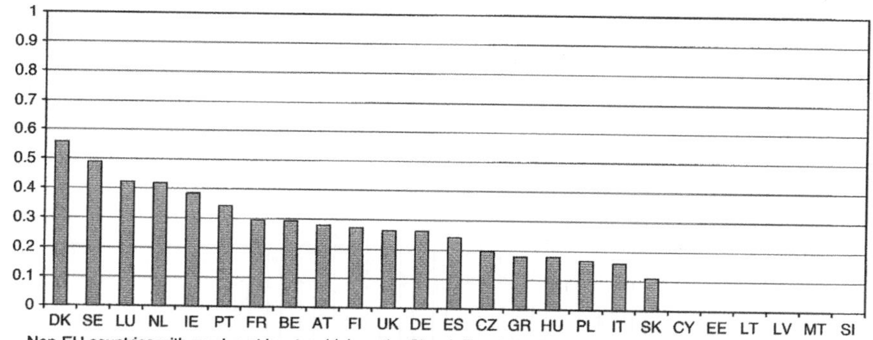

Non-EU countries with a value at least as high as the Slovak Republic: IS 1, JP 0.61, NO 0.46, CH 0.39, CA 0.29, AU 0.27, US 0.26, MX 0.14. For country codes, see Appendix 5.A.1.
To obtain non-normalized indicators: take the inverse and multiply by 0.52.
Number of countries with available data: 28.

Source: OECD Education at a glance 2003, table A13.1.

Target 3.1: Strengthening the links with working life, research and society at large.

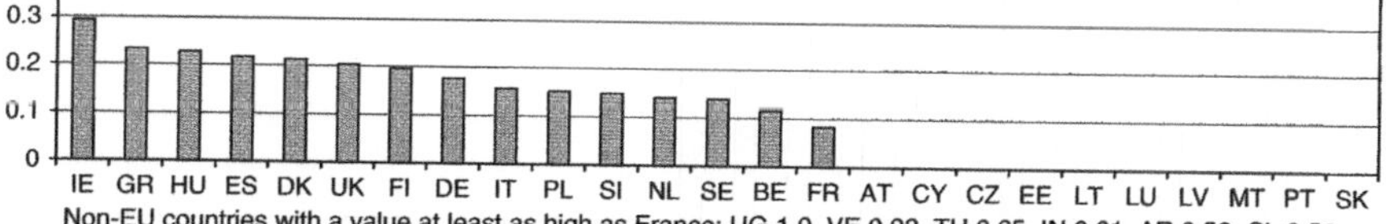

Non-EU countries with a value at least as high as France: UG 1.0, VE 0.93, TH 0.65, IN 0.61, AR 0.58, CL 0.56, KR 0.50, NZ 0.47, BR 0.45, MX 0.42, CN 0.41, US 0.39, IS 0.39, AU 0.34, CA 0.29, NO 0.28, CH 0.25, IL 0.24, ZA 0.19, TW 0.15, HK 0.11, HR 0.11, RU 0.09. For country codes, see Appendix 5.A.1.
To obtain non-normalized indicators: multiply by 29.3.
Number of countries with available data: 39.

Source: Global Entrepeneurship Monitor 2003.

Target 3.2: Developing the spirit of enterprise.

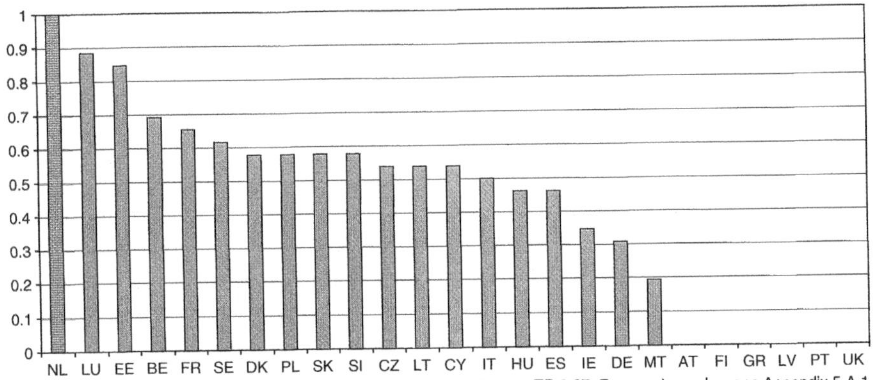

Non-EU countries with a value at least as high as Malta: IS 0.54, HR 0.54, TR 0.27. For country codes, see Appendix 5.A.1.
To obtain non-normalized indicators: multiply by 2.6.
Number of countries with available data: 22.

Source: Eurostat database, www.europa.eu.int.

Target 3.3: Improving foreign language learning.

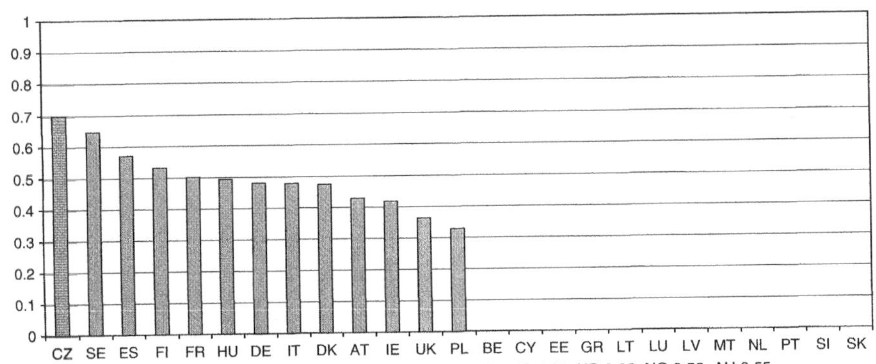

Non-EU countries with a value at least as high as Poland: NZ 1, IS 0.66, KR 0.62, NO 0.59, AU 0.55, JP 0.52, US 0.44, CH 0.42. For country codes, see Appendix 5.A.1.
To obtain non-normalized indicators: multiply by 258.5.
Number of countries with available data: 22.

Source: OECD Education at a glance 2004, table C 3.1.

Target 3.4: Increasing mobility and exchange.

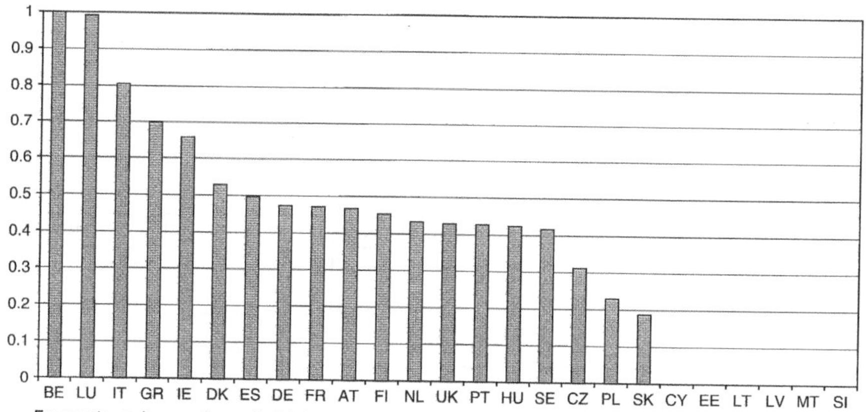

For country codes, see Appendix 5.A.1.
To obtain non-normalized indicators: multiply by 90.8.
Number of countries with available data: 19.
Source: www.elections2004.eu.int.

Target 3.5: Strengthening the European cooperation.

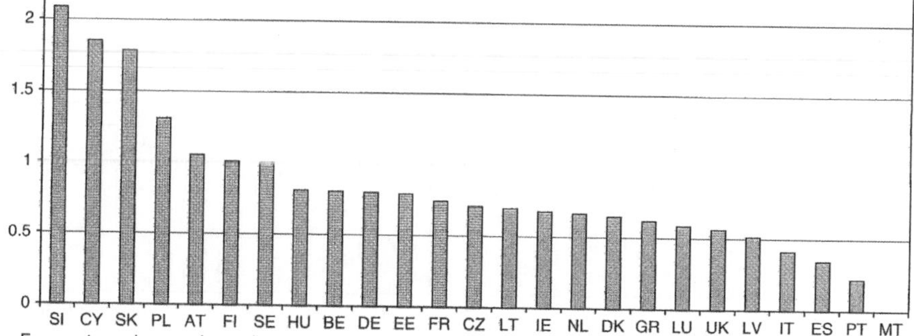

For country codes, see Appendix 5.A.1.
To obtain the rate in % of early school leavers in 2000: take the inverse and multiply by 10.
Source: Eurostat Labour Force Survey data for 2002 from the Official Journal of the European Union, note 2004/C 104/01 "Education & Training 2010".

Reference Level 1: Early school leavers.

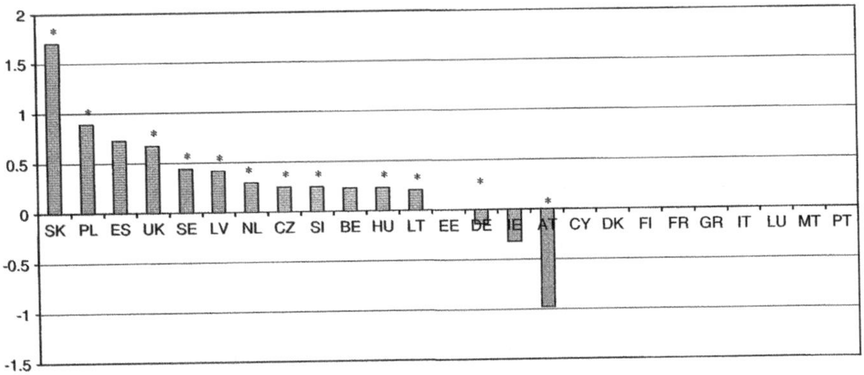

For country codes, see Appendix 5.A.1.
Note: * indicates that the female share has increased.
To obtain the percentage change in the number of graduates between 2000 and 2003: multiply by 3.
Source: Eurostat database, www.europa.eu.int.

Reference Level 2: Graduates in science and technology.

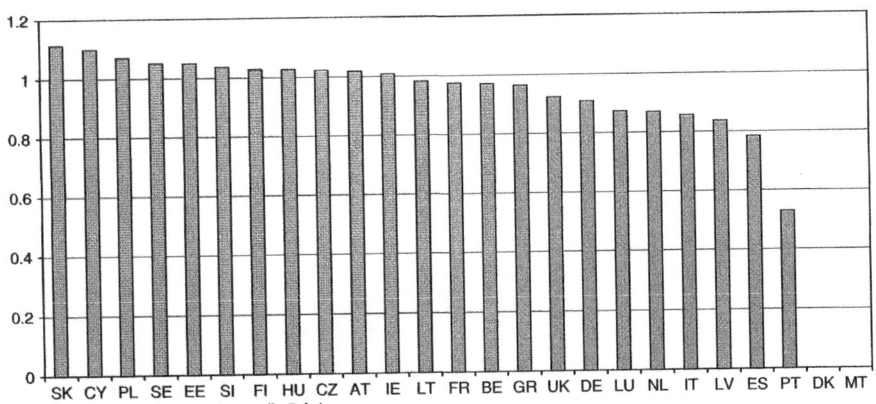

For country codes, see Appendix 5.A.1.
To obtain the percentage of 22-year olds with at least upper secondary school in 2002: multiply by 85.
Source: Eurostat Labour Force Survey 2002.

Reference Level 3: Upper secondary education attainment.

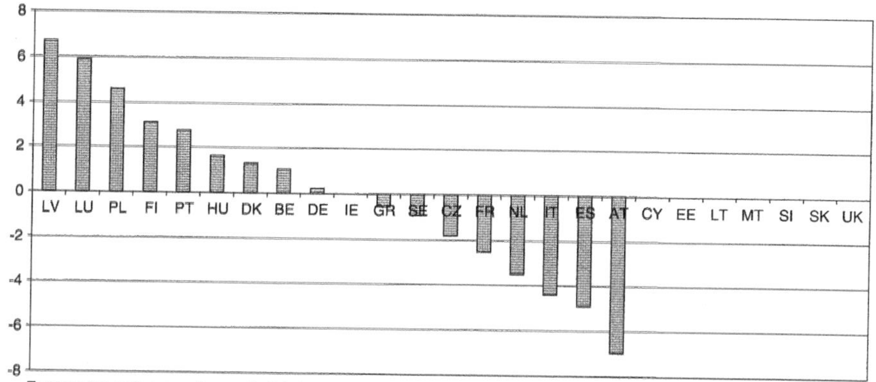

For country codes, see Appendix 5.A.1.
To obtain the relative change in share of low-achievers between 2000 and 2003 in %: multiply by -3*((1/5)/10)*100.
Source: OECD PISA 2000, 2003. www.pisa.oecd.org.

Reference Level 4: Key components.

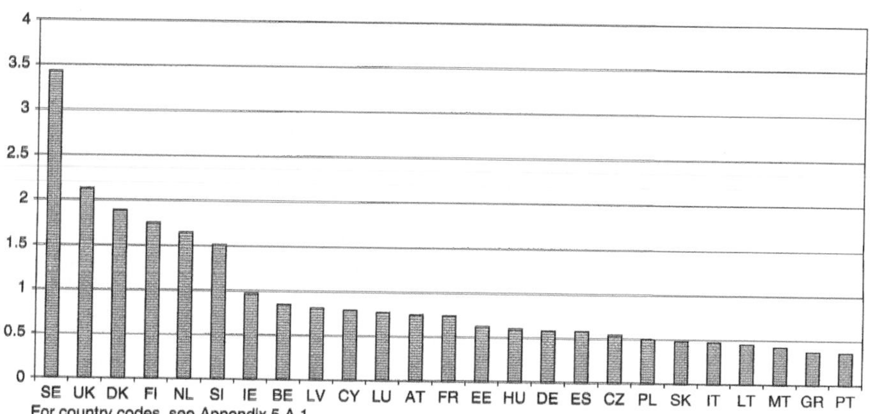

For country codes, see Appendix 5.A.1.
To obtain the share, in %, that participated in education or training: multiply by 10.
Source: Eurostat Labour Force Survey, www.europa.eu.int.

Reference Level 5: Lifelong learning—adult participation in education and training.

Chapter 6

Transparency in Bankruptcy Law: A Perspective on Bankruptcy Costs across Europe

Karin S. Thorburn

6.1 Introduction

When operating cash flow drops, a leveraged firm may fail to have trouble meeting its debt obligations. With default imminent, bankruptcy law determines the restructuring options available to the distressed firm. The law allocates control rights to various claimholders and decides the extent to which financial markets participate in the reorganization of the firm. Different procedures imply various costs for the financially distressed firm and its creditors. The greater the costs imposed by the bankruptcy code, the higher is the firm's *ex-ante* cost of raising capital. The optimality of a code is ultimately determined by its ability to minimize total costs.

Bankruptcy costs are of several different types. There are direct costs for the administration of the firm through the proceedings and indirect costs from damages incurred to the business when filing. Another set of costs stems from *ex-post* inefficiencies in the redeployment of the firm's assets as well as *ex-ante* inefficiencies in managers' investment decisions. A transparent bankruptcy code reduces the uncertainty about the outcome of the procedure. Creditors can better predict their recovery if debt contracts are strictly enforced. When transparency reduces the uncertainty related to default, the availability of capital *ex-ante* increases (as discussed in Chapter 1).

Corporate and Institutional Transparency for Economic Growth in Europe

ISBN: 0-08-044665-5

There is a wide variation in the bankruptcy systems across Europe. The UK receivership code gives significant powers to creditors, while the French code eliminates creditor influence over the reorganization of the firm. In Germany, firms get a three-month grace period to restructure. In Sweden, the distressed firm is immediately auctioned off. Most other European countries have some variation or combination of these four codes.

What types of costs are associated with the different bankruptcy systems and which system minimizes total costs? Creditor-friendly codes, honoring claimants' contractual rights, have been accused of excessively closing down viable firms, selling assets at depressed prices. Moreover, a harsh treatment of top management may encourage managers to delay filing and invest in high-risk value-reducing projects in a bet on staying out of bankruptcy. Debtor-friendly codes, on the other hand, might allow inefficient continuation of non-profitable firms by removing the true residual claimholders—creditors—from the reorganization process in favor of a broader set of stakeholder interests.

Empirical evidence suggests that the Swedish system of mandatory bankruptcy auctions constitutes a relatively low-cost procedure. The process is speedy and direct costs are low. There is no evidence in support of delayed filings, asset sales at depressed prices or excessive termination of viable firms. The creditor-oriented UK system produces comparable recovery rates, perhaps implying total costs of a similar magnitude.

The French reorganization system, in contrast, appears to impose relatively high costs on distressed companies. Few firms survive bankruptcy as a going concern, recovery rates are low and the proceedings last much longer. There is some evidence that German banks tend to coordinate their efforts in order to facilitate voluntary restructurings outside of the formal procedure.

Despite the seemingly attractive features of creditor-oriented bankruptcy systems like the Swedish auction code, current reform efforts in Europe aim at strengthening the provisions for reorganization. Nevertheless, extant evidence suggests that such changes may be potentially damaging and possibly lead to increased costs for firms to finance their businesses.

This chapter is organized as follows: Section 6.2 describes the nature of various bankruptcy costs and discusses the potential costs associated with different types of systems. Section 6.3 describes bankruptcy law in the UK, France, Germany, and Sweden. A discussion of the costs relevant to the different codes and their magnitude as well as a review of the empirical evidence is found in Section 6.4. Section 6.5 discusses recent reform in Europe and Section 6.6 concludes.

6.2 Bankruptcy Systems and Their Potential Costs

6.2.1 Bankruptcy Costs

Bankruptcy costs have several components. The most straight-forward element is the direct costs for legal and advisory fees incurred during the reorganization process. Moreover, there are indirect costs generated by e.g. unproductive use of management time, departure of key employees, and loss of critical suppliers and customers, which reduce the value of the business. Since these costs increase with the time that the firm spends in bankruptcy, the swiftness of the procedure is critical.

Another set of *ex-post* costs relate to the efficiency of the redeployment of assets. Optimally, the bankruptcy procedure should allocate the distressed firm's assets to their highest-value use i.e. a sound business suffering from an inadequate capital structure should be maintained as a going concern while only rehabilitating the balance sheet. On the other hand, economically distressed operations that have poor long-term prospects should be liquidated (i.e. broken up in pieces) and the resources transferred to more productive use. I classify inefficient allocation of assets as a cost since it reduces the total value of the firm.

The next cost category concerns *ex-ante* investment inefficiencies resulting from agency conflicts between the firm's debt and equityholders prior to filing. As Jensen and Meckling (1976) point out, equityholders of a financially distressed firm have an incentive to invest in high-risk projects that can yield a significant payoff, albeit with a very low probability. Such risk-shifting activities may be undertaken in a desperate attempt to entirely avoid bankruptcy. However, if unsuccessful, the value of the filing firm's assets may end up being severely reduced. Again, such investment inefficiencies on average reduce firm value and I therefore include them in the total bankruptcy costs.

Since the design of bankruptcy law affects the magnitude of all these costs, the formal rules determine the size of the total pie that the claimholders get to split. Moreover, by deciding the relative bargaining strength of various claimants, the code affects the outcome of the reorganization. The more transparent the procedure is for the firm's claimholders, the better the outcome can be predicted. When the uncertainty about the payoff of debt claims in bankruptcy is high, creditors may be reluctant to provide financing to the firm *ex-ante*, increasing the firm's cost of raising necessary capital. Lack of transparency increases such uncertainty and is therefore costly to the firm.

The anticipated payoffs to the various claimants in their turn create incentives for the different parties to reach agreements out-of-court. The lower the payoff expected in the formal proceedings, the stronger incentives creditors have to reach a voluntary agreement. The relative frequency of workouts therefore depends on the total bankruptcy costs as well as the distribution of these costs between the different claimants. Ultimately, the specific costs imposed by any bankruptcy code affect firms' *ex-ante* cost of raising new capital and its choice of capital structure.

6.2.2 Bankruptcy Systems

In the absence of a first-best system, we observe a wide range of different bankruptcy codes. Each country provides a unique set of insolvency rules that in interplay with the institutional environment determines the outcome of distressed restructurings.

At the extreme, two distinct systems stand out: reorganization and auction codes. A reorganization code provides a framework for claimholders to negotiate a necessary restructuring of the firm's capital structure and operations. Incumbent management typically stays at the helm of the firm, while creditor rights are scaled back. A prominent example of a reorganization code is the Chapter 11 of the US Bankruptcy Code. An auction code, in contrast, mandates a sale of the firm either as a going concern or piecemeal.[1] The fate of management is up to the buyer in the auction and creditor rights are at the forefront.

Proponents of the auction code point to the benefits from letting the market decide on the valuation and allocation of the bankrupt firm's assets. The highest bidder in the auction, whose own money is at stake, gets to determine whether the assets are worth more continuing as a going concern or redeployed in other uses. This increases the transparency of the auction process. Moreover, the cash settlement in the auction facilitates strict adherence to absolute priority rules.

Adversaries to auctions, on the other hand, claim that the markets for distressed firms' assets are illiquid.[2] High-valuation bidders might abstain from bidding in the auction due to liquidity constraints and excessive transactions costs, resulting in a suboptimal allocation of assets to inferior uses. Furthermore, the harsh treatment of management in the auction procedure may induce managers to delay filing and engage in costly risk-shifting behavior.[3] On the contrary, it is often argued that a reorganization code protecting management provides incentives to file early, thereby saving firm value and increasing the likelihood of a successful reorganization.

---

[1]The auction code is often referred to as a liquidation code. In that context, however, liquidation implies that the assets are redeployed through a sale and not necessarily a termination of the operations.

[2]See e.g. Aghion, Hart, and Moore (1992) and Shleifer and Vishny (1992).

[3]See e.g. White (1996) and Hart (2000).

Obviously, reorganization codes suffer from their own weaknesses. Negotiations decide the valuation as well as how to restructure the assets and what to pay various creditors. Combining all these decisions into one negotiated solution risks lengthening the bankruptcy procedure with an associated increase in direct and indirect costs as well as a decrease in the transparency of the proceedings. Moreover, leaving substantial control rights with incumbent management, whose incompetence may potentially have caused the default, opens for inefficient continuation decisions and impedes a perhaps necessary change in management. The mere existence of an option for a management-friendly reorganization allows self-interested managers to avoid filing for a disciplining auction procedure also when a piecemeal liquidation of the assets is optimal.

In sum, auction and reorganization bankruptcy codes impose different types of costs on distressed firms. While regulators, employees, and management tend to favor reorganization codes arguing that it saves job opportunities, the relative efficiency of different bankruptcy systems remains an empirical question.

6.3 Bankruptcy Codes across Europe

There is substantial variation in the legal procedures facing distressed firms across Europe. The UK code is geared toward protecting secured creditors, with little focus on the interests of other claimants. France explicitly puts preservation of employment at the forefront, restricting the firm's equity and debtholders from participating in the reorganization. German law allows distressed firms a three-month grace period to reorganize, and in Sweden bankrupt firms are put up for sale in an auction.[4]

I describe below the bankruptcy codes in the UK, France, Germany, and Sweden. These countries provide a good representation of the codes that exist across Europe in different variations.

6.3.1 The United Kingdom

UK companies have access to several court-supervised procedures. In the predominant procedure (*receivership*), a secured creditor appoints a receiver representing the interest of the appointing creditor. When the creditor's claim is

[4]In La Porta, Lopez-de-Silanes, Shleifer, and Vishny (1998), France scores 0 for the protection of creditor rights, while the UK gets the highest score of 4 and Sweden gets a 2. Under the old bankruptcy code, replaced in 1999, Germany scores 3.

secured by floating charge collateral, an administrative receiver gets full control over the firm and can take actions to reorganize the firm or sell assets without asking permission from other creditors or the court.[5] In a majority of cases, the firm is sold as a going concern or liquidated piecemeal.

There is no automatic stay of debt. Creditors secured with fixed liens on particular assets have the right to repossess their collateral, even if the assets are vital for the firms' operations. The receiver realizes the security and, after deducting his expenses and paying any higher priority claims, uses the proceeds to pay off the appointing creditor. Any excess balance is distributed to the remaining claimholders according to the absolute priority of their claims. Unsecured creditors have little influence over the procedure.

There are also two court-administered reorganization procedures, Administration and—for small firms—Company Voluntary Arrangements (CVA), which give the firm temporary relief from its creditors. A secured creditor can veto these procedures, however, and instead appoint a receiver. Thus, in practice, the court can appoint an administrator that represents all creditors only in the absence of secured creditors.

6.3.2 France

France is the country in Europe that perhaps provides the strongest provisions for court-supervised reorganization of distressed firms. Notably, the French bankruptcy code (*redressement judiciare*) removes debtholders and equityholders from the reorganization process in favor of a court-appointed administrator.[6] The reorganization is geared toward preservation of job opportunities. The objectives of the administrator are, in order of priority, to keep the firm's operations as a going concern, maintain employment, and satisfy creditor claims. In fact, employees get to appoint their own representative, while creditors are represented by a court officer.

The administrator evaluates the prospects for reorganization and the court offers creditors altered claims in place of their old impaired debt claims. The court cannot force the creditors to write down claims, but it can redefine the terms of the loan, including maturity. Thus, in practice, creditors often prefer to accept a write-down with prompt repayment to a long-delayed promised repayment in full. Creditors cannot reject the court's decision and can raise their concerns only

---

[5]The collateral of a floating charge claim includes e.g. inventory, accounts receivables, working capital, and intangible assets.

[6]French insolvency law also provides a separate proceeding for liquidation (*liquidation judiciare*) and a rarely used procedure for renegotiation of debt contracts prior to default (*reglément amiable*).

through the court-appointed creditor representative. The approval of secured creditors is not required to confirm a reorganization plan or to sell their collateral.

The firm receives protection from its creditors during the bankruptcy process. Debt payments are stayed and the administrator can raise new super-priority financing without the consent of creditors. In the event of a sale of the firm, the court can choose a bidder offering a lower price but providing better prospects for continuing the operations and upholding employment. Moreover, the government places its own claims and employee claims first in priority to the proceeds from a sale of collateral, effectively imposing a deviation from absolute priority rules.[7]

6.3.3 Germany

The current German bankruptcy code (*Insolvenzordnung*) took effect in 1999.[8] A court-appointed administrator supervises the bankrupt firm and has three months to contrive a plan of reorganization. The plan outlines the reorganization of the firm, including a possible sale of the firm as a going concern or a piecemeal liquidation. The approval of creditors is required for the plan to be implemented. Creditors vote on the plan with a simple majority rule. The court may cram down the plan on a dissenting class of creditors as long as the plan leaves the class better off than piecemeal liquidation. There is an automatic stay of creditor claims during the three-month reorganization period. The firm can raise new debt with super-priority subject to creditor approval.

6.3.4 Sweden

Sweden has a mandatory auction system. The proceeding is run by a court-appointed bankruptcy trustee with fiduciary responsibility to all creditors. The trustee's main task is to organize the sale of the firm in an auction. The winning bidder in the auction determines whether the firm is economically viable as a restructured going concern or whether the firm's assets are to be liquidated piecemeal. The method of payment is restricted to cash and creditors are paid according to the absolute priority of their claims.

In contrast to the UK, the Swedish code restricts the liquidation rights of creditors: bankruptcy filing triggers automatic stay of debt payments and prevents

[7]Certain types of collateral, like receivables and guarantees, are exempt from this rule.

[8]Prior to 1999, German insolvency law offered an auction liquidation process (*konkursordnung*) and a rarely used procedure for the reorganization of unsecured claims (*vergleichsordnung*).

repossession of collateral. These provisions help protect the firm as a going concern throughout the bankruptcy process. It is possible to raise super-priority debt to finance the firm's ongoing activities until the final sale. In practice, firms tend to cover operating expenses by incurring new trade credits with super-priority. The incumbent management team typically stays to run the operations while in bankruptcy.

Swedish bankruptcy law has a provision for composition (*ackord*), which allows a renegotiation of unsecured debt claims. Secured debt and priority claims (taxes and wages) must be offered full repayment and junior creditors at least 25 percent of their claim. As a result, this procedure is hardly ever feasible. A new reorganization law was enacted in 1996. The new law shares many of the weaknesses of the old composition procedure, however, and is rarely used (Buttwill & Wihlborg, 2004). Thus, in Sweden, court-supervised renegotiation of the firm's debt contracts is effectively not an option.

6.4 Costs Relevant to Different Codes and Their Relative Magnitude

Having outlined the various bankruptcy codes, I now turn to a discussion of the potential costs associated with the different systems and survey relevant empirical evidence.

6.4.1 *Inefficient Continuation and Liquidation*

Different parties may have diverging incentives with respect to the continuation of the bankrupt firm. A manager with substantial private benefits of control, for instance, may favor continuation of the firm's operations, also if a piecemeal sale of the assets yields higher revenues. Similarly, even if the present value of expected cash flows exceeds the piecemeal liquidation value, a secured creditor may favor a sale in pieces for proceeds barely covering the secured claim simply to avoid the uncertainty associated with a continuation of the firm. The allocation of control rights in bankruptcy determines which incentives will be allowed to influence the fate of distressed firms.

The French code, with its explicit objective to keep operations as a going concern and preserve jobs, has a propensity to allow continuation of inefficient firms. Excessive continuation is less likely in German bankruptcy since it requires creditor approval of the reorganization plan. The three-month moratorium instead risks being too short to permit a reorganization of the firm, possibly forcing premature closure of economically viable firms.

The UK code provides little protection of the operations from creditors in the form of automatic stay or super-priority financing. In combination with leaving the continuation decision to secured creditors, who have little incentive to maximize firm value above the secured claim, the UK system risks inefficiently terminating viable firms.[9] Franks and Nyborg (1996), however, argue that the incidence of inefficient piecemeal sales may be greatly reduced if the creditor appointing the receiver has large private benefits of control associated with the survival of the firm.

In the Swedish system, unlike the UK, the business is protected from creditors while in bankruptcy, facilitating a continuation of the operations. With the buyer in the auction determining how to best use the firm's assets, there are no systematic continuation or liquidation inefficiencies resulting from conflicts of interest between the bankrupt firm's claimholders.[10]

Overall, the French bankruptcy code seems susceptible to excessive continuation, while the UK and German codes might suffer from too many terminations and piecemeal sales. If the perceived inefficiencies play out in the data, the rate of firm survival should be higher in France than in the UK and Germany, with Sweden falling in between. Extant empirical evidence does not support this prediction, however.

Kaiser (1996) reports that only 15 percent of French firms survives bankruptcy as a going concern, while almost half of the UK firms are sold as going concerns or successfully restructure through administrative receivership. Franks and Sussman (2005) report that 60 percent of filing firms survive the UK receivership code as a going concern. Including both bankruptcy filings and voluntary workouts, Davydenko and Franks (2004) find a lower fraction of piecemeal liquidations for distressed firms in the UK than in Germany and France, with liquidation ratios of 43, 57, and 62 percent, respectively.

Thorburn (2000) shows that three-quarters of small Swedish firms filing for bankruptcy are auctioned as going concerns, with the remaining one-quarter being liquidated piecemeal. The probability for a going concern sale increases in the fraction of intangible assets, perhaps because these assets generate little value in a piecemeal liquidation. Moreover, to assess the quality of the continuation decision, Eckbo and Thorburn (2003) examine the operating profitability of the firms emerging from Swedish bankruptcy. They document that auctioned firms perform at par with their industry competitors for several years.

---

[9]Franks, Nyborg, and Torous (1996) suggest that the strong control rights allocated to creditors in the UK receivership code result in excessive liquidations and underinvestment.

[10]As discussed in Section 6.4.3, however, assets may be allocated inefficiently due to market failure.

To sum up, the Swedish and the UK systems do not appear to suffer from the perceived risk of excessively terminating viable firms. Swedish bankruptcy auctions typically produce a going concern sale of the firm. A large number of UK firms in receivership are reorganized or sold as going concerns. In contrast, while rigged to safeguard firm survival, the French bankruptcy code seems to fail in this respect. Indeed, survival rates for bankrupt firms are much lower in France and Germany than in Sweden and the UK. Thus, in terms of excessive continuation or termination of financially distressed firms, the Swedish system appears to impose relatively low costs along with the UK system.

6.4.2 Delayed Filing

A potential benefit of a management-friendly bankruptcy law is that it could encourage managers to file relatively early while there is still substantial going-concern value worth saving. The French code allows management to continue running the firm and endorses a continuation of the firm, hence promoting early filing. In contrast, a code-treating management harshly risks providing incentives for management to delay filing and undertake value-reducing investments. The creditor-oriented bankruptcy codes in the UK and Sweden could belong to the latter category, possibly suffering from extensive risk-shifting activities.

Eckbo and Thorburn (2003) argue that managers' incentives to preserve private benefits of control will counteract potential risk-shifting incentives. In an attempt to increase the joint likelihood that the firm survives as a going concern and current management gets to stay at the helm, managers will implement a conservative investment policy prior to filing. For a sample of Swedish bankruptcy filings, Eckbo and Thorburn (2003) show that the probability that the incumbent manager continues to run the auctioned firm increases in a measure for his private benefits of control. Bidders screen managers on quality in the rehiring decision and CEOs suffer large income declines conditional on bankruptcy filing. The evidence supports the notion that managers' motivation to retain control may reduce the temptation to risk shift.

Most European countries hold directors and managers personally liable with civil and criminal penalties if they fail to file timely or inform creditors when the firm becomes insolvent. To the extent that such laws are enforced, the penalties may well trigger prompt action offsetting any tendencies to delay filing, also under a creditor-oriented system.

In sum, while potentially a substantial cost to distressed firms, there is little evidence that managers tend to delay bankruptcy filing under any code. Motives to retain control and significant personal penalties help counteract risk-shifting incentives, encouraging managers to act promptly.

6.4.3 Asset Fire Sales

A common objection to auctioning off distressed firms is the concern that markets are illiquid, forcing fire sales at depressed prices. When financial distress is industry wide, industry insiders may lack the financial resources to participate in the auction. Moreover, bidding costs might be substantial due to uncertainty about the distressed firm, deterring potential bidders from entering.

Bankruptcy codes using the market mechanism to allocate the distressed firm's assets—here the codes in Sweden and the UK—are subject to concern about asset fire sales. This issue may be particularly prominent in the UK, where the firm's operations receive little protection against creditors and the receiver has to act expeditiously selling the business as a going concern.

Studying Swedish bankruptcies, Stromberg (2000) finds that the probability of the old owner repurchasing the firm increases with operating profitability and industry leverage, and decreases with non-specific assets. He suggests that repurchases help avoid costly asset fire sales in periods of industry distress.

Eckbo and Thorburn (2005) model the participation of a secured creditor who has an impaired debt claim on the bankrupt firm. The more impaired the secured claim, the greater incentive has the creditor to provide financing to competing bidders in the auction, thus increasing expected recovery. Eckbo and Thorburn (2005) show that Swedish bankruptcy auctions are characterized by bid competition and that the bankrupt firm's bank frequently finances bids. Premiums paid by the winning bidder tend to be higher in auctions where the secured creditor expects a low recovery under piecemeal liquidation. Importantly, premiums do not vary systematically with fire-sales variables. Eckbo and Thorburn (2005) argue that secured creditors' incentives to finance a bidder may counteract potential problems with asset fire sales.

Overall, while bankruptcy auctions risk forcing asset sales at depressed prices, evidence from Sweden suggests that incentives of secured creditors and old owners may increase auction demand, effectively raising prices and balancing fire-sales tendencies.

6.4.4 Direct and Indirect Costs

Direct bankruptcy costs are a function of the number of officials and lawyers involved in the procedure and the time that the restructuring takes. Indirect bankruptcy costs are difficult to measure but are also increasing in the duration of the formal process. The French reorganization process is likely to extend much longer than the quicker auction codes and the German reorganization process with its three-month limit.

Thorburn (2000) estimates the direct costs in Swedish bankruptcy to average 6 percent of pre-filing book value of assets, with an average of 4 percent for the one-third largest firms in her sample. When measured as a fraction of the market value of assets in bankruptcy, costs average 19 percent with a median of 13 percent. The direct costs decrease with firm size and increase with measures of industry distress, suggesting that trustees increase their sales effort in periods when auction demand is relatively low. Importantly, the auction is speedy with an average time from filing to sale of the assets of only two months, implying relatively low indirect costs.

For a sample of small-to-medium sized financially distressed UK companies transferred to their bank's workout unit (BSU), Franks and Sussman (2005) report direct costs averaging 33 percent of asset values. They suggest that the lack of competition among receivers may explain the high direct costs and point to much lower costs (mean 14 percent) when the Royal Bank of Scotland recently required receivers to tender for their appointments. While I am not aware of any empirical evidence on the duration of UK bankruptcy procedures, Franks et al. (1996) suggest that the UK receivership code is speedy. The firms in Franks and Sussman (2005) spend an average of 7.5 months in the BSU.

The value of assets remaining at the end of the bankruptcy process reflects all the different costs imposed on the financially distressed firm, including possible investment inefficiencies and fire sales. This value is split between the firm's creditors. The higher the total costs of bankruptcy, the lower are creditor recovery rates. A comparison of creditor recovery rates across countries is therefore interesting in itself.

In Swedish bankruptcy, creditors' claims are paid with the cash generated in the auction. Thorburn (2000) reports average recovery rates of 35 percent (median 34 percent). Recovery rates are higher in going concern sales (mean 39 percent) than in piecemeal liquidations (mean 27 percent). Secured creditors receive on average 69 percent (median 83 percent).

Franks and Sussman (2005) find average bank recovery rates in the UK of around 75 percent (median 100 percent). They observe that banks liquidate collateral to prices close to the secured claim, and argue that secured creditors take little interest in generating excess proceeds to cover more junior claims. The average bank studied by Davydenko and Franks (2004) recovers 69 percent (median 82 percent) in UK bankruptcy, 47 percent (median 39 percent) in French proceedings, and 59 percent (median 61 percent) under the German code.[11]

[11]The firms in Davydenko and Franks (2004) filed for bankruptcy during the period 1984 through 2003. Thus, most of the German firms filed before the current code took effect in 1999.

In sum, Swedish auction bankruptcy is a speedy procedure with relatively low direct costs. Direct costs in the UK are higher, possibly as a result of less competition among receivers. To the extent that secured creditors' recovery rates reflect the total costs imposed on financially distressed firms, the French reorganization code appears to be comparatively costly while the market-based systems in the UK and Sweden better protect the value of the firm and the German system falls in between.

6.4.5 Out-of-court Solutions

Bankruptcy law provides incentives for claimholders to restructure out-of-court. The higher the costs of the formal procedure the more inclined are creditors to negotiate an agreement outside the court system. In the UK and Sweden, where creditors are well protected and costs appear relatively low, one should expect comparatively few out-of-court restructurings. In contrast, the lack of creditor right protection under the French bankruptcy code should encourage creditors to participate in voluntary workouts.

For small UK firms that default on their debt, Davydenko and Franks (2004) find that 75 percent enter formal bankruptcy with the remaining 25 percent of firms reorganizing out-of-court. Surprisingly, the fraction of defaulted firms filing for bankruptcy is similar in Germany (78 percent) and somewhat higher in France (87 percent). Franks and Sussman (2004) observe that UK banks rarely make concessions to small firms in financial distress.

When large distressed UK companies issue new equity, banks behave differently. Franks and Sanzhar (2003) show that UK banks make concessions for one-third of publicly traded distressed firms issuing equity. These concessions include forgiveness of principal, debt for equity swaps and provisions for new loans. Concessions are offered to firms with higher leverage and greater debt impairment, representing situations where the expected wealth transfer to debt holders is larger.

An important impediment to out-of-court agreements is holdout problems among dispersed creditors. The likelihood of a coordination failure seems especially low in Germany, where the debt typically is concentrated with a house bank that often also has an equity interest. According to Kaiser (1996), most German firms with a chance of survival are reorganized through an out-of-court workout. Elsas and Krahnen (2002) study the role of lending relationships for private workouts of financially distressed firms in Germany. They find that banks are more likely to participate in a voluntary restructuring when the bank holds a secured claim and is a house bank. Brunner and Krahnen (2004) show that German bank lenders often coordinate their reorganization efforts by forming a bank pool upon the onset of financial distress.[12] The probability of bank pool formation increases with the number of bank relationships and the degree of distress.

Buttwill and Wihlborg (2004) report a rate of firm bankruptcy filings per employee that is six to seven times higher in Sweden than in Germany and the UK. It is possible that the widespread use of the formal process is a manifestation of relatively low bankruptcy costs in the Swedish system. However, eliminating filings of Swedish firms with zero employees and adjusting the German rates for rejections by the court yields similar bankruptcy filing rates across Germany and Sweden.

To sum up, while statistics on bankruptcy filings is readily available, systematic data on informal negotiations are scarce. The existing evidence suggests that the fraction of distressed firms negotiating a workout is lower in France than in Germany and the UK, possibly because French firms have few reasons to not seek bankruptcy protection from their creditors. Moreover, there is some evidence that German banks coordinate their efforts to facilitate restructurings out-of-court.

6.4.6 Ex-ante *Effects*

Creditors anticipating high costs associated with the restructuring of a financially distressed firm have incentives to take measures *ex-ante* in order to protect their claim and hence reduce the expected costs. Such measures could imply less debt in the capital structure, higher interest margins, and stricter requirements for collateral. In light of the relatively harsh treatment of creditors in French bankruptcy, one would expect comparatively high-interest spreads charged by banks and other lenders and a high degree of collateralization.

Davydenko and Franks (2004) show that debt collateralization rates at loan origination are highest in France and lowest in Germany, with the UK in between. Pre-distress interest margins, however, are similar in France and the UK and highest in Germany, with an average margin of 224, 223, and 290 basis points, respectively. While unexpected, somewhat surprising, it is possible that the higher degree of collateralization makes it feasible for French banks to charge similar margins as UK banks. I am not aware of any comparable evidence for Sweden.

Acharya, Sundaram, and John (2005) argue that the allocation of control rights in bankruptcy determines the impact of asset specificity on the firm's optimal

---

[12] Banks strike a formal contractual pool arrangement for 45 percent of the firms studied in Brunner and Krahnen (2004). The sample, which consists of distressed and potentially distressed mid-sized companies, is collected from credit files of the largest German commercial banks.

capital structure. When assets are specific, piecemeal liquidation values are low and a forced piecemeal sale is relatively costly to the firm. On the other hand, when assets are non-specific, the costs from an inefficient continuation of the firm are relatively high. As a result, firms with high asset specificity will choose a relatively lower debt-level under a creditor-friendly system, which has a bias toward inefficient terminations, than under a reorganization-oriented code. In contrast, firms with low asset specificity will choose a relatively lower debt level under a debtor-oriented code, which risks allowing excessive continuation. For a sample of UK and US firms, Acharya, Sundaram, and John (2005) find debt ratios consistent with their predictions.

While rational creditors take *ex-ante* measures to reduce the expected costs of financial distress, there is limited cross-country evidence to this point. French banks take more collateral than bank lenders in the UK and Germany, possibly reflecting their poor standing in French bankruptcy. Furthermore, the specificity of assets determines the cost of different types of bankruptcy systems and can thus help explain firms' choice of debt level.

6.5 Recent Reform

The European Union (EU) encourages its member countries to strengthen the provisions for court-supervised reorganization and to facilitate entry into these procedures.[13] The last decade has seen substantial reform of insolvency laws throughout Europe, all aimed at facilitating reorganization.

Germany's current law took effect in 1999 and Sweden added reorganization provisions in 1996. France is in the process of enacting new regulation. Reformed UK insolvency procedures took effect in 2003. The new UK law cuts back the rights of creditors secured by floating charge, including that to appoint an administrative receiver.[14] Holders of floating charge claims issued prior to September 15, 2003, however, retain the same rights as before.

Spain adopted new reorganization-oriented bankruptcy legislation in 2004. Austrian officials recently announced that they in the fall of 2005 will present a draft of a new bankruptcy law designed along the lines of Chapter 11 of the US Bankruptcy Code. To save Parmalat, Italy adopted new insolvency provisions in 2003 available for large firms. The procedure, which aims at preserving employment, allows firms to freeze their debts without declaring bankruptcy.

---

[13]See European Commission (2003). The EU also recommends that courts organize specialized insolvency sections.

[14]Moreover, while access is restricted, the CVA now allow small firms a moratorium.

In 2000 the EU Council adopted the Regulation on Insolvency Proceedings, which came into force in 2002. It establishes common rules for cross-country insolvency proceedings but does not seek to harmonize law between different EU countries. Broadly, the regulation provides that main insolvency proceedings are opened in the member state where the firm has its "center of main interest" (COMI). These proceedings have universal scope and encompass all assets and creditors worldwide. Secondary proceedings may be opened in one or more other member states. Such proceedings are limited to winding up the assets in that country and run parallel to the main proceedings.

Deciding where the COMI is located has proved difficult and has given rise to disputes that has lead to delays in the coordination of pan-European insolvency proceedings. Applications for COMI have been challenged by local courts and one case was recently taken to the European Court of Justice.[15]

6.6 Conclusions

Failure is an inevitable part of doing business when using some degree of debt financing. To eliminate coordination problems among creditors, all countries provide bankruptcy regulation governing the restructuring of financially distressed firms. The design of the bankruptcy system, however, varies considerably across countries. Some codes mandate an auction of the bankrupt firm, while other codes prescribe a reorganization of the distressed firm's claims in a formal renegotiation procedure.

This chapter describes the bankruptcy codes in the UK, France, Germany, and Sweden. In the UK, secured creditors appoint a receiver who restructures or sells the firm. In France, creditors are removed from a court-administered reorganization process. German firms get a three-month grace period to restructure their claims, while in Sweden bankrupt firms are sold in a mandatory auction.

Critics of the auction system warn that assets are sold at depressed prices; viable firms are inefficiently terminated; and managers destroy firm value by delaying bankruptcy filing. In contrast, a debtor-friendly reorganization code could encourage early filing, permitting firms to continue operating as going concerns.

Extant empirical evidence refutes allegations that auctions fail to allocate assets efficiently. Incentives of creditors and managers may promote prompt filing and

[15]Irish and Italian courts have both purported that Eurofood IFSC, an Irish-incorporated company which is part of the Parmalat group, is within their own jurisdiction.

counteract fire-sale tendencies. Direct costs are low and the Swedish auction procedure is speedy. In contrast, the French bankruptcy code seems to fail reorganizing distressed firms successfully. Creditor recovery rates are much lower than in the other countries and few firms survive bankruptcy as a going concern.

There is an increasing use of market mechanisms in US reorganizations and asset sales are a dominant feature of Chapter 11 proceedings today. Half of all publicly traded US firms filing for bankruptcy in 2002 were resolved trough a sale of the assets. Of the remaining cases, half were negotiated prior to filing with the judge confirming the reorganization plan and half were reorganized through traditional court-supervised negotiations (Baird & Rasmussen, 2003).

Interestingly, the trend in Europe goes in the opposite direction. Despite the seemingly attractive features of bankruptcy auctions, the EU encourages its member countries to strengthen the procedures for reorganization. Most countries in Europe have adopted reorganization provisions over the last decade, weakening creditor rights in formal bankruptcy proceedings.

It is questionable whether this development is sound. Lower costs of bankruptcy translate into lower costs for raising capital *ex-ante*. It is possible that the changes in insolvency law currently undertaken in Europe will imply less transparency and higher expected costs of resolving financial distress, thus increasing firms' costs of financing their operations. Before initiating further changes, regulators should take a closer look at the evidence.

References

Acharya, V. V., Sundaram, R. K., Rangarajan, K. S., & John, K. (2005). *On the capital-structure implications of bankruptcy codes*. Working Paper. New York University. Cross-Country Variations in Capital Structures: The Role of Bankruptcy Codes. CEPR Discussion Papers: 4916.

Aghion, P., Hart, O., & Moore, J. (1992). The economics of bankruptcy reform. *Journal of Law, Economics and Organization, 8*, 523–546.

Baird, D. G., & Rasmussen, R. K. (2003). Chapter 11 at twilight. *Stanford Law Review, 56*(3), 673–699.

Brunner, A., & Krahnen, J. P. (2004). *Multiple lenders and corporate distress: Evidence on debt restructuring*. CEPR Working Paper no. 4287.

Buttwill, K., & Wihlborg, C. (2004). *The efficiency of the bankruptcy process. An international comparison*. Working Paper. Copenhagen Business School.

Davydenko, S. A., & Franks, J. R. (2004). *Do bankruptcy codes matter? A study of defaults in France, Germany, and the UK*. Working Paper. London Business School.

Eckbo, B. E., & Thorburn, K. S. (2003). Control benefits and CEO discipline in automatic bankruptcy auctions. *Journal of Financial Economics, 69*, 227–258.

Eckbo, B. E., & Thorburn, K. S. (2005). *Bidding in mandatory bankruptcy auctions: Theory and Evidence*. Working Paper. Dartmouth College. CEPR Discussion Papers: 4873.

Elsas, R., & Krahnen, J. P. (2002). *Collateral, relationship lending and financial distress: An empirical study on financial contracting*. Working Paper. Goethe-Universität Frankfurt.

European Commission. (2003). *Best project on restructuring, bankruptcy and a fresh start*. Final report of the expert group, available at http://europa.eu.int/comm/enterprise/entrepreneurship/support_measures/failure_bankruptcy/

Franks, J. R., & Nyborg, K. G. (1996). Control rights, debt structure, and the loss of private benefits: The case of the UK insolvency code. *Review of Financial Studies*, *9*, 1165–1210.

Franks, J. R., Nyborg, K. G., & Torous, W. (1996). A comparison of US, UK, and German insolvency codes. *Financial Management*, *25*, 86–101.

Franks, J. R., & Sanzhar, S. V. (2003). *How do firms overcome the debt overhang problem?* Working Paper. London Business School.

Franks, J. R., & Sussman, O. (2005). Financial distress and bank restructuring of small-to-medium size UK companies. *Review of Finance*, *9*, 65–96.

Hart, O. (2000). Different approaches to bankruptcy. In: *Governance, equity and global markets*. Proceedings of the Annual Bank Conference on Development Economics in Europe, June 21–23, 1999. Paris: La Documentation Francaise.

Jensen, M. C., & Meckling, W. (1976). Theory of the firm: Managerial behavior, agency costs, and capital structure. *Journal of Financial Economics*, *3*, 305–360.

Kaiser, K. M. J. (1996). European bankruptcy laws: Implications for corporations facing financial distress. *Financial Management*, *25*, 67–85.

La Porta, R., Lopez-de-Silanes, F., Shleifer, A., & Vishny, R. W. (1998). Law and finance. *Journal of Political Economy*, *106*, 1113–1155.

Shleifer, A., & Vishny, R. W. (1992). Liquidation values and debt capacity: A market equilibrium approach. *Journal of Finance*, *47*, 1343–1366.

Stromberg, P. (2000). Conflicts of interest and market illiquidity in bankruptcy auctions: theory and tests. *Journal of inance*, *55*, 2641–2692.

Thorburn, K. S. (2000). Bankruptcy auctions: Costs debt recovery and firm survival. *Journal of Financial Economics*, *58*, 337–368.

White, M. (1996). The cost of corporate bankruptcy: A U.S.–European comparison. In: J. Bhandari, & L. Weiss (Ed.), *Corporate bankruptcy: Economic and legal perspectives* (Chapter 30, pp. 467–500). Cambridge: Cambridge University Press.

Chapter 7

Economic Growth and the Governance of the Financial Sector in the EU: What Role for Regulatory Transparency?

Jean-Pierre Casey

7.1 Introduction

Since the 1970s, Europe has witnessed a steady deceleration in economic growth, a disappointing performance that has led it to fall significantly behind the United States in both relative and absolute terms. Whereas the EU and the U.S. were growing at approximately even rates throughout the 1970s (averages of 3.0% and 3.2%, respectively), during the 1990s, the gap widened: EU growth had slowed to 2.1% compared with the U.S. rate of 3.6% (Sapir et al., 2003). In the absence of higher growth, the long-term sustainability of the European social welfare model is threatened by the trinity of challenges that are its deteriorating demographic landscape, increased competition from abroad in the context of global trade liberalization, and the costs of enlargement. Until higher growth rates are achieved, recovering a sustained path of economic growth ought therefore to remain the overriding policy objective in the European Union. A search for possible answers to the growth dilemma has arisen in the context of the Lisbon Agenda, which had set out in the year 2000 to transform the EU into the world's most "dynamic and competitive economy by the year 2010."[1] Nevertheless, the

---

[1]In March 2000 at the Lisbon European Council, the EU Heads of States and Governments agreed to make the EU "the most competitive and dynamic knowledge-driven economy by 2010" and outlined a program at the EU level to achieve this ambitious target.

Corporate and Institutional Transparency for Economic Growth in Europe

ISBN: 0-08-044665-5

Lisbon Agenda, which is a program designed to promote growth at the *EU level*, is handcuffed by the fact that the EU member states have refused to cede economic instruments (monetary policy aside) to supranational governance in the EU, while at the same time being undermined by a gaping coordination failure: member states expect to free-ride on the positive spillovers generated by growth-enhancing structural reforms carried out by their neighbours, hoping thereby to sidestep the political and short-run economic costs of domestic reform.

In light of the unfavourable progress made thus far on the Lisbon Agenda in the face of the aforementioned upcoming challenges, other avenues to help accelerate growth, however small, cannot continue to remain unexploited. This paper will concentrate on one such avenue — unlocking the growth potential of the internal market for financial services by improving the EU-wide governance of the financial sector — in a wider matrix of factors that can contribute to enhanced growth outcomes in the EU. We focus on the internal market for services because the tertiary sector[2] today accounts for the lion's share of production in the EU: 70%, compared with only 57% in 1980 (Sapir et al., 2003, p. 29). Surprisingly, however, less than 5% of production in most services sectors is exported to other EU member states (Kox, Lejour, & Montizaan, 2004). In other words, despite market integration having the potential to unleash important pro-competitive effects conducive to economic growth, this enormous potential remains totally under-exploited. Within the class of services, particular emphasis on the *financial sector* is warranted not only by the unique and vital role it plays in the economy by channelling resources to their most productive uses and by facilitating the diversification of risk, but also due to its importance in the European economy. In line with the unifying theme of the book, this paper will focus on how one of the central pillars of economic governance, namely transparency, can contribute to higher rates of economic growth in Europe by fostering better governance of the financial sector EU-wide and a smoother functioning of the internal market for financial services.

The present chapter is structured as follows. After a discussion of how improved governance of the financial sector — and the role of transparency in particular — can lead to higher economic growth, the chapter will address the following issues: the need for greater regulatory transparency in an age of global and regional integration (obviously with specific emphasis on the EU); what role transparency plays in the entirely new EU regulatory framework for financial services that began to be put into place in the year 2001; and how vertical transparency (i.e.,

[2] In the literature, the terms "primary", "secondary" and "tertiary" sectors commonly refer to agriculture, manufacturing and services, respectively. They represent the breakdown by category of economic output in the very broadest sense.

between the regulator and the regulated) and horizontal transparency (i.e., among regulatory/supervisory authorities) in the EU contribute to enhanced policy predictability, credibility and accountability and thus feed back into economic growth.

7.2 The Role of Governance in Determining Growth Outcomes

Though it may appear self-evident, the realization that the quality of the institutional climate in which markets operate is related to the efficiency of resource allocation was long taken for granted by economists. Legal and political institutions were assumed as given. In the past, the institutional environment was typically subsumed in the theoretical literature into the catch-all *ceteris paribus* conditions—and therefore not subjected to economic analysis—since economists used to believe institutions were less important for efficiency and growth than ensuring relative prices properly reflected prevailing supply and demand conditions (Rodrik, 1999). With the birth of public choice theory (Buchanan & Tullock, 1962) and its derivative, the "new institutional economics" (Williamson, 1975), economic analysis began to be applied to fields that traditionally had not been subjected to it, with a view to explaining human behaviour as a sequence of "rational choices." This school of thought seeks to explain what institutions are, how they arise, what purposes they serve and how they may be reformed (Klein, 2000, p. 456). With the emergence of these new schools of thought, the public sector, which had long been perceived as the guardian of economic stability and efficiency, gradually came to be seen—when it intervened too much in the economy—as a potential threat to the efficiency, stability and liquidity of markets, since, like the firm, it is seen to be composed of rational, utility-maximizing agents who first and foremost aim to optimize their own welfare. Only subject to this condition will public servants perhaps advance the public good, according to this theory. Though it may represent a dismal view of the human person, such a theory does have useful applications for regulatory policy. No longer was it taken for granted that the regulator would act as a "benevolent dictator," who, as an "enlightened" public servant, would seek to maximize public welfare. Rather, absent an appropriate incentive structure, the regulator, acting in his own self-interest, was likely to be "captured" by vested interests and could be led to distort economic activity (see e.g. Olson, 1965). In light of this new understanding of the role of the public sector in the economy, it was considered vital to ensure that civil servants faced an incentive structure that was compatible with the advancement of the public good. How closely the two are matched will often determine the quality of governance in a jurisdiction.

Thus, there came to be a consensus: institutions matter for economic growth (North, 1994). Indeed, there is now "widespread agreement among economists studying economic growth that institutional quality holds the key to prevailing patterns of prosperity around the world" (Rodrik, 2004, p. 1). Institutional quality is even perceived by some economists as *primus inter pares* among explanatory variables motivating long-term growth (Rodrik, Subramanian, & Trebbi, 2004). In a broad sense, "institutional quality" can be interpreted not only as the stability of the political system and the soundness of the legal framework governing the interaction between the legislative, judicial, executive branches of government and their ties with regulatory bodies, but also the manner in which these institutions interact, the quality of legislation and regulation produced (i.e., are they designed with certain key regulatory principles in mind?), and their democratic accountability. The quality of market-supporting institutions therefore depends to a critical degree on establishing appropriate incentive structures for workers in the public sector in order to ensure efficient economic outcomes — and therefore growth.

The combination of legal structures and incentive schemes that contribute to a high standard of institutional quality is more commonly referred today as "good governance." With respect to the financial sector, good governance can be thought of as a set of policies that are conducive to economic efficiency, market liquidity and financial stability, while not compromising certain key non-economic objectives of financial market regulation such as ensuring an equitable income distribution and preventing the facilitation of fraud, money laundering and terrorist financing. Often, an environment of institutional opacity breeds cronyism, wider corruption and a regulatory "leviathan" that will impede market-driven outcomes with distortive command- and control-type policies. Transparency in the work of public bodies, including financial market regulatory authorities, is therefore a crucial pillar of good governance. Theoretically, if good governance is a key determinant of economic growth — which recent theoretical and empirical literature increasingly demonstrate to be the case (see e.g. Olson, Sarna, & Swamy, 2000) — then, as a pillar of good governance, enhanced transparency in the design and implementation of regulation as well as in the exercise of regulatory discretion, must have a positive impact on growth.

Although most of the academic research on policy uncertainty and its impact on financial markets has focused on the response of asset prices and investment to (unexpected) interest rate changes or to outright regime shifts in monetary policy (Locarno & Massa, 2005), important lessons can be drawn from this literature — because it pioneered the analysis of the economic effects of policy uncertainty — which could be applied to the actions of regulatory and supervisory authorities as well. By improving the communication channels running from the

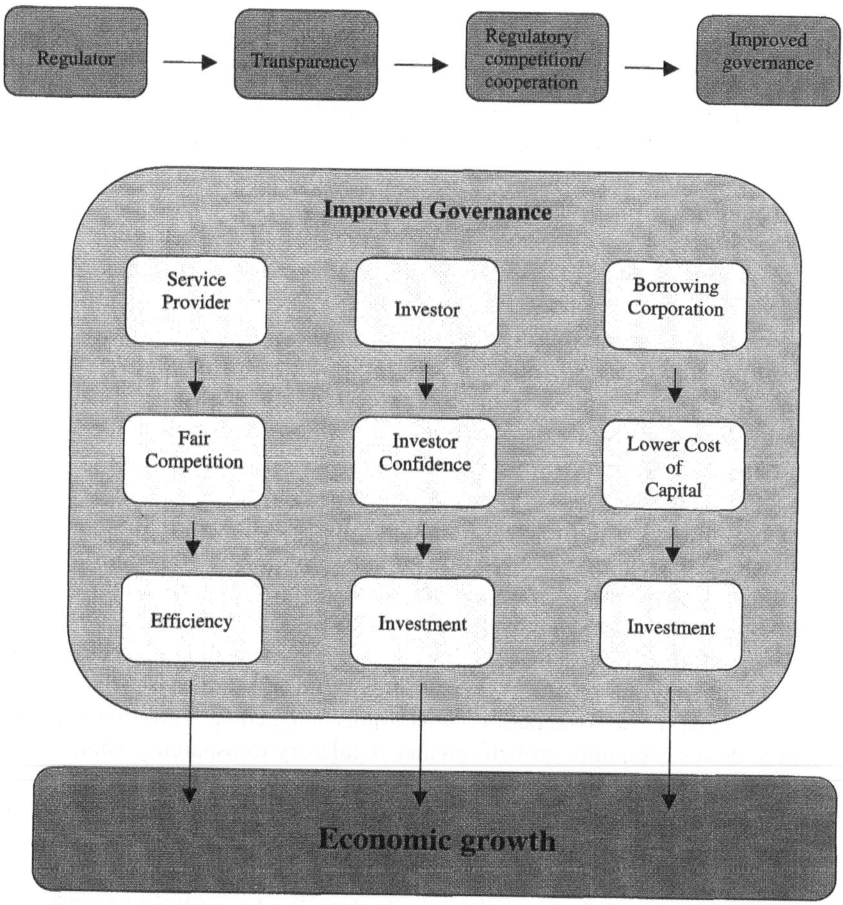

Figure 7.1: Transparency, governance and economic growth linkages.

regulator to the regulated, transparency plays an important role in policy continuity, in policy certainty and in policy credibility.

As shown in Figure 7.1, there are primarily four channels through which improved governance as a result of increased regulatory transparency can feed back into higher economic growth: a competition effect, a cost-of-capital effect, an investor confidence effect and a regulatory competition/coordination effect. Within the context of liberalized international trade, such as the EU's internal market, the *competition effect* arises from greater regulatory transparency leading to a certain levelling of the playing field of cross-border service provision (see also Chapter 3). In general, domestic incumbents enjoy significant competitive advantages over foreign competitors in their home market due to their market power and (relatively) high market share(s), better knowledge of the domestic market through their experience with fluctuations in local demand and supply conditions, their greater familiarity with local customs, traditions and legal structures. In addition, whether through ties with domestic regulators or simply through greater familiarity with the prevailing regulatory framework, domestic firms benefit from important information advantages on upcoming or existing regulation over foreign competitors. Transparency therefore contributes to market efficiency by removing various obstacles to free competition that derive from differences in access to information for foreign firms compared with rival domestic firms.

The greater the uncertainty surrounding the regulatory regime in which a firm operates, the higher the risk-adjusted discount rate a firm will use to discount the stream of future cash flows a proposed project is expected to generate (see Chapter 1). In other words, greater policy certainty yields welfare gains for society in the form of a *cost-of-capital effect*. Evidently, the higher the risk premium that is added to the risk-free discount rate, the lower the value of the expected cash flows and the greater the probability that the net present value of an investment will be negative or too low for the firm to accept it, leading to a fall in investment. Conversely, as transparency reduces regulatory uncertainty, firms are more confident about incurring large sunk costs for important long-term investments in technology and capital goods. In other words, there is a direct link between regulatory transparency and the total value of projects in which firms will decide to invest in a given period, other things being equal. Thus, to the extent investment drives economic growth, greater regulatory transparency should lead to higher growth rates.

The *investor confidence effect* derives from the notion that investor sentiment influences equity risk premia, which feeds back into the cost of capital. The so-called "equity premium puzzle" (see Mehra & Prescott, 1985) is a special case of the fact that asset prices are more volatile than can be explained by "fundamental" shocks (Evans & Kenc, 2004). In other words, investor sentiment has a non-negligible economic impact. This recognition drove the important recent research that has been produced in the field of behavioural finance (see e.g. Shiller, 2003). In a sense, the equity risk premium captures the price of uncertainty. Policy uncertainty is an important component in the wider matrix of uncertainty, which investors must try to "price" (or quantify the risk they are undertaking) if they are rational investors (see e.g. Oxelheim, 1990, 1996). For example, Evans and Kenc (2004) show that the explanatory capacity of existing models of risk premia in foreign exchange markets — found as a component of the differentials between domestic and foreign interest rates — can be significantly improved when policy uncertainty is added into the mix. As discussed in Chapter 1 an increased risk premia will deter firms from investing, since increases in the risk premium raises the cost of capital for firms, discouraging investment. On the other hand, a lower risk premia, e.g. accompanying enhanced investor confidence, will reduce the cost of capital for firms and encourage investment.

The *regulatory competition/coordination effect* derives from the realization that the degree to which regulators interact in todays environment consists of a balance of competition and coordination, or "co-opetition." In an increasingly globalized economy, the action of regulators is based upon a mixture of reactions to national preferences, regional developments and global tendencies. Which course of action national regulators decide to take for each of their functions will depend on how they balance their response to these various influences, such that social welfare in their respective jurisdictions is maximized.[3] In some cases, social welfare is improved in a dynamic of competition between regulators, such that they face pressure to maximize the efficiency of government interventions in the economy. In others, negative spillovers from outright regulatory competition could result in a dynamic that is detrimental to welfare globally.

Within certain bounds, competition between regulatory regimes can be healthy. A high degree of international cooperation between regulators replicates the dangers of excessive regulatory intervention at the national level: a (unaccountable) regulatory leviathan with monopoly authority, which does not need to pay great attention to the quality of regulation, and an opaque entity subject to capture by special interest groups. This scenario has the ability to reduce welfare by excluding some economic choices that free market competition would have enabled market participants to choose from, not to mention that excessive regulatory convergence at the international level leaves little room for innovation in securities market regulation. To begin with, a common standard or regulatory regime enjoying a monopoly does not come under pressure from competing regimes, so there is little incentive for regulators to improve their regime or to introduce better standards when they cooperate closely at the international level. In addition, there is an inherent risk in "benevolent planners" choosing what they believe to be the most appropriate market structure, because they may impose the wrong market structure and respond inadequately to changes in demand and to the introduction of new technologies, which may warrant a need to radically alter the market structure (Harris, 2003, p. 529). Recent research on securities markets

[3]This naturally assumes a "benevolent dictator" regulator as opposed to a myopic one driven only by self-interest.

in the field of law and economics has focused on optimal regulatory regimes. According to Geradin and McCahery (2003), the complexity of financial markets and the challenges governments face are such that sophisticated regulatory strategies are necessary to promote the public interest, and quite often, these will demand an optimal mix of regulatory competition and cooperation or co-opetition. Regulatory transparency can help establish this mix, since regulatory regimes are directly comparable when fully transparent. Thus, transparency in national regulatory practices within the EU can help establish more efficient rules and balance legislation that is harmonized at the EU level with a healthy degree of regulatory competition.

7.3 The Need for Regulatory Transparency in an Age of Global and Regional Integration

Spurred by large-scale cross-border capital flows, international competition leading a worldwide trend towards deregulation, and impressive rates of financial innovation, the globalization of financial markets in the past quarter century has altered the nature of their regulation and supervision, largely relegated to the discretion of national authorities prior to 1980. Such a model is no longer sustainable today, since spillovers from domestic-oriented policies have the potential to spread through financial contagion to neighbouring, and indeed far away, jurisdictions. In recent years, a series of events in the financial economy — most notably, the violent maelstrom of international financial crises that swept across the globe from Mexico to East Asia to Brazil to Russia to Turkey to Argentina — has triggered an intense debate between stakeholders worldwide, central banks, regulatory/supervisory authorities, business executives, politicians, investors and academics alike, on how to reform the international financial architecture. In the wake of these crises, these various stakeholders interested in promoting the stability and efficiency of financial intermediation agree that transparency, in its various components, is vital for the proper functioning of financial markets.

Transparency is recognized today as contributing in a crucial manner to several key objectives of financial regulation, most notably stability and efficiency. In fact, the objective of transparency had reached such high priority that it was to become the "golden rule" of the reformed, post-1997 international financial system (Camdessus, 1999). Transparency, in other words, has become the symbol of good governance in an increasingly inter-connected international financial marketplace characterized by multiple (and overlapping) levels of regulation and the necessary frequent consultations between national authorities within the context of international policy coordination. The oil greasing outputs of the international policy process actors — such as the Financial Stability Forum, CPSS, Basle Committee, IOSCO and G-10 meetings — are facilitating consensus-building through frank dialogue and comparisons of best practices between regulatory/supervisory authorities.

Parallel to the rapidly changing landscape of international finance in the past 20 years, a long-standing movement to deepen European economic integration[4] accelerated in the very same period. By the mid-1980s, several other neighbouring countries had joined the customs union established by the original six, and there was a political consensus that widening and deepening the (very fragmented) internal market prevailing in the European Economic Community was essential to restoring economic growth to Europe, which suffered for years from the undesirable mix of low growth and high unemployment, known as "eurosclerosis." The project crystallized after the 1985 publishing of the now famous White Paper,[5] which culminated in the 1992 Maastricht Treaty creating the European Union. This push towards deeper economic integration was made possible by the new legislative instrument of majority voting in the Council of Ministers (previously done through unanimity),[6] as well as by the new legal concept of mutual recognition, which was established by case law precedents of the European Court of Justice.[7] Armed with these instruments, Jacques Delors and Lord Cockfield were able to push through 282 directives and regulations in a seven-year period, in order to dismantle existing non-tariff barriers to trade in Europe. But despite the declaration at Maastricht, the creation of a Single Market in goods and services still remains an ongoing project, as even the European Commission itself recognizes: [. . .] "creating a genuinely integrated market is not a finite task, but rather an ongoing process, requiring constant effort, vigilance and up-dating" (European Commission, 2003, p. 4). This statement rings particularly true in the case of integrating services markets, which have lagged considerably behind goods markets in terms of the results

---

[4]Although the project of European integration really began with the Treaty of Paris in 1951, which instituted the European Coal and Steel Community, economic integration began in earnest with the 1957 Treaty of Rome establishing a customs union between Belgium, France, Germany, Italy, Luxembourg and the Netherlands.

[5]"Completing the Internal Market," White Paper from the Commission to the European Council (Milan, 28–29 June 1985) COM (85) 310.

[6]As a result of the 1987 Single European Act, qualified majority voting was introduced in the Council of Ministers, which greatly facilitated the ambitious legislative program to lay down common rules underpinning the operation of the single market. Unanimity voting was nevertheless preserved in several highly sensitive areas, such as taxation.

[7]Notably the 'Dassonville' (ECJ, 11 July 1974, case 11/74) and 'Cassis de Dijon' (ECJ, 20 February 1979, case 120/78) cases.

thus far achieved. Financial services (outside of the wholesale segment) are no exception.

Part of the reason financial market integration—especially in the retail segment—has not advanced as quickly as it should in the EU is that services markets liberalization was always treated as a second-class citizen behind the opening up of goods markets. Although the free movement of services was supposed to be a pillar of the internal market since the 1957 Treaty of Rome, the process of liberalizing financial services is rendered especially difficult in Europe by the large spaces carved-out from the freedom of establishment and movement principles by generous interpretations of the "general good" clause. In its role as interpreter of the Treaties, the European Court of Justice has repeatedly highlighted in case law the primacy of community law over national jurisprudence and has established the principles of free movement and freedom of establishment as overriding imperatives that cannot be undermined by national regulations. An "opt-out" clause to these principles—known as the "general good" clause—was nevertheless reserved, but was only deemed justified in cases of "imperious need."[8] What exactly the Court meant by "imperious need" was the subject of much debate, especially as there were cases where the general good clause—invoked to ensure consumer/user protection and financial stability—had been abused for protectionist purposes.

Even though the European Commission has repeatedly tried to harmonize rules across the EU for cross-border takeovers, banking consolidation across borders within the EU is a regular victim of the general good exception, the most recent example being the proposed takeover of Antonveneta by the Dutch bank ABN-AMRO, a move that was vetoed by the governor of the Italian central bank. As a result of the uncertainty surrounding the conditions under which the general good clause can be invoked, the European Commission published three non-binding (albeit influential) communications, one each for establishing a common for the treatment of "general good" questions related to banking, insurance and investment services, so as to ensure as close as possible to a uniform application of general good measures across the EU (Tison, 2000). Enhanced institutional transparency of this form has helped to increase the efficiency of financial regulation and supervision, but the non-binding nature of these communications leads one to question whether these measures are in fact adequate in the absence of clearer pronouncements by the Court of Justice to further circumscribe the concept of the general good: "legal uncertainty surrounding the

---

[8]The "imperious need" was established in the Cassis de Dijon case as the counterpart to the principle of mutual recognition, since the Court sought to mitigate the potential recriminations that would arrive from such a "liberal" interpretation of the EC Treaties and leave the door open for derogations (see Tison, 2000).

interpretation of the general good-clause in the banking and financial services directives has emerged as one of the most controversial interpretation issues in the operation of the directives" (Tison, 2000, p. 1). Legal uncertainty can only be pared down if national regulators–supervisors render their decision-making processes more transparent and they themselves are held accountable by parliamentary authorities. Recent proposed reforms following the latest Italian financial scandal go along these lines.[9]

Aside certain non-regulatory barriers to trade (such as taxation, accounting standards and legal structures) impeding full financial market integration, the completion of the single market for financial services depends to a large degree on whether political will exists within national administrations to dismantle often protectionist regulatory barriers to trade. One way to circumvent this problem is to increase transparency in supervisory practices at the national level. Nevertheless, how to overcome coordination failures remains a critical challenge: no regulatory authority would wish to be a first mover by facilitating foreign takeovers through enhanced regulatory transparency, since it could be considered politically unacceptable for corporate symbols of national pride to be taken over by foreign firms if such moves could not be counterbalanced by similar reverse scenarios. How exactly to overcome this coordination problem is a difficult question, not least because there are also questions of subsidiarity, confidentiality and other legal constraints which may limit the degree to which regulatory proceedings are rendered transparent. The objection that greater regulatory transparency would lead to unacceptable breaches of confidentiality between the regulator and the regulated is not valid as a general criticism against greater transparency *per se*, because policy certainty does not require the divulging of sensitive proprietary information: it only requires that the criteria for examining the validity of e.g. foreign takeover bids are pre-established and that a set framework exists for *ad-hoc* decisions, so as to preserve policy flexibility without resorting to opacity. Such a code of conduct for regulators would increase the accountability of regulatory authorities while enhancing policy certainty and quality.

Thus, the need for transparency in regulatory policy is all the more essential in Europe because of the unique legal framework of the European Union, in which supranational legislation is implemented by national governments and policed by

[9]For example, the Bank of Italy continues to be characterized by an archaic, opaque governance structure. The bank governor enjoys a life appointment and the Banks' shares are held by the banks it regulates (!). Three well-known Italian economists, Alberto Alesina, Guido Tabellini and Luigi Zingales recently tabled a proposal to reform the Bank of Italy by re-allocating the portfolio of competences between the Bank of Italy the Consob (Regulated markets watchdog) and the Tesoro (Ministry of Finance), increasing collegiality in decision-making processes, and fixed appointments for the central bank governor (Barber, 2005).

national courts, unless and until a clear violation of EU law is detected, in which case the European Commission would launch infringement proceedings that could end up in the European Court of Justice. Transparency in the implementation of EU laws by national legislatures as well as in the exercise of discretion by national supervisory authorities in their oversight of banks, investment firms and insurance firms, is therefore critical in such a complex regulatory–supervisory nexus that relies so heavily on decentralized implementation and enforcement. How transparent these processes are rendered will very likely affect the degree to which rules underpinning the internal market are uniform, and to what extent EU member states play by the rules.

7.4 Transparency in the New EU Financial Regulatory–Supervisory Framework

Seven years after the Treaty of Maastricht—which was supposed to have created a single market—it had become obvious to the Commission that progress made in the field of financial services integration was unacceptable. As a result, the Commission, acting in its role as "guardian of the Treaty" launched its celebrated Financial Services Action Plan (FSAP) in 1999 to give renewed impetus to the drive for deeper financial market integration within the EU. The FSAP comprised a set of some 42 directives, which sought to lay down a set of rules by which EU financial services firms could compete within a single market on an equal footing. These directives were buttressed by complementary legislative measures, such as the introduction of uniform accounting standards (mandatory application of International Financial Reporting Standards (IFRS)[10] for all listed companies across the EU since January 2005), ongoing review and reform of national bankruptcy law and initiatives to design a modern regulatory framework for company law.

The logic of the FSAP and its derivatives was simple: unless financial regulation at the national level could be (sufficiently) harmonized, it would be impossible to harness the potential benefits for capital markets promised by the introduction of a single currency. But if national regulators do not transpose EU directives into national law promptly and accurately, the FSAP will remain nothing more than a façade. Likewise for supervisors, since efficiency-enhancing cross-border mergers/takeovers of financial institutions, effective global risk monitoring, and credible crisis prevention and management cannot be expected to function well in the absence

---

[10]EU Regulation 1606/2005 sought to harmonize the accounting rules used in reporting requirements for firms listed on EU stock exchanges. IFRS rely heavily on fair value, as opposed to historical cost, accounting, which will represent a fairly dramatic step for the GAAP of some EU member states. See also Chapter 10.

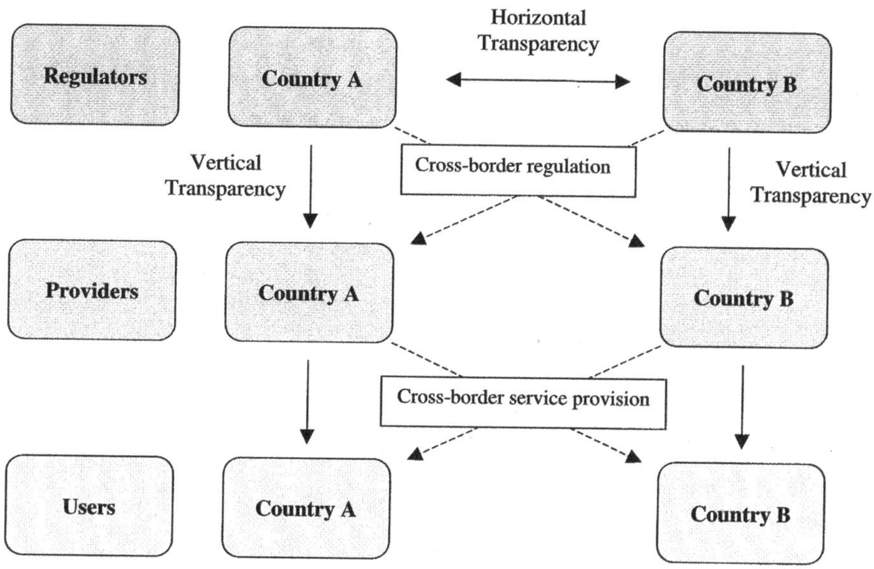

Figure 7.2: Transparency for economic efficiency and stability.

of close cooperation between member states' respective authorities on the basis of mutual trust. As the latticework which binds and strengthens ties between the various tiers of legislation/regulation/supervision in the EU's multi-institutional, multi-level governance structure, transparency is instrumental in ensuring that a coherent approach among all public sector players at various levels is achieved (*horizontal transparency*) and that sufficient account is taken of stakeholders' interests, i.e., communication channels running from regulatory authorities to the market and civil society (*vertical transparency*) — see Figure 7.2.

To complement such an ambitious legislative program as the FSAP, as well as to ensure its sound and coherent implementation on a national level, a new regulatory and supervisory framework was established along the lines of the recommendations of the Lamfalussy Committee of Wise Men,[11] because it was

[11]The French Presidency of the EU Council took the initiative to constitute a Committee of Wise Men to discuss the regulation of European securities markets, more precisely to improve the mechanisms to adapt to market changes and to come to a greater convergence in practices. On 17 July 2000, the Council of Finance Ministers of the EU (Ecofin) agreed with the mandate and composition of a group chaired by Alexandre Lamfalussy. The Group reported a few months later. Among the main recommendations were the need for framework legislation, broad implementing powers for committees, strengthened cooperation between national regulators and stronger enforcement (the "four levels," see Figure 7.2). This was endorsed by the Copenhagen European Council (March 2001).

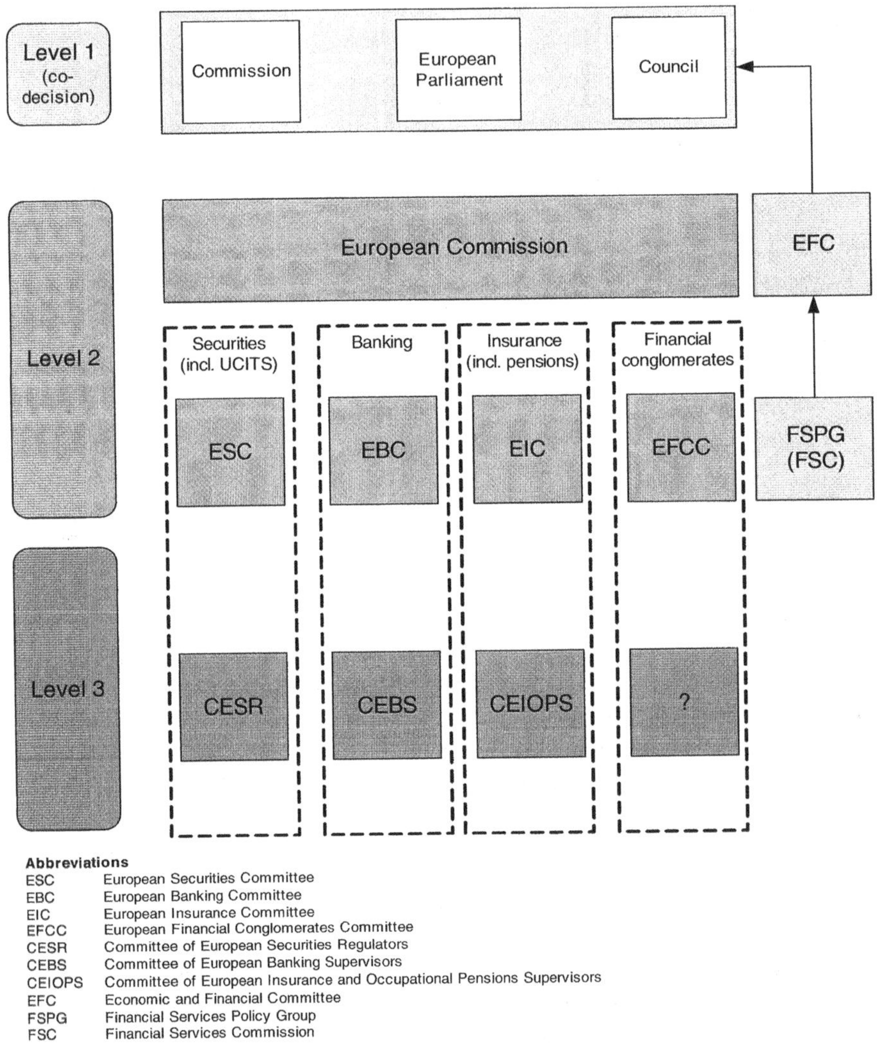

Figure 7.3: The EU's new (post-2001) financial regulatory structure.

considered that the current structures of supervisory cooperation were inadequate to deal with greater cross-border integration and conglomeration in the financial sector. The new framework was organized around four levels (Figure 7.3). Framework directives are prepared in Level 1 following the co-decision procedure, in which the Council of Ministers and European Parliament act on a proposal from the Commission. Level 2 consists in the drafting of detailed implementing measures of framework directives in Committees of experts that are chaired by the European Commission.[12] Nevertheless, member state authorities have an important — if circumscribed — role to play, as they retain their regulatory role by voting (by qualified majority) on the draft implementing measures put forward by the Commission in the Level 2 Committees (Lannoo & Casey, 2005). Level 3 was created to facilitate convergence of supervisory practices across the EU, such that consistent implementation of EU directives at the national level could be ensured. In this way, investors would be confident that investor protection standards were equivalent across the EU, and service providers would be comforted that the level playing field created by legislation actually was emerging in practice. Finally, at Level 4, the Commission enforces Community law with the various instruments at its disposal.

The new procedure, as applicable to securities markets, was rapidly extended to banking and insurance as well. In December 2002, the Ecofin Council accepted the findings of another report by the Economic and Financial Committee (EFC). In particular, the Council "reaffirmed its clear preference for implementing arrangements based upon the Lamfalussy framework to all financial sectors." The EU structure for financial sector regulation and supervision would henceforth be constituted of three separate sectoral committees, plus a fourth committee dealing with matters related to financial conglomerates; furthermore, the Council decided that EFC would remain the primary source of advice on issues related to economic and financial affairs and financial stability issues, whereas a new Financial Services Committee (FSC), replacing the Financial Services Policy Group (FSPG), would advice the Council and the Commission on financial market regulatory issues, and coordinate the work of the different Lamfalussy Committees (Lannoo & Casey, 2005). The Commission's decisions establishing the new Committees were taken in November 2003 and the directive conferring the regulatory powers to the Level 2 committees was adopted by the European Parliament in April and the EU Council in May 2004.[13] Hence, within a few years, the whole structure was re-drawn.

The fact that EU financial regulatory structures were fundamentally re-drawn in less than five years renders the need for transparency in their functioning all

[12]This process is known as "comitology" in Euro-speak.

[13]Proposal for a Directive of the European Parliament and of the Council amending Council Directives 73/239/EEC, 85/611/EEC, 91/675/EEC, 93/6/EEC and 94/19/EC and Directives 2000/12/EC, 2002/83/EC and 2002/87/EC of the European Parliament and of the Council, in order to establish a new financial services committee organizational structure.

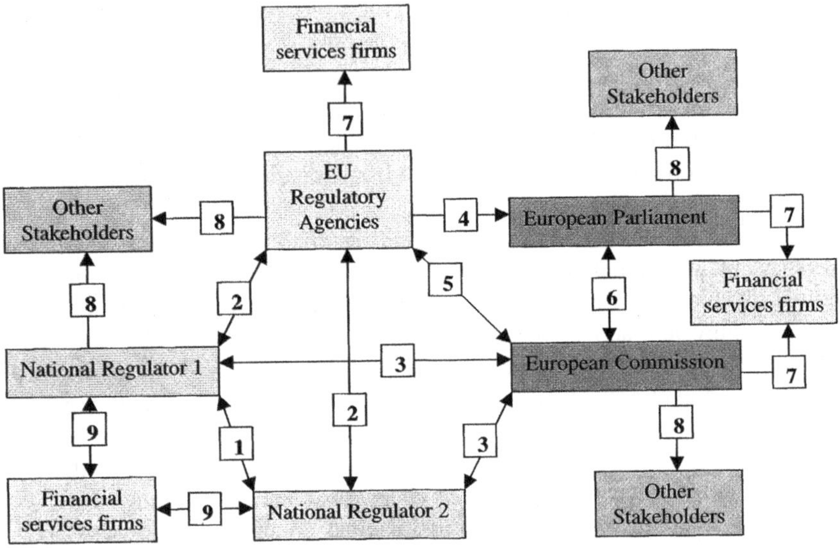

Figure 7.4: Communication linkages in EU financial services regulation.

the more pressing. The European Parliament has been a powerful advocate of transparency and accountability in the new regulatory committees.[14] Transparency is also vital due to the sheer complexity of the network of regulatory authorities. Figure 7.4 describes the communication linkages that exist between the various actors in the EU financial regulatory nexus and which necessitate transparency.

Possibly the most beneficial aspect of the new approach to financial services regulation in the EU described above is that it has significantly increased the co-operation among supervisory authorities. Not only do ministry of finance representatives have to sit together when discussing draft directives, supervisors now also meet to discuss implementing measures. Although supervisors already met before, this was largely limited to the presidents of the supervisory commissions, in the context of the pre-Lamfalussy regulatory committees. Today, also the specialists meet on a regular basis in *ad-hoc* committees dealing with specific matters. This development should certainly have a positive effect on the quality of European financial regulation and levelling the regulatory playing field. It

[14]Currently, the Parliament is locked in a power struggle with the Commission on its right to "call-back" legislation drafted in committee work, a right which it currently does not enjoy but would have had if the Constitution had been adopted.

Channels of communication

1. Between national regulators: In a single market, regulatory and supervisory authorities from different member states often need to cooperate closely; transparency is therefore of the essence in preserving systemic stability and in reducing protectionist impediments to a single market for financial services.
2. Between national regulators and EU regulatory agencies: In Level 2 of the new Lamfalussy procedure for drafting securities market (now also insurance and banking) legislation, national regulators maintain a regulatory capacity at the EU level. Coordination of Level 2 and Level 3 committee work is essential, particularly Level 3 committees' advice and input as regards to the detailed technical implementing measures drafted in Level 2.
3. Between national regulators and the European Commission: In order for the Commission to exercise its role of "guardian of the Treaties" effectively, it relies on national regulatory authorities to provide it with timely and accurate information on the state of the implementation of EU law. Likewise, it is important for the Commission to communicate clearly what it expects from the member states and which legislative measures may satisfy certain provisions in the directives.
4. From EU regulatory agencies to the European Parliament: The Parliament has recently become more assertive in its exercise of parliamentary control over powers it has delegated to the Commission (which in turn delegates it to committees of experts). Therefore, greater transparency in the "comitology" process will reduce inter-institutional conflicts that can reduce the quality of EU legislation, delay its drafting and ultimately hinder the competitiveness of EU firms.
5. Between EU regulatory agencies and the European Commission: Since the Commission chairs the technical committees in which implementing measures are decided, it is important that the two properly coordinate and agree to a common strategy. In addition to leading to a smoother operation of the technical work, transparency can help defuse conflicts, such as the ongoing power struggle between the Committee of European Securities Regulators (CESR) and the European Commission, in which CESR sees the Commission as wanting to control its agenda too closely.
6. Between the European Parliament and the Commission: In the EU, the Commission has the sole right of initiative on legislation, which it drafts before it is reviewed and voted on following the co-decision procedure in which both the European Parliament and the Council of Ministers decide on its merits. Proper communication between the Commission and the Parliament is therefore of the essence to ensure quality legislation. Particularly important is the

role of transparency in the "comitology" process whereby the Parliament and the Council delegate the drafting of technical bits of legislation to the Commission. Today, it insists on preserving its right to call back technical implementing measures drafted in Lamfalussy Level 2 committees for a second reading in the Parliament—a right it would have had if the EU Constitution had been adopted. Transparency should help defuse inter-institutional tensions.

7. Between EU Parliament/Commission/regulatory committees and financial services firms: In order for EU firms to maintain their competitiveness in global markets, it is essential that regulatory initiatives adhere to certain key principles, such as ensuring that they are based on clear evidence of market failure—or widely agreed upon societal objectives—regulatory impact analyses, and follows a *de minimis* approach.

8. From EU Parliament/Commission/regulatory committees and national regulators to other stakeholders: A perceived lack of legitimacy has given rise to a crisis of confidence in the European project, seen in the dual French and Dutch rejections of the EU Constitution in the spring of 2005. A major component of this is a fundamental lack of trust in EU institutions due to the so-called "democratic deficit," an important component of which is the notorious lack of transparency that characterizes some of the EU institutions' (often budgetary) operations. Greater transparency will help to enhance legitimacy and lend greater public support to the far-reaching legislative actions that may still be necessary to complete the single market for financial services.

9. Between national regulators and financial services firms: In the context of the EU's internal market, much of the legislation in member states concerning securities regulation and the regulation of other financial services is decided in Brussels. Nevertheless, legislation is often drafted on the basis of minimal harmonization with mutual recognition (home country control). This model allows member states to "top-up" their national regulatory frameworks with stricter standards, so long as these measures do not impede the free movement of services. But this ability in effect roughens what was supposed to be a smooth playing field. In order for domestic firms to compete effectively on the EU level, they should be aware of the rulebook in competing regulatory regimes into which they may wish to migrate. Therefore, greater regulatory transparency can underpin a healthy degree of regulatory competition and lead to greater resource efficiency.

increases the degree of regulatory harmonization and reduces the possibility for host-country restrictions. At the same time, supervisors are aware that their respective financial centres are in competition with each other and that they need to ensure that regulation is in line with market needs.

7.5 Vertical and Horizontal Transparency in EU Financial Regulation

7.5.1 Vertical Transparency

As the EEC pushed for the completion of the internal market with renewed vigor in the wake of the 1985 White Paper that preceded the Single Market Act, command- and control-type regulation was seen to give excessive discretion to national regulators, thereby effectively chocking the dynamic market forces that would make integration a reality. As a result, there was a marked shift — also propelled by global competitive forces — to a more market-oriented approach to regulation, an essential step towards creating a single market within the EEC. At the same time, the abysmal failure of the centrally planned economy, witnessed in the collapse of the Soviet Union and its communist satellites, only served to reinforce this realization. Since then, market self-determination has been recognized in the EU as a principle to which national regulators should adhere.

Yet after the initial removal of barriers on a national level as a result of the single market programme, the implementation of the FSAP measures has led a tendency towards re-regulation in the field of financial services *at the EU-level.* Evidently, a number of legislative measures were essential components of completing the internal market for financial services. But re-regulation at the European level, evidenced for example in the application of the maximum harmonization[15] principle (as opposed to minimum harmonization *cum* mutual recognition),[16] could threaten the very ability of financial services firms to compete for available

---

[15]This explanation is taken from Lannoo and Casey (2005). Under [the maximum harmonization] approach, member states cannot introduce additional requirements other than those specified in the directive. [. . .] The reliance on maximum harmonization emerged in response to the difficulties, which providers have faced with additional host country restrictions in cross-border provision of financial services in the EU. Under the minimum harmonization approach, followed in the EU's single market programme, minimum standards for free provision of services are set under EU law, and additional national rules subject to mutual recognition.

[16]In the mid-1980s, the European Commission decided to aggressively pursue market integration with a new legislative-regulatory framework called minimum harmonization with mutual recognition. Under this approach, called the "New Approach", instead of technical details being harmonized at the EU level, the simple concept of accepting the standards set by regulatory authorities in other member states was advanced. This new approach precluded the need to engage in slow, intense and highly detailed negotiations on technical standards in the Council of Ministers. Mutual recognition, as established by case law precedents of the European Court of Justice, meant that standards set in other member states had to be granted equivalence when products adhering to these standards crossed borders. In other words, home country control, as opposed to host country control, became firmly established as a key principle the European Commission would henceforth protect.

pools of capital (and service provision) in the global contest to attract foreign financial flows. For this reason, calls for focusing on market-oriented solutions such as self-regulation and market discipline, combined with an emphasis on enforcing current regulations rather than further burdening firms with additional layers of regulation, have recently multiplied.

An important manifestation of the Commission's determination to improve vertical transparency materialized in the June 2002 White Paper on Governance,[17] in which the EU Commission formally proposed an action plan for "simplifying and improving the regulatory environment." It marked a major initiative (at least in the rhetorical sense) at the EU level to reduce the burden of regulation for firms. This proposal was followed up in December 2004 by a joint statement on "Advancing regulatory reform in Europe,"[18] by a foursome group of EU Council presidencies (Ireland, Netherlands, Luxembourg and United Kingdom), which has since been extended to include two more (Austria and Finland). By establishing a common theme, the string of six rotating Council presidencies signing up to the statement (or the equivalent of three years) will ensure continuity in the impetus the Council gives to the policymaking process in Brussels.

The seriousness with which the new approach to regulation is taken is evidenced in the numerous and extended consultation processes that precede any initiative at the European level. For example, the Investment Services Directive review process has lasted for more than two years, with hundreds of responses and continued dialogue with the private sector. With the burden of proof now upon the regulator to demonstrate that the benefits of legislative initiatives outweigh the costs, regulatory impact assessments have gained a new significance in the policy process. At the end of 2005, there are some 900 pieces of legislation in the pipeline in the EU Council of Ministers and the Parliament, all of which will be subject to cost–benefit analyses.

Vertical transparency in the primary stage of EU legislation, or Lamfalussy[19] Level 1 in the case of financial services, banking, insurance and pensions legislation,

---

[17]European Governance: Better Lawmaking, COM (2002) 275 (5 June 2002) June 2002 White Paper on Governance.

[18]*Advancing regulatory reform in Europe*: A joint statement of the Irish, Dutch, Luxembourg, UK, Austrian and Finnish Presidencies of the European Union, 7 December 2004.

[19]The Lamfalussy Process was designed to enhance the speed and flexibility of the legislative process in the EU. Prior to its introduction, it would take about three years for a directive to be implemented, from the consultative stage to the transposition deadline. It breaks the legislative process down into four components: Level 1, or the framework directive, which is supposed to only include the central provisions, or objectives of the planned legislation; Level 2, or the implementation phase, in which specialized Committees draft the more technical implementing measures and are not subjected to extensive and time-consuming parliamentary scrutiny (unless the Treaty establishing a Constitution

has been extended to Level 2 implementation measures for framework legislation, where consultations with industry associations and market participants are the norm as well. In Level 3, the multi-lateral instances governing the process of convergence in financial market governance, as in the case of CESR (Committee of European Securities Regulators), CEBS (Committee of European Banking Supervisors), CEIOPS (Committee of European Insurance and Occupational Pension Supervisors), and the planned supervisory committee for financial conglomerates, are all very transparent, as their informative websites amply demonstrate.

Better communication between the Commission and member states' regulatory authorities, i.e., a form of vertical transparency (that is, from the supranational level of governance to the national level) is also vital in ensuring that the most important phase of the FSAP, Level 4, or enforcement, is effective. Certain measures have already been taken by the Commission to ensure greater transparency in the transposition process whereby member states convert EU law into national law. Thus, specialized "transposition workshops" have been organized and chaired by the Commission to ensure a uniform and proper transposition of EU directives. At the same time, the Commission resorts to the public display of transposition tables, an instrument that can be used for "naming and shaming" the laggards who fail to transpose EU law properly and in a timely fashion. These instruments, geared at increasing transparency, are all the more important as Phase I of the FSAP draws to a close. Thirty-nine out of the 42 directives originally planned have in 2005 been adopted through the co-decision procedure.[20] Although the Commission was able to achieve 93% of the legislative program before the promised mid-2004 deadline, a single market is not created from EU legislative initiatives alone. Much more important still is the ability and willingness of the Member States to implement the legislation in a timely and accurate manner and above all to enforce it. So far, the FSAP record is at best mixed, since the rate of transposition of FSAP directives as of the fall of 2005 remains pitifully low.[21] The accountability of national legislators in the EU member states would

---

for the EU is adopted, in which case the EU Parliament would win a "call-back" provision to validate the work of the technical committees); Level 3, in which national supervisors exert peer pressure on each and compare best practices too arrive at some form of convergence in practices and Level 4, the enforcement phase to ensure that indeed member states are properly implementing EU legislation. The Ecofin Council of November 2004 has since enlarged its applicability to include other financial sectors, including banking, insurance and pensions.

[20]The three remaining ones are the 3rd Capital Adequacy and 10th and 14th Company Law Directives.

[21]With a view to buttressing the Lisbon Agenda with a vibrant single market, the Commission had set a target transposition rate of 98.5%. But as of May 2005, the best performers (Austria, Denmark, Germany and Ireland) were just barely over 80%. On the other hand, the efforts of some other Member States can be characterized as none other than miserable, led by the Netherlands and Greece (just over

be enhanced through greater transparency that will incentivize them to perform better in terms of transposing EU law into national legislation.

The increased degree of vertical transparency, which today has become a *modus operandi* within the EU institutions and their offspring, will enhance the accountability of regulators, since it subjects them to the scrutiny of market participants. At the same time, transparency will enhance the credibility of regulators: the policy process will be recognized by all stakeholders as one that is participatory and visible. Confidence-building is the ultimate aim of vertical transparency. Better transparency between regulators and markets will enhance efficiency by facilitating the process of identifying market failures and finding the most appropriate policy or market (read self-regulatory) instrument for redressing them.

7.5.2 *Horizontal Transparency in the EU*

There can be no question that regulatory barriers to trade constitute the greatest impediment to the necessary rationalization of the European banking, asset management and clearing and settlement industries. In a recent paper, the European Commission has highlighted the key obstacles to the cross-border provision of financial services, following the discussion on the abuse of supervisory powers to prevent cross-border mergers that was held between European Ministers of Finance at the Scheveningen European Council (fall 2004). These include

- Opaque decision-making processes. "An institution based in another Member State might only have a partial understanding of all the parameters at stake, some of them not formalized. Such a situation might constitute a significant failure risk, as a potential bidder might not have a clear understanding of who might approve or reject a merger or acquisition proposal" (European Commission, 2005, p. 3).
- Approval process by supervisors. "The complexity of the numerous supervisory approval processes in the case of a cross-border merger can also pose a

40%). Many new member states are struggling, although one must appreciate the enormity of the task that lies before them to implement the existing acquis as well as to keep up to date on the latest FSAP measures. Some directives have been plagued with horrid transposition rates: According to the Commission transposition tables, not a single Member State notified the Commission about the Conglomerates Directive; the Accounting Provisions of Company Law and Market Abuse Directives (MAD) achieved implementation of below 5% and barely above 10%, respectively, at the time of the transposition deadline. In fact, only one country, Lithuania, had complied with the October 2004 deadline set in the MAD. The directives on winding up of credit institutions (40%) and fair value accounting fared better (just below 50%), but were still not implemented by a majority of Member States.

risk to the outcome of the transaction as some delays must be respected and adds to the overall uncertainty. In particular, in the case of a merger between two parent companies with subsidiaries in different countries, 'indirect change of control' regulations may require that all the national supervisors of all the subsidiaries must approve the merger" (European Commission, 2005, p. 7).

- Multiple reporting requirements. "In some cases, combined with a lack of transparency in terms of requirements and definitions, [multiple reporting requirements] may also impose a significant and costly administrative burden on cross-border groups. Indeed, a cross-border merger might cause heavier reporting requirements compared to those imposed on the two entities that are being merged. Instead of creating cost synergies as in a domestic merger, a cross-border might even create additional costs" (European Commission, 2005, pp. 7–8).
- Political interference. "Some Member States may promote a 'national industrial policy,' aiming at the creation of 'national champions'. Among possible justifications, some may argue that such a policy may ensure adequate financing of the national economy. Such interference might not require formal powers or rules to materialize. Indeed, as evidenced in the previous sections, there are many obstacles to overcome to carry through a cross-border merger that it is realistic to think that no cross-border merger can be achieved if there is a strong political opposition" (European Commission, 2005, p. 9).

Part of the problem arises from a fundamental lack of trust between national regulators/supervisors, wherein they do not believe their counterparts in other EU member states can guard systemic stability and ensure investor protection as effectively as they can, leading to a certain reticence to allow home country control to operate as it should. It is highly likely that a lack of proper coordination mechanisms, including regular and detailed information exchanges, is a critical feature in the culture of mistrust. As such, it should be pared down through the application of horizontal transparency. Trust-building between national regulators/supervisors, must therefore be considered the ultimate aim of horizontal transparency. The latter is a signalling mechanism whereby regulators from one member state indicate to their colleagues in other member states that they are not engaging in unfair regulatory competition, that is, harmful competition in which they pass on the negative externalities of their policies to their neighbours (such as financial instability through lax supervision of financial institutions).

Horizontal transparency is especially vital in the supervision of financial institutions with cross-border operations, and as evidenced by its inclusion in Principle 1 of the Core Principles on Effective Banking Supervision (Basle

Committee on Banking Supervision, 1997).[22] The need for transparency is pressing in the context of increased European financial market integration, which requires consistent implementation of EU legislation and optimal convergence of supervisory practices. The importance of supervisory transparency and accountability has been stressed by the Basle Committee and by the new capital adequacy directive. This will require supervisors to make disclosures that allow meaningful comparisons of supervisory rules and practices across Europe. In its consultative paper (CP05) CEBS defined supervisory transparency as a comprehensive policy of transparency. Its aims are to make information related to prudential supervision available in a timely manner to all interested parties, including credit institutions, investment firms, other market participants, other supervisors and consumers. The proposed framework is meant only to provide information. It is not meant to limit in any way the ability of individual national supervisors to act in a flexible, timely and independent manner when required. The supervisory disclosure framework has two main goals: enhancing the effectiveness of supervision and helping to promote a level-playing field throughout Europe.

It is clear that in the context of implementing Basel II in Europe, transparency is essential to more efficient and effective information exchanges in the context of the supervision of large groups established and operating in different Member States as well as to promote the comparison of regulatory/supervisory best practices. Various policy measures, such as the concept of a "lead supervisor" advocated by the European Financial Services Roundtable, can neither be efficient nor effective in the absence of horizontal transparency. Thus, horizontal transparency is an essential pillar of a sound macro-prudential framework in terms of the supervision of regulated entities as well as self-regulated organizations.

7.6 Conclusion

The simultaneity of the aforementioned tandem of paradigm shifts — one exogenous (the globalization of financial markets), the other endogenous (policy-driven EU financial integration) — has posed important new challenges for national reg-

[22]Principle 1 states that "an effective system of banking supervision will have clear responsibilities and objectives for each agency involved in the supervision of banks." This requirement is developed further in the Core Principles Methodology, the implementation guide used by the IMF and the World Bank in their joint Financial Sector Assessment Program. The Core Principles Methodology states that supervisory agencies should set out their objectives, should be subject to regular review of their performance against their responsibilities and objectives through a transparent reporting and assessment process, and should ensure that information on the financial strength and performance of the industry under their jurisdiction is publicly available.

ulators and supervisors within the EU. Whether the twin objectives of creating an operational internal market and maintaining a regulatory framework that can withstand the forces of global arbitrage are compatible remains an open question. Some believe that rigorous internal competition will be the springboard for global competitiveness. Others fear that the rules necessary to ensure the emergence of an internal-level playing field may lock up resources that EU financial services firms would otherwise have invested in the development of innovative products and processes, thereby detracting from their ability to compete in global markets. In an age where capital flows are footloose, finding the optimal policy mix that can reconcile the push for ever deeper integration within the EU with the imperative of creating a flexible regulatory architecture remains a daunting outstanding challenge for public authorities.

This chapter has argued that in the face of the twin paradigm shifts described above, regulators in the EU, whether at the national or supranational (intra-EU) levels, will have to find a middle ground between competition and cooperation, or "co-opetition." The interdependence of markets has reached a point where the need to coordinate policy responses is essential, particularly for large economic regions whose regulatory initiatives are susceptible to spillover effects that impact other regions. At the same time, a healthy degree of regulatory competition ensures that regulatory authorities act in a way that is predictable, credible, proportionate and accountable. Transparency is an essential vector of the co-opetition equilibrium, since it engenders public confidence in regulators (the vertical transparency component) and it builds trust between supervisors (the horizontal transparency component). Together, these two dimensions of transparency highlight its importance throughout the policy process.

As explained throughout this chapter, part of the reason the EU internal market for services is not functioning properly lies in the extensive regulatory barriers to trade that impede cross-border service provision and efficiency-enhancing cross-border consolidation in the form of mergers and takeovers. These barriers have amounted to an absence of a true "mutual recognition culture" (Pelkmans, 2002) and hence prevent the system of home country control from working effectively. A culture of mutual recognition will only arise in financial services if greater trust emerges between national supervisors. At the wholesale level, national protectionism often takes the guise of a prudential precautionary principle, whereas at the retail level, it is buttressed by the myth that investor protection is always better achieved by the home member state. Both forms of protectionism are choking the emergence of a truly integrated financial market. Greater regulatory transparency can vitally contribute to rectifying this situation.

Cross-border consolidation, especially in the areas of asset management, clearing and settlement and banking activities, is essential to improving the efficiency of financial services provision in Europe—and hence in driving improved growth outcomes. By underpinning the key objectives of financial regulation and supervision, namely, stability, efficiency and public confidence in markets, transparency contributes to, and improves, the quality of regulation and supervision of financial institutions. Transparency remains an indispensable facet of effective supervision in the EU pyramid of overlapping tiers of governance. In its vertical component, transparency enhances the ability of public authorities to identify market failures and to react to them in the most efficient manner, and in its horizontal component, transparency renders enhanced cooperation between regulators/supervisors more credible. As a result, market quality, the quality of bank intermediation and the quality of regulation/supervision can all improve markedly, yielding efficiency gains that translate into welfare improvements. In addition, greater transparency will enhance the legitimacy of EU institutions and regulatory agencies and therefore allow them greater flexibility as proper democratic controls are ensured.

To the extent that greater policy credibility and transparency will boost investor confidence, reduce borrowing costs for corporations and improve the efficiency of service provision, improved governance of the EU financial sector should yield a material growth increase in the EU at a time when the trinity of challenges that are ageing, global competition and the costs of enlargement are weighing down on public finances. Better governance of the EU's "single" market for financial services can only help to realize the unexploited potential of this powerful engine for economic growth.

References

"Advancing regulatory reform in Europe": A Joint Statement of the Irish, Dutch, Luxembourg, UK, Austrian and Finnish Presidencies of the European Union, 7 December 2004. http://www.hm-treasury.gov.uk/media/95A/52/6presidencies.pdf.

Barber, T. (2005). Call for ownership reforms at Bank of Italy. Financial Times, August 24.

Basle Committee on Banking Supervision. (1997). Core principles on effective banking supervision http://www.bis.org/publ/bcbs30a.pdf.

Buchanan, J. M., & Tullock, G. (1962). *The calculus of consent: Logical foundations of constitutional democracy*. Ann Arbor: University of Michigan Press.

Camdessus, M. (1999). Stable and efficient financial systems for the 21st century: A quest for transparency and standards. Address at the XXIVth annual conference of the international organization of securities commissions (IOSCO), Lisbon, Portugal, May 25.

European Commission. (2002). Governance: Better lawmaking. White Paper on Governance. COM(2002)275, June 5. http://europa.eu.int/comm/governance/white_paper/index_en.htm.

European Commission. (2003). The internal market — Ten years without frontiers. http://europa.eu.int/comm/internal_market/10years/docs/workingdoc/workingdoc_en.pdf.

European Commission. (2005). *Obstacles to cross-border mergers and acquisitions in the financial sector*. DG Internal Market and Services — April 2005 IPM Survey on Obstacles to Cross-Border Mergers and Acquisitions. http://europa.eu.int/comm/internal_market/finances/docs/cross-sector/mergers/consultation_en.pdf.

Evans, L., & Kenc, T. (2004). FOREX risk premia and policy uncertainty: A recursive utility analysis. *Journal of International Financial Markets, Institutions & Money, 14*, 1–24.

Geradin, D., & McCahery, J. (2003). Regulatory competition and regulatory co-opetition. In: J. Jordana, D. Levi-Faur, & D. Vogel (Eds), *The internationalization of regulatory reform* (pp. 296–300). London: Elgar.

Harris, L. (2003). *Trading and exchanges*. New York: Oxford University Press.

Klein, P. G. (2000). New institutional economics. In: B. Bouckeart, & G. De Geest (Eds), *Encyclopedia of law and economics* (pp. 456–489). Cheltenham, U.K.: Edward Elgar.

Kox, H., Lejour, A., & Montizaan, R. (2004). The free movement of services within the EU. CPB Document no. 69, October. http://www.cpb.nl/eng/pub/document/69/doc69.pdf.

Lannoo, K., & Casey, J. -P. (2005). *EU financial regulation and supervision beyond 2005*. Report for a CEPS task force. http://shop.ceps.be/BookDetail.php?item_id=1199.

Locarno, A., & Massa, M. (2005). Monetary policy uncertainty and the stock market. CEPR Discussion Paper DP4828.

Mehra, R., & Prescott, E. (1985). The equity premium: A puzzle. *Journal of Monetary Economics, 15*, 145–162.

North, D. (1994). Institutions matter. Washington University Working Paper. http://ideas.repec.org/p/wpa/wuwpeh/9411004.html.

Olson, M. Jr. (1965). *The logic of collective action*. Cambridge, MA: Harvard University Press.

Olson, M. Jr., Sarna, N., & Swamy, A. V. (2000). Governance and growth: A simple hypothesis explaining cross-country differences in productivity growth. *Public Choice, 102*(3–4), 341–364.

Oxelheim, L. (1990). *International financial integration*. Heidelberg: Springer.

Oxelheim, L. (1996). *Financial markets in transition – globalisation, investment and economic growth*. London: Routledge and International Thomson Press.

Pelkmans, J. (2002). Mutual recognition in goods and services: An economic perspective. Bruges European Economic Papers no. 2, College of Europe, Bruges, December.

Rodrik, D. (1999). Institutions for high-quality growth: What they are and how to acquire them. NBER Working Paper no. 7540. http://ksghome.harvard.edu/~drodrik/institutions.pdf.

Rodrik, D., Subramanian, A., & Trebbi, F. (2004). Institutions rule: The primacy of institutions over geography and integration in economic development. *Journal of Economic Growth, 9*(2), 131–165.

Rodrik, D. (2004). *Getting institutions right*. Harvard University Kennedy School of Government. http://ksghome.harvard.edu/~drodrik/ifo-institutions%20article%20_April%202004_.pdf.

Sapir, A., Aghion, P., Bertola, G., Hellwig, M., Pisani-Ferry, J., Rosati, D., Viñals, J., & Wallace, H. (2003). *An agenda for a growing Europe: Making the EU economic system deliver*. Report of an Independent High-Level Study Group established on the initiative of the President of the European Commission.

Shiller, R. (2003). From efficient market theory to behavioral finance. *Journal of Economic Perspectives*, *17*(1), 83–104.

Tison, M. (2000). Unraveling the general good exception: The case of financial services, financial law institute. In: M. Andenas, & W. -H. Roth (Eds), *Free movement of services*. Oxford: Oxford University Press.

Williamson, O. E. (1975). *Markets and hierarchies: Analysis and antitrust implications*. New York, NY: Free Press.

Chapter 8

Bank Insolvency Procedures and Market Discipline in European Banking

Apanard Angkinand and Clas Wihlborg

8.1 Introduction

The potential role of market discipline in the regulatory and supervisory framework for the financial sector has received increasing attention in recent years. While many academics have emphasized market discipline for a long time,[1] regulatory bodies until recently have viewed their own activities as substitutes for market discipline in the banking sector in particular. The Basel Committee's proposal for a new Capital Accord for Credit Institutions (Basel II) represents a deviation from this view in that it considers discipline as the Third Pillar of the Capital Adequacy Framework. Although the actual proposal does not go far, its view of market discipline as an integral aspect of the regulatory framework — and one that can be enhanced by regulatory measures — represents a break in regulatory philosophy.

Capital requirements may contribute to market discipline themselves by forcing banks to risk shareholder capital in lending activities. This disciplinary effect presumes that shareholders do not perceive themselves as implicitly protected by potential bailouts in case of bank failures.

Many academics have argued for the inclusion of mandatory subordinated debt in the capital requirements in order to strengthen market discipline *per se*,

[1]The "narrow banking" proposal (Litan, 1991; Pierce, 1991) represents one attempt to enhance market discipline for credit institutions.

Corporate and Institutional Transparency for Economic Growth in Europe

ISBN: 0-08-044665-5

and to provide information to supervisors about the financial health of banks.[2] Similarly, partial deposit insurance schemes could contribute to the awareness of the risk of bank failures. Others emphasize the role of regulation and supervision within a strong institutional environment in coping with the moral hazard induced by explicit and implicit guarantees of banks' creditors (see, for example, Demirgüç-Kunt and Huizinga, 2004).

One aspect of market discipline related to the motivation for this chapter is the issue of credibility of non-insurance of subordinated debt holders, other non-insured depositors, and shareholders. For a group of creditors to be convincingly non-insured, explicit and implicit insurance schemes for financial sector firms need to be limited, and each creditor group must know the order of priority of its claim in case of bank failure. Thus, transparency of distress resolution procedures by means of *ex ante* rules and enforcement powers is a requirement for market discipline. Without credible non-insurance stakeholders need not worry about the probability of bank failure, and banks will not compete for depositors funds by striving to be the best risk evaluators and managers.

In this chapter, we discuss bank crisis resolution procedures in Europe and test empirically the hypothesis that market discipline in Europe is enhanced by the existence of credibly non-insured creditors of banks. We argue that the credibility of non-insurance depends strongly on the degree of coverage of deposit insurance schemes, and on the existence of transparent, institutionally supported distress resolution procedures for banks, including explicit procedures for the liquidation of insolvent banks. As in Angkinand and Wihlborg (2005) we expect there to be an optimal degree of coverage of deposit insurance that maximizes market discipline and minimizes the probability of banking crisis.

The relevance of this paper within the framework for analysis of transparency set out in the introductory chapter, lies in the relation between the rules and regulation of financial institutions and the cost of capital of non-financial firms. The regulatory and legal framework for financial institutions and its transparency affect the level of, as well as the relative cost of, debt by influencing the incentives of bankers to manage and price credit risk in an efficient manner.

---

[2]The idea of using subordinated debt as an instrument of disciplining banks goes back to the 1980s, in particular to proposals made in the U.S. by the Federal Deposit Insurance Corporation (1983) and by Benston, Eisenbeis, Horvitz, Kane, and Kaufman (1986). A more recent elaboration can be found in Calomiris (1999). The idea was part of a joint statement by a subgroup of the Shadow Financial Regulatory Committees of Europe, Japan, and the U.S. (1999, 2001), a statement by the European Shadow Financial Regulatory Committee (2000), and it was a key, specific element in recent proposals from the U.S. Shadow Financial Regulatory Committee (2000, 2001).

In the following, reasons for the increasing attention to market discipline within the regulatory framework and the role of insolvency procedures are discussed in Section 8.2. We describe briefly the existing (lack of) procedures for dealing with banks in distress in the EU in Section 8.3. In Section 8.4 we develop the model to be tested and specific hypotheses. We test whether the probability of banking crisis in a country falls as the credibility of non-insurance increases. The data described in Section 8.5 cover 17 Western European countries between 1985 and 2003. In this section the proxy for credibility of non-insurance is explained. We also test whether the quality of institutions in the 17 countries affect credibility. The empirical results are discussed in Section 8.6. The relation between probability of banking crisis and explicit deposit insurance schemes is described for Western and Eastern European countries. Conclusions follow in Section 8.7.

8.2 The Role of Market Discipline and Insolvency Procedures[3]

Commercial banking has long been considered special because of a perceived high risk of market failure, and because most creditors are explicitly or implicitly insured to safeguard against losses in case banks fail. The rationale for this insurance is to be found in banks' role in the payment system and the risk of contagious bank runs. Without going into the economic validity of the risk of bank runs and contagion, it is a fact that supervisory authorities and governments in all countries offer a degree of insurance of banks' creditors. There is explicit deposit insurance in many countries, and expected bailouts imply a degree of implicit insurance. This implicit insurance may be extended to shareholders as well.

The insurance of banks' or other financial institutions' creditors implies that the latter need not monitor risks. If, in addition, the insurance is not priced, then banks have incentives to deliberately take on high risk–high return assets.[4] Furthermore, under any system wherein banks do not compete by means of risk evaluation skills there is a high likelihood that these skills will be "under-developed" since banks tend to resort to volume competition rather than quality and price competition. Thereby, the financial system as a whole may fail to take

---

[3]This section is based on Benink and Wihlborg (2002).

[4]See, for example, Dewatripont and Tirole (1994) and Freixas and Rochet (1997) for expanded treatments of the economics of bank regulation.

important risks into consideration even if bankers do not have the explicit intention to accept excessively risky assets.

Capital requirements in excess of the willingly held equity capital are intended to ensure that shareholders have a stake in all projects, and, thereby, to reduce incentives for risk-taking. The capital requirement for a particular asset determines its cost of capital for a bank. Thus, if assets with different risk–return characteristics have the same capital requirement, banks favor those assets that offer a relatively high expected rate of return. They can engage in "risk arbitrage" and choose relatively risky assets offering the highest expected return among those with a certain cost of capital. The Basel I Capital Adequacy Rules (Basel Committee on Banking Supervision, 1988) have been criticized severely for having too few asset risk classes, "risk buckets". Thereby, Basel I provides incentives for risk arbitrage.

The regulatory dilemma that the Basel Committee has had to struggle with is that if supervisors specify risk buckets that are too broad, as in Basel I, then a bank's expertise can be used for risk arbitrage, while if they specify risk buckets too narrowly, then the incentives for banks to develop expertise in risk assessment—their presumed comparative advantage—would be weakened.

The proposed solution to the regulatory dilemma of either allowing regulatory arbitrage with broad risk buckets, or removing incentives for banks to develop risk-assessment expertise, is to allow banks to use their own internal ratings as the basis for risk-weighting of assets. Basel II (Basel Committee, on Banking Supervision, 2004) allows relatively sophisticated, international banks to use internal ratings of loans as a basis for capital requirements. Any approach taken by a bank to evaluate risk must be evaluated and accepted by the bank's supervisory authority.

Opportunities for risk arbitrage may exist under an "internal ratings standard" as well, because risk weights are based on banks' private information rather than on external, verifiable variables. A major problem facing the supervisors is to check the truthfulness of even estimates of probabilities of default. Even the banks face great difficulties to translate their own ratings into probabilities of default. Both the European Commission and the Basel Committee recognize the potential scope for "gaming and manipulation" (see European Commission, 1999) within an internal ratings standard as the one proposed in Basel II.

Two "pillars" of the capital adequacy framework, supervision, and market discipline, carry the weight of having to limit excessive risk-taking and raise the consciousness and quality of risk assessment in the banking community. Under Basel II most of the burden of controlling banks' internal risk assessment procedures is placed on Pillar 2, i.e. on expanded and active supervision. Supervisory authorities are expected to build up their expertise substantially in both quantitative and qualitative terms. In fact, supervisors are expected to work closely with the banks when they develop and upgrade their internal risk-scoring models. The very close cooperation envisioned between banks and supervisors is naturally intended to reduce the information- and knowledge asymmetry between banks and supervisors. However, banks will always be able to make decisions based on private information. The intensified involvement of supervisors could instead lead to greater "regulatory capture" in the sense that supervisors identify themselves more strongly with the banks they supervise.

The implication of this discussion is that the need for market discipline as an instrument to induce banks to hold sufficient capital (in total or relatively) for their portfolios of risky assets is arguably stronger under the proposed new Basel II accord. By market discipline we mean that market participants' choices of depository institutions give banks incentives to assign capital costs to credits that reflect the banks' best evaluation of credit risk from the point of view of share- and debt holders, including depositors. To a particular cost of capital for a loan corresponds a choice of debt and equity financing, including a certain amount of equity held against a loan. If banks' creditors are insured, their choices of depository institutions will be less sensitive to perceptions about banks' risk-taking. Therefore, shareholders have an incentive to use too much low-cost debt financing to finance relatively risky loans.

Market discipline should also enhance incentives to compete by means of credit-evaluation and pricing skills. Unintended underestimation of risk seems to have been an important element of banking crises in, for example, the Scandinavian countries and Japan. Regulators have generally been unable to detect this kind of underestimation. There is obviously no guarantee that market discipline will resolve this problem; but it increases the likelihood that market participants will detect underestimation of risk, since banks' risk-taking and procedures for assessing credit come under the scrutiny of a large number of observers with stakes in the banks. Rating agencies naturally play a role as producers of information that uninsured depositors and other creditors demand.

The European Commission and the Basel Committee rely on information disclosure to enforce market discipline. However, effective market discipline requires not only that information is available to some observers, but also that the observers value the information, and are able to impose a cost on the bank that releases negative information (or abstains from releasing positive information). As long as depositors and other creditors of banks are insured, or implicitly expect to be bailed out, information about potential credit losses is not going to be a major concern to creditors. Another aspect is that the disclosed information is going to be more relevant and effective if the choice of disclosed information is based on demand for information in the market place.

By putting their faith in rules for information disclosure alone to create market discipline, the European Commission and the Basel Committee neglect that the amount and truthfulness of information available in the market place depend on incentives on the demand as well as supply side for information. Demand for information is likely to influence both the quantity and the quality of information supplied by the banks themselves, ratings agencies, and other analysts.

An indirect method for imposing market discipline is for regulators to use information in the market risk premium on an uninsured portion of the bank's debt to assess a risk-premium on claims of insured creditors. By requiring banks to issue a minimum amount of "credibly uninsured" subordinated debt, regulators may obtain not only a discipline device, but also an information device for imposing costs on banks in proportion to asset risk.[5] In principle the yield spread on subordinated debt could be used to determine a deposit insurance premium for the bank. The effective pricing of deposit insurance would essentially make capital requirements unnecessary even for banks that are "too big to fail". An alternative route for the regulator is to use the information in the yield spread to adjust capital requirements and to intervene in the activities of banks approaching distress ("prompt corrective action").

The arguments in favor of subordinated debt are based on the assumption that the subordination is credible and that the holders of subordinated debt will not be bailed out when a bank faces distress. Any other mechanism that would make banks' creditors credibly non-insured would essentially have the same disciplinary effects as subordinated debt. In the following we argue that the credibility of non-insurance of holders of subordinated debt, as well as of non-insured depositors, is enhanced substantially by the existence of well-specified, *ex ante*-determined insolvency procedures for banks. Deposit insurance, subordinated debt, and prompt corrective action procedures are aspects of insolvency procedures.

The role of insolvency procedures for financial firms is in principle the same as for non-financial firms. There are important differences between banks and non-financial firms, however. First, banks supply liquidity. A large part of the liabilities of banks are very short term and they play an important role in the payment mechanism. These liabilities may be subject to bank runs if creditors fear non-repayment. Second, a large part of the short-term liabilities are inter-bank liabilities that may contribute to contagion among banks if one bank fails. Third,

---

[5]Subordinated debt proposals were mentioned in footnote 2. Recently, the literature analyzing the proposals has been growing rapidly. Examples are Federal Reserve Board (1999, 2000), Federal Reserve Board and Department of the Treasury (2000), Calomiris (1999), Evanoff and Wall (2000, 2001), Sironi (2000a,b), and Benink and Benston (2001), and additional references below.

creditors of banks in particular are diverse and many. Thus, banks do not generally have one or a few large creditors with a strong interest in resolution of distress. For non-financial firms a large creditor (a bank) often takes the lead in restructuring distressed firms informally or formally in countries with effective restructuring laws like Chapter 11 in the USA.[6]

For the reasons mentioned, regular bankruptcy law is not often applied in cases when banks face distress. The USA and a few other countries have implemented bank-specific insolvency procedures. Most other countries simply do not allow banks to fail. Although many economists have argued that the fear of contagion of a bank failure is exaggerated, few governments are willing to test this belief.

One response to the fear of contagion is deposit insurance. The USA with its relatively complete deposit insurance coverage is actually the country that seems most likely to allow banks to fail. Partial deposit insurance schemes, as the ones mandated in the EU, provide a level of protection for small investors but they may not substantially reduce the risk of contagion. Therefore, the governments' incentives to bail out depositors, and even shareholders, remain.

The recurrence of bank failures across the world suggests that a combination of preventive and remedial measures is needed. A regulatory authority facing an actual or perceived threat to the banking system is compelled to respond in order to eliminate the risk of bank runs. The authority or its government may bail out banks fully or partially—even nationalizing the banking sector, as in Norway in the late 1980s. Other solutions include (a) debt restructuring, (b) a mix of government and more or less voluntary private assistance, and (c) the creation of specialized agencies to take over bad loans, such as the Resolution Trust Corporation in the USA.

Even though these solutions may assist in restoring a functioning market, they tend to be assembled by regulators, central banks, and governments in times of crises. Therefore, they fail to provide the sector with transparent, predictable consequences in cases of mismanagement or excessive risk-taking. When the crisis occurs the political pressures to resolve it by protecting strong interest groups are high. *Ex ante* knowledge of these political pressures lead to expectations of bailouts. Thus, generally acceptable rules for resolving banking crises must be determined *ex ante* in order to make statements about a non-bailout policy credible. Furthermore, the non-bailout policy must be politically acceptable. This acceptability can be achieved by limiting the non-insurance of creditors to a certain amount per deposit, or by limiting the non-insurance to particular groups of creditors.

[6]See Wihlborg and Gangopadhyay with Hussain (2001) for a discussion of formal and informal insolvency procedures. See also Chapter 6 in this volume.

Transparent, pre- and well-specified insolvency procedures for banks could increase the credibility of no bailout policies, enhance market discipline and thereby reduce the probability of banks facing distress, and where distress occurs, prevent one bank's failure to have contagion effects.

The European Shadow Financial Regulatory Committee (1998) proposed the following characteristics of distress resolution procedures to achieve the objectives discussed:

1. There should be pre-specified trigger capital ratios for pre-specified regulatory or legal action (prompt corrective action).
2. If a bank's capital is depleted it must be closed and liquidation promptly initiated. This trigger point may actually be set at a positive capital ratio given uncertainty about asset values.
3. Priority among creditors must be pre-specified in such a way that claims with high liquidity value are given priority.
4. Valuation procedures should be made transparent.
5. Since liquidation takes time, claims on banks with high liquidity value can remain liquid only if other banks or the central bank are organized *ex ante* to provide temporarily the liquidity held up during the liquidation process. Banks may have incentives to organize such arrangements, if clear liquidation procedures exist, but if they do not, then regulators must make sure that arrangements exist.
6. The central bank should be prepared to provide exceptional liquidity only under conditions where a bank's failure may create systemic problems. The lender of last resort function should not be extended to insolvent banks.
7. The authorities managing a crisis must be made independent of *ad hoc* political pressures in order to enhance the credibility of the intervention process.

8.3 Distress Resolution Procedures in Europe

As noted few countries have administrative or legal rules specifying procedures for resolution of distress of a bank. The USA with its high coverage deposit insurance system has been leading in the creation and implementation of pre-specified rules. The Federal Deposit Insurance Corporation Improvement Act (FDICIA) of 1991 sets trigger capital ratios for specific "prompt corrective actions" by banks and regulatory authorities. There are four trigger points at which the FDIC in particular must take action or order the bank to take certain actions. The Fed's ability to act as "Lender of Last Resort" has been strongly restricted unless there is substantial systemic risk. Questions remain, however, about the ability and willingness of the Fed and the FDIC to follow the prompt corrective action procedures if the bank in distress is considered "too big to fail".

The American procedures can be compared to Chapter 11 of the bankruptcy code for non-financial firms. This legislation is primarily aimed at restructuring rather than liquidation and the same can be said about the FDICIA. The legislation therefore has certain disadvantages in that it does not provide much guidance for liquidation of banks. Thereby, it does not provide strong incentives for private initiatives to enter contractual arrangements *ex ante* for how to resolve liquidity problems or inter-bank claim settlements. Nevertheless, it increases the credibility of both the insurance of depositors and the non-insurance of depositors beyond the pre-specified amounts.

Norway is another country with pre-specified distress resolution procedures for banks. Already before the Norwegian banking crisis there were rules for "public administration" of banks in distress. The procedures are more similar to liquidation procedures than to restructuring procedures and the distressed bank is not expected to remain under public administration for long. Perhaps because of the concentration of the Norwegian banking industry, no bank can be allowed to fail. As a result, the public administration procedures were not employed during the crisis in the late 1980s. Instead the banks were nationalized. They were re-privatized again several years later. In spite of some revisions of the procedures after the banking crisis, the spirit of the law is unchanged. From the perspective of those responsible for financial system stability the procedures should be used as little as possible. Instead, the Norwegian Financial Supervisory Authority has obtained stronger powers to intervene when a bank approaches distress. This intervention is not strongly rule based as in the USA.

The Norwegian case illustrates that it is not merely the existence of predetermined insolvency procedures that matter. The banking industry in Norway—like in many other small countries—is dominated by few banks. Therefore, each bank tends to be "too big to fail" making any crisis systemic in the eyes of authorities. If so, liquidation of a distressed bank is not a politically acceptable alternative and liquidation procedures will not be enforced. Thereby, they lose credibility.

In the vast majority of countries there are no formal distress resolution procedures for banks. Regular bankruptcy laws apply in principle on banks. In some countries insolvency law may include procedures that are particularly suitable for banks. In particular, the UK insolvency law includes a procedure called "administration" designed to enable reconstruction of a firm. An administrator can be appointed by either a group of creditors or a court to lead a distressed firm. The administration procedures are similar to Chapter 11 in several ways except that the administrator takes over management functions. In administration the firm is protected from actions by creditors, while negotiations with creditors are ongoing (see also Chapter 6 in this volume). The intention of administration is to be short lived and the administrator can enter new agreements with the purpose of avoiding liquidation.

After 1997, the British FSA has been given strong authority to issue rules for banks with the purpose of ensuring financial stability. The FSA can force a bank to enter bankruptcy or administration proceedings. It has the right to issue opinions about the result of administration proceedings. The division of responsibility between the FSA, the Bank of England, and the Ministry of Finance has been specified in a "Memorandum of Understanding". However, the distress resolution procedures for the FSA are not as clearly rule-based as in the USA.

The issue of crisis management for banks has been addressed by the EU. In particular, the coordination problem arising when an international bank faces distress has led to some activity with respect to development of principles for crisis resolution. Since most major banks within the EU have some international activity, these principles are the closest the EU comes to insolvency procedures for banks.

In a "Report on Financial Crisis Management" the Economic and Financial Committee[7] states that "there is no blueprint for crisis management" and as a general principle "private institutions should be involved as much as possible in both crisis prevention and, if this fails, in crisis management . . . If financial losses occur, the firm's shareholders should bear the costs and its management should suffer the consequences. For this reason, the winding down of the institution may be a sensible strategy." EU crisis management procedures do not become more specific than this.

The report emphasizes information sharing, coordination, and solutions on a very general level. On the issue of coordination and the assignment of responsibility for decision making with respect to crisis management the report states that "the presumption in international banking supervision is that the home country authorities are responsible for decisions on crisis management". However, "the principle of home country control is not directly applicable to foreign subsidiaries, as the host country authorities are obliged to treat these as domestic institutions with their own legal identity. In the event of a crisis at a foreign subsidiary, the host country supervisor—which is in fact the subsidiary's home country supervisor—can take any preventive measure envisaged in this context." Since most international activity takes place in subsidiaries there is very little guidance in these statements.

[7]Economic Paper No 156 (July, 2001) from The Economic and Financial Committee.

Other sections of the report refer to alternative solutions in a bank crisis. Private sector solutions are "preferred" but "liquidity support might have to be granted in order to stabilise the troubled institution or the market as a whole in order 'to buy time'. In a less volatile environment, public measures may then be considered, if the winding-down of the institution is not a viable option." Competitive implications of crisis management measures are also discussed in a separate section.

The implication for crisis management of these very general principles is that central banks, financial supervisors, and responsible ministries in home and host countries will become involved when a bank with international activities faces distress. Burden sharing easily becomes a major concern in negotiations rather than long-term consequences for incentives of stakeholders in banks. The lack of clear and transparent procedures in combination with the need to act quickly and the political incentives to protect depositor groups creates a system where the authorities are obliged to support the distressed bank.

As a country experiencing a severe banking crisis in the early 1990s, Sweden has had a debate about distress resolution procedures during the 1990s. The Swedish banking crisis was essentially resolved by the issuance of a blanket guarantee for all bank creditors. Even shareholders were indirectly bailed out by this guarantee. Before the crisis there was neither formal deposit insurance nor any bank distress resolution procedures. Depositors and other creditors were nevertheless correct in assuming that they were implicitly insured.

In 2000 a government committee proposed specific legislation for a separate insolvency law for banks, much in the spirit of the Shadow Committee proposal described above. Specifically, the proposal for "public administration" contained a mixture of the American and the Norwegian rules. Like the American FDICIA the purpose of the proposed procedures was primarily to make restructuring possible. Liquidation procedures were also clearly specified. For example, the liquidity problem was addressed directly. The proposal is "resting" after being positively received although some reservations on specifics were expressed by, for example, the Swedish FSA.

The internationalization of Swedish banks have also created a need for "Memoranda of Understanding" between Swedish and foreign authorities with respect to banking supervision. The merger of four major Nordic banks into the pan-Nordic Nordea necessitated agreements among authorities in Sweden, Denmark, Norway, and Finland. There is a Nordic Memorandum of Understanding and there is a specific Memorandum with respect to supervision of Nordea. Furthermore, the dominating ownership role of Swedish banks in Estonia has led to a Memorandum of Understanding between the Estonian and the Swedish Financial Supervisory Authorities.

The principles laid down in the Nordic memoranda are similar to and refer to the EU principles discussed above. The Swedish Estonian memorandum refer more directly to "Crisis; bankruptcy; winding-up" in the following paragraph:

> The Estonian and Swedish authorities shall inform each other, without delay, if they become aware of any pending crisis concerning particular credit institutions with cross-border establishments in the other country or if the crisis is limited to a particular cross-border establishment. Also crisis, which may indirectly affect credit institutions, shall be subject to the exchange of information. In either case, the host country authority shall collaborate with the home country authority if supervisory countermeasures are to be taken by the latter. Moreover, the host country maintains the right to apply its own procedures concerning the winding up and reorganization of cross-border establishments to cross-border establishments that are on the verge of bankruptcy.

These principles with respect to crisis management are hardly more transparent than those for the EU as a whole. If a crisis occurs, *ad hoc* solutions must be developed quickly in committees including central banks, financial supervisors, and ministries in the countries concerned.

The conclusion of this overview of insolvency procedures for banks in Europe is that transparent rules that could enhance the credibility of non-insurance of creditor groups are lacking. There is also little variation across countries. There is some variation in terms of independence of supervisory authorities and more general institutional quality reflecting, for example, the efficiency of the legal system with respect to contract enforcement. These institutional characteristics may have an impact on, for example, the degree to which "private solutions" will be sought in line with the stated principles of the EU. In the empirical section below, we ask whether institutional characteristics of EU countries affect the credibility of non-insurance of banks' creditors.

8.4 Testing for the Relationship between Credibility of Non-insurance and Market Discipline

We test the effect of the credibility of non-insurance on the market discipline in the banking sector by using a sample of 17 European countries during the period of 1985–2003. Following Angkinand and Wihlborg (2005), AW in the following,

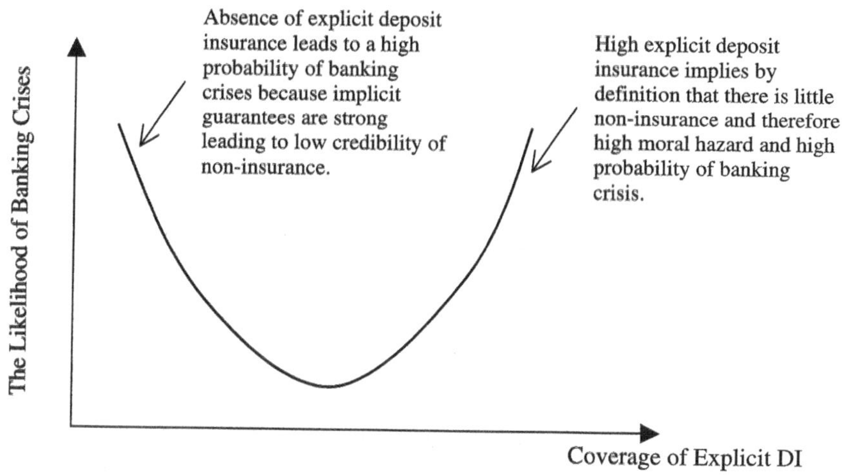

Figure 8.1: The relationship between explicit deposit insurance, credibility of non- insurance and banking crises.

we measure the extent of market discipline by using country-level data for the probability of banking crises, which is expected to be higher for a country that lacks market discipline. Lacking a direct proxy for credibility of non-insurance we argue as in the mentioned paper that there is a U-shaped relationship between credibility of non-insurance and explicit deposit insurance coverage. Thus we also expect U-shaped relationships between degree of moral hazard and explicit deposit insurance coverage, and between the probability of banking crisis and explicit deposit insurance coverage. Figure 8.1 from AW illustrates the hypothesized relationships.

The U-shaped curve in the figure can be viewed as the vertical sum of an upward sloping relation between explicit deposit insurance and moral hazard at a given level of implicit guarantees, and a downward sloping relation showing how the credibility of non-insurance declines with lower explicit coverage. Extensive non-insurance has no credibility. In other words, if explicit deposit insurance is non-existent or very low, moral hazard will be high. The reason is that the fear of contagion in a crisis, as well as considerations of consumer protection, compels authorities to intervene rapidly to guarantee depositors' funds by bailing out the bank. Thereby it can remain in operation. Shareholders may or may not be bailed out but depositors will. A common response in this situation is to issue a blanket guarantee to all creditors. On the other hand, if explicit deposit insurance is complete or nearly so, the moral hazard will be generated by the explicit insurance itself. Credible non-insurance requires partial insurance of depositors. The coverage must be high enough that the non-insurance does not have severe political ramifications and that contagious bank runs are not likely to occur.

Angkinand and Wihlborg (2005) find that the implied positive quadratic relationship between probability of banking crisis and explicit deposit insurance coverage is significant in a panel data analysis of banking crises in 140 countries, as well as subsamples, for the period of 1985–2003. In this paper we focus on 17 European countries covered by available data.

Hypothesis 1. *The probability of banking crisis (reflecting strength of moral hazard incentives) in individual European countries is minimized at an intermediate level of explicit deposit insurance coverage, where the credibility of non-insurance of some creditor groups is high.*

We have argued that insolvency procedures could enhance the credibility of non-insurance but we cannot test this proposition directly since there is no variation across the countries with respect to this variable. We will introduce other institutional characteristics that may influence the credibility of non-insurance below. In the figure, higher credibility of non-insurance at a given level of explicit coverage causes the U-shaped curve to shift down and more so for low levels of explicit coverage where the credibility is very low.

Hypothesis 2. *Institutional characteristics, such as the existence of ex ante insolvency procedures for banks, contributing to credibility of non-insurance reduces the probability of banking crisis for a given level of explicit insurance coverage, and the reduction is greater the lower the level of explicit coverage.*

There exists a substantial literature on the relationship between deposit insurance, the probability of banking crisis, and the output costs of banking crises. This literature is reviewed in AW.[8] It suffices to note that most empirical studies indicate that the probability of banking crisis is an increasing function of deposit insurance coverage. The relationship is not always significant, however. Output costs of banking crises, on the other hand, tend to be declining with higher explicit coverage but this result is controversial. The results in AW confirm that if the analysis is constrained to a linear relation between probability of banking crisis and explicit deposit insurance coverage then a positive relationship is found but if the quadratic formulation is allowed for, then the U-shaped relation is obtained.

[8]Examples are Angkinand (2005), Demirgüç-Kunt and Detragiache (1998, 2002), Demirgüç-Kunt and Kane (2002), Eichengreen and Areta (2000), Gropp and Vesala (2001), Hoggarth and Reidhill (2003), Honohan and Klingebiel (2003), Hutchison and McDill (1999), and Hoggarth, Jackson, and Nier (2005).

Angkinand (2005) analyses the impact of institutional variables such as Law and Order, Supervisory Power, and Corruption on the relationship between probability of banking crisis and deposit insurance. She finds limited but significant impact of some institutional variables. For example, corruption tends to be positively associated with banking crisis. We return to institutional variables when Hypothesis 2 is tested below.

Now, we turn to empirical methodology and data. Following AW logit regressions are estimated on the following banking crisis model:

$$L_{i,t} = \ln\left[\frac{P_{i,t}}{1-P_{i,t}}\right] = \alpha + \beta_k x_{k,i,t} + \delta_1 DI_{i,t} + \delta_2 (DI^2_{i,t}) + \varepsilon_{i,t} \quad (8.1)$$

where $P_{i,t} = prob(BC_{i,t} = 1 \mid x_{i,t},\ DI_{i,t}) = \dfrac{1}{1 + e^{-(\alpha + \beta_k x_{i,t} + \delta_1 DI_{i,t} + \delta_2 DI^2_{i,t})}}$, $BC_{i,t}$ is a banking crisis dummy variable, which takes a value of 1 in a crisis year, and 0 if there is no banking crisis. $\ln[P_{i,t}/1 - P_{i,t}]$ is the odd ratio of the logit estimation, where $P_{i,t}$ is the probability that a banking crisis occurs, or when $BC_{i,t}$ equals to 1. The subscript *i* refers to a country and *t* indicates time. To test our U-shaped relationship hypothesis, we enter the variables for explicit deposit insurance coverage (*DI*), in a banking crisis regression in a quadratic functional form. If there is evidence supporting the hypothesis of the U-shaped relationship, then the estimated coefficient of squared term (δ_2) should be positive and significant, and the estimated coefficient of linear term (δ_1) should be negative and significant.

The banking crisis dummy is obtained from the World Bank database used in most of the empirical work on the subject (see Caprio and Klingebiel, 2003). The judgment of whether a country has had a banking crisis or not a particular year is somewhat subjective. The crisis must have been serious enough to have had a potential impact on GDP but it need not have been systemic.[9] We will actually distinguish between systemic banking crises and those that were not considered systemic by the World Bank analysts.

In the equations above, *x* is a *k*-element vector of control variables; real GDP per capita, real GDP growth rate, the ratio of money supply to international reserves, the ratio of domestic credit provided by banking sector to GDP, and the ratio of current account to GDP. The current account surplus is expected to reduce the probability of crises. The ratio of M2 to foreign reserves and the growth rate of the ratio of domestic credit to GDP are expected to have a positive relationship

---

[9]The failure of one of thousands of small, US commercial banks or of a very local German Sparkasse would not constitute a banking crisis.

with the probability of crises. The increase in the money supply relative to reserves and the credit growth rate reflects the expansion of credits that may contribute to unsustainable rise in asset prices and the bank exposure to foreign exchange risk, which may increase the likelihood of financial crises.[10] ε_i is the error term.

We also test whether the credibility of non-insured deposits can be enhanced in a country with strong institutional environments including prudent financial regulation and supervision, independence of political pressure, and high quality of domestic institutions. We test this hypothesis from the following model specifications:

$$L_{i,t} = \ln\left[\frac{P_{i,t}}{1-P_{i,t}}\right] = \alpha + \beta_k x_{k,i,t} + \delta_1 DI_{i,t} + \delta_2(DI_{i,t}^2) \quad (8.2)$$
$$+ \phi(Institution \times DI_{i,t}^2) + \theta(Institution) + \varepsilon_{i,t}$$

Each regression includes the same set of control variables previously discussed, institutional variable, and the interaction term between an institutional variable and the squared term of partial deposit insurance variable.[11] The positive summation of ϕ and δ_2 indicates the U-shaped relationship between the probability of crises and the extent of deposit insurance coverage. If a strong institutional environment increases the credibility of non-insured depositors as Hypothesis 2 suggests, the expected negative impact on the probability of banking crisis should be revealed through a negative ϕ and a negative θ.

8.5 Data

Summary statistics for the non-institutional variables are presented in Table 8.1, dates of banking crises in the 17 countries are presented in Table 8.2 and characteristics of the deposit insurance systems and the financial regulatory environment are shown in Table 8.3.

8.5.1 Data on Banking Crises

The country-level data for banking crisis dates for 17 European countries between 1985 and 2003 are from Caprio and Klingebiel (2003), who compile the data based

[10] A lag of the ratio of current account to GDP and credit growth is used in the estimation.

[11] The interaction term between an institutional variable and the linear term of partial deposit insurance variable is not included, since it leads to the failure of the prediction in logit regressions.

Table 8.1: Summary statistics.

Variable	Observations	Mean	Stdandard deviation	Minimum	Maximum
Banking crisis dummy	323	0.121	0.326	0	1
Real GDP per capita[†]	306	250.852	88.882	74.713	468.949
Real GDP growth rate	306	0.027	0.022	−0.060	0.112
M2 to reserve	312	0.134	0.097	0.028	0.554
Credit growth$_{t-1}$	312	0.029	0.152	−0.544	1.537
CA to GDP$_{t-1}$	322	0.005	0.039	−0.104	0.156
Explicit DI	323	0.892	0.311	0	1
Comprehensive DI	323	1.406	0.678	0	2
Compreh. DI × Compreh. DI	323	2.433	1.639	0	4
Coverage per GDP	323	1.732	1.961	0	7.60
CovGDP × CovGDP	323	6.833	15.035	0	57.76
Coverage per deposit	323	2.667	3.363	0	11.80
CovDeposit × CovDeposit	323	18.387	41.664	0	139.24

Note: Comprehensive DI (Compreh. DI) = interbank + foreign currency + no coinsurance; Coverage per GDP (CovGDP), coverage limit-to-GDP per capita; Coverage per Deposit (CovDeposit), coverage limit-to-total deposits per GDP per capita.

[†]The unit of real GDP per capita is a hundred U.S. dollar.

Table 8.2: Dates of banking crises (1985–2003).

Country	Systemic banking crises	Non-systemic banking crises
Austria	—	—
Belgium	—	—
Denmark	—	1987–1992
Finland	1991–1994	—
France	—	1994–1995
Germany	—	—
Greece	—	1991–1995
Iceland	—	1985–1986, 1993
Ireland	—	—
Italy	—	1990–1995
Netherlands	—	—
Norway	1987–1993	—
Portugal	—	1986–1989
Spain	1985	—
Sweden	1991	—
Switzerland	—	—
U.K.	—	—

Source: Caprio and Klingebiel (2003).

on the published financial sources and interviews with experts (see Table 8.2). We use the data of banking crises, which are classified into both systemic and non-systemic (i.e. smaller or borderline) crises. A systemic banking crisis is defined as the situation when much or all of bank capital is exhausted, and a non-systemic or smaller banking crisis is identified when there is evidence of significant banking problems such as a government intervention in banks and financial institutions.

8.5.2 *Data on Partial Deposit Insurance*

Data for deposit insurance variables are from the database of Deposit Insurance around the World published by Demirgüç-Kunt and Sobaci (2000) at the World Bank.[12] We use three variables to capture the partial extent of coverage limit of

[12]The data for the ratio of coverage limit per GDP and the ratio of coverage limit to deposits are taken from Claessens, Klingebiel, and Laeven (2004), who also construct these variables based on the World Bank Deposit Insurance database.

Table 8.3: Designs of explicit deposit insurance system and characteristics of the financial regulatory environment.

	Date enacted	Foreign currency deposit	Inter-bank deposit	Co-insur-ance	Cov per GDP	Cov per deposit	Blanket guarantee	DI-funds	Prompt corrective power	Capital regu-latory index	Official super-visory power
Austria	1979	Yes	No	Yes	0.9	1.1	No	N/A	5	10	13
Belgium	1974	Yes	No	No	1	1	No	N/A	0	6	10
Denmark	1988	Yes	No	No	1.2	2.3	Yes	0.17	2	8	9
Finland	1969	Yes	No	No	1	2.1	1993–1998	0.3	1	5	6
France	1980	Yes	No	No	3.1	4.6	Yes	N/A	0	4	7
Germany	1966	Yes	No	Yes	0.9	1	Yes	N/A	0	6	9
Greece	1993	Yes	No	No	0	0	No	0.27	0	7	12
Iceland	1985	Yes	No	Yes	0.7	1.8	No	0.01	3	6	5
Ireland	1989	Yes	No	Yes	0.9	1	No	0.2	0	4	11
Italy	1987	Yes	No	No	6	11.4	1993–2001	N/A	0	5	7
Netherlands	1979	Yes	No	No	0.9	0.9	No	N/A	0	7	5
Norway	1961	Yes	No	No	7.6	11.8	Yes	2	1	N/A	9
Portugal	1992	Yes	No	Yes	0	0	No	0.3	0	7	14
Spain	1977	Yes	No	No	1.5	1.9	No	0.3	3	10	9
Sweden	1996	Yes	No	No	0	0	1992–1996	1	0	3	8
Switzerland	1984	No	No	No	0.5	0.42	No	N/A	0	N/A	14
U.K.	1982	Yes	No	Yes	1.3	1.2	No	N/A	0	6	11

Data for deposit insurance variables is from Demirgüç-Kunt & Sobaci, 2000. Cov per GDP is the ratio of coverage limit to GDP per capita; Cov per deposit is the ratio of coverage limit per deposits per capita. Data for blanket guarantee, DI-Funds (deposit insurance funds-to-total assets (%)), prompt corrective power, capital regulatory index, and official supervisory power is from the World Bank database of Financial Regulation and Supervision, compiled by Barth, et al, 2004.

deposit insurance. The first variable, called the *comprehensive deposit insurance (Comprehensive DI)*, is constructed by aggregating dummy variables of various designs of deposit insurance coverage. These dummies are the foreign currency deposits covered (which is equal to 1 for explicit deposit insurance that protects foreign currency deposits, and 0 otherwise), the interbank deposits covered (which is equal to 1 for explicit insurance that protects interbank deposits, and 0 otherwise), and the no-coinsurance dummy (which is equal to 1 if the explicit system has no coinsurance, and 0 otherwise). The second variable is *coverage per GDP* (or CovGDP), which measures the coverage limit per deposit relative to GDP per capita, and the third variable is *coverage per deposit (CovDeposit)*, which measures the coverage limit per deposit relative to total deposits per GDP per capita.[13] Table 8.3 reports deposit insurance data for 17 European countries in our sample.

8.5.3 Data for Bank Regulation and Supervision, Institutional Quality, and Political Independence Variables

We use variables to measure institutional environments from two datasets: the database of Regulation and Supervision of Banks around the World, compiled by Barth, Caprio, and Levine (2004), and the International Country Risk Guide (ICRG). These variables are separated into three groups. For each variable a higher value indicates a stronger institutional environment. The first group measures characteristics of financial regulation and supervision. Three variables are employed from Barth et al.'s dataset. These variables are *prompt corrective power (PCP)*, which indicates the existence of bank solvency trigger points for intervention and the authorities' power to intervene, *official supervisory power (Ospower)*, which measures the extent of supervisory authority power in taking actions to prevent and resolve financial problems, and *capital regulatory index (Crindex)*, which captures the extent of capital requirement stringency.[14,15] The

---

[13]For observations prior to the establishment of a formal deposit insurance system (the database of Deposit Insurance contains the dates in which a formal explicit deposit insurance system was established across countries in each country), the dummy for partial deposit insurance is assigned a value of 0, indicating the potential existence of implicit deposit guarantee.

[14]The official supervisory power variable is scaled 0–16, based on 16 surveyed questions; higher score indicates greater supervisory power. The capital regulatory index is scaled 0–9 on the basis of 9 surveyed questions.

[15]The data from Barth et al. are primarily available from 1999, so the extent of regulations and supervisions is assumed not varying overtime. Barth et al. also compile historical data for some regulation and supervision variables and find that those variables have only marginal change over time.

variables in the second group capture the extent of independence of crisis management from *ad hoc* political pressures. Two variables are *court involvement (Courtinv)* and *political independence of supervisory authority (Indpoli)*. These variables are also from Barth et al.'s dataset and shown in Table 8.3. The last group measures the quality of domestic institutions, which are *rule of law (Law)*, *corruption (Corrupt)*, and *bureaucratic quality (Bureaucracy)*. These variables are compiled by the ICRG.[16]

The data for economic and financial variables, which are controlled in the models, are from the International Financial Statistics and World Development Indicators, the World Bank.

8.6 Empirical Results for the Probability of Banking Crisis and Explicit Deposit Insurance

Table 8.4 reports regression results for the effect of explicit deposit insurance coverage on the probability of banking crises. The three variables for partiality of explicit deposit insurance, which are defined in Section 8.4, enter the regressions in both a linear and quadratic functional form. The regression in column 1 shows that the 0/1 dummy for explicit deposit insurance alone does not explain the likelihood of banking crises for the sample of European countries during the period of 1985–2003.[17] All European countries have explicit deposit insurance systems toward the end of the period but not throughout the estimation period beginning in 1985. Columns 2–7 report regression result when taking into account the cross-country difference of deposit insurance coverage. Columns 2, 4, and 6 show the results with linear specification as in most of the literature. For all proxies of coverage the coefficient for explicit coverage is positive and significant. However, when the quadratic term is introduced in columns 3, 5, and 7 the linear term becomes negative for two proxies for explicit coverage and very small and insignificant in the third case (column 7). At the same time the quadratic term enters positively in all three cases and significantly for two proxies of explicit coverage in columns 3 and 5. Thus, the hypothesized quadratic relationship is strongly supported when explicit deposit

[16]The rule of law and corruption variables are scaled 0–6. The bureaucratic quality variable is scaled 0–4.

[17]The negative sign of estimated coefficient of the explicit deposit insurance dummy is consistent with Gropp and Vesala (2001). They use the sample of European countries and find that explicit deposit insurance systems decrease banks' risk-taking incentives.

Table 8.4: Results of logit analysis of the probability of banking crisis.

	(1)	(2)	(3)	(4)	(5)	(6)	(7)
Constant	−0.170	−1.086	−0.821	−0.773	−0.090	−0.680	−0.535
	(0.878)	(1.044)	(1.024)	(0.842)	(1.033)	(0.838)	(0.996)
Real GDP per capita	−0.002	−0.002	−0.000	−0.004	−0.005	−0.005	−0.005
	(0.003)	(0.003)	(0.003)	(0.003)	(0.003)	(0.003)	(0.004)
Real GDP growth rate	−20.419**	−19.872**	−16.544*	−23.795**	−24.527**	−23.923**	−24.163**
	(8.767)	(9.003)	(10.112)	(10.262)	(10.025)	(10.267)	(10.115)
M2 to reserve	−6.434	−6.101	−5.149	−3.946	−2.502	−2.806	−2.514
	(4.292)	(4.106)	(4.112)	(3.344)	(3.562)	(3.186)	(3.271)
Credit growth$_{t-1}$	−2.338	−2.279	−1.390	−3.269*	−3.326*	−3.122*	−3.224*
	(1.548)	(1.519)	(0.999)	(1.848)	(1.907)	(1.841)	(1.885)
CA to GDP$_{t-1}$	−13.380**	−16.529**	−21.753***	−16.742**	−17.028*	−17.133**	−17.400**
	(6.645)	(6.854)	(7.378)	(6.814)	(6.794)	(6.847)	(6.809)
No. of Banks	0.002*	0.002	0.001	−0.000	−0.000	−0.002	−0.002
	(0.001)	(0.001)	(0.001)	(0.001)	(0.001)	(0.001)	(0.001)
Explicit DI	−0.331						
	(0.500)						
Comprehensive DI		0.545	−4.295***				
		(0.350)	(1.355)				

(Compreh. DI × Compreh. DI)			2.248***				
			(0.641)				
CovGDP				0.386***	−0.325		
				(0.088)	(0.438)		
(CovGDP × CovGDP)					0.093*		
					(0.055)		
CovDeposit						0.298***	0.179
						(0.057)	(0.308)
(CovDeposit × CovDeposit)							0.010
							(0.024)
No. of observations	289	289	289	289	289	289	289
% Correctly predicted	86.51	87.51	88.24	88.24	87.54	88.58	88.58
Wald Chi-square	27.14	31.22	38.73	48.47	51.80	54.82	56.45
Prob > Chi-square	0.000	0.000	0.000	0.000	0.000	0.000	0.000
Pseudo R^2	0.114	0.130	0.202	0.183	0.199	0.212	0.213
Log-likelihood	−101.281	−99.535	−91.258	−93.366	−91.596	−90.147	−90.033

*, **, *** indicate significance level of 10%, 5%, and 1%, respectively. The numbers in parentheses are robust standard errors of estimated coefficients. Subscripts $t-1$ indicate the value of variable enters regression with one year preceding crisis year, respectively.

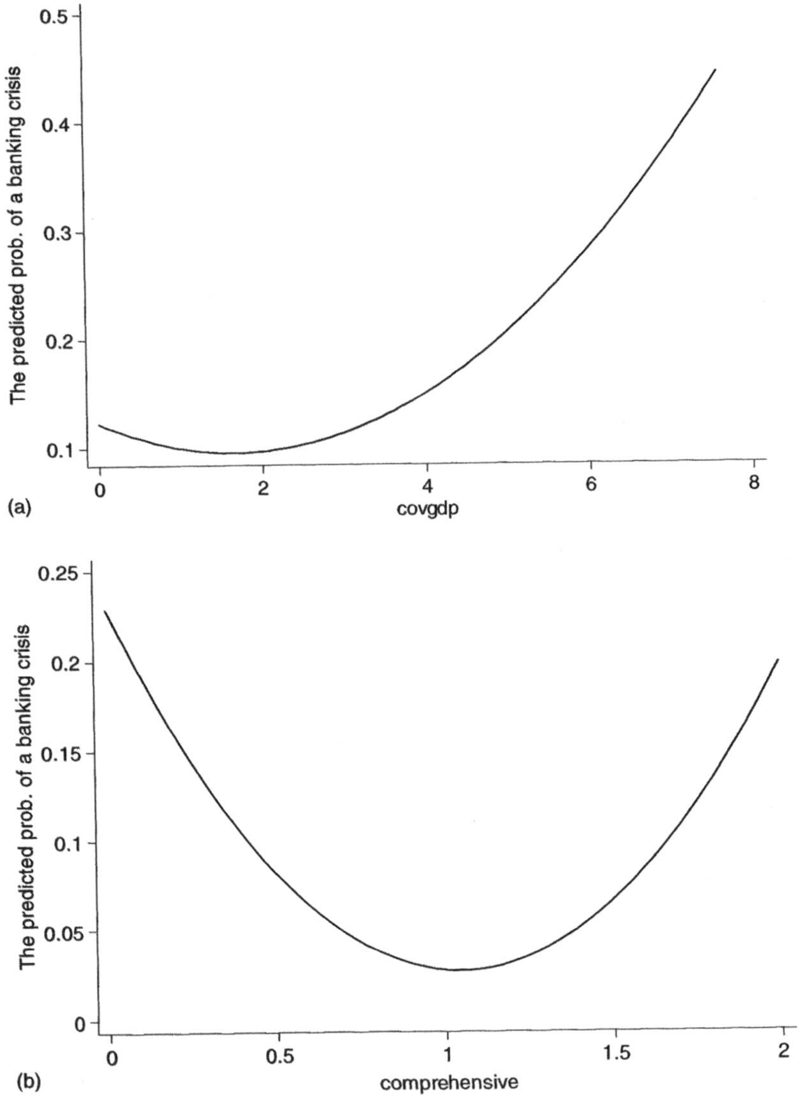

Figure 8.2: The predicted probability of banking crises and coverage of explicit deposit insurance measured as (a) coverage GDP per capita ratio and (b) comprehensiveness in terms of deposit types (range 1–4). Western European Countries (1985–2003).

insurance coverage is measured by the Comprehensive DI variable and by coverage limit per GDP per capita (*CovGDP*). When using the coverage limit per deposit (*CovDeposit*) the coefficients still imply a U-shaped curve (i.e. the linear term has a negative sign and the squared term has a positive sign), but these estimates are not significant. In addition, by looking at the goodness of fit of the models, the Wald Chi-square test points to the superiority of the quadratic estimation. For control variables, the coefficients of real GDP growth rate and the ratio of current account to GDP are negative and statistically significant suggesting that on average countries with high economic growth and a current account surplus experience lower probabilities of banking crises.

Figure 8.2 shows the U-shaped relationship for the European countries. In Figure 8.2a, the coverage limit per GDP/capita (covgdp) measures coverage of explicit insurance. In Figure 8.2b, the Comprehensive DI proxy consisting of a summation of dummy variables is used. It can be seen that the minimum probability of crisis occurs for a value of 1 for Comprehensive DI and a value slightly below 2 for covgdp. The mean Comprehensive DI-value for the countries is 1.4 as shown in Table 8.1, while the mean covgdp value is 1.74. Thus, the probability of banking crisis in Europe could be reduced by a reduction of the types of deposits covered by insurance, while the coverage limit per deposit seems close to the minimum point.

Regression results in Table 8.5 explore institutional environments that might contribute to the increasing credibility of non-insured deposits and then market discipline. Each regression includes the same economic and financial variable as those used in Table 8.4, but they are not reported. In each case explicit coverage is captured by the Comprehensive DI proxy.

Columns 1–3 focus on the regulation and supervision in the financial sector. The significant positive coefficients for PCP and Crindex alone do not support the hypothesis that stronger corrective action power and capital requirement stringency reduce the probability of banking crisis. However, the significant negative coefficients for the variables when they interact with the squared term for explicit coverage indicates that the U-shaped relationship between the probability of crisis and the coverage of explicit deposit insurance becomes flatter in countries with stronger corrective action powers and capital requirement stringency. This result is consistent with Hypothesis 2. Increased flatness can be interpreted to mean that changes in explicit coverage have less of an effect on implicit insurance and the credibility of non-insurance.

Turning to the other institutional variables we observe that higher quality of rule of law and higher quality of the bureaucracy also increase the flatness of the

Table 8.5: Results of logit analysis for explicit deposit insurance coverage and institutional variables (control variables are not reported).

	(1)	(2)	(3)	(4)	(5)	(6)	(7)	(8)
Comprehensive DI	−5.504***	−4.405**	−4.650***	−3.917***	−4.234***	−4.700***	−3.895***	−3.257**
	(1.305)	(1.753)	(1.561)	(1.254)	(1.426)	(1.410)	(1.348)	(1.405)
Comp DI-square	2.928***	2.596**	3.180***	2.252***	2.332***	2.346***	2.085**	0.730
	(0.622)	(1.289)	(0.913)	(0.589)	(0.729)	(0.943)	(0.857)	(1.101)
(PCP ×	−0.158**							
Comp DI-square)	(0.082)							
PCP	0.503***							
	(0.194)							
(Ospower ×		−0.029						
Comp DI-square)		(0.061)						
Ospower		0.122						
		(0.061)						
(Crindex ×			−0.139**					
Comp DI-square)			(0.060)					
Crindex			0.416**					
			(0.202)					
(Courtinv ×				−0.161				
Comp DI-square)				(0.236)				
Courtinv				−0.256				
				(0.887)				

(Indpoli ×					−0.278			
Comp DI-square)					(0.240)			
Indpoli					0.582			
					(0.851)			
(Law × Comp						(0.009)		
DI-square)						(0.115)		
Law						0.716*		
						0.384		
(Corrupt ×							−0.004	
Comp DI-square)							(0.146)	
Corrupt							0.579	
							(0.607)	
(Bureaucracy ×								0.306
Comp DI-square)								(0.209)
Bureaucracy								−1.187*
								(0.660)
No. of observations	289	289	253	289	289	277	277	277
% Correctly	88.58	88.58	88.54	87.54	87.89	86.28	88.09	88.09
Wald Chi-square	47.49	52.63	33.89	43.00	48.60	40.23	37.72	37.82
Prob > Chi-square	0.000	0.000	0.002	0.000	0.000	0.000	0.000	0.000
Pseudo R^2	0.211	0.204	0.196	0.214	0.208	0.213	0.201	0.211
Log-likelihood	−90.245	−90.976	−77.243	−89.835	−90.560	−88.636	−89.923	−88.803

Note: Comp DI-square = Comprehensive DI × Comprehensive DI; PCP, prompt corrective power; Crindex, capital requirement index; Ospower, official supervisory power. *, **, *** indicate the significance level of 10%, 5%, and 1% respectively. The number in parentheses are robust standard errors of estimated coefficients.

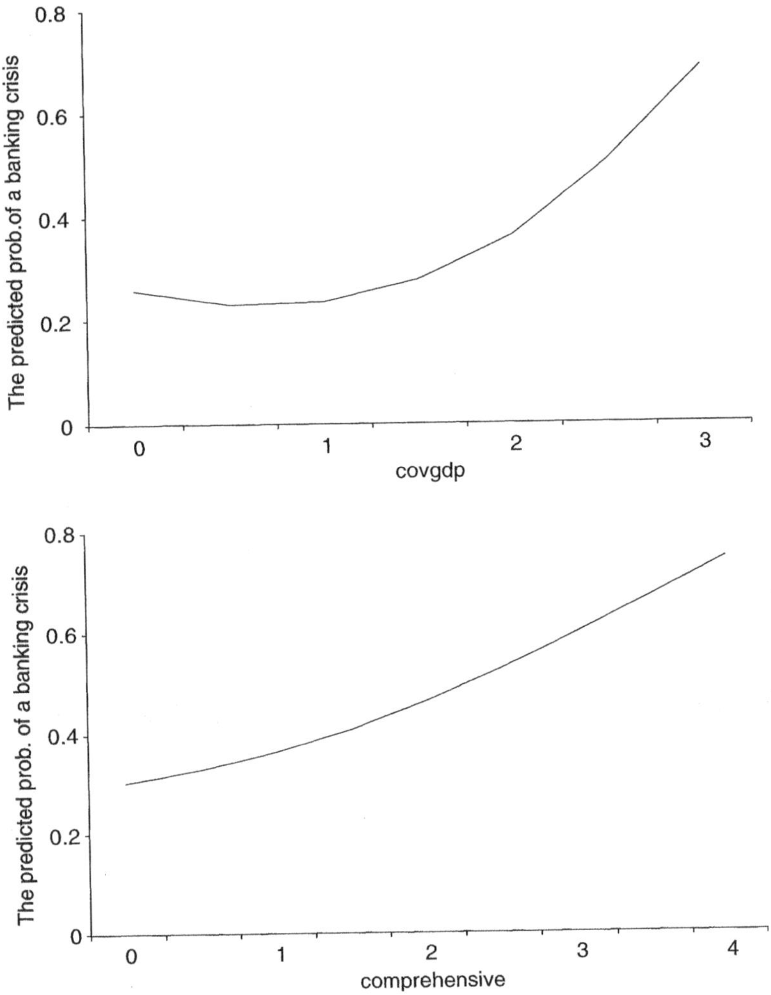

Figure 8.3: The predicted probability of banking crises and the coverage of explicit deposit insurance. Eastern European countries based on coefficient estimates for emerging market economies in Angkinand and Wihlborg (2005). *Notes*: (1) Eastern European countries include Estonia, Hungary, Lithuania, Poland, Slovakia Republic, and Slovenia. The predicted values are estimated based on a sample of 35 emerging market economies. (2) Covgdp is the ordinal data of deposit insurance coverage to GDP per capita. The value of this variable is assigned based on a value of the coverage to GDP per capita ratio, which is equal to 0 if there is no explicit deposit insurance coverage, 1 if the coverage to GDP per capita ratio is between 0 and 5, 1.5 if the coverage to GDP per capita ratio is between 5 and 10, 2 if the coverage to GDP per capita ratio is between 10 and 15, 2.5 if the coverage to GDP per capita ratio is greater than or equal to 15, 3 if there is blanket deposit guarantee. (3) Comprehensive DI variable is the summation of four dummy variables (see section 8.5.2).

quadratic relationship but these variables surprisingly shift the probability of crisis upward. The estimated coefficients for the interactive terms remain negative, although insignificant, when the squared comprehensive DI is interacted with Ospower, Courtinv, Indpoli, and Corrupt variables. These results for the institutional variables and therefore for Hypothesis 2 are not very strong. It is possible that there is not sufficient variation among the 17 European countries to identify significant effects.

All results so far refer to Western Europe since data of Eastern Europe exist only for recent years. Nevertheless, as a final exercise we want to compare the relationship between probability of banking crisis and explicit deposit insurance coverage in Western and Eastern Europe. For this purpose, we compare our results presented in Figure 8.2 with results for emerging market economies estimated in Angkinand and Wihlborg (2005). We assume that these results are valid for Eastern European countries. Then we plug in actual values for all variables except deposit insurance coverage for a group of Eastern European countries and draw the curve describing the relationship between probability of banking crisis and coverage of explicit deposit insurance for these countries. Figure 8.3 shows the emerging market relation using data for Estonia, Hungary, Lithuania, Poland, Slovakia Republic, and Slovenia.

Comparing Figures 8.2 and 8.3 it can be seen that the minimum probability of banking crisis is much lower in Western (0.03) than in Eastern Europe (0.25) as we would expect. Furthermore, the explicit deposit insurance coverage that minimizes the probability of banking crisis is lower in Eastern than in Western Europe. For the Comprehensive DI proxy based on dummies for types of depositors we actually cannot identify the minimum probability point, but for the covgdp proxy the minimum probability in Eastern Europe occurs when covgdp takes a value below 1. The corresponding minimum probability coverage in Western Europe in Figure 8.2a is close to 2.

The difference between Eastern and Western European banking systems is substantial since the Eastern European systems are still relatively immature. Also, the institutional framework is weaker. These differences explain the higher minimum probabilities in Eastern Europe. It may seem surprising, however, that the explicit deposit insurance coverage that minimizes the probability of banking crisis is lower in Eastern Europe. This observation would imply that credibility of non-insurance is obtained at a relatively low level of explicit deposit insurance coverage. In other words, lack of explicit coverage does not cause expectations of bail outs to the same degree in Eastern as in Western Europe. This difference is not explained by differences in *ex ante* distress resolution procedures but it may be explained by a greater political acceptability of losses for depositors in Eastern Europe.

8.7 Concluding Remarks

We have argued that banks' risk-taking and credit allocation can be made more efficient by means of enhanced market discipline. Strong market discipline in the banking system requires that there are groups of creditors of banks that are credibly non-insured. Such credibility requires transparent *ex ante* determined distress resolution procedures for banks and a politically acceptable level of non-insurance. An overview of distress resolution procedures for banks in Europe reveal that they are generally not rule based. Therefore, a sudden banking crisis is likely to be met with *ad hoc* measures that often include blanket guarantees of creditors or bail outs of distressed banks. We argue that the lower the coverage of explicit deposit insurance the stronger is the implicit insurance. On these grounds, we hypothesize that there is an intermediate level of explicit deposit insurance coverage that maximizes the credibility of non-insurance of groups of creditors. At this level market discipline is relatively strong, moral hazard incentives relatively weak and the probability of banking crisis relatively low. Thus, we expect a U-shaped relation between explicit deposit insurance coverage and the probability of banking crisis.

In the empirical part of the paper the U-shaped relationship is confirmed for 17 Western European countries using data for the period of 1985–2003. We take this as evidence that there is an intermediate level of explicit deposit insurance coverage that minimizes the probability of banking crisis by maximizing the credibility of non-insurance of groups of depositors and other creditors of banks.

In a comparison of Eastern and Western Europe, we found that the minimum probability of banking crisis is higher in Eastern than in Western Europe, and that the explicit deposit insurance coverage that minimizes the probability of crisis is lower in Eastern than in Western Europe.

Institutional variables describing powers of financial supervisors to take corrective action for distressed banks and powers to intervene more generally to influence banks' risk-taking, as well as variables describing the quality of legal and political institutions were introduced to test the hypothesis that the credibility of non-insurance of creditors increases with transparency of rules for supervisors and legal enforcement. The results for these variables were weak, perhaps because there is not sufficient variation in these qualities among the Western European countries, or because the number of countries included in the study is insufficient to identify influences of institutions. A few variables capturing quality of institutions were found to reduce the impact of changes in explicit deposit insurance coverage on the credibility of non-insurance. This result is consistent with our hypothesis but the same quality variables were found to increase the probability of banking crisis in contradiction to our hypothesis.

References

Angkinand, A. (2005). *Deposit insurance and financial crises: Investigation of the cost-benefit tradeoff*. Working Paper. Claremont Center for Economic Policy Studies, Claremont Graduate University.

Angkinand, A., & Wihlborg, C. (2005). *Deposit insurance coverage, credibility of non-insurance and banking crisis*. Working Paper. No. 010, Center for Law, Economics and Financial Institutions, CBS (LEFIC), Copenhagen Business School.

Barth, J. R., Caprio Jr., G., & Levine, R. (2004). Bank regulation and supervision: What works best? *Journal of Financial Intermediation, 13*, 205–248.

Basel Committee on Banking Supervision. (1988). *International convergence of capital measurement and capital standards*. Basel.

Basel Committee on Banking Supervision. (2004). *Basel II, international convergence of capital measurement and capital standards, a revised framework*. Basel.

Benink, H. A., & Benston, G. J. (2001). *The future of banking regulation in developed countries: Lessons from and for Europe*. Working Paper. Erasmus University, Rotterdam, and Emory University, Atlanta.

Benink, H., & Wihlborg, C. (2002). The new Basel capital accord; making it effective with stronger market discipline. *European Financial Management*, (March), *8*, 103–115.

Benston, G. J., Eisenbeis, R. A., Horvitz, P. M., Kane, E. J., & Kaufman, G. G. (1986). *Perspectives on safe and sound banking*. Cambridge, MA: MIT Press.

Calomiris, C. W. (1999). Building an incentive-compatible safety net. *Journal of Banking and Finance, 23*, 1499–1520.

Caprio Jr., G., & Klingebiel, D. (2003). *Episodes of systemic and borderline financial crises*. The World Bank.

Claessens, S., Klingebiel, D., & Laeven, L. (2004). *Resolving systemic crises: Policies and institutions*. Policy Research Working Paper Series 3377. The World Bank.

Demirgüç-Kunt, A., & Detragiache, E. (1998). The determinants of banking crisis in developed and developing countries. *IMF Staff Papers, 45*, 110–131.

Demirgüç-Kunt, A., & Detragiache, E. (2002). Does deposit insurance increase banking system stability? An empirical investigation. *Journal of Monetary Economics, 49*, 1373–1406.

Demirgüç-Kunt, A., & Huizinga, H. (2004). Market discipline and deposit insurance. *Journal of Monetary Economics, 51*, 375–399.

Demirgüç-Kunt, A., & Kane, E. J. (2002). Deposit insurance around the globe: Where does it work? *Journal of Economic Perspectives, 16*, 175–195.

Demirgüç-Kunt, A., & Sobaci, T. (2000). *Deposit insurance around the world: A database*. The World Bank.

Dewatripont, M., & Tirole, J. (1994). *The prudential regulation of banks*. Cambridge, MA: MIT Press.

Economic and Financial Committee of the EU. (2001). Report on financial crisis management. *Economic Papers, 156*.

Eichengreen, Barry, & Carlos Arteta (2002). Banking crisis in emerging markets: Presumptions and evidence. In: Mario, I. Blejer and Marko Skreb (Eds) *Financial policies in emerging markets*. Cambridge, MA: MIT Press.

European Commission. (1999). *A review of regulatory capital requirements for EU credit institutions and investment firms*. Brussels.

European Shadow Financial Regulatory Committee. (1998). *Resolving problem banks in Europe*. Statement No 1. London.

European Shadow Financial Regulatory Committee. (2000). *Internal ratings capital standards and subordinated debt*. Statement No. 7. Brussels.

Evanoff, D. D., & Wall, L. D. (2000). Subordinated debt and bank capital reform. In: G. G. Kaufman (Ed.), *Research in financial services: Private and public policy, 12*, 53–119.

Evanoff, D. D., & Wall, L. D. (2001). *Measures of the riskiness of banking organizations: Subordinated debt yields, risk-based capital and examination ratings*. Paper. Federal Reserve Banks of Chicago and Atlanta.

Federal Deposit Insurance Corporation. (1983). *Deposit insurance in a changing environment: A study of the current system of deposit insurance pursuant to Section 712 of the Garn-St Germain Depository Institution Act of 1982*. Washington, DC.

Federal Reserve Board. (1999). *Using subordinated debt as an instrument of market discipline*. Staff Study No. 172. Washington, DC.

Federal Reserve Board. (2000). *Improving public disclosure in banking*. Staff Study No. 173. Washington, DC.

Federal Reserve Board and Department of the Treasury. (2000). *The feasibility and desirability of mandatory subordinated debt*. Washington, DC.

Freixas, X., & Rochet, J.-C. (1997). *Microeconomics of banking*. Cambridge, MA: MIT Press.

Gropp, R., & Vesala, J. (2001). *Deposit insurance and moral hazard: Does the counterfactual matter*? European Central Bank Working Paper No. 47, March.

Hoggarth, G., Jackson, P., & Nier, E. (2005). Banking crisis and the design of safety nets. *Journal of Banking and Finance*, *29*, 143–159.

Hoggarth, G., Reidhill, J., & Sinclair, P. (2003). Resolution of banking crises: A review. *Financial Stability Review*, (December), *15*, 109–123.

Honohan, P., & Klingebiel, D. (2003). The fiscal cost implications of an accomodating approach to banking crises. *Journal of Banking and Finance*, *27*(8), 1539–1560.

Hutchison, M., & McDill, K. (1999). Are all banking crises alike? The Japanese experience in international comparison. *Journal of the Japanese and International Economies*, *13*, 155–180.

Litan, & Robert, E. (1991). *The Revolution in U.S. Finance*. Washington, D.C.: The Brooking Institution.

Pierce, J.L. (1991). *The Future of Banking*. Yale University Press, New Haven.

Shadow Financial Regulatory Committees of Europe, Japan, and the U.S. (1999). *Improving the Basel Committee's New Capital Adequacy Framework*. Joint Statement. New York.

Shadow Financial Regulatory Committees of Europe, Japan, Latin America, and the U.S. (2001). *Reforming bank capital regulation*. Joint Statement. Amsterdam.

Sironi, A. (2003). *Testing for market discipline in the European banking industry: Evidence from subordinated debt issues*. *Journal of Money, Credit, and Banking*, (June), *35*(3), 443–472.

Sironi, A. (2001). *An analysis of European banks SND issues and its implications for the design of a mandatory subordinated debt policy*. *Journal of Financial Services Research*, (Oct.–Dec.), *20*(2–3), 233–266.

U.S. Shadow Financial Regulatory Committee. (2000). *Reforming bank capital regulation*. Statement No. 160. Washington, DC.

U.S. Shadow Financial Regulatory Committee. (2001). *The Basel Committee's Revised Capital Accord Proposal*. Statement No. 169. Washington, DC.

Wihlborg, C., Gangopadhyay, S. with Hussain, Q. (2001). *Infrastructure requirements in the area of bankruptcy*. Brookings-Wharton Papers on Financial Services.

Chapter 9

Legal Determinants of the Return on Equity[1]

Davide Lombardo and Marco Pagano

9.1 Introduction

Understanding the determinants of the international cross-section of stock returns has proved a daunting task for research to date. The explanatory power of the International Capital Asset Pricing Model (ICAPM) is typically found to be quite low (see, among others, Solnik, 1977 and Ferson & Harvey, 1994). In this chapter, we ask whether a better understanding of this topic can be achieved by combining the traditional asset pricing approach with the law and finance approach — two strands of literature so far disjoint.

In principle, the law and its enforcement can affect both the demand for equity by investors and the supply of equity by companies. On the investors' side, the law (including the degree of mandated corporate transparency) affects the auditing costs incurred by shareholders to monitor management, and therefore their required return on equity. On the firms' side the law, by imposing for example stringent transparency requirements, can limit the share of corporate resources that managers can divert to their benefit: this allows firms to pledge a higher payout to investors and thereby raise more external finance, for a given set of investment opportunities.

[1]The views expressed in this article are the authors' only, and are not necessarily shared by the IMF or its Executive Board.

Corporate and Institutional Transparency for Economic Growth in Europe

ISBN: 0-08-044665-5

In addition, a well-functioning legal environment can expand the set of profitable investment opportunities, and thereby firms' desired amount of equity finance.

Through all these channels — whether on the demand or on the supply side — better legal and judicial institutions are associated with broader equity markets. This squares with the cross-country evidence by La Porta, Lopez-de-Silanes, Shleifer, and Vishny (1997, 1998) (henceforth LLSV). They document that external equity financing correlates with the degree of respect for the law, the quality of judicial enforcement and the legal protection of minority shareholders' rights. An obvious question then arises: do these differences also explain cross-country differentials in risk-adjusted expected returns? Using a simple model, we show that the answer to this question largely depends on the degree of international integration of equity markets.

In a perfectly integrated world market, the return required by investors on any country's stock market does not vary with the amount of equity issued by local companies, since that country's idiosyncratic risk is spread across the whole world's investor base. As a result, if differences in legal institutions affect only firms' *supply* of equity, they do not matter for the equilibrium rate of return, which is pinned down by a perfectly elastic demand for shares. But the law may affect also the *demand* side of the market, as investor-friendly legal institutions that protect property rights and increase corporate transparency can reduce shareholders' auditing costs, and thereby their required risk-adjusted return. Therefore, under international financial integration, the correlation between risk-adjusted returns and the quality of legal institutions should be either zero or negative.

If instead international equity markets are segmented, the relationship between risk-adjusted returns and the quality of the legal framework is more complex. In addition to the demand-side effects just described, also supply-side effects now matter for equilibrium returns. Since the risk-bearing capacity of domestic investors is limited, companies must pay a higher expected return if they want to raise more equity. Therefore, to the extent that the law affects firms' supply of equity, it will also affect equilibrium returns.

Therefore, with segmented equity markets, the correlation between the quality of the legal system and expected returns may well be positive, for two reasons. First, with stricter limits to managerial opportunism (including greater transparency requirements in corporate law and regulations) companies will be able to raise more equity. Second, fair legal rules and a trustworthy judicial system may widen the menu of enforceable contracts, increase corporate profitability and hence boost firms' equity issuance. In both cases, companies will have to offer higher expected returns, in equilibrium.

In the second part of the chapter, we bring the model to the data. Our most robust finding is that the risk-adjusted return on equity is positively associated with the efficiency of the judicial system and the rule of law, and is negatively associated with corruption of government officials. Therefore, the data reject the hypothesis that legal variables do not matter for expected returns, as well as the hypothesis that they matter mostly via demand-side effects (i.e. by affecting the rate of return required by investors). The estimated correlations are instead consistent with the joint hypothesis that equity markets are segmented and that the law affects equilibrium returns mainly via the supply of equity. Our evidence is consistent with much of the empirical literature on capital market integration (see for example Roll, 1992; Heston & Rouwenhorst, 1994 and Bekaert & Harvey, 1995). In this respect, our results suggest, for example, that as EU countries with a weaker institutional setting converge toward the EU average, their firms may be expected to pay higher returns, as their profitability and, consequently, their supply of shares increase. Moreover, as their financial markets fully integrate into the Euro area (possibly also as a result of the institutional harmonization), firms in these countries should enjoy a reduction in the cost of capital.

In the context of the basic approach of this book, this chapter studies how the system of laws and their enforcement influences the two-way relationship between domestic and foreign investors at one end and corporations at the other, with a focus on the equity market. The chapter also discusses how the legal system can affect the cost of capital for firms, and hence their real investment behavior and, ultimately, economic growth.

The analysis in this chapter contributes to the growing empirical literature on law and finance, and especially to the interpretation of the seminal work by LLSV. They interpret the positive correlation between the quality of legal institutions and the breadth of stock markets as evidence that good institutions reduce agency problems between managers and shareholders. However, our model stresses that this positive correlation may arise from several other channels, not all of which are related to the agency costs of external finance. In addition, our approach controls for risk in assessing the correlation between institutional variables and asset returns. LLSV (2002), using international company-level data, found that the cash-flow/price ratio is negatively related to shareholder rights protection, and interpret this as resulting from less severe agency problems. But their correlation could be driven by an omitted risk variable. If, for example, countries with better protection of shareholder rights are also safer investment havens for international investors, then companies in those countries will fetch higher valuation irrespective of agency problems.[2]

[2]In our data, for instance, stock market returns are negatively correlated with judicial efficiency when one does not control for risk, but the relationship becomes positive when one controls for risk.

The structure of the chapter is as follows. Section 9.2 lays out our analytical framework and the hypotheses to be tested. In Section 9.3, we present the empirical methodology and report on the results obtained with secondary market returns. In Section 9.4, we use an alternative approach, based on dividend yields as a measure of expected returns. Section 9.5 concludes.

9.2 The Model

In this section, we present a simple extension to the traditional ICAPM to illustrate the channels through which legal variables may affect the equilibrium rate of return on equity, and set out the hypothesis to be tested in the empirical analysis. Legal institutions can affect both investors' demand for equity and firms' supply of equity. An investor-friendly legal environment raises investors' appetite for equity by tempering agency problems between managers and shareholders. This can happen in two ways: by constraining managerial private benefits or by reducing the resources needed to monitor management. On the other side of the market, better law enforcement may increase companies' propensity to issue equity by lowering their cost of contracting, and thereby raising their profits. The model highlights that the equilibrium relationship between legal institutions and expected returns crucially depends on the degree of international financial integration.

Consider a world with two countries: the "home" country, populated by N_h domestic investors, and the "rest of the world", populated by N_w investors, where N_w is a large number. A fraction $1 - \lambda$ of the N_w foreign investors cannot access the home market due to transaction or information costs (see, for example, Gordon & Bovenberg, 1996). Their asset demand is subscripted by f. The remaining λN_w foreigners can access also the home equity market, and their asset demand is subscripted by g (for "global" investors). Thus, λ is an index of international integration ($\lambda = 0$ implying complete segmentation, $\lambda = 1$ full integration). Asset demands have two subscripts: the first refers to the country and the second to the investor's type (e.g., x_{hg} denotes the global investors' holdings of the home stock).

The gross return on home equity $\tilde{R}_h$ is a random variable with mean $1 + \mu_h$ and standard deviation σ_h. Symmetrically, the gross return on the world portfolio $\tilde{R}_w$ has mean $1 + \mu_w$ and standard deviation σ_w. The correlation between the two gross returns is ρ.

The return $\tilde{R}_h$ is the cash flow per dollar of initial investment in home equity, net of any private benefits taken by the company's management. We assume that this cash flow can be entirely appropriated by managers as private benefits, unless shareholders pay legal and auditing costs c per dollar invested in home market equities.[3] One can think of these costs as lawyers' and accountants' fees needed to verify the truthfulness of the company's accounts. However, payment of these fees does not fully eliminate the agency problem. Managers can still divert a fraction d of the investments' proceeds to their benefit. Therefore, the cost c merely ensures that not less than a fraction $1 - d$ of the total returns is paid to shareholders.

Since the focus of the analysis is on the home equity market, we assume that in the foreign market there are neither agency problems nor auditing costs to secure payment from managers. Both assumptions are irrelevant to our results and just simplify the notation.

9.2.1 *Investors' Portfolio Choice*

Assuming mean–variance utility, the representative j-type investor ($j \in \{h,g,f\}$) solves

$$\underset{x_{hj},\,x_{wj}}{\text{Max}}\ E(\widetilde{W}_{1j}) - \frac{b}{2}\,Var(\widetilde{W}_{1j}) - cx_{hj} \qquad (9.1)$$

where $\widetilde{W}_{1j}$ is investor j's terminal wealth, b an index for the investors' degree of risk aversion, and x_{hj} and x_{wj} are the amounts invested in the home and world market, respectively. The foreign investor with no access to the domestic market, i.e. investor f, has the additional constraint of zero home equity holdings $x_{hf} = 0$.

Combining the first-order conditions of the different types of investors, we express the home market excess return as

$$\mu_h - r = \beta_h(\mu_w - r) + c + b(\sigma_h^2 - \beta_h^2\sigma_w^2)\frac{X_h^D}{N_h + \lambda N_w} \qquad (9.2)$$

where $\beta_h \equiv \sigma_{hw}/\sigma_w^2$ and $X^D \equiv N_h x_{hh} + \lambda N_w x_{hg}$ is the total demand for home market equity (see Appendix 9.A.1 for derivations). Eq. (9.2) shows how the traditional ICAPM predictions are modified by agency problems and legal variables. In addition to the familiar reward for world covariance risk (the first term involving "beta"), the required excess return includes two additional terms: a compensation for auditing costs borne by shareholders (c), and a reward for

[3] We envision a situation in which the financial resources contributed by managers and controlling shareholders are insufficient to operate companies, so that the marginal investor is an outside shareholder.

home-country idiosyncratic risk (the last term). Therefore, the equation nests three models:

(i) The standard ICAPM, with perfect capital mobility and no role for legal variables, where these two additional terms are absent.
(ii) An "extended ICAPM", with perfectly integrated markets but differential auditing costs. In this case, the last term drops out as home-country idiosyncratic risk is fully diversified away ($\lambda = 1$), but national risk-adjusted returns differ *in equilibrium* because of differences in auditing costs c, just as they would because of different national tax rates.[4]
(iii) A segmented markets model, where the home-country risk premium is increasing in per-capita exposure to domestic equity $X_h^D/(N_h + \lambda N_w)$.

9.2.2 Supply of Equity by Companies

We assume a continuum of entrepreneurs, each endowed with an investment opportunity requiring full outside financing. The gross return per unit of physical capital invested in project j (for $j \in [1, 2, \ldots, J]$) is a random variable, with expectation $1 + \pi_j$, and variance σ^2. The cost of a unit of physical capital is standardized at 1. Each investment project j has a maximum size s. Projects are ranked according to their profitability: for $j \geq j'$, $\pi_j \leq \pi_{j'}$. For each j, there are $n(j)$ entrepreneurs with projects yielding π_j, and therefore $N(j) = \int_0^j n(s)ds$ entrepreneurs with projects yielding at most π_j. All projects are perfectly correlated, so that in the investors' eyes they are perfect substitutes, and in equilibrium must pay the same expected rate of return.

The projects' profitability is increasing in the efficiency of the legal and judiciary institutions, measured by an index ℓ. A reduction in the resources needed to enforce contracts expands the production opportunity set of companies, and thereby their profitability. Formally, we assume that $\pi_j = \pi_j(\ell)$, where π_j is increasing in ℓ.

Investors anticipate that managers will divert a fraction d of the company's cash flow, if the auditing cost c is incurred. Therefore, shareholders expect the company to distribute cash in the amount of $(1 + \pi_j)(1 - d)$ per share, and accordingly the price of a share in project j is

$$p_j = \frac{(1 + \pi_j)(1 - d)}{1 + r^e} \tag{9.3}$$

where r^e denotes the required rate of return, common across companies.[5]

---

[5]While treated parametrically by firms, the expected return r^e is a variable to be determined in equilibrium.

[4]Recall that N_w is very large relative to N_h, so that the last term tends to zero as λ goes to 1, and the demand for equity is perfectly elastic.

Profit-maximization in perfectly competitive markets and no barriers to entry requires Tobin's Q to equal 1 for the marginal company j^*

$$p_{j^*} = 1 \Leftrightarrow 1 + \pi_{j^*} = \frac{1 + r^e}{(1 - d)} \tag{9.4}$$

Eq. (9.4) implicitly defines the cost of equity capital, π_{j^*}. The aggregate supply of equity (X_h^S) is decreasing in the cost of capital π_{j^*} and therefore in the required return r^e:[6]

$$X_h^S = \int_0^{j^*} sp_j \, dN(j) \tag{9.5}$$

The equilibrium rate of return and quantity are determined by the intersection of the demand schedule in Eq. (9.2) and the supply schedule in Eq. (9.5), i.e. by the condition that $X_h^D = X_h^S$. This amounts to equating the rate of return r^e anticipated by entrepreneurs with the expected rate of return required by investors, μ_h.

An important insight of the model is that, with agency costs, the return paid to shareholders falls short of the return on firms' investments (the cost of equity capital). Rewriting Eq. (9.4) as

$$r^e = \pi_{j^*} - d(1+\pi_{j^*})$$

we see that agency costs operate just like a tax, driving a wedge between the two. As a result, their equilibrium values can move in opposite directions following an institutional change.

9.2.3 Effects of the Legal System

The legal system of the home market can affect the equity market in three different ways. First, the legal environment determines the auditing costs that shareholders must incur to secure any payment from managers. For example, greater transparency and better accounting standards lower the cost of monitoring the company's performance, by reducing the need for expert advice by accountants, lawyers and financial analysts. Similarly, the availability of class action suits and the possibility of voting by mail reduce the costs of shareholder

[6] The aggregate supply of equity, X_h^S, is decreasing in r^e for two reasons. First, the price of each share is decreasing in the required rate of return r^e, from Eq. (9.3). Second, the upper integration limit j^* in Eq. (9.5) is itself decreasing in r^e, from Eq. (9.4): as the required rate of return increases, the profitability of the marginal project must increase, so that fewer projects can be financed.

activism. In our model, a reduction in auditing costs is captured by a lower value of the parameter c.

Second, the law may constrain the fraction of corporate profits that managers are able to divert, i.e. the parameter d. For instance, more stringent transparency requirements and legal limits to managerial discretion concerning asset sales or merger agreements may curtail the scope for dilution of shareholders' income rights.

Finally, apart from its effects on the agency problem between managers and shareholders, better law enforcement may benefit companies by reducing the cost of enforcing contracts with customers and suppliers, thus raising corporate profits. Our model captures this by an increase in the index of legal and judicial efficiency ℓ, which raises the marginal productivity of capital and therefore equity issuance by firms.

The three effects are illustrated graphically in Figures 9.1–9.3. In each figure, the top panel portrays the case of international integration: the required excess return on equity is a horizontal line, whose height reflects only covariance risk and the cost of auditing management. The bottom panel, instead, refers to segmented equity markets: the excess return on equity is upward sloping, because it also includes the home-country risk premium.

In all three figures, the maximum return on investment that companies can pay for each possible level of equity funding is a downward sloping line, reflecting the decreasing marginal productivity of capital: we label it the "cost-of-capital" schedule. To the extent that managers extract private benefits, however, companies pay out only a fraction of their profits to shareholders. Therefore, the "net return paid by firms" schedule lies below the cost-of-capital schedule. The vertical distance between the two is d, the private benefits per dollar invested.

Equilibrium occurs where the excess return required by shareholders equals the net return paid out by companies, as in point A. The corresponding cost of capital to the company (point B) determines the capital budgeting decisions of its management. Notice that, while we can hope to infer the equilibrium return on equity from stock-market data, the corresponding value of the cost of capital is unobservable.

Figure 9.1 shows how cross-country differences in the auditing costs c borne by shareholders affect the equilibrium. In countries where, possibly as a result of greater corporate and policy transparency, they pay lower auditing costs to monitor management, investors require a lower return. In these countries, the equilibrium is at a point like C, whereas it is at a point like A if auditing costs are higher. In countries where auditing is more cost effective, the equilibrium rate of return is correspondingly lower, the cost of capital is lower and the quantity of external equity is larger. As the two panels show, the qualitative effects of different auditing costs do not depend on the degree of international integration.

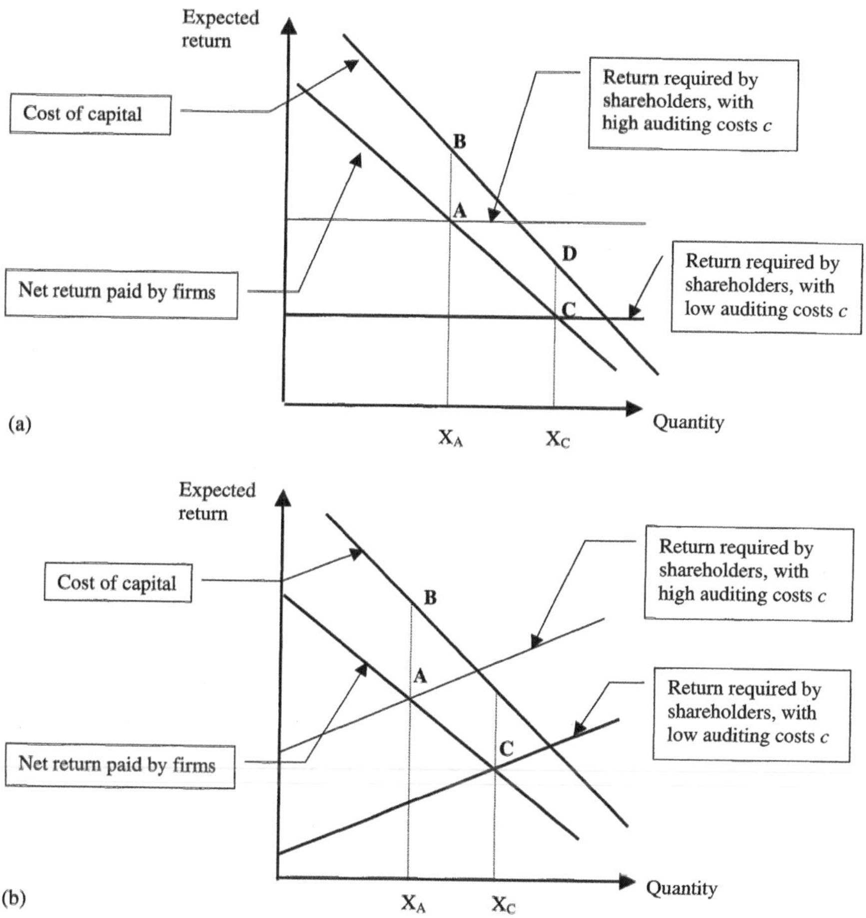

Figure 9.1: Differences in auditing costs under (a) international integration and (b) international segmentation. *Note*: The figure shows the effects of cross-country differences in auditing costs c with integrated equity markets (Panel A) and with segmented equity markets (Panel B). In both panels, points A and C represent the equilibrium in countries with high and low auditing costs, respectively. The figure shows that the cross-country correlation between auditing costs and equity returns is positive, irrespective of the degree of financial integration.

Figure 9.2 illustrates how the equilibrium is affected by the ability of the legal system to constrain managerial private benefits. For a given level of auditing costs, countries with lower private benefits (lower d) feature a smaller wedge

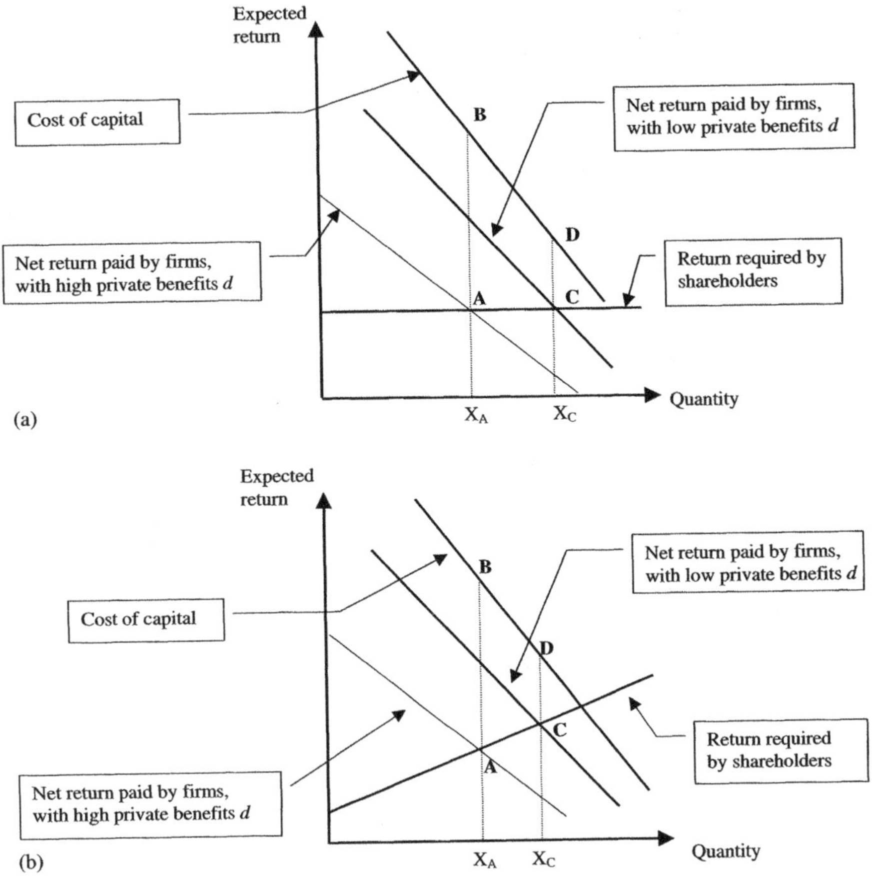

(a) (b)

Figure 9.2: Differences in private benefits with (a) integrated markets and (b) segmented markets. *Note*: The figure shows the effects of cross-country differences in private benefits *d* with integrated equity markets (Panel A) and with segmented equity markets (Panel B). In both panels, points A and C represent the equilibrium in countries with low and high private benefits, respectively. The figure shows that the cross-country correlation between private benefits and returns to shareholders is zero with integrated markets, and negative with segmented markets.

between the cost of capital and the return paid to shareholders. In low-private-benefit countries, the equilibrium is at a point like C instead of A. Under financial integration (Panel A), differences in private benefits have no effects on the risk-adjusted rate of return earned by investors. If markets are segmented (Panel B), countries with high shareholder protection feature a higher return on equity (point A) than low-protection ones (point C). Intuitively, in low-private-benefit countries companies issue more equity; therefore, the equilibrium amount of country risk to be borne is larger.

Irrespective of the degree of financial integration, a lower d results in a higher amount of equity (X_C instead of X_A). It also results in a lower cost of capital (point D instead of B), highlighting that cross-country differences in shareholder protection can produce qualitatively different (even opposite) effects on the required return on equity and on the cost of capital.

Finally, Figure 9.3 depicts the effects of differences in the degree of judicial efficiency. Other things equal, in countries where contract enforcement is more effective the return on investment is larger. Companies can then afford to pay a higher cost of capital: both the cost-of-capital schedule and the net-return schedule lie higher than in countries with less efficient enforcement. Under financial integration the equilibrium rate of return does not depend on the quality of judicial enforcement (Panel A). If instead stock markets are not fully integrated, judicial efficiency correlates positively with the rate of return on equity, while the correlation with the cost of capital is ambiguous (Panel B). Irrespective of the degree of financial integration, the amount of external equity correlates positively with judicial efficiency.

9.2.4 *Test Strategy*

The model relates equilibrium expected returns to the quality of legal institutions, measured along several dimensions. Its predictions, as summarized in Table 9.1, can be used to formulate two testable hypotheses:

(1) *The ICAPM holds in its standard form*: risk-adjusted expected returns are not correlated with international differences in legal institutions. Stock market returns (as measured by the excess return denominated in US dollars relative to the US risk-free rate) depend only (and linearly) on that country's beta with respect to the world market portfolio.

(2) *The ICAPM holds only in its extended form*: markets are internationally integrated, but equilibrium risk-adjusted returns may differ because of institutional differences. The prediction here is that returns are either uncorrelated or negatively correlated with the quality of legal institutions (first column of Table 9.1). The negative correlation arises if poor legal institutions impose costs on shareholders, who require correspondingly higher returns in equilibrium.

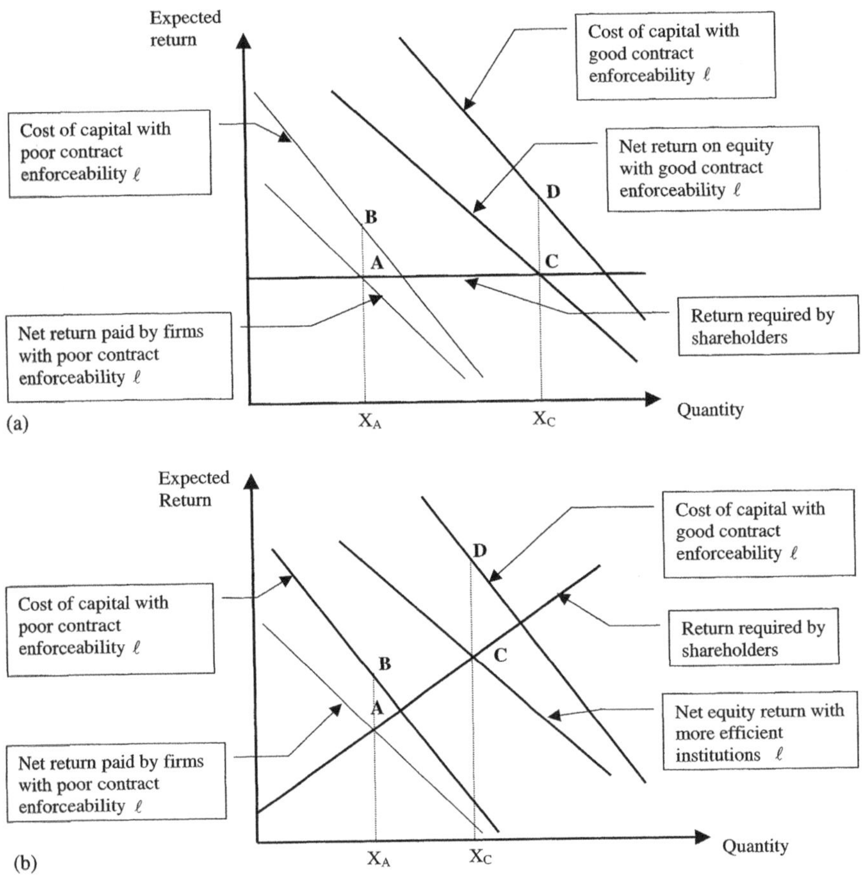

Figure 9.3: Differences in contract enforceability with (a) integrated markets and (b) segmented markets. *Note*: The figure shows the effects of cross-country differences in contract enforceability ℓ (and resulting differences in profitability) with integrated (Panel A) and segmented equity markets (Panel B). In both panels, points A and C denote the equilibrium in countries with good and poor contract enforceability, respectively. The figure shows that the cross-country correlation between contract enforceability and equity returns is zero if markets are integrated, while it is positive if markets are segmented.

An upshot of this analysis is that a positive correlation between the quality of legal institutions and the return on equity implies the rejection of the second, less stringent hypothesis, and *a fortiori* of the first one. It is a symptom of international

Table 9.1: Testable predictions.

Institutional features	**Correlation with equilibrium expected returns**	
	With integrated markets	**With segmented markets**
Effectiveness of shareholders' monitoring (low auditing costs c in Figure 9.1)	Negative (extended ICAPM)	Negative
Shareholder protection (low private benefits d in Figure 9.2)	Zero (standard/extended ICAPM)	Positive
Contract enforceability (high judicial efficiency ℓ in Figure 9.3)	Zero (standard/extended ICAPM)	Positive

Note: The table summarizes the predicted correlations between institutional cross-country differences and equilibrium expected excess returns on equity, using the comparative statics results illustrated in Figures 9.1, 9.2 and 9.3.

market segmentation. In Table 9.1, this outcome corresponds to the cells in the shaded area.

9.3 Stock Market Returns and Legal Variables

In this section, we lay out our empirical methodology to implement the test strategy just described on a sample of secondary market returns for developed and emerging countries, and then we present our results. The key challenge that we face in the estimation is to correct observed returns for risk, so as to infer the effect of institutional variables on equilibrium expected returns.

9.3.1 Methodology

To relate the risk-adjusted rate of return on equity to institutional variables, we use the Generalized Least Squares methodology proposed by Litzenberger and Ramaswamy (1979). This is a refinement of the Fama–Macbeth (1973) approach, widely used in explaining the cross-section of stock returns.

This method involves (i) estimating, for each month t and country i, the "betas" with respect to the relevant risk factors on a preceding sample and (ii) estimating, for each month *t*, a cross-sectional regression of excess returns on the estimated betas, on estimates of residual risk and — in our case — on institutional variables. The final estimated coefficients are the time average of the coefficients obtained in step (ii), taking into account the relative precision of the estimates (as explained below). Under the assumption of normality of excess returns, these "averaged" coefficients, once divided by their standard deviations, are distributed as *t*-statistics, thus allowing simple *t*-tests for inference purposes.

More specifically, this procedure involves estimating an empirical model of the form

$$r_{it} = \gamma_{0t} + \sum_{k=1}^{K} \gamma_{kt} x_{ikt} + \varepsilon_{it}, \; i = 1, 2\ldots, N, t = 1, 2\ldots, T \tag{9.6}$$

where r_{it} is the excess return on country index *i* for month *t*, x_{ikt} the *k*th component of the vector x_{it}, which includes the sensitivities of country *i*'s return to the relevant risk factors at time *t* and (a vector of) the institutional variables for country *i*, and ε_{it} a disturbance with variance possibly changing across *i* and *t*. *N* is the number of countries included in the estimation sample and *T* the number of time data points (i.e. the number of monthly observations used in the estimation). In Eq. (9.6), the sensitivities for month *t* are estimated over the previous five years of monthly data (i.e. on the data for months $t-60$ up to $t-1$).

The original Fama–Macbeth procedure consists of estimating Eq. (9.6) cross-sectionally for each month, so as to obtain a time series of estimated coefficients $\hat{\gamma}_{kt}$ for γ_k, $k=1, \ldots, K$. If each of the estimates is assumed to be drawn from a stationary distribution, then the pooled estimates $\hat{\gamma}_k$ are

$$\hat{\gamma}_k = \frac{1}{T} \sum_{t=1}^{T} \hat{\gamma}_{kt} \tag{9.7}$$

and their variance is

$$Var(\hat{\gamma}_k) = \frac{\sum(\hat{\gamma}_{kt} - \hat{\gamma}_k)^2}{T(T-1)} \tag{9.8}$$

However, this procedure does not take into account that the slope coefficients in the cross-sections for different months are estimated with different precision. The refinement proposed by Litzenberger and Ramaswamy (1979) addresses exactly this problem. They show that, if the monthly estimators $\hat{\gamma}_{kt}$ are serially uncorrelated, the pooled GLS estimators $\hat{\gamma}_k$ are the weighted means of the monthly estimates, where the weights are inversely proportional to the variances of these estimates. Specifically,

$$\hat{\gamma}_k = \sum_{t=1}^{T} Z_{kt}\hat{\gamma}_{kt}, \quad \text{where } Z_{kt} = \frac{[Var(\hat{\gamma}_{kt})]^{-1}}{\sum_{t=1}^{T}[Var(\hat{\gamma}_{kt})]^{-1}} \tag{9.9}$$

and

$$Var(\hat{\gamma}_k) = \sum_{t=1}^{T} Z_{kt}^2 \, Var(\hat{\gamma}_{kt}) \tag{9.10}$$

9.3.2 Baseline Estimation Results

In Table 9.2, we report the results from this estimation procedure for a sample of 28 developed and emerging markets for the time interval from January 1987 to July 2001 (a total of 175 cross-sectional regressions).[7,8]

In column 1, we report the baseline specification, which allows the beta with respect to the world market portfolio to have a different impact on expected returns in emerging markets. The estimated market price for covariance risk is positive, though not significantly different from zero.[9]

In column 2, we add idiosyncratic risk and an index of institutional quality to the specification.[10] Idiosyncratic risk is measured by the mean-squared error of the first-stage regressions. The quality of institutions is proxied by an index of the efficiency of the judicial system. We allow the estimated impact of these variables to differ across the subsamples of developed and emerging markets. Finally, we include two measures of the degree of shareholder protection, namely, the "anti-director rights" index and the "one-share/one-vote" dummy variable proposed by LLSV.

In this specification, the estimated market price for risk is positive and significantly different from zero in the developing markets' subsample. For these markets, also idiosyncratic risk is priced, which is a departure from the ICAPM. Moreover, the coefficient of the judicial efficiency index is positive and statistically different from zero: in countries with more efficient judicial systems the stock market pays a significantly higher excess return. This effect is also

---

[7]See Appendix 9.A.2 for a description of the data used throughout the chapter.

[8]In the choice of the sample, we tried to include the maximum number of markets and the longest possible time period, while requiring data to be available for the same time interval for all markets. To balance these conflicting desiderata, we included all markets for which coverage in the MSCI and EMDB databases starts on or before 1982. We use the first five years of data to estimate the betas. Thus, we run the Lintzerberger–Ramaswamy estimation procedure beginning in January 1987.

[9]The estimated coefficients on beta may fail to pass the statistical significance test in this formulation due to non-linearities in the relationship between excess returns and betas. We have considered a quadratic form for beta (along the lines of the specification used by the original Fama–Macbeth (1973) article). Although there is some evidence of non-linearity, the results for the institutional variables reported below are qualitatively unaffected.

[10]Descriptive statistics for returns and institutional variables are reported in Tables 9.A.1 and 9.A.3 in Appendix 9.A.2.

Table 9.2: Average slopes of monthly cross-sectional regressions of returns on beta, residual risk and institutional variables.

Regressors	**1**	**2**	**3**	**4**	**5**	**6**	**7**
Institutional variable used		**Judicial efficiency**	**Judicial efficiency**	**Rule of law**	**Rule of law**	**Corruption**	**Corruption**
Beta	0.0005 (0.30)	−.003 (−1.25)	0.003 (1.46)	0.002 (0.69)	0.003 (1.39)	−0.003 (−1.14)	0.003 (1.32)
Beta*EMDB	−0.00002 (−0.01)	0.012 (3.07)	0.004 (1.16)	0.005 (1.07)	0.005 (1.45)	0.011 (2.51)	0.005 (1.50)
Residual risk	—	−0.61 (−1.23)	—	−0.19 (−0.38)	—	−0.25 (−0.50)	—
(Residual risk)*EMDB	—	1.12 (2.12)	—	0.77 (1.43)	—	1.05 (1.89)	—
Quality of institutions	—	0.002 (4.01)	—	0.002 (3.21)	—	0.002 (3.45)	—
Quality of institutions in emerging markets	—	−0.0003 (−1.01)	—	0.001 (1.11)	—	0.0001 (0.01)	—

Institutions*residual risk	—	—	−0.011 (−0.22)	—	−0.050 (−1.03)	—	−0.007 (−0.13)
Institutions*residual risk*EMDB	—	—	0.090 (1.61)	—	0.116 (1.99)	—	0.080 (1.29)
One-share/one-vote	—	−0.006 (−3.17)	−0.005 (−2.71)	−0.003 (−1.45)	−0.004 (−2.30)	−0.001 (−0.67)	−0.004 (−2.49)
Anti-director rights	—	0.0002 (0.52)	—	—	—	—	—
Constant	0.004 (2.67)	0.001 (0.04)	0.003 (1.66)	−0.014 (−2.19)	0.004 (2.36)	−0.012 (−1.74)	0.003 (2.28)
Number of observations in cross-sectional regressions	28	28	28	28	28	28	28

Note: Monthly total excess returns in US dollars for equity markets present in the MSCI and EMDB databases from January 1982 are regressed each month on the explanatory variables for the period from January 1987 to July 2001. The safe rate of return is the yield on the 30-day maturity government bond with closest maturity. (*Source*: "Fama files" from CRSP database.) For each market, beta at time t is estimated from a first-stage market model regression on months $t-1$, $t-2$, ..., $t-60$. Residual risk is the mean squared error of the first-stage regression. EMDB is a dummy variable for emerging markets. All other variables are from LLSV (1998). Coefficients and standard errors are computed with pooled GLS estimators. *T*-statistics are reported underneath the estimated coefficients.

economically significant: a change in judicial efficiency from its mean (8.345) to its maximum is associated with a 447 basis-points increase in the annual rate of return. The effect is large even for already developed countries; for example, a change in judicial efficiency from the mean value of the European countries in the sample (8.92) to its maximum is associated with a 289 basis-points increase in the annual average rate of return.[11] This finding is a rejection of the ICAPM, even in its extended form, and it represents evidence of international market segmentation.

The measures of shareholder rights protection appear instead to have considerably different effects. The coefficient of the "one-share/one-vote" variable is negative and significant, indicating that, controlling for the efficiency of the judicial system, aligning shareholders' control rights with their cash-flow rights reduces the required return. A possible interpretation is that the "one-share/one-vote" provision reduces the scope for insiders' opportunism, and hence the equilibrium auditing costs borne by outside shareholders. In contrast, the summary indicator of shareholders' legal protection proposed by LLSV (1998) — the "anti-director rights" index — plays no role in the determination of risk-adjusted expected returns.[12]

According to the model presented in Section 9.2, institutional variables should affect equilibrium returns via their interaction with idiosyncratic risk (see Eq. 9.2). Accordingly, in the specification of column 3 we interact the judicial efficiency index with residual risk. We find some evidence in support of the model's prediction, especially in the subsample of emerging markets. The coefficient is positive, though only marginally significant at the 10 percent confidence level. In the subsample of developed markets, the coefficient is not significantly different from zero.

Columns 4 and 5 repeat the specifications of columns 2 and 3, but use the "rule-of-law" index as an alternative measure of institutional quality. The results are qualitatively unchanged, with three minor differences: (i) the coefficient of idiosyncratic risk is not statistically different from zero in either subsample; (ii) the positive correlation between the rule of law and expected returns is stronger in

---

[11]For comparison, the average annualized return in the sample is 11.6 percent. The effect reported in the text is obtained by adding the estimated effect of the institutional change to the sample average monthly return, annualizing it (with compounding), and subtracting off the 11.6 percent average annualized return.

[12]Similarly, the dummy variables for the origin of the legal systems do not have any explanatory power in conjunction with the other institutional variables, particularly with the rule-of-law index, and for brevity we do not report the corresponding specifications. Finally, to rule out collinearity between these institutional variables, we estimated the specifications in Table 9.2 also excluding the "one-share/one-vote" dummy and the "anti-director rights" index, with no qualitative change in the results.

emerging markets; and (iii) in the emerging markets subsample, the interaction term is significantly different from zero at the 1 percent level.

Finally, in columns 6 and 7 we use the "corruption" index to measure the quality of institutions. (Note that the indicator is inversely proportional to the presence of corruption.) The results are very similar to those obtained with the judicial efficiency index. In specifications that we do not report for brevity, we also investigate the relationship between risk-adjusted returns and other indices of institutional quality, such as the risk of expropriation and the quality of accounting standards. The risk of expropriation enters the specification with coefficients very similar to those of judicial efficiency, rule of law and corruption. In contrast, risk-adjusted returns appear to be uncorrelated with the quality of accounting standards.

To summarize, Table 9.2 documents a positive correlation between the quality of the institutional framework and risk-adjusted expected returns. This finding represents a rejection of the ICAPM, even in its extended form, and is evidence of segmentation in equity markets: as argued above, with perfectly integrated equity markets, the quality of the institutional environment is expected to affect negatively (if at all) the risk-adjusted return on equity.

Two caveats should be mentioned when interpreting these results. First, Ferson and Harvey (1997) argue that, before concluding that a significant coefficient of a variable other than beta represents a rejection of the traditional CAPM, one needs to ensure that the variable itself has no informational content for the cross-section of the true betas. In terms of our exercise, good institutions may translate into higher expected returns because institutional quality has informational content for betas. However, our measures of institutional quality do not change over time. Hence, it is hard to ascribe their correlation with expected returns to their impact on time-varying betas.[13]

Second, the estimated correlations may suffer from a sample selection bias similar to that studied by Jorion and Goetzmann (1999), because equity markets may fail to exist in countries were institutional quality is very low. However, the results in Table 9.2 indicate that the positive correlation between risk-adjusted returns and institutional quality is, if anything, stronger in emerging markets than in developed ones. Therefore, barring non-monotonicity in the underlying relationship, the sample selection bias is unlikely to be responsible for our findings.

---

[13]There is no reason to expect that we systematically underestimate beta in countries with good institutions and overestimate it in countries with poor institutions, as would be required to interpret the positive effect of institutions on expected returns along the lines of compensation for "hidden" risk.

9.3.3 *Extending the Estimation Time Interval*

In Table 9.3, we assess the robustness of our results to the extension of the sample along the time dimension. Unfortunately, this constrains the analysis to the subsample of developed markets, for most of which return data are available since

Table 9.3: Average slopes of monthly cross-sectional regressions of returns on beta, exchange rate risk and institutional variables in developed markets.

Regressors	**1**	**2**	**3**	**4**	**5**
Institutional variable used		**Judicial efficiency**	**Judicial efficiency**	**Rule of law**	**Corruption**
Beta	−0.001 (−0.68)	−0.0001 (−0.15)	−0.001 (−0.35)	0.001 (0.76)	−0.0001 (−0.03)
Exchange risk factor	−0.002 (−2.37)	−0.003 (−2.89)	−0.003 (−2.63)	−0.003 (−2.53)	−0.001 (−1.49)
Residual risk	—	−0.493 (−1.60)	—	−0.560 (−1.70)	−0.140 (−0.47)
Quality of institutions	—	0.001 (2.78)	—	0.001 (1.71)	0.001 (2.78)
Institutions* residual risk	—	—	−0.035 (−1.17)	—	—
Constant	0.006 (3.67)	−0.005 (−1.16)	0.007 (4.38)	−0.016 (−2.18)	−0.007 (−1.32)
Number of observations in the cross-section	18	18	18	18	18

Note: Monthly total excess returns in US dollars for the markets of the MSCI database are regressed each month on the explanatory variables for the period from February 1975 to July 2001. For each month and market, both beta and the exchange rate risk sensitivity are estimated on the previous 60-month period. The safe rate of return is the yield on the 30-day maturity government bond with closest maturity. (*Source*: "Fama files" from CRSP database.) All other variables are from LLSV (1998). Coefficients and standard errors are computed with the pooled GLS estimators. *T*-statistics are reported underneath the estimated coefficients.

January 1970.[14] As a further check, we amend the baseline CAPM to account for possible failures of the Purchasing Power Parity (PPP) hypothesis. If the PPP does not hold, the real exchange rate risk of each country is an additional risk factor priced on world stock markets.[15]

Column 1 reports the estimates of the baseline CAPM specification, augmented with the exchange rate risk factor. As in Table 9.2, the linear term in beta is not statistically different from zero.[16] Column 2 adds the residual risk variable and the index of judicial efficiency. Risk-adjusted returns are positively correlated with judicial efficiency, although the coefficient is smaller than the corresponding coefficient in Table 9.2. Neither the coefficient of residual risk nor its interaction with judicial efficiency in column 3 is statistically different from zero, in line with the results obtained for the subsample of developed countries in Table 9.2. Finally, the exchange rate risk factor does appear to be priced according to the predictions of the theory (see footnote 15). Replacing judicial efficiency with alternative measures of the quality of institutions (rule of law or corruption) yields virtually identical results, in both size and precision, as illustrated by the estimates in columns 4 and 5.

9.4 Dividend Yields and Legal Variables

Dividend yields are an alternative measure of the returns on a country's stock market. Bekaert and Harvey (2000) and Errunza and Miller (2000), among others, rely on the dividend yield as a measure of the cost of capital. As pointed out by Bekaert and Harvey (2000, p. 9), "the dividend yield has the advantage of being directly measurable — that is, it need not be pre-estimated — and being a stationary variable". By its nature, however, this measure needs to be adjusted, in an international comparison, for different inflation and growth prospects.

[14]The estimation sample ranges from February 1975 to July 2001, and covers 18 countries. We exclude Finland, Ireland and New Zealand, which enter the MSCI database in 1988. However, their inclusion does not affect materially the estimation results.

[15]Adler and Dumas (1983), Harvey (1991) and Dumas and Solnik (1995), among others, show that exchange rate risk is indeed priced for developed markets. Ferson and Harvey (1993, 1994) recommend the use of a two-factor model, by adding to the traditional world market portfolio the return on a portfolio of deposits in different currencies, with weights reflecting the world trade structure. The real exchange rate index used in Table 9.3 is constructed in such a way that an increase means a *depreciation* of the US dollar. Hence, theory predicts the sign of its coefficient to be negative. This is because a positive correlation between the real exchange rate index and the return on the world market portfolio provides hedging (i.e. the exchange rate *appreciates* when the world market portfolio falls).

[16]As in the previous subsection, there is some evidence of a non-linear impact of betas on returns, which however does not materially affect the other coefficient estimates.

9.4.1 Methodology

Under fairly general assumptions, the stock market price index in country i at time t, $P_{i,t}$, is the expected value of discounted dividends from the component stocks

$$P_{i,t} = E_t \sum_{j=1}^{\infty} \frac{D_{i,t+j}}{(1+ k_{i,t+j})^j} \tag{9.11}$$

where E_t is the expectation conditional on information known at time t, $D_{i,t+j}$ the dividend paid out by the companies listed in country i at time $t+j$, and $k_{i,t+j}$ the per-period risk-adjusted discount factor between time t and $t+j$ relevant for the stream of dividends from country i. The simplest version of this valuation approach assumes k_i to be constant and $E_t\,(D_{i,t+j}) = D_{i,t}(1 + g_i)^j$, where $D_{i,t}$ is the current dividend and g_i a constant growth rate specific to country i. The expected dividend yield then becomes

$$\frac{D_{i,t}}{P_{i,t}} = k_i - g_i \tag{9.12}$$

Based on the model of Section 9.2, required rates of return on equity may depend on the interest rate, on covariance risk, and on institutional variables, such as the quality of the legal and judicial systems and the degree of minority shareholders' protection

$$k_i = \alpha r_i + \eta \beta_i + \gamma \ell_i \tag{9.13}$$

where r_i is the yield on a long-term "risk-free" domestic security,[17] β_i the country's vector of betas with respect to the relevant risk factors, ℓ_i a vector of variables proxying for the quality of legal institutions and the degree of investor's protection in country i. If the standard ICAPM holds, then $\alpha = 1$, η is the market price for risk, and $\gamma = 0$. Substituting Eq. (9.13) in (9.12), one obtains the following expression for the dividend yield

$$\frac{D_{i,t}}{P_{i,t}} = \alpha r_i + \eta \beta_i + \delta g_i + \gamma \ell_i. \tag{9.14}$$

Being predicated on the constancy of the expected returns and dividend growth, this basic version of the Gordon growth model is not realistic, but its qualitative

[17]The nominal domestic interest rate must be included, since our estimates of the expected growth in earnings per share are in nominal terms and the dividend yields are denominated in different currencies. As a result, we must allow for different yields to reflect different expected inflation rates, even if all other factors were the same across markets.

implications carry through to a setting where expected returns (k_i) and dividend growth rates (g_i) vary over time. Bekaert and Harvey (2000) generalize the model to this case and derive a regression specification by linearizing the structural model around mean expected returns and dividend growth rates. Hence, we estimate the following regression, with time-varying returns, betas and dividend growth rates

$$\frac{D_{i,t}}{P_{i,t}} = \alpha r_{i,t} + \eta \beta_{i,t} + \delta g_{i,t} \, \gamma \ell_i + \varepsilon_{i,t} \tag{9.15}$$

The expected coefficient of the dividend growth rate is quite different depending on the process that generates it. In the deterministic constant-growth Gordon model one should expect $\delta = -1$. But Bekaert and Harvey (2000, p. 583) show that $\delta = 0$ "when dividend growth follows a white noise process, not an unreasonable approximation to the dividend growth process, and expected returns are constant".

Eq. (9.15) requires an estimate for β_{it}, which we obtain from a first-stage regression as explained in Section 9.3. In the estimation, we allow for cross-market correlation and heteroskedasticity for the errors ε_{it} as well as for autocorrelation of the error terms within each country.

9.4.2 Results

Our empirical results are reported in Table 9.4. We estimate Eq. (9.15) using an unbalanced panel of monthly observations on the dividend yields for 18 developed and seven emerging markets. Appendix 9.A.2 provides details on the time-series interval of each dividend yield series as well as descriptive statistics by country (in Table 9.A.2).

Table 9.4 reports the coefficient estimates of various specifications, which include different institutional variables in the vector ℓ. As in Table 9.2, the specification of column 1 includes three sets of explanatory variables: (i) the determinants of the dividend yield suggested by the Gordon model (i.e. the domestic government bond yield, the market beta, the dividend growth rate and the exchange risk factor); (ii) idiosyncratic risk, which should play a role only with segmented markets; and (iii) legal variables capturing the quality of institutions and the degree of investors' protection, such as legal origin dummies, the "one-share/one-vote" dummy and the "anti-director rights" variable. We cannot include country-fixed effects because our institutional variables do not vary over time and would otherwise be unidentified. However, country-specific variation in the dependent variable is at least partly controlled for by our legal variables.

Consistently with the model, the coefficients of both the domestic government bond yield and of the beta are positive, though the latter is not precisely estimated,

Table 9.4: Dividend yields, risk and institutional variables in developed markets.

Regressors	**1**	**2**	**3**	**4**
Institutional variable used	**Judicial efficiency**	**Judicial efficiency**	**Rule of law**	**Corruption**
Dividend growth rate	0.003 (1.01)	0.002 (0.67)	0.003 (1.11)	0.003 (0.99)
Risk-free rate	0.001 (2.21)	0.0003 (2.26)	0.001 (2.34)	0.0005 (2.25)
Beta	0.005 (1.13)	0.005 (0.99)	0.008 (1.68)	0.005 (1.34)
Exchange risk factor	−0.003 (−2.17)	−0.004 (−2.69)	−0.003 (−2.25)	−0.002 (−1.61)
Residual risk	0.042 (0.10)	—	−0.009 (−0.02)	0.042 (0.11)
Quality of institutions	0.005 (3.39)	—	0.004 (7.50)	0.005 (6.37)
Quality of institutions* residual risk	—	−0.028 (−0.46)	—	—
One-share/one-vote	−0.008 (−2.47)	−0.008 (−2.05)	−0.002 (−0.56)	−0.006 (−2.47)
Anti-director rights	0.001 (0.70)	—	—	—
French origin	0.007 (1.18)	−0.006 (−1.47)	−0.001 (−0.36)	0.001 (0.56)
German origin	−0.009 (−1.34)	−0.014 (−4.68)	−0.013 (−3.22)	−0.014 (−3.07)
Scandinavian origin	−0.017 (−5.78)	−0.015 (−5.94)	−0.019 (−6.56)	−0.021 (−6.08)
Constant	−0.29 (1.43)	0.030 (5.15)	−0.016 (−2.22)	−0.019 (2.62)
Number of observations	4473	4473	4473	4473
R^2	0.367	0.210	0.365	0.393

Note: Monthly dividend yields are from the IBES global aggregates database (Thomson Financial). The dividend yield is the weighted average yield based on the indicated annual dividend (IBES datatype: ADVYLD). The risk-free rate is obtained from IFS. The dividend growth rate is the percent change of the dividend over the previous year. Beta for market i in month t is estimated from market model regressions of market i's excess return on the world market excess return in months $t-1, ..., t-60$. Institutional variables are from LLSV (1998). The data are an unbalanced panel from developed and emerging markets (see Appendix 9.A.2 for the list of markets included and for the time interval of each series). T-statistics corrected for both heteroskedasticity and within-country autocorrelation are reported underneath the estimated coefficients.

and the coefficient of the exchange risk factor is negative. In line with the prior by Bekaert and Harvey (2000), dividend growth does not carry a statistically significant coefficient.[18] As in Table 9.2, judicial efficiency has a large and positive correlation with returns: firms in countries with a higher degree of judicial efficiency pay a higher risk-adjusted dividend yield. A change in judicial efficiency from its sample mean (8.64) to its maximum (10) is associated with an increase of 70 basis points in the dividend yield.[19] This finding represents further evidence of international market segmentation.

The other coefficients in the baseline specification of column 1 also parallel closely the corresponding results of Table 9.2: the coefficient of residual risk is not significantly different from zero, while that of the "one-share/one-vote" dummy is negative.

In column 2 we enter residual risk and judicial efficiency only interactively, in keeping with the specification of Eq. (9.2), but the estimated coefficient is not significantly different from zero, while the other estimates are virtually unaffected.

These results are largely confirmed when the index of judicial efficiency is replaced by the rule-of-law index or the corruption score. This is shown in columns 3 and 4, which reproduce the specification of column 1 with these two alternative variables.[20] Other things equal, the dividend yield is significantly higher in more law-abiding and less corrupt countries.

In the various specifications of Table 9.4, legal origin variables enter with a consistent pattern: firms in German and the Scandinavian countries pay a lower risk-adjusted return than firms in Anglo-Saxon countries. If, as maintained by LLSV, shareholders are better protected in Anglo-Saxon countries than elsewhere, this is another piece of evidence against the ICAPM, even in its extended formulation described in Section 9.2. This is because, if markets were integrated, one would have expected companies in Anglo-Saxon countries to be rather the ones paying the lowest returns. An interpretation of this seemingly counterintuitive finding in line with our model in Section 9.2 is that the

[18]We also controlled for the differential tax treatment of dividends, by including the variable "Dividend Tax Preference" from LLSV (2000). This variable is defined as the ratio of the net-of-taxes value to outside shareholders of 1 dollar in earnings distributed out as dividends to the net-of-taxes value of 1 dollar of earnings retained in the firm. It is meant to capture the extent of tax disadvantage borne by dividends relative to capital gains. Its estimated effect is never significantly different from zero, and therefore we omit it from our reported results.

[19]In our sample, the average dividend yield is 0.032, its standard deviation is 0.015 and its range is between 0.0035 and 0.11.

[20]These two specifications do not include the "anti-director rights" index. If included, the coefficient of this variable is not significantly different from zero and all the other results are unaffected. We do not report these specifications for brevity.

English-country dummy captures some unmeasured social characteristic that enhances company profitability.

9.5 Concluding Remarks

In this chapter, we have explored the effects of legal institutions on the equilibrium returns on equity. We have presented an extension of the standard ICAPM to account for both demand- and supply-side effects. On the demand side, strong protection of shareholder rights reduces the auditing costs incurred by shareholders to monitor management, and therefore increases their demand for equity. On the supply side, legal rules that constrain managerial diversion of corporate resources (for example, stringent corporate transparency standards) allow companies to pledge a higher payout to investors and thereby issue more shares; in addition, better legal enforcement can expand the investment opportunities of firms, again increasing their share issuance.

The model highlights that, in contrast with the demand-side effects, the supply-side effects of legal institutions on returns are muted if equity markets are internationally integrated, since in this case the demand for shares is perfectly horizontal. We show that for this reason, with integrated markets, the cross-country correlation between the quality of legal institutions and equilibrium returns must be either zero or negative.

However, in our empirical analysis, we document a significant positive correlation, which is robust to changes in the length of the time sample, in the geographical coverage of the sample, in the proxies for institutional quality and even in the measures of equity returns (secondary market returns or dividend yields).

This suggests that supply effects are far from muted, and hence that equity markets are not fully integrated: in countries with better legal rules, more effective enforcement and less widespread corruption, firms issue more equity, thereby raising those countries' equilibrium risk premia. The positive correlation uncovered in the data, in other words, underscores the limited risk-bearing capacity of local investors in segmented markets. From the European perspective, our results suggest that, to the extent that new accession countries raise the quality of their institutional setting as they prepare to join the EU, their firms may be expected to pay higher returns, as their profitability and, consequently, their supply of shares increase. Over the medium term, however, as their financial markets fully integrate into the Euro area (possibly also as a result of the institutional harmonization), firms in these countries should enjoy a reduction in the cost of capital. This result sheds new light on the findings reported by LLSV (1997). The positive correlation between the quality of legal institutions and the breadth of stock markets may result from several channels, not all of which are related to the agency costs of external finance. For instance, in countries where contracts are more readily enforced, firms' profitability may be higher and therefore firms may issue more shares.

From a policy point of view, our findings suggest that, as countries strengthen their legal and judicial institutions, their firms may have to pay higher returns to attract additional equity financing. But, far from representing a drawback, this may just mean that firms are becoming more profitable and investment is expanding. But the extent to which institutional development will translate in greater investment and share supply will in turn depend on how integrated these countries are in international equity markets.

Our analysis leaves a number of issues open to further inquiry. First, an intriguing issue is which precise mechanism generates the positive correlation between the efficiency of judicial enforcement of contracts and the return on equity. A second task is to test the robustness of our results on more disaggregated data. Third, a fascinating line of research involves endogenizing the evolution of the institutional framework, so as to understand why some countries end up having and retaining "bad" institutions.[21]

Acknowledgments

We thank for their comments Kent Daniel, John Griffin, Ted Eisenberg, Tullio Jappelli, Giovanna Nicodano, Andrei Shleifer and seminar participants at HEC, LSE, NYU, Stanford University, the University of Salerno, the JFI Olin Symposium in Law and Finance at Cornell University, the EEA 1999 Meetings in Santiago de Compostela, the AFA 2000 Meetings in Boston, the workshop on Financial Markets, the Legal System and Judicial Enforcement at the University of Naples and the WFA 2000 meetings in Sun Valley, Idaho. Lombardo acknowledges support by grants from ISFSE-CNR and the Olin Program in Law and Economics at Stanford University Law School. The Olin Program also supported the purchase of data. Pagano acknowledges support from the Italian Ministry of University and Scientific and Technological Research (MURST).

This chapter is produced as part of a CEPR research network on The Industrial Organization of Banking and Financial Markets in Europe, funded by the European Commission under the Training and Mobility of Researchers Programme (Contract No ERBFMRXCT980222).

[21]For a step in this direction see Pagano and Volpin (2005).

References

Adler, M., & Dumas, B. (1983). International portfolio selection and corporation finance: A synthesis. *Journal of Finance*, *38*(3), 925–984.

Bekaert, G., & Harvey, C. R. (1995). Time-varying world market integration. *Journal of Finance*, *50*(2), 403–444.

Bekaert, G., & Harvey, C. R. (2000). Foreign speculators and emerging equity markets. *Journal of Finance*, *55*(2), 565–613.

Dumas, B., & Solnik, B. H. (1995). The world price of foreign exchange risk. *Journal of Finance*, *50*(2), 445–479.

Errunza, V., & Miller, D. (2000). Market segmentation and the cost of capital in international equity markets. *Journal of Financial and Quantitative Analysis*, *35*, 577–600.

Fama, E. (1984). Term premiums in bond returns. *Journal of Financial Economics*, *13*(4), 529–546.

Fama, E., & Macbeth, J. D. (1973). Risk, return, and equilibrium: Empirical tests. *Journal of Political Economy*, *71*(May–June), 607–636.

Ferson, W. E., & Harvey, C. R. (1993). The risk and predictability of international equity returns. *The Review of Financial Studies*, *6*(3), 527–566.

Ferson, W. E., & Harvey, C. R. (1994). Sources of risk and expected returns in international equity markets. *Journal of Banking and Finance*, *18*(4), 775–803.

Ferson, W. E., & Harvey, C. R. (1997). Fundamental determinants of national equity market returns: A perspective on conditional asset pricing. *Journal of Banking and Finance*, *21*(11–12), 1625–1665.

Gordon, R. H., & Bovenberg, A. L. (1996). Why is capital so immobile internationally? Possible explanations and implications for capital income taxation. *American Economic Review*, *86*(5), 1057–1075.

Harvey, Cambell. (1991). The world price of covariance risk, *Journal of Finance*, *46* (1), (March), 111–157.

Heston, S. L., & Rouwenhorst, K. G. (1994). Does industrial structure explain the benefits of international diversification? *Journal of Financial Economics*, *36*, 3–27.

Jorion, P., & Goetzmann, W. (1999). Global stock markets in the twentieth century. *Journal of Finance*, *54*(3), 953–980.

La Porta, R., Lopez-de-Silanes, F., Shleifer, A., & Vishny, R. W. (LLSV). (1997). Legal determinants of external finance. *Journal of Finance*, *52*, 1131–1150.

La Porta, R., Lopez-de-Silanes, F., Shleifer, A., & Vishny, R. W. (LLSV). (1998). Law and finance. *Journal of Political Economy*, *106*(6), 1113–1155.

La Porta, R., Lopez-de-Silanes, F., Shleifer, A., & Vishny, R. W. (LLSV). (2000). Agency problems and dividend policies around the world. *Journal of Finance*, *55*(1), 1–33.

La Porta, R., Lopez-de-Silanes, F., Shleifer, A., & Vishny, R. W. (LLSV). (2002). Investor protection and corporate valuation. *Journal of Finance*, *57*(3), 1147–1170.

Litzenberger, R. H., & Ramaswamy, K. (1979). The effect of personal taxes and dividends on capital asset prices: Theory and empirical evidence. *Journal of Financial Economics*, *7*(2), 163–196.

Morgan Stanley Capital International (MSCI, 2005). MSCI index calculation methodology (last updated November 2005). Available from http.//www.msci.com/equity/index2.html
Pagano, Marco., & Paolo F. Volpin. (2005). The political economy of corporate governance, *The American Economic Review, 95* (4), (September), 1005–1030.
Roll, R. (1992). Industrial structure and the comparative behavior of international stock market indices. *Journal of Finance, 46*, 3–41.
Standard and Poor's (2005). The S&P Equity Markets Indices (November 2005).
Solnik, B. H. (1977). Testing international asset pricing: Some pessimistic views. *Journal of Finance, 32*(2), 503–512.
Thomson Financial. I/B/E/S/Global Aggregates. (www.thomson.com)

Appendix 9.A.1 Derivation of Eq. (9.2)

In this appendix, we spell out the derivations involved in obtaining Eq. (9.2) in the text. The problems of the representative home investor and of the representative global investor are

$$\underset{x_{hj},\, x_{wj}}{\text{Max}}\ E(\widetilde{W}_{1j}) - \frac{b}{2}\, Var(\widetilde{W}_{1j}) - cx_{hj}, \quad j = \{h, g\} \tag{9.A.1}$$

where $\widetilde{W}_{1j}$ is the value of investor j's terminal wealth, x_{hj} and x_{wj} are the amounts she invests in the home and the world market, respectively. The expected value of terminal wealth is

$$E(\widetilde{W}_{1j}) = (W_{0j} - x_{hj} - x_{wj})\,(1 + r) + x_{hj}\,(1 + \mu_h) + x_{wj}\,(1 + \mu_w) \tag{9.A.2}$$

and its variance is

$$Var(\widetilde{W}_{1j}) = \sigma_h^2 x_{hj}^2 + \sigma_w^2 x_{wj}^2 + 2\sigma_{hw} x_{hj} x_{wj} \tag{9.A.3}$$

where σ_{hw} is the covariance between the home and the world market.

Rearranging the first-order conditions of the above maximization problem, one obtains

$$\mu_h - r = c = b\sigma_h^2 x_{hj} + bb_{hw} x_{wj} \tag{9.A.4}$$

$$\mu_w - r = b\sigma_w^2 x_{wj} + b\sigma_{hw} x_{hj} \tag{9.A.5}$$

Finally, the portfolio choice problem of the foreign investors who cannot diversify is

$$\underset{x_{ww}}{\text{Max}}\ E(\widetilde{W}_{1f}) - \frac{b}{2}\, Var(\widetilde{W}_{1f}) \tag{9.A.6}$$

subject to

$$E(\widetilde{W}_{1f}) = (W_{0f} - x_{wf})\,(1 + r) + x_{wf}\,(1 + \mu_w) \tag{9.A.7}$$

and

$$Var(\widetilde{W}_{1f}) = \sigma_w^2 x_{wf}^2 \tag{9.A.8}$$

The first-order condition yields

$$\mu_w - r = b\sigma_w^2 x_{wf} \tag{9.A.9}$$

We define the total investment in the two stocks h and w, respectively as

$$N_h x_{hh} + \lambda N_w x_{hg} = X_h \tag{9.A.10}$$

$$N_h x_{wh} + \lambda N_w x_{wg} + (1 - \lambda)\, N_w x_{wf} = X_w \tag{9.A.11}$$

Multiplying Eq. (9.A.4) first by N_h (setting $j=h$) and then by λN_w (setting $j=g$), substituting from Eqs. (9.A.10) and (9.A.11), and adding up, one obtains

$$(N_h + \lambda N_w)\,(\mu_h - r) = (N_h + \lambda N_w)c + b\sigma_h^2 X_h + b\sigma_{hw} \times (X_w - (1 - \lambda)N_w x_{wf}) \tag{9.A.12}$$

Similarly, multiplying Eq. (9.A.5) by N_h (with $j=h$), (9.A.5) by λN_w (with $j=g$) and (9.A.9) by $(1-\lambda)N_w$, substituting again from Eqs. (9.A.10) and (9.A.11), and adding up, one obtains

$$(N_h + N_w)\,(\mu_w - r) = b\sigma_w^2 X_w + b\sigma_{hw} X_h \tag{9.A.13}$$

Replacing x_{wf} from Eq. (9.A.9) and X_w from Eq. (9.A.13) into Eq. (9.A.12) and rearranging, we obtain Eq. (9.2) in the text.

Appendix 9.A.2: Data Sources and Definitions

Secondary Market Returns

We draw monthly equity indices from January 1982 to July 2001 for 18 developed countries from Morgan Stanley Capital International (MSCI, 2005).[22] We

[22]The MSCI indices are broadly representative of each country's market composition. Virtually, all the stocks (99 percent) can be traded by foreign and domestic investors. As noted by Harvey (1991), the returns computed on the basis of these indices are highly correlated with widely quoted country indices, such as the NYSE value-weighted return (calculated by the CRSP) for the USA, or the Nikkei 255 index for Japan.

use the MSCI value-weighted World Index as the market portfolio for developed countries.[23] The indices for seven emerging markets are drawn from the Emerging Market Database (EMDB), originally introduced by the International Finance Corporation (IFC) and now offered by Standard & Poor's (S&P). Table 9.A.1 reports country-level summary statistics for the estimation period used in Table 9.2 (January 1987–July 2001).[24]

Both MSCI and EMBD indices are value-weighted and calculated with dividend reinvestment, and both data sets extend to July 2001. Returns are computed as percentage changes of the indices expressed in US dollars. Tables 9.A.1 and 9.A.2 report the average returns from the MSCI and the EMBD databases, respectively. Excess returns are calculated using the yield on the US Treasury bill closest to 30 days to maturity on the last trading day of the month, drawn from the CRSP government bond file (see Fama, 1984).

The exchange rate risk factor is the nominal effective trade-weighted exchange rate index of the US dollar vis-à-vis 20 industrial countries (IFS series 111 ... NEUZF ...). The change in the log of this index approximates the excess return on a trade-weighted portfolio of foreign-currency bonds; assuming that the trade weights are known and that a trade-weighted combination of foreign currency deposit rates in the 20 countries is close to the US bill rate.[25] A positive change in the index indicates a depreciation of the dollar.

Dividend Yields, Dividend Growth Rates and Yields on Government Bonds

Monthly dividend yields for a sample of 18 developed countries and seven emerging markets are drawn from the IBES global aggregates database, available from Thomson Financial.[26] The extension of the sample for each country is indicated in Table 9.A.2. The dividend growth rate is the percent change of the dividend over the previous year, computed by netting the change of the

[23]We also used the value-weighted average of the excess returns on all the markets in the MSCI and EMDB databases that are active in that month, with no qualitative change in results.

[24]For EMDB methodology, see S&P (2005). The selection criteria of the components of the MSCI and the EMDB national indices are similar, though not identical. Bekaert and Harvey (1995) describe the EMDB indices and briefly compare the EMDB and MSCI methodologies.

[25]Ferson and Harvey (1993) adopt a mimicking portfolio approach, i.e. they construct a portfolio that is maximally correlated to the change in the log of G-10, and they compute its excess return. When they use this portfolio excess return instead of the simple change in the log of G-10, they obtain similar results.

[26]The dividend yield is defined as "weighted dividend yield based on the indicated annual dividend" (IBES datatype: ADVYLD).

Table 9.A.1: Summary statistics: annualized return.*

Country	Arithmetic mean	Geometric mean	Standard deviation
Panel A: European countries			
Austria	0.072	0.044	0.240
Belgium	0.130	0.113	0.177
Canada	0.111	0.092	0.188
Denmark	0.153	0.134	0.192
France	0.125	0.104	0.201
Germany	0.103	0.081	0.209
Greece	0.233	0.153	0.417
Italy	0.074	0.044	0.243
Netherlands	0.148	0.134	0.162
Norway	0.115	0.083	0.247
Spain	0.136	0.109	0.230
Sweden	0.162	0.129	0.255
Switzerland	0.131	0.114	0.183
UK	0.128	0.112	0.178
–Average	*0.130*	*0.103*	*0.223*
Panel B: Non-European developed markets			
Australia	0.114	0.085	0.229
Hong Kong	0.175	0.125	0.311
Japan	0.039	0.008	0.251
Singapore	0.112	0.071	0.281
USA	0.149	0.137	0.154
–Average	*0.118*	*0.085*	*0.245*
Panel C: Non-European emerging markets			
Argentina	0.402	0.176	0.761
Brazil	0.274	0.095	0.598
Chile	0.219	0.182	0.273
India	0.086	0.035	0.323
Jordan	0.051	0.040	0.145
Korea	0.100	0.013	0.433
Mexico	0.287	0.182	0.430
Thailand	0.100	0.004	0.437
Zimbabwe	0.216	0.138	0.388
–Average	*0.193*	*0.096*	*0.421*

Note: All European countries except Greece are classified as developed markets in this paper. The distinction is based on the source of data (see Appendix 9.A.2).

*Summary statistics for the estimation sample used in Section 9.3.2. The sample is a balanced panel for the time interval between January 1987 and July 2001.

Table 9.A.2: Summary statistics: dividend yields.

Country	Mean*	Standard deviation*	Starting date*	Ending date*	Number of observations
European countries					
Belgium	0.039	0.016	February 1975	July 2001	318
Denmark	0.019	0.005	May 1981	December 1988	92
France	0.039	0.015	February 1975	July 2001	318
Germany	0.025	0.009	July 1975	July 2001	313
Greece	0.028	0.013	January 1991	July 2001	126
Ireland	0.028	0.005	February 1993	January 1999	72
Italy	0.024	0.008	March 1977	July 2001	293
Netherlands	0.052	0.012	December 1975	August 1990	155
Portugal	0.031	0.009	March 1993	March 1999	84
Spain	0.033	0.011	March 1988	July 2001	161
Sweden	0.023	0.007	January 1983	July 2001	223
Switzerland	0.020	0.007	January 1980	July 2001	259
UK	0.044	0.011	February 1975	July 2001	318
Non-European countries					
Australia	0.040	0.009	February 1975	July 2001	318
Brazil	0.025	0.022	July 1975	July 2001	64
Canada	0.032	0.011	February 1975	July 2001	318
Hong Kong	0.030	0.008	December 1992	July 2001	93
Malaysia	0.021	0.007	February 1990	July 2001	138
Mexico	0.019	0.008	May 1990	July 2001	135
New Zealand	0.048	0.006	February 1993	July 2001	102
Philippines	0.010	0.005	February 1990	July 2001	138
South Africa	0.027	0.004	February 1988	July 2001	42
Thailand	0.041	0.004	January 1988	September 1999	22
Turkey	0.051	0.033	February 1992	July 2001	53
USA	0.035	0.014	February 1975	July 2001	318

Note: All European countries except Greece are classified as developed markets in this paper. The distinction is based on the source of data (see Appendix 9.A.2).

*Mean value, standard deviation, starting and ending date of the series of dividend yields used in the estimation for Section 9.4.2 and Table 9.4.

corresponding stock price index P from the change in dividend yield D/P, according to the identity

$$\frac{\Delta D}{D} \equiv \frac{\Delta(D/P)}{D/P} + \frac{\Delta P}{P} + \frac{\Delta(D/P)}{D/P}\,\frac{\Delta P}{\Delta P}$$

The yield on government bonds used in the estimation of Eq. (9.15) is drawn from the IFS database.

Institutional Variables

The variable "Judicial Efficiency" is an assessment of the "efficiency and integrity of the legal environment as it affects business, particularly foreign firms". It is produced by the country-risk rating agency Business International Corporation and is an average between 1980 and 1983, ranging from 0 to 10, with higher values associated with higher efficiency levels. Summary statistics for this and some of the other variables described in this section are shown in Table 9.A.3.

Other variables that we use were constructed by LLSV (1998). Among these, the index "anti-director rights" captures the degree of legal protection from expropriation by the managers and controlling shareholders granted to minority shareholders. The dummy variable "one-share/one-vote" equals one if in the country concerned ordinary shares are required to carry only one vote per share and zero otherwise. The variables "French Origin", "German Origin", "Scandinavian Origin"and "English Origin" indicate the "family" to which the legal system of a given country belongs.

Most other legal and institutional variables used here are produced by the rating agency International Country Risk (ICR). Each variable is measured as the average of the months of April and October of the corresponding ICR monthly index between 1982 and 1995, and ranges on a scale from 0 to 10 (in some cases, by rescaling the original ICR indices). The variable "rule of law" is ICR's "evaluation of the legal and order tradition in the country", with lower scores for countries with weaker legal and order tradition. "Corruption" is an assessment of the degree of corruption in the government, with lower scores indicating higher corruption. The variable "Risk of Expropriation" reflects ICR's evaluation of the risk of "outright confiscation" or forced nationalization, with lower scores indicating higher risk.

Finally, the variable "Quality of Accounting Standards" is drawn from International Accounting and Auditing Trends (Center for International Financial Analysis & Research, Inc.), and measures the quality of companies' annual reports along seven general dimensions (general information, income statements, balance sheets, funds flow statement, accounting standards, stock data and special items). In our complete sample of developed and emerging markets, it ranges between 24 and 83, with a mean of 61 and a standard deviation of 13.5.

Table 9.A.3: Summary statistics: institutional variables (from LLSV 1998).

	Judicial efficiency	Rule of law	Corruption	Risk of expropriation	Accounting standards	Anti-director rights
Panel A: European countries						
Austria	9.5	10.0	8.6	9.7	54.0	3.0
Belgium	9.5	10.0	8.8	9.6	61.0	0.0
Denmark	10.0	10.0	10.0	9.7	62.0	3.0
France	8.0	9.0	9.1	9.7	69.0	3.0
Germany	9.0	9.2	8.9	9.9	62.0	1.0
Greece	7.0	6.2	7.3	7.1	55.0	2.0
Italy	6.8	8.3	6.1	9.4	62.0	1.0
Netherlands	10.0	10.0	10.0	10.0	64.0	3.0
Norway	10.0	10.0	10.0	9.9	74.0	4.0
Spain	6.3	7.8	7.4	9.5	64.0	3.0
Sweden	10.0	10.0	10.0	9.4	83.0	3.0
Switzerland	10.0	10.0	10.0	10.0	68.0	2.0
UK	10.0	8.6	9.1	9.7	78.0	5.0
–Average	*8.9*	*9.2*	*8.9*	*9.5*	*65.8*	*2.5*
Panel B: Non-European developed markets						
Australia	10.0	10.0	8.5	9.3	75.0	4.0
Canada	9.3	10.0	10.0	9.7	74.0	4.0
Hong Kong	10.0	8.2	8.5	8.3	74.0	5.0
Japan	10.0	9.0	8.5	9.7	65.0	3.0

(*Continued*)

Table 9.A.3: (*Continued*).

	Judicial efficiency	**Rule of law**	**Corruption**	**Risk of expropriation**	**Accounting standards**	**Anti-director rights**
Singapore	10.0	8.6	8.2	9.3	78.0	4.0
USA	10.0	10.0	8.6	10.0	71.0	5.0
–Average	*9.9*	*9.3*	*8.7*	*9.4*	*72.8*	*4.2*
Panel C: Non-European emerging markets						
Argentina	6.0	5.4	6.0	5.9	45.0	5.0
Brazil	5.8	6.3	6.3	7.6	54.0	3.0
Chile	7.3	7.0	5.3	7.5	52.0	4.0
India	8.0	4.2	4.6	7.8	57.0	3.0
Jordan	8.7	4.4	5.5	6.1		1.0
Korea	6.0	5.4	5.3	8.3	62.0	2.0
Mexico	6.0	5.4	4.8	7.3	60.0	1.0
Thailand	3.3	6.3	5.2	7.4	64.0	3.0
Zimbabwe	7.5	3.7	5.4	5.6		3.0
–Average	*6.5*	*5.3*	*5.4*	*7.1*	*56.3*	*2.8*
Sample statistics						
Mean	8.3	8.0	7.7	8.7	64.9	3.0
Standard deviation	1.9	2.1	1.9	1.4	9.2	1.3
Minimum	3.3	3.7	4.6	5.6	45.0	0.0
Maximum	10.0	10.0	10.0	10.0	83.0	5.0

Note: All European countries except Greece are classified as developed markets in this paper. The distinction is based on the source of data (see Appendix 9.A.2).

Chapter 10

The European Adoption of International Financial Reporting Standards—Effects on Corporate Transparency

Magnus Bild and Walter Schuster

10.1 Introduction

Accounting in Europe is undergoing a fundamental change because from 2005 onwards all listed companies within the European Union (EU) will be required to apply International Financial Reporting Standards (IFRSs) in their consolidated financial statements. In this chapter, we aim to analyse the effects of adopting IFRSs (IASB, 2004) on corporate transparency.

A common theme for all the contributions to this volume is the link between institutional transparency and economic growth in Europe. Transparency is important for the capital formation process, where funds raised are allocated directly to financial markets and to financial intermediaries and then used for real investment producing economic growth (Oxelheim, 1996). In this process different actors can be identified: savers/investors, corporate decision makers, politicians/regulators and international politicians/regulators. This chapter deals directly with transparency between corporate decision makers and investors (via financial markets) i.e. corporate transparency. Bushman, Piotroski, and Smith (2004) define corporate transparency as the availability of firm-specific information to those outside publicly traded firms. We interpret this as the ability of outsiders to evaluate a firm's operations (see also Chapter 12 in this volume). Accounting information, in turn, in the form of financial statements and additional disclosures, arguably represents the most important source of firm-specific information to outsiders.

Corporate and Institutional Transparency for Economic Growth in Europe

ISBN: 0-08-044665-5

In this context, it is necessary to elaborate further on the meaning of transparency. Bushman et al. (2004) view corporate reporting, i.e. the periodic disclosure of firm-specific information on a voluntary or mandatory basis, as one information mechanism related to corporate transparency.[1] Moreover, they identify two aspects of corporate reporting directly related to the financial reporting standards: financial disclosure intensity and accounting principles used.

Additional information enhances transparency. However, substituting one accounting method for another does not necessarily improve transparency, i.e. the availability of firm-specific information to outsiders and their ability to evaluate a firm's operations, which depend on the characteristics of the respective methods. Thus, replacing a set of national standards by another set of "international" standards that are uniform across countries does not necessarily improve transparency. Of course, it is often argued that IFRSs represent a coherent set of high-quality standards, which therefore would improve transparency. Even assuming this to be true, the gains from improved transparency would nevertheless have to be compared to the cost of getting this transparency.[2]

Furthermore, it is not sufficient just to look at accounting standards. These accounting standards interact with other contextual factors, such as institutional factors, information mechanisms or important actors' rationales. The effects of adopting a new set of standards could well be constrained by such other factors (Ball, Ashok, & Wu, 2003).[3] Generally, one might hypothesize that a specific set of standards will work well under certain conditions, and that a country-specific GAAP has evolved together with other country-specific factors (Stolowy, Ding, Hope, & Jeanjean, 2005). If that is the case, the introduction of IFRSs will affect corporate transparency differently across countries.

Bushman et al. (2004) point out that most prior research on corporate transparency isolates individual aspects of financial reporting or analysts' behaviour, while they themselves view corporate transparency as an output from a system of interrelated mechanisms. They then try to find improved measures of corporate transparency[4] that will enable more powerful tests of the economic consequences of the widespread availability of such information.

---

[1]Two other categories are private information acquisition and information dissemination.

[2]In an ideal case information is costless to all participants. In reality, there are costs to collect, disclose and interpret the information.

[3]Ball et al. (2003) study the interaction between accounting standards and the incentives of managers and auditors and show that even if a country has high-quality standards, financial reporting quality is not high when preparers' incentives imply low quality.

[4]They select country-level variables from various databases and use factor analysis to find such improved measures. For corporate reporting variables their source is the Centre for Financial Analysis and Research's (CIFAR) International Accounting and Auditing Trends (CIFAR, 1995).

Because a number of mechanisms interact, it is not certain that a particular method or set of standards will increase corporate transparency even if it seems more informative, in and of itself, than an alternative.[5] In addition, we argue that an increased knowledge of corporate transparency, in terms of a descriptive explanation of a number of such important relations, is necessary for making inferences (e.g. for standard setting) about the association between corporate transparency and various economic phenomena. Basically, this is a variation of the observation made by Holthausen and Watts (2001, p. 3), regarding much of the accounting literature on value relevance, i.e. unless the underlying theories are descriptive of accounting, standard setting and valuation, the value-relevance literature's reported associations between accounting numbers and common equity valuations offer few implications or inferences for standard setting; they are mere associations.

The purpose of this chapter is to analyse the European adoption of IFRS and its effects on corporate transparency. We will look at the interaction between the abovementioned other factors and the accounting standards; compare IFRSs to national standards in terms of fundamental characteristics; and discuss the effects of adopting IFRSs on corporate transparency given the existence of these other factors.

The chapter is organized as follows. In Section 10.2, our focus is on an individual aspect of financial reporting. Corporate transparency can be viewed in terms of individual aspects of financial reporting (Aggarwal & Simkins, 2004)[6] as well as on a more comprehensive level (Bushman et al., 2004). We look at the accounting for business combinations and at how corporate transparency is affected by the introduction of IFRS 3 (IASB, 2004). The acquisition of another company is perhaps the one single event that most powerfully affects the profitability of a company, and the introduction of IFRS 3 is one of the most controversial changes associated with the application of IFRSs.[7]

In Section 10.2.1, we briefly describe the major changes in the accounting for business combinations. In the new method, there is no amortization of goodwill and thus no information about its useful life. Potentially, this constitutes a loss of transparency. Whether this is actually the case depends on whether the lost information revealed something important about the expected value creation of

---

[5]E.g. measuring assets at fair value rather than historical cost.

[6]Aggarwal and Simkins (2004) examine the relation between voluntary disclosures of currency derivative's usage and cost of capital/shareholder value.

[7]Regarding accounting principles, Bushman et al. (2004) focus on the extent to which financial statements are consolidated and general reserves are used. Consolidated statements are viewed as more informative and the existence of general reserves as less informative. Although important, these two might be seen as "easy" ones, and in more economically developed countries non-consolidation and general reserves are not particularly common.

takeovers to external stakeholders. To answer this question, we develop in Section 10.2.2 a conceptual framework that relates expected value creation to the amortization period of goodwill, taking into consideration the fact that takeovers are subject to different business logics and hence that variations in amortization periods across acquisitions are expected. We then examine empirically the historical association between amortization period and takeovers of different strategic types. Section 10.2.3 describes the sample selection for this empirical analysis. The hypotheses are presented in Section 10.2.4, the results in Section 10.2.5, and the discussion in Section 10.2.6.

In Section 10.3, we keep the focus on the new standard for business combinations and analyse its effects on expected profits. The expected consequences for takeover activity and prices paid are discussed in view of the findings in the mergers and acquisitions literature about the financial outcome of takeovers in general.

In Section 10.4, we look more closely at the concept of corporate transparency from a behavioural perspective, extending our analysis to important actors' rationales and how they interact, considering the processes of preparation and use of accounting information. Doing this, it is reasonable to also expand the analysis to the global level.[8] The object of analysis is the whole set of IFRSs and the ultimate concern is with the consequences for resource allocation in general. Of course, to investigate the consequences of the adoption of IFRSs considering the processes of preparation and use of accounting information is an immense task (Walton, 2004, p. 8), and the analysis is of an exploratory nature. Concluding remarks and policy recommendations are put forward in Section 10.5.

10.2 The Effects on Corporate Transparency of the New Standard on Business Combinations

In this section we analyse the effect on transparency of changing the standard on business combinations.

10.2.1 The Accounting Standards for Business Combinations

In most EU countries, the previous accounting practice for acquired goodwill was one of systematic amortization. Of the 25 member countries, 12[9] are represented

---

[8] Even though IFRS 3 is not atypical, the picture it gives is not complete.

[9] Austria, Belgium, Denmark, Finland, France, Germany, Italy, Netherlands, Portugal, Spain, Sweden and the UK.

in the Transnational accounting project.[10] In seven of these countries, this practice of systematic amortization was required and in the other five it was an allowed alternative. Since the allowed amortization period varied across the 12 countries, there were considerable differences in the treatment of goodwill on a more detailed level.

In contrast to that, IFRS 3 requires goodwill acquired in a business combination to be measured at cost less any accumulated impairment losses. Consequently, goodwill is not amortized systematically, but must instead be tested for impairment annually (or more frequently). The impairment test requires an estimate of expected cash flows to a unit. The new method is characterized by increased complexity.

In terms of corporate transparency, the loss of systematic amortization entails the loss of any information it may have provided. On the other hand, we get the impairment procedure. We argue that the old accounting regime included something similar, to the extent that impairments roughly correspond to write-downs in the old regime.[11] The net effect is a potential loss of transparency. To further investigate this potential loss, we will continue to develop a framework that relates goodwill to the value created by a firm's operations.

10.2.2 Goodwill—Abnormal Profits—Strategy

One common view is that takeovers are motivated by the prospects of obtaining an advantageous competitive position. Acquiring firms would be willing to pay for reaching that position as long as the expected net present value of the decision is non-negative. Undertaking a takeover endeavour on such premises means that there are expectations of abnormal profits.

The abnormal profits will be manifested in goodwill. The origin might be found inside the target company—consolidation goodwill—or in the interaction between buyer and target—combination goodwill (Johnson & Petrone, 1998). The useful life of goodwill will depend on the persistence of the abnormal profits,

---

[10]The Transnational Accounting project is used by e.g. d´Arcy (2001). It systematically sets out the financial accounting rules and practices of several countries based on descriptions given by local accounting professors and local professionals in each country. The information on individual countries and the IASC is summarized in the Reference Matrix, so that each country's complete accounting rules are presented in the tabular form and the rules on any particular accounting problem can be read for all the countries covered by TRANSACC. It provides information on each accounting method under review of the following form: required, allowed and forbidden.

[11]In general, fixed assets had to be written down if they had values that were lower than their book values and the decrease was permanent. It must of course be acknowledged that the procedures for arriving at a devaluation of assets are different now than before.

which, we argue, will depend on the time it will take the competitors to achieve the same position and remove the competitive advantage, the likelihood that technological development will erode the position, and the stability of customers' demand (Capron & Pistre, 2002; Chatterjee, 1986; Barney, 1988). Thus, we conceptually link abnormal profits, competitive position and amortization period.[12]

It seems reasonable to assume that the persistence of the abnormal profits and hence the useful life of goodwill depends on the acquisition type. A long amortization period should be used for takeovers where the deal leads to a unique position that is both difficult and costly to imitate. A short amortization period should be used for acquisitions where the competitive advantage is negligible and/or erodes quickly.[13]

In our strategic discussion we assume that goodwill is a function of abnormal profits alone. However, from a strict accounting perspective, goodwill may also arise as a consequence of, for instance, overpayment or non-recognizable assets. We disregard these alternative sources of accounting goodwill, i.e. we assume there are no differences between the fair values and the book values of the acquired net assets.

Acquisitions are initiated for various reasons and conducted in different manners. The resource-based view states that the outcome of a takeover is likely to depend on the takeover's attributes (Barney, 1988). Researchers have attempted to capture this variation by presenting takeover classification schemes based on strategic characteristics. Hitt, Harrison, Ireland, and Best (1988) developed an approach inspired by Barney (1988). We have chosen to build on a seminal paper in the field, which distinguishes between horizontal, vertical, concentric and conglomerate acquisitions (Ansoff & Weston, 1962). Similar categories have been used for practical purposes by the Federal Trade Commission (FTC), and are still discussed in empirical research on M&A outcomes (King, Dalton, Daily, & Covin, 2004; Campa & Kedia, 2002; Palich, Cardinal, & Miller, 2000).

We define five takeover types in the following way. A *horizontal* takeover is one where the parties operate at the same position in the same value chain. They provide identical products or services in the same or different markets. A *vertical* takeover is one within the same value chain where there exists, or could potentially exist, a supplier–customer relationship. The vertical integration can either

[12]A broad empirical study where profitability is linked to competitive position is in McGahan and Porter (2002).

[13]We assume that the buyer not only attains control and consolidates the target company, but also that the buyer acquires such a stake that extraction of synergies is practically possible. In Sweden that means that 90% of the number of shares must be acquired, otherwise the minority owners in the target company have some legal protection.

be *forward* or *backward* oriented. In a *concentric* acquisition, the parties belong to different value chains but have highly similar production or distributional technologies or customers. A *conglomerate* takeover is one where the parties belong to different value chains. There are no buyer–seller relationship, no technical or distributional relationship, and the parties do not deal with identical products.

Walter and Barney (1990) found empirically that the managerial acquisition motives are different in the five takeover types. Based on their research, and commonly proposed takeover motives in press releases, we make the following division. Horizontal deals are explained by motives such as economies of scale, critical mass, synergies, market share and geographical expansion. Integration backwards is distinguished by, for instance, an interest in handling critical relations, in securing production input and in cutting transaction costs between suppliers and customers. Integration forward is, among other things, characterized by an interest in handling critical relations, in securing demand for production output, in taking care of service and after market activities, in cutting transaction costs between suppliers and customers and in getting closer to the final customer as a stimulus for production development. Concentric acquisitions might be driven by an idea to sell new products to the same customer group or by using established distribution channels for new products. Conglomerate acquisitions are normally motivated by arguments of risk reduction.

We argue that the useful life of goodwill should reflect the business logic of the underlying strategic decision. The time period should be longest in horizontal, and to some extent vertical, takeovers where combination goodwill can be at hand. It is probably shorter in concentric acquisitions and even more so in conglomerate takeovers, where consolidation goodwill dominates.

It has however been questioned whether the amortization period conveys any information about the useful life of goodwill, and hence of abnormal profits, to external stakeholders, i.e. whether it has positive effects on corporate transparency. That question is at the centre of our empirical study below.

10.2.3 Sample Selection

We searched for industries characterized by high takeover activity covering all strategic types and with substantial goodwill items. Several industries fitted the description, most clearly so IT, mechanical engineering, and power generation. We chose to focus on listed Swedish IT firms' acquisitions.

The M&A activity in the IT industry peaked around the turn of the millennium. Many Swedish firms attained leading positions in Europe through numerous transactions, turning Kista, a suburb of Stockholm, into an IT hub second only to Silicon Valley. Many of the companies were active in the goodwill debate, not seldom proposing alternative accounting methods. This means that the management of these firms has discussed goodwill on a detailed level and that many of them presumably were knowledgeable when setting the amortization scheme.

We delimited the time period to 1997–2001. During that period more than 50 IT companies were listed at the Stockholm Stock Exchange. The differences between the companies were of such a kind that they could disturb our search for a correlation between strategic type, abnormal profits and useful life of goodwill. To control for that risk we divided the sample into the three sub-industries that are used by convention: (a) IT and Internet consultants, (b) software firms, and (c) hardware and distributors. The sub-industries face different business conditions. Consultancy operations are most dependent on individual employees when it comes to customer contacts. This human capital is usually loosely knitted to the company. Hardware firms and retailers are in the opposite situation. Software firms benefit from routines and processes that to a larger extent belong to the organization. Hence, they are less dependent on individuals. A complete list of the companies in the sub-industries, following a classification by the Swedish business weekly *Affärsvärlden*, is presented in Appendix 10.A.2.

We established a gross list of takeovers made by the listed IT companies. Our starting point was a list compiled by the Swedish M&A journal *Förvärv & Fusioner*. We compared it to and adjusted it for information in annual reports and press releases. From the gross list we excluded takeovers that were accounted for with the pooling of interest method, acquisitions where we did not have information on the useful life of goodwill, small transactions, direct takeovers, and finally acquisitions that could be seen as intra-family restructurings. We ended up with a list of 79 takeovers made by 17 acquirers in 15 different countries representing all five takeover types. By limiting the study to only one industry and to a period often referred to as a boom period for that industry, we advocate caution whenever the results are to be generalized to other industries and periods.

The strategic classification of the takeovers is critical to our approach. Press releases and annual reports were the initial sources of information. The stated takeover motives were analysed using the findings of Walter and Barney (1990). The relevant descriptions were however missing for some takeovers and unclear for others. Consequently, we did not manage to classify all the takeovers with a reliable degree of accuracy. Our way of solving the problem was to ask industry and transaction experts to help us complement and double-check the strategic classifications. They represented various perspectives and kinds of experience; one financial analyst specialized on the IT industry, one investment banker who was involved in several deals on the list, and one executive with more than 25 years of experience as CEO, President and owner of several companies in the industry. We met them individually and explained our classification scheme. They got the list with the 79 takeovers and carried out their own classification. In those cases where all the experts and we did not arrive at the same classification, we discussed the issue further until we agreed. These people, we argue, have a better overview of the industry than the CEO or CFO of the individual company, which would have constituted an alternative expertise for complementing our incomplete classifications. Hence, we are able to secure a certain degree of internal consistency in the classifications.

It is not trivial to make an ex-post strategic classification of the 79 acquisitions that we have selected. Memory of the industrial development fades and it is sometimes hard to recall the exact circumstances of each decision. We have attempted to classify each acquisition following the strategy the buyer had at the time of the deal, but as will be explained below in some cases we have had to moderate that position a bit. It is also worth mentioning that similar takeovers made by the same company can be classified differently. For instance, an IT consultant's acquisition of its first advertising agency might be a concentric deal, but when the second advertising agency is taken over it is likely to be a horizontal acquisition. That is a difference in classification that may not be compatible with the way companies choose amortization periods for these deals. For each takeover case, we have used the original amortization scheme. Hence the subsequent prolongation of the period that was made by one acquirer was left without notice.

10.2.4 Hypotheses

It follows from the reasoning in Section 10.2.2 that we expect to find that

- the amortization period depends on the acquisition's strategic characteristics.,
- horizontal takeovers are associated with a longer useful life of goodwill than, in order, vertical, concentric and conglomerate acquisitions.

We further argue that a takeover's strategic value and useful life is likely to depend on the sub-industry. Thus, we also expect to find that

- the amortization periods are longer for retailers and for hardware and software companies than for consultancy firms,
- the ranking order of the average useful life between the five acquisition types is the same for the three sub-industries.

10.2.5 Results

It is clear from Table 10.1—presenting the frequency of amortization periods over the different strategic types—that a horizontal takeover amortized over 10

Table 10.1: Frequency of different strategic types of acquisitions and amortization periods.

Strategic type	**Amortization period for goodwill**			**Total**
	5	**10**	**20**	
Horizontal	13	34	7	54
Forward		6		6
Backward		1		1
Concentric	1	6	3	10
Conglomerate	1	5	2	8
Total	15	52	12	79

years is the typical deal. But at the same time there is considerable variation. We have examples of all useful lives and all strategic types, although there are no observations for all combinations.

It is striking that the longer amortization periods are used in cases where we did not expect them to be frequent. The other side of the coin is that the shortest useful life is predominantly attached to the strategic type where we rather expected it to be rare. The fact that the number of acquiring firms was restricted to 17 necessitates a careful interpretation of the results. Two examples illustrate this. It appears at first glance that there is a widespread use of 10-year amortization schemes for takeovers that lead to an integration forward. But six of the transactions were made by the same acquirer. Second, all horizontal takeovers with a 5-year amortization scheme were made by the same acquirer. Yet, that company not only used a useful life of 5 years, but also applied a 20-year useful life in one of its horizontal acquisitions.

We know that some acquirers have the same useful life for all takeovers, while others apply a continuum. The question is whether this difference is a reflection of the strategically different deals made by these companies. In Table 10.2 we present the situation for those acquirers that made at least two acquisitions. Two positions can be explained by our strategic reasoning, the bottom-left and the upper-right. The position one expects to observe most often is at the bottom-left, i.e. companies that make acquisitions of the same strategic type should use one and the same amortization period. The position at the upper-right is also in line with our expectations as long as the differences in amortization period reflect differences in strategic type of the underlying takeovers. However, for the two companies in that cell we cannot detect any such relationship.

Table 10.2: The combinations of amortization period and type of strategic acquisitions.

Amortization period	Type of strategic acquisitions	
	One category	**Several categories**
Continuum	Information Highway	Framfab, Sigma
Single	IMS Data, Adera	Enea Data, Intentia, Know IT, MSC Konsult

The other two positions in Table 10.2, i.e. the bottom-right and the upper-left, are difficult to explain by our strategic reasoning. The one at bottom-right could, however, be understood in the light of our overall finding that strategic characteristics do not seem to determine the applied useful life for goodwill. It may be the case that a corporate goodwill policy states one useful life of goodwill regardless of the strategic character of the deal. The position at the upper-left cannot be explained on the basis of our reasoning.

So far, our discussion has concerned the entire sample of 79 acquisitions. The question is if a division into sub-industries and the dimension domestic/cross-border would change our overall findings. When it comes to the sub-industries, 66 of the 79 takeovers were made by consultancy firms. Typically, the consultants made horizontal takeovers (52 of the 66 cases). The remaining 13 acquisitions in the study were made by software firms. The strategic type was typically non-horizontal among these firms. Six of the 13 cases were integrations forward (all made by one acquiring firm), five concentric, and two horizontal. Despite the differences in strategic type, the sub-industries use similar amortization periods for goodwill.

We also checked whether there were any systematic differences between the domestic takeovers (60% of the sample) and the cross-border ones (40% of the sample). We could not detect any significant patterns. On a more detailed level there were, however, some differences. The distribution of amortization periods is somewhat different. A larger portion of the cross-border deals was amortized over 20 years. Forward integration was over-represented, and conglomerate acquisitions under-represented among the cross-border transactions.

In summary, we do not find any strong support for the general hypothesis that amortization period would depend on strategic characteristics. Specifically, we do not observe the expected ranking order between the various types of strategic acquisitions or sub-industries. Against that background we conclude that there is probably no loss of transparency when systematic amortization of goodwill is abandoned as IFRS 3 is introduced.

10.2.6 Discussion

The mismatch between our expected findings and the observations in our analysis calls for discussion. Could it be that our model is univariate and hence does not catch the impact of other variables? In a multivariate analysis we could have included variables such as the size of the goodwill item and the profitability of the acquiring company. The size of the goodwill item for a particular takeover is, unfortunately, usually not disclosed. Bearing that in mind, we have exposed our data to tests of robustness.

Claiming that the choice of amortization period could be affected by size and profitability is in line with the earnings management literature. In our context, earnings management might mean that companies' choice of amortization period is influenced by a propensity to enhance net profits. Healy and Wahlen (1999) found that earnings management occurs for a variety of reasons, such as influencing the stock market, increasing management compensation and reducing the likelihood of violating lending agreements. In the context of accounting for business combinations, studies of earnings management have indicated that managers prefer the consolidation method that leads to the highest post-merger earnings (Aboody, Kaznik, & Williams, 2000), and that in a purchase analysis, the valuation of acquired assets (and hence the residual value of goodwill) offers scope for managerial discretion (Higson, 1998, p. 157).

In a previous study (Bild & Schuster, 2003), we analysed the earnings management behaviour of 52 IT companies listed at the Stockholm Stock Exchange during the period 1997 through 2001. Among the 52 companies were those 17 acquirers that are the focus of this chapter. The magnitude of the goodwill phenomenon is illustrated in Figure 10.1. We see that the relative size of goodwill, scaled against sales, increases over the period 1998–2001. The development is most accentuated for the top quartile of the listed IT companies. It is obvious that net profits are very sensitive for the choice of amortization period.

We have already seen that amortization periods varied across acquirers and takeovers in the sample of 17 acquirers (Appendix 10.A.1) and that goodwill-to-sales increased among the 52 listed companies (Figure 10.1). If earnings management was practiced, it would also mean that the amortization period increased. In Figure 10.2, we see that the median amortization period (AP)[14] was fairly stable over the years, but that the top 10 per cent extended gradually.

---

[14]For companies that used several useful lives for their different goodwill items, the average amortization period had to be calculated. In short, we divided the accumulated acquisition cost for goodwill by the annual amortization of goodwill. There are measurement problems involved, which are developed in Bild and Schuster (2003).

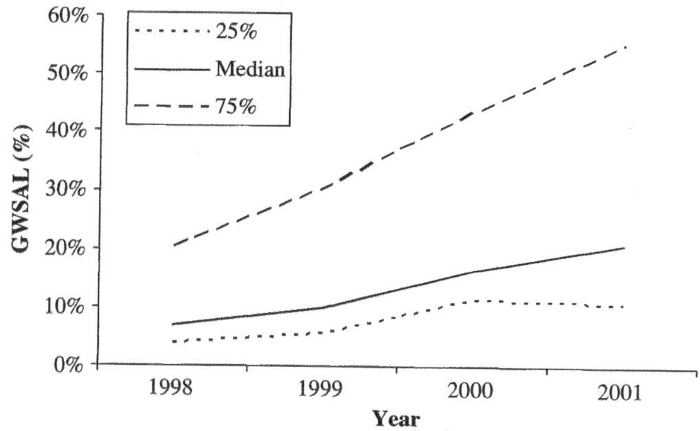

Figure 10.1: Goodwill to sales for the IT companies 1998–2001.

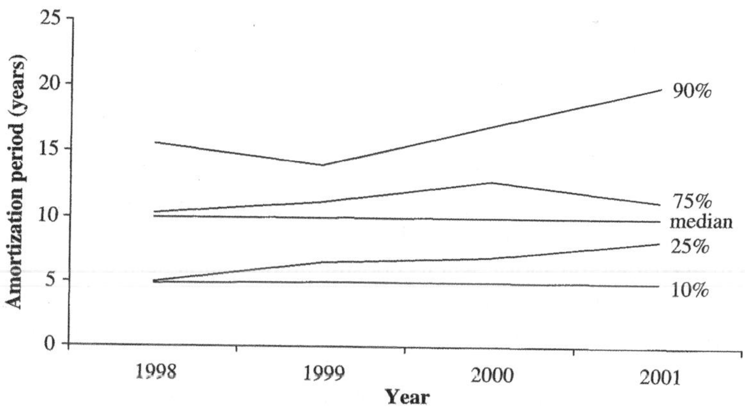

Figure 10.2: Amortisation period, 1998–2001.

The questions we asked, among others, were whether the length of the AP was correlated to the companies' profitability and/or financial position. In other words, were the longer APs used by unprofitable and/or financially weak firms? To investigate that issue, we defined two measures, the EBITA-margin (EBITAM) and the Equity-to-Sales-ratio (EQSAL). EBITAM was defined as 'operating profit before amortization and write-down of goodwill to sales'. EQSAL was defined as 'average book equity (before amortization and write-downs of goodwill at year end) to sales'.

We computed the correlations between AP and EBITAM and EQSAL, respectively. The Pearson correlation coefficient for EBITAM and AP is generally weak and the sign changed over the years. We also analysed the lagged correlation between AP and EBITAM the coming year, but it did not change the results. The Pearson correlation coefficient for EQSAL and AP was weak and varied over the years. A negative correlation would have been consistent with the hypothesis that higher risks entail longer amortization periods.

To conclude, there was no strong support for the idea that earnings management could explain the length of the amortization period. That, in turn, could mean that a multivariate analysis of goodwill amortization periods would not necessarily provide different conclusions than those derived from our univariate analysis of Section 10.2.5.

Another topic to discuss is whether we should have compared the amortization period of goodwill to the financial outcome of takeovers, instead of theory-deduced expected persistent competitive advantage. There are many indications that horizontal acquisitions actually develop more unfavourably than conglomerate deals (Bild, 1998). This is perhaps due to a tendency for overpayment and/or a troublesome post-acquisition process (Sirower, 1997). These findings suggest hypotheses quite the opposite of ours. Horizontal acquisitions should have the shortest amortization periods and conglomerate acquisitions the longest. Looking at our data from this perspective, we cannot find support for the alternative hypotheses.

We can understand the absence of a pattern if management tends to balance theory and general takeover outcomes, i.e. our hypotheses and the alternative one outlined in the paragraph above, when choosing amortization period for goodwill. The reasoning would be that the management knows that horizontal takeovers have the largest return potential and therefore they deserve a long amortization period. But at the same time management are well aware of the risk of a poor outcome due to overpayment, post-acquisition integration problems and competitors' strategic reactions. In any individual case, it is not possible to observe how, and if, this balance is applied, since we do not know how the two dimensions are weighted. Furthermore, the transparency for an external user would be low since there is no robust link between the strategic type of takeover and the choice of amortization period.

Finally, as was previously stressed, it must be emphasized that we have studied only one industry during a limited period of time, where the business conditions were rather special. This does of course impact our ability to generalize our findings of a lack of transparency to other industries and other time frames. However, it must be emphasized that the spirit of this chapter is to bring up on an explorative-basis issues of transparency in relation to the adoption of IFRS.

10.3 The Consequences of IFRS 3 for Reported Profits and M&A Activity

The change to IFRS 3 does not have cash flow implications for the amalgamated entity. Financial theorists claim that the change of standard therefore lacks economic consequences (Watts & Zimmerman, 1986). It does, however, impact the group's net income. If profit figures are deemed important by external users of accounting information, there are reasons to analyse how the group's net income is affected.

We limit our analysis to the effects on net profit related to goodwill.[15] They are

(a) Net profit *increases or is constant* compared to the previous method. If total impairment losses equal total amortization, the total net profit will be the same in the long run. However, there is a measurement problem related to internally generated goodwill, which in some cases will lead to constant book values for goodwill.[16] If this is the case, total impairment will be lower than total amortization in the long run and consequently total net profit will be higher.
(b) Net profit is *reported earlier* compared to the previous method. Even if total impairment losses equal total amortization, net profit will be reported earlier. This conclusion rests upon the assumptions that write-downs were required by the previous method as a complement to amortization if necessary and that the carrying value of goodwill by the new method could never be lower compared to the previous method.
(c) Net profit is *more volatile* compared to the previous method. Assuming that total net profit is the same, the net profit is more volatile since amortizations of an equal amount each year are replaced by impairment losses in some years.

At face value, (a) and (b) may be considered to be positive effects, while (c) is negative. The expected net effect is positive. The net effects may be considered to be so attractive that we see an increase in takeover activity and/or higher purchase prices for target companies (Runsten, 2004). Both potential consequences are worrying since we know that takeovers in general have no, or even negative, value consequences for the buying company (King et al., 2004). These losses do not,

[15]The new method requires the identification of separable assets to a larger extent. The effect on net profit depends on the amortization period for these. If the amortization period for identifiable, separable assets is equal to the amortization period for goodwill in the previous method, the net profit is not affected by the change to the extent that goodwill is replaced by separable assets.

[16]In the impairment test, existing book values are compared to expected cash flows. Since the expected cash flows include effects from events after the acquisition (internally generated goodwill), it is possible that no impairment is registered even though the goodwill attributed to the acquisition has decreased in value.

however, translate into welfare losses of mergers and acquisitions. Numerous studies conclude that we are dealing with a zero-sum-game, where losses for the buyer are balanced by gains for the seller, at least if transaction costs are disregarded.[17] If transaction costs are included, we cannot reject that M&A activity could actually destroy value and thus be detrimental for resource allocation in a society. Considering the financial outcome of takeovers, there is a risk that IFRSs reduces transparency in one important sense. Namely, that decisions that destroy value are portrayed in a way that lead to higher profits.

The indications in this section rest upon a functional fixation on an all-inclusive concept of income, i.e. comprehensive income (CI). It is CI that becomes more volatile. Other income concepts, before impairments but after amortization, become more stable. Earnings Before Interest Taxes Depreciation and Amortization (EBITDA) will be constant. Even though a focus on CI has merit as a robust measure, a richer descriptive picture has to consider that the economic consequences of this change in net profit could be expected to depend upon analysts' interpretation of this accounting information. In general, a study of the economic consequences of the introduction of a new standard requires a more comprehensive analysis of the processes of preparation and use of accounting standards.

10.4 The Effects on Corporate Transparency of the Adoption of the Whole Set of IFRSs

So far, we have restricted our analysis of the effects of IFRSs on corporate transparency to the standard on business combinations, focusing on individual aspects such as choice of amortization period and change of expected net income in simplified settings. In this section, we extend the analysis to the processes of preparation and use of accounting information. An increased knowledge of corporate transparency in terms of a descriptive explanation of important actors' rationales and relations between those actors is necessary for making specific inferences e.g. for standard setting purposes.[18]

10.4.1 Interplay between Actors

In general, it is the processes of preparation and use of accounting information that make up the setting for corporate transparency. An analysis of these processes

---

[17] Roll (1986) is an early advocate for this view.

[18] It should be recognized that accounting information sometimes also has direct consequences. Among these are consequences on taxes, bonus programmes, prices in regulated markets and debt covenants.

gives descriptive relevance to observed associations between single phenomena. Characteristic of these processes is a rather complicated interplay between various actors.[19] We choose to describe this interplay in terms of a number of trade-offs and the need for a long-term balance between different legitimate interests. In our analysis of the interplay between various actors, we focus on management, auditors, analysts, ultimate users and standard setters.[20]

The primary task of management is to manage the entity. From this point of view it is important that the way managers see their businesses corresponds to the way in which they present it to the outside world. The primary task of the auditors is to verify the accounting information. One issue is the scope of the audit, e.g. whether the auditors task just is to verify that a specific method follows the relevant standard, or if they also should assess whether the use of a specific method gives "a true and fair view", which is related to the ability of outsiders to evaluate a firm's operations, i.e. transparency.

The analysts are interpreters that collect and process accounting information that then serves as a base for the ultimate users. Ultimate users are of different kinds. In IFRS seven different categories are explicitly identified.[21] Often investors are placed foremost and their perceived needs are treated as a benchmark for the other categories (Barth, Beaver, & Landsman, 2001, p. 77).

The standard setters are also a part of this process. A standard setter confronted with an accounting issue has three options: (1) to prescribe a specific method, (2) to allow more than one method (with or without stating any explicit preference for one of them e.g. a benchmark method and an allowed alternative method), and (3) to decide not to regulate (but perhaps require additional disclosure). A standard setter needs compliance. If the necessary compliance is not attained, the standard setter will be replaced by other means of regulation.

This process of preparation and use is characterized by a number of trade-offs. From a management perspective there is a trade-off between external users demand for additional information and other factors that affect the companies' supply of additional information, such as the complexity of the issues, the confidentiality

---

[19]In Section 10.3, the effects of transactions on net income were analysed. These effects depend upon the applied accounting standards. The consequences of these will in turn depend on how this accounting information is interpreted by various users.

[20]It is rather common to distinguish between preparers and users of accounting information. Even though we sometimes make this distinction, we do not use it to categorize the actors. Some actors, such as auditors, do not fit easily into any category. Others fit into both, management do not only prepare accounting information but also use it e.g. for benchmarking and controlling purposes.

[21]Investors, employees, lenders, suppliers and trade creditors, customers, governments and their agencies and the public.

interest in regard of competitors and management control of different organizational levels within the company.[22]

External users' view on disclosure is characterized by their wanting more information, rather than less. In the absence of balancing factors regarding external users' demand for information (as opposed to management and standard setters), there is a risk that too much data with unclear information content is demanded and supplied.

From a standard setting perspective, there has to be a balance between preparers' and users' interests. A standard setter has to consider the preparers' environment as well as users' requirements when developing standards. Starting from a company view, it is important that the standard setter's choice is based on an understanding of the role that the transactions have in a business and control setting. If, on the other hand, the starting point for the standard setter is the capital markets requirements, company practices are less important, but the working of the capital markets more so. A standard setter has to make a trade-off between level of specification and compliance (Johansson & Oestman, 1995). The more flexible the rules are, the better the compliance. The existence of severe sanctions produces a better formal compliance, but also requires more unambiguous standards, while at the same time preparers get more hesitant to accept these.

To conclude, the processes of preparation and use of accounting information that make up the setting for corporate transparency are characterized by a number of trade-offs and there is a need for a long-term balance between different interests.

10.4.2 Characteristics of IFRSs

In Section 10.3, we analysed the expected effects on net income in a simplified setting. Doing this for the whole set of standards is difficult. So instead we identify the general characteristics of IFRSs to give some indications. The IFRSs are constantly changing. These changes are reflected in current standards (new standards and existing standards that recently have been changed) and working projects (new standards, amendments of existing standards and general issues). One advantage of including working projects is that they say more about current

---

[22]The idea that the extent of (voluntary) disclosure involves balancing the costs and benefits of disclosure is found in Aggarwal and Simkins (2004). Disclosure enhances value. However, there are also costs to collect and disseminate information. Factors that have been hypothesized or shown to influence disclosure costs include political costs and agency costs (Watts & Zimmerman, 1986), and also strategic costs (Admati & Pfleiderer, 1998). To our knowledge, the management control dimension has not received much attention in the literature in this context. In our opinion, it is fundamental.

thought. On the other hand, they may be a forum for exploring ideas that in the end will not be accepted. We focus on current standards but make references to working projects when appropriate.

We analyse the introduction in terms of common recognition and measurement principles and complexity.[23] Regarding common recognition and measurement principles IFRS brings an increased frequency of fair values (Barker, 2004, p. 159), which together with an all-inclusive concept of income (see below), is expected to have substantial effects on net profit.

The increased frequency of fair values is analysed in terms of which assets and liabilities are reported at fair value and when they are reported at fair value (at initial recognition and/or subsequently). Important categories of assets reported at fair value are financial instruments, investment property and agricultural products. In the long term, the scope is expected to increase even more.[24]

Regarding the time dimension most assets[25] are still reported at acquisition cost at initial recognition. Already Paton and Littleton (1940) argued that historical cost is not important in the sense of consideration given, but as a measure of fair value at the time of acquisition. However, when it comes to the recognition of profit, there is a subtle difference between the measurement of assets received and the consideration paid. If the fair value of assets received is deemed to exceed consideration paid, you could argue that there is a profit. In the long term, the use of fair values at initial recognition is expected to increase.[26]

---

[23]Another important dimension is changes in the institutional setting. The consequences of these could be expected to vary across countries, which have had different systems before the change.

[24]The IASB and FASB Boards are exploring an 'asset and liability approach' to defining revenue and specifying the criteria for the recognition of revenue (FASB, 2005). That approach focuses on identifying and measuring increases in assets and decreases in liabilities arising from contracts with customers. The Boards have developed a draft conceptual model for identifying the assets and liabilities that arise from contractual rights and obligations. In addition, the Boards have adopted a working principle that requires assets and liabilities affecting revenue to be measured at fair value.

[25]The same applies for liabilities that the company incurs.

[26]In the working project on business combinations (IASB, 2005a) it is said that "In a business combination the total amount to be recognised by the acquirer should be the fair value of the business over which it obtains control. Assuming an exchange of equal values, the fair value of the consideration given by the acquirer generally is more clearly evident than the fair value of the acquirer's interest in the business acquired . . . In rare circumstances a business combination is not an exchange of equal values such that the fair value of the acquirer's interest in the business acquired exceeds the consideration given for that interest. In such cases, the excess of the fair value of the acquirer's interest in the business acquired over the consideration given for that interest should be recognised as a reduction in the total amount of goodwill . . . Any excess remaining after the total goodwill has been reduced to zero *should be recognized immediately in profit or loss* (our emphasis) at the date of acquisition".

The full impact of fair values on net profit is realized through an application of an all-inclusive concept of income. Currently, there are a number of cases where changes in assets and liabilities bypass the income statement and go directly to equity (available for sale securities, pensions, etc.). In the long term, the frequency of this is expected to decrease.[27]

The expected effects on total net profit of the use of fair values and CI are not apparent. However, an increased volatility in profits and an earlier recognition of profits could be expected.[28] The adoption of IFRS also leads to an increased complexity in a number of respects. Not only are the recognition and measurement rules more complex. There are also substantial additional disclosure requirements.

10.4.3 Consequences of the Adoption of IFRSs on the Preparation and use of Accounting Information

The consequences of the adoption of IFRSs on corporate transparency will depend on the processes for preparation and use of accounting information. We will now analyse how the trade-offs that we have identified are affected by the increased complexity and the use of fair values and CI.

Regarding the increased complexity, from a management perspective this makes it more difficult for companies to have the necessary knowledge internally. They have to rely on external consultants and become more dependent on the auditors. However, the complexity is sometimes such that the auditors in turn have to rely on external consultation, e.g. the big auditing firms' international accounting desks in London. The increased complexity paired with an uncertainty about the scope of the audit leads to an increased use of assessment suppliers, i.e. companies specialized in valuation of some kind.[29]

A primary consequence is that the process of preparation of accounting information becomes more distant from the business operations, which the information represents. A secondary consequence will be that there is an increased gap between financial reporting and management control. This might mean that the corporate transparency does not increase.

Regarding fair value and CI, from a management perspective this could widen the gap between financial reporting and management control. From an analyst's

---

[27]The project on Reporting Performance (IASB, 2005b).

[28]For an early empirical indication, FT 18 April 2005 refers to an UBS analysis of 27 companies that have restated their 2004 earnings under the new rules showing profit swings of 12 % on average.

[29]Real estate is an old area that has been complemented by e.g. various intangible assets such as customer lists.

perspective, the predictive function of accounting is dominant. The analysts do not have direct access to the management's business model. If information about fair values replaces information about future cash flows, the analysts are not better off. They want information to predict values, not the values *per se*. Information about fair values renders them more dependent on the preparers. This might mean that transparency does not increase.

The focus on CI instead of a more restricted income concept (such as net income or earnings) gives sophisticated analysts/investors the opportunity to pick and choose. It is motivated by the risk of otherwise missing important items, that there is no unambiguous foundation for some other concept of income and that performance cannot be captured in a single number. This might not be as good for other users. It is perhaps the necessity of making a choice that is beneficial for transparency through the processes of preparation and use of accounting information. There is an explicit stand in a classification, a write-down, etc. It is originally made by the accountants, confirmed by the CEO, verified by the auditors, scrutinized by monitors, discussed in media and assessed in qualitative terms by analysts. In a number of steps different actors are forced to argue for their stand and the issue at hand gets a detailed treatment. An absence of classification does not give the same room for argumentation. The same is true for a valuation at expected value.[30] Thus, transparency might not increase.

This development towards fair values could be expected to continue. The argument of internal system consistency, which traditionally has favoured acquisition cost over fair value, is not as valid as it once was (at some point, the argument for internal system consistency could actually be used to support fair value measurements). Ultimately, with a gradually increasing complexity and the use of fair values together with CI, there is a risk of institutionalizing primitive concepts of income closely related to the cash flow of the period, which could jeopardize the status of profit as a measure of performance and the legitimacy of accrual accounting. Transparency might even decrease.

The economic consequences of an increased volatility of profits and an earlier recognition of profits are of course difficult to establish. However, as noted above, there are direct consequences. One important feature of many of these is that they are not at all, or only to a limited extent, reversible. Bonuses paid out are not repayable, repayment of taxes is often covered by restrictions, and premature repayments of loans are not reversed.[31] Since these are outflows, a potential

---

[30]Fair values are not just market values, but in some cases values according to economic theory.

[31]Of course, many other consequences of accounting information where there is an element of interpretation are also irreversible.

consequence is a reduction of corporate wealth, i.e. the aggregate purchasing power available to a firm for strategic purposes (Donaldson, 1984).

From a standard setting perspective, IASB has been under fire. Critics have questioned, whether the advantages of IFRSs in terms of improved transparency are large enough to offset the higher costs associated with the much-increased complexity. We have gone beyond that and asked, whether there will be improved transparency. Our analysis indicates that transparency will not always increase; in some cases it might even decrease. Of course, the consequences of the adoption of IFRSs are elusive and could be expected to differ across countries. The trade-offs that characterize the preparation and use of accounting information will change. This will affect the balance between various legitimate interests with unclear long-term consequences on resource allocation. These processes related to the preparation and use of accounting information have to be more closely studied. At the same time there is a large demand for more limited studies within the framework of a descriptive model.

10.5 Concluding Remarks and Policy Recommendations

We believe that IFRSs is basically a positive force in its harmonizing of financial reporting. A successful progress would enhance transparency and in the end foster more profitable growth in European industries. To reach that end, it is important that standard setting is dealt with in today's manner, i.e. that politicians leave the standard setting process to the IASB and allow for national standard setting bodies to continue to play an active part within the IFRS context.

We do however question whether transparency, and hence the prospects for growth, are best supported by an increasingly complex reporting system characterized by an aspiration for more fair values and CI. That is not to say that we oppose fair values in general. Fair values are appropriate for assets that are actively traded on a well-functioning market. For other than such assets, reporting only fair value could counteract the underlying objectives of the IFRSs project. Hence, we recommend a temporary stop in the adoptation to fair values. The stop would allow time for reflection and deep analyses of the consequences of applying IFRSs.

Acknowledgement

The authors are grateful to Stefan Engqvist, Robert Holm and John Wattin for assistance with strategic classifications of takeovers in the IT industry, and to *Förvärv & Fusioner* for lists of takeovers by IT companies.

References

Aboody, D., Kaznik, R., & Williams, M. (2000). Purchase versus pooling in stock-for-stock acquisitions: Why do firms care? *Journal of Accounting and Economics, 29*(3), 261–286.

Admati, A. R., & Pfleiderer, P. C. (1998). *Forcing firms to talk: Financial disclosure regulation and externalities*. Stanford University Working Paper no 1470. https://gsbapps.stanford.edu/researchpapers/detail1.asp

Aggarwal, R., & Simkins, B. J. (2004). Evidence on voluntary disclosures of derivatives usage by large US companies. *Journal of Derivatives Accounting, 1*(1), 61–81.

Ansoff, H. I., & Weston, J. F. (1962). Merger objectives and organization structure. *Quarterly Review of Economics and Business, 2*(3), 49–58.

Ball, R., Ashok, R., & Wu, J. S. (2003). Incentives versus standards: Properties of accounting income in four East Asian Countries. *Journal of Accounting and Economics, 36*(1–3), 235–270.

Barker, R. (2004). Reporting financial performance. *Accounting Horizons, 18*(2), 157–172.

Barney, J. B. (1988). Returns to bidding firms in mergers and acquisitions: Reconsidering the relatedness hypothesis. *Strategic Management Journal, 9*(Special Issue), 71–78.

Barth, M. E., Beaver, W. H., & Landsman, W. R. (2001). The relevance of the value-relevance literature for financial accounting standard setting: Another view. *Journal of Accounting and Economics, 31*(1–3), 77–104.

Bild, M. (1998). *Valuation of takeovers*. Stockholm: EFI.

Bild, M., & Schuster, W. (2003). Amortization of goodwill: Strategic rationales or earnings management? Working paper. Stockholm School of Economics. Presented at the 26th annual congress of the European Accounting Association, Sevilla.

Bushman, R. M., Piotroski, J. D., & Smith, A. J. (2004). What determines corporate transparency? *Journal of Accounting Research, 42*(2), 207–252.

Campa, J. M., & Kedia, S. (2002). Explaining the diversification discount. *Journal of Finance, 57*(4), 1731–1762.

Capron, L., & Pistre, N. (2002). When do acquirers earn abnormal return? *Strategic Management Journal, 23*(9), 781–794.

Center for International Analysis and Research (CIFAR). (1995). *International accounting and auditing trends*. Princeton, NJ: CIFAR Publications Inc.

Chatterjee, S. (1986). Types of synergy and economic value: The impact of acquisitions on merging and rival firms. *Strategic Management Journal, 7*(2), 119–139.

d'Arcy, A. (2001). Accounting classification and the international harmonisation debate—an empirical investigation. *Accounting, Organizations and Society, 26*, 327–349.

Donaldsson, G. (1984). *Managing corporate wealth—the operation of a comprehensive financial goal system*. New York: Praeger.

FASB. (2005). *Revenue recognition*. http://www.iasb.org/current/iasb.asp?showPageContent=no&xml=16_19_67_09092003.htm. November 4, 2005.

Healy, P. M., & Wahlen, J. M. (1999). A review of the earnings management literature and its implications for standard setting. *Accounting Horizons, 13*(4), 365–383.

Higson, C. (1998). Goodwill. *British Accounting Review, 30*(2), 141–158.

Hitt, M. A., Harrison, J. S., Ireland, R. D., & Best, A. (1988). Attributes of successful and unsuccessful acquisitions of US firms. *British Journal of Management*, *9*(2), 91–114.

Holthausen, R. W., & Watts, R. L. (2001). The relevance of the value-relevance literature for financial accounting standard setting. *Journal of Accounting and Economics*, *31*(1–3), 3–75.

IASB. (2004). *International financial reporting standards*. London: IASCF.

IASB. (2005a). *Business combinations (Phase II)—purchase method procedures*. http://www.iasb.org/uploaded_files/documents/16_10_buscom2-ps.pdf. November 4, 2005.

IASB. (2005b). *IASB activities—performance reporting*. http://www.iasb.org/current/iasb.asp?showPageContent=no&xml=16_19_67_09092003.htm. November 4, 2005.

Johansson, S., & Oestman, L. (1995). *Accounting theory—integrating behaviour and measurement*. London: Pitman Publishing.

Johnson, L. T., & Petrone, K. R. (1998). Is goodwill an asset? *Accounting Horizons*, *12*(3), 293–303.

King, D. R., Dalton, D. R., Daily, C. M., & Covin, J. G. (2004). Meta-analyses of post-acquisition performance: Indications of unidentified moderators. *Strategic Management Journal*, *25*(2), 187–200.

McGahan, A. M., & Porter, M. E. (2002). What do we know about variance in accounting profitability? *Management Science*, *486*(7), 834–851.

Oxelheim, L. (1996). *Financial markets in transition. Globalization, investment and economic growth*. London: Routledge and International Thomson Press.

Palich, L. E., Cardinal, L. B., & Miller, C. C. (2000). Curvilinearity in the diversification-performance linkage: An examination of over three decades of research. *Strategic Management Journal*, *21*(2), 155–174.

Paton, W. A., & Littleton, A. C. (1940). *An introduction to corporate accounting standards*. American Accounting Association, Sarasota, Fla.

Roll, R. (1986). The Hubris Hypothesis of corporate takeovers. *Journal of Business*, *59*(2), 197–216.

Runsten, M. (2004). Vinst, vinstförväntningar och aktiekursrörelser mot bakgrund av de finansiella styrprocesserna. In: J. Lind, & W. Schuster (Eds), *Redovisningens teori, praktik och pedagogik—En vänbok till Lars Östman* (pp. 119–156). Stockholm: EFI.

Sirower, M. L. (1997). *The synergy trap: How companies lose the acquisition game*. New York: The Free Press.

Stolowy, H., Ding, Y., Hope, O. K., & Jeanjean, T. (2005). Differences between domestic accounting standards and IAS: Measurement, determinants and implications. Working paper presented at European Accounting Association conference, May 17–20, Gothenburg, Sweden.

Walter, G. A., & Barney, J. (1990). Management objectives in mergers and acquisitions. *Strategic Management Journal*, *11*(1), 79–86.

Walton, P. (2004). IAS 39: Where different accounting models collide. *Accounting in Europe*, *1*, 5–16.

Watts, R. L., & Zimmerman, J. L. (1986). *Positive accounting theory*. Englewood Cliffs: Prentice-Hall.

Interviews:

Stefan Engkvist, February 24, 2003
Robert Holm, May 23, 2003
John Wattin, June 17, 2003

Appendix 10.A.1: Strategic Classifications

Acquirer	Target company	Target nationality	Source	Date of source (yymmdd)	Useful life	Strategic type
Adera	GCI Interactive Europé	SE	FT/Res	000207/10	10	H
Adera	Itage	SE	Dir	000417	10	H
Adera	Nucleus	UK	Res/DI	000915/6	10	H
AU-System	Svenska Teknikbolaget	SE	BIT	010116	10	H
Connova Group	Billiant	SE	Wm/Dir	011106/7	10	C
Enea Data	Redina Informatik	SE	UNT/CS	990824/30	10	H
Enea Data	TekSci	USA	FT	000202	10	H
Enea Data	Epact	SE	Dir	000306	10	H
Enea Data	Polyhedra	UK	Dir/TO	010327	10	C
Framfab	Netsolutions	SE	FT/Res/SvD	990331/0408/13	10	H
Framfab	Networkers	DK	CS	990512	10	H
Framfab	Production Medialab	SE	Dir/DR	990921	10	G
Framfab	Hypernode	SE	FLT	990924	10	H
Framfab	Wcube	F	DR	990929	10	H
Framfab	Vivid Edge	UK	FT	991029	10	H
Framfab	Springway	SE	SvDSyD	991118	10	H
Framfab	Guide Konsult	SE	DI/DN	991203/04	10	H
Framfab	Mindfact Interaktive Medien	D	Dir	991203	10	H
Framfab	eBizApps.com	USA	TT	991216	10	H
Framfab	Tecma	SE	FLT	000403	20	G

Framfab	Halbye, Kaag & Parners	DK	DR/Vis	000419	20	G
Framfab	NetlinQ	NL	Dir/FT	000502/3	20	H
Framfab	NettX Consulting	DK	AP/CS	000819/23	20	H
Framfab	Arexus	BUL	Dir	000918	20	H
Framfab	Marknadsföring & Reklambyrån Marknad	SE	AR	9905xx	10	G
HiQ International	Wise Network	DK	Dir	000124	10	H
IFS	Effective Management Systems	USA	Dir/CS	990901/3	20	H
IMS Data	Stadab Norrköping	SE	CS/DT	970513/29	10	H
IMS Data	Office Data	SE	CS	971028	10	H
Information Highway	Next Generation	SE	Dir	970827	5	H
Information Highway	Strateg Communication	SE	CS	970926	5	H
Information Highway	Abricom	SE	Dir/CS	971007/10	5	H
Information Highway	Dexpertgruppen	SE	CS	980330	5	H
Information Highway	Liga Systems & Software Scandinavia	SE	CS	980330	5	H
Information Highway	Info-Expert	N	Dir	980716	5	H

(Continued)

Acquirer	Target company	Target nationality	Source	Date of source (yymmdd)	Useful life	Strategic type
Information Highway	Interaction Design	N	FLT/FT	990716/0817	5	H
Information Highway	Veritema	SE	TT/Dir/FT	990927/7/8	5	H
Information Highway	ELK	DK	Dir/CS	991123/4	5	H
Information Highway	Netmill	SF	DI/CS	991124	5	H
Information Highway	Bergsnov, Mellbye & Rosenbaum	N	SvD	991217	5	H
Information Highway	Berens Partner	D	FLT/CS	000321/2	20	H
Information Highway	Netgain	SE	FLT	000329	5	H
Information Highway	Jevinger Interactive	SE	Dir	000517	5	H
Intentia	BCM Systems	AUS	TT/CS	970822/9	10	F
Intentia	Vimex	PL	Dir	970826	10	F
Intentia	Movex Software	E	CS	970926	10	F
Intentia International	PM Sims	DK	DI	980328	10	C
Intentia International	Sigma	AT	CS	980527	10	F

Intentia International	Professional Software Consultants	USA	Dir	980608	10	F
Intentia International	Logosoft	D	Dir	981123	10	C
Intentia Europe	Intentia Switzerland	CH	CS	000918	10	F
Know IT	Infosys	SE	CS	980206	10	H
Know IT	Candeo Nord-konsult i Luleå	SE	Dir/CS	980316/23	10	H
Know IT	Openinfo Gränssnitt	SE	Dir	980318	10	C
Know IT	UniCation	SE	Dir	980605	10	H
Know IT	Ergosoft i Sverige AB	SE	Dir	980915	10	G
Know IT	Tamscan	SF	Dir	990312	10	H
Know IT	Dalsys	SE	Dir/CS	990319/0407	10	H
Know IT	ES Solutions	SE	AR	1998/99	10	H
Know IT	Datakonkret	SE	Dir	990521	10	H
Know IT	Moderna System i Karlstad	SE	SvD	991104	10	H
Know IT	The Natural Advantage TnaSE	CS	991119	10	G	
Know IT	Accson Interactive Design	SE	Dir	000224	10	G
Know IT	Complit CS System	SE	Dir	000303	10	H
Know IT	Umeå IT Center	SE			10	B

(Continued)

Acquirer	Target company	Target nationality	Source	Date of source (yymmdd)	Useful life	Strategic type
MSC Konsult	Elektrosoft i Stockholm	SE	Dir	981015	5	C
MSC Konsult	Lexicon Liljeholmen	SE	Dir	981203	5	G
M2S	Prokoda	D	DI	000408	20	C
Netwise	Ineo	SE	BIT	010205	10	H
Prevas	Profac	SE			10	H
Sigma	Benima Ferator Engineering	SE	SvD/SyyD	980922	20	H
Sigma	Cadato Engineering	SE	FLT/DI	991007/8	10	H
Sigma	Måldata	SE	SvD/TT	991215/6	20	C
Sigma	Teleca Ltd	UK	FT	000417	20	C
Sigma	Intelia	F	FLT/DI	000817/8	20	H

Sigma	High Tech Engineering	SE	DI	001016	10	H
Sigma	QIS Systems	D	BIT	010104	10	H
Sigma	Frontec Research & Technology	SE	BIT	010220	10	H
Teligent	Bull (division OpenVoice)	SE	Dir	991222	10	C

H, Horizontal; F, Forward; B, Backward; C, Concentric; G, Conglomerate.

Source 1: Förvärv & Fusioner. Takeovers by acquirers belonging to industry codes Ed and Ks.

Source 2: Various media: Aftenposten (AP), Annual Report (AR), BIT, Computer Sweden (CS), Datateknik (DT), Direkt (Dir), Dagens Industri (DI), Dagens Nyheter (D) Aftenposten (AP), Annual Report (AR), BIT, Computer Sweden (CS), Datateknik (DT), Direkt (Dir), Dagens Industri (DI), (F) Dagens Nyheter (DN), Dagens Reklamnyheter (DR) Finanstidningen (FT), Förenade Landsorts Tidningar (FLT), Resumè (Res), Svenska Dagbladet (SvD), Sydsvenska Dagbladet (SyD), Telekom Online (TO), Tidningarnas Telegrambyrå (TT), Upsala Nya Tidning (UNT), Vision (23), Waymaker (WM). Online (TO), Tidningarnas Telegrambyrå (TT), Upsala Nya Tidning (UNT), Vision (23), Waymaker (WM).

Appendix 10.A.2: Sub-Industry Classification.

Consultancy firms	Software firms	Hardware and retailing firms
Adcore	Connova	C Technologies
Adera	Enlight	Gandalf
AU-System	Iar Systems	Multi Q
Cell Network	IBS	Scribona
Cyber Com	IFS	Sectra
Dimension	Intentia	
Enea	Jeeves	
Framfab	M2S	
Frontec	Netwise	
HIQ	Nexus	
Icon	Nocom	
IMS Data	Orc Software	
Kipling	Pricer	
Know It	Protect Data	
Mind	Readsoft	
Modul 1	Teligent	
Mogul.com	Trio	
MSC		
Novotek		
Prevas		
Proact		
Pronyx		
Resco		
RKS		
Sigma		
Softronic		
Teleca		
Tietoenator		
Turnit		
WM-data		

Chapter 11

Corporate Transparency and Risk Management Disclosure of European Issuers in the United States

Söhnke M. Bartram, Georg Stadtmann and Markus F. Wissmann

11.1 Introduction

The introduction of the Sarbanes-Oxley Act (SOX) in the United States changed the reporting environment of international companies significantly and had a worldwide impact on institutional and corporate transparency. The importance of SOX originates in part from its influence on non-U.S. companies. First, being mandatory for American and foreign companies alike that have their shares listed on a U.S. stock exchange, it directly affects cross-listed companies. Second, the U.S. corporate governance system may serve as a blueprint for other countries that intend to reform their own reporting regulation. This is likely to indirectly affect companies all over the world — even if not listed in the United States — as a result of convergence of foreign reporting standards with U.S. rules, including SOX.

The likely effects on companies that have been identified so far are twofold. On the one hand, recent evidence in the United States shows that the implementation of SOX significantly increases costs of publicly listed companies. This makes equity markets a less-attractive source of funding, which could induce companies to avoid these requirements. This has been empirically confirmed by Leuz, Triantis, and Wang (2004), who show that an increasing number of U.S. companies deregister their common stock as a result of SOX. However, this

Corporate and Institutional Transparency for Economic Growth in Europe

ISBN: 0-08-044665-5

observation is not limited to U.S. companies. Recent surveys of lobbying institutions show that many foreign companies cross-listed in the United States consider delisting from a U.S. exchange in order to avoid the burden imposed on them by SOX (Fischer zu Cramburg, Hannich, & Ziegert, 2004). In addition, complying with both SOX and domestic regulation can be particularly burdensome when domestic legislation is in conflict with SOX, such as the German co-determination rules (Perino, 2003).[1]

On the other hand, stricter rules resulting from SOX enhance transparency and the trustworthiness of financial reporting, which improves the credibility of a company in the equity markets. In addition, the requirements on the quality of internal reporting mechanisms are useful for large international companies that have a variety of businesses with complex reporting structures. It provides market participants and managers with the assurance that the system of internal controls ensures a true and fair view of the financial position of a company. With regard to corporate risk management, this pertains also to the financial risks the firm is exposed to and the hedging decisions it has taken as a response, e.g., in terms of derivative instruments and/or foreign currency debt. A more accurate reporting system thus increases the transparency and effectiveness of the risk management program.

Since the effect of SOX on companies is thus far from clear and is an empirical issue, this chapter investigates how SOX impacted corporate transparency and the statutory risk disclosure of European issuers in the United States. It follows the link between transparency, risk, and cost of capital as outlined in Chapter 1. We examine whether SOX is complementary to and consistent with the existing national standards that foreign issuers are obliged to comply with in addition to SOX. Furthermore, we elaborate on the perceived cost and benefits of the Act for cross-listed companies. To address these questions, we analyze the responses to a questionnaire by German companies that are cross-listed on the New York Stock Exchange (NYSE). The issues covered by the questionnaire relate to financial reporting in general (such as risk disclosure and changes thereof due to SOX), a cost–benefit analysis of the recent regulatory changes (such as synergies with German reporting standards and additional costs imposed by SOX), and the potential impact of the new regulation on risk management in particular. The results indicate that companies consider potential benefits as small and limited in scope. This implies that the marginal effect of SOX is an increase in the costs associated with cross-listings. As a result, raising equity capital at NYSE — and

[1]However, the SEC addressed this problem and regards the employee representative in the supervisory board as independent.

probably in the United States in general — became less attractive for European companies owing to SOX.

The results in this chapter have broad implications pertaining to other areas, such as issues around capital structure. Aggarwal and Kyaw (Chapter 12), for instance, show within this volume that corporate debt levels depend on the design of institutional transparency. In particular, changes in transparency that reduce the agency conflict between shareholders and management are associated with lower levels of debt. Changes in transparency that reduce the exposure of debt holders to operating risk, however, are associated with higher levels of debt. If SOX achieves its original purpose to better align management action with shareholder value, it will likely lead to less debt and more equity finance of the companies that are subject to it. As far as cross-listed, foreign companies are concerned, however, it is shown here that this very same legislation made the U.S. stock market a less attractive place to raise additional equity finance. Rather than reducing relative debt levels, this could lead leverage to either stay constant or to increase. Therefore, these offsetting effects may make an *ex ante* prediction of the effect of SOX on corporate capital structures difficult, as both of these effects seem to be present.

The analysis by Bild and Schuster in Chapter 10 is also closely related to this chapter. They examine how international harmonization of national accounting standards influences overall transparency in the context of the adoption of the International Financial Reporting Standards (IFRS) in Europe. Converging national accounting standards implies changes to the individual national accounting rules, which leads to the indirect effect SOX has on non-U.S. companies mentioned earlier. Finally, this chapter relates to Gugler, who in Chapter 3 analyzes issues of companies that operate in multiple jurisdictions. The lesser the international law is harmonized the higher the costs, complexity and uncertainty for these companies. The introduction of SOX is one example of additional complexity inflicted on cross-listed, foreign companies, which also demonstrates that legal systems in which companies operate can change significantly over time.

The remainder of this chapter is structured as follows: Section 11.2 provides an overview of SOX and discusses the effects on U.S. companies. Furthermore, it discusses implications for both foreign companies raising equity capital in the United States and different national corporate governance systems. Abstracting from the analysis of NYSE-listed German firms, Section 11.3 discusses implications for German companies that are cross-listed on a U.S. stock exchange. In particular, the German and the U.S. corporate governance regimes are compared with an emphasis on implications for risk management and internal control. A discussion of the survey of German companies cross-listed on NYSE complements the analysis. In Section 11.4, an overview of the discussion about deregistration of foreign issuers is provided, which is directly linked to disclosure requirements as a result of SOX. Finally, Section 11.5 summarizes the results and concludes the chapter.

11.2 The Sarbanes-Oxley Act

11.2.1 Key Provisions of SOX with respect to Corporate Transparency

Following the high-profile accounting scandals and bankruptcies, such as Enron and WorldCom, the U.S. legislature set up a law named after its initiators, Senator Paul Sarbanes and member of Congress Michael Oxley — the Sarbanes-Oxley Act (SOX). The Act was passed by the U.S. Congress on January 23, 2002 and became effective on July 30, 2002. It reshaped the landscape of corporate governance in the United States dramatically (Axarlis, 2004). SOX already emphasized strong shareholder rights by making management more accountable and control mechanisms more effective through increased mandatory disclosure and supervision and by making top management personally liable.

One important part of the new law intends to better align management action to shareholders' interests and to improve the effectiveness of management supervision. Title III of SOX defines corporate responsibilities, a major aspect of which is presented in Section 301, which seeks to reduce conflicts of interest of those who represent shareholders, i.e., corporate directors. The rules explicitly require directors to be independent. This rule is further detailed in that directors must not accept any kind of compensation from the company whose board they oversee. Another important part of SOX is Section 302. It states that the CEO and CFO have to certify their financial report every quarter. In particular, they have to confirm the truthfulness of all information and the absence of any misleading statements in the report. Section 906 goes on by listing the punishment both executives face if they get caught to knowingly certify wrong or misleading information: a fine of up to USD 1 million and a prison term of up to 10 years. If willfully certified wrong, the penalties increase up USD 5 million and 20 years imprisonment.

Other parts of SOX are concerned with the quality of financial data. Section 407, for instance, defines what constitutes a "financial expert" and requires the company to disclose whether it has one on its audit committee (SEC, 2003b). Requirements regarding additional financial disclosure are set out in Title IV. The executive certification mentioned in the previous paragraph requires an effective way of recording, processing, summarizing, and analyzing internal information to make sure that the certified financial information disclosed in the financial reports is correct (SEC, 2003a). This point is addressed in Section 404, which requires management to assess the effectiveness of internal control systems and publish a report thereof with the annual financial figures. The general characteristic of internal control of financial reporting is defined in the final rule by the Securities and Exchange Commission (SEC) as[2]

> A process designed by, or under the supervision of, the registrant's principal executive and principal financial officers, or persons performing similar functions, and effected by the registrant's board of directors, management and other personnel, to provide reasonable assurance regarding the reliability of financial reporting and the preparation of financial statements for external purposes in accordance with generally accepted accounting principles and includes those policies and procedures that:
>
> - Pertain to the maintenance of records that in reasonable detail accurately and fairly reflect the transactions and dispositions of the assets of the registrant;
> - Provide reasonable assurance that transactions are recorded as necessary to permit preparation of financial statements in accordance with generally accepted accounting principles, and that receipts and expenditures of the registrant are being made only in accordance of the registrant;
> - Provide reasonable assurance regarding prevention or timely detection of unauthorized acquisition, use or disposition of the registrant's assets that could have a material effect on the financial statements" (SEC, 2003a, p. 9).

Next to defining the nature of internal control, Section 404 requires the company to identify and address weaknesses in its system of internal control and financial reporting. Therefore, to comply with SOX, companies are obliged to establish and maintain information systems that support and allow for effective risk management (Menzies, 2004).

In addition to internal controls of financial reporting, the SEC requires what it calls proper disclosure controls. Unlike internal controls, which focus on the

[2]This definition incorporates the framework developed by COSO, the Committee of Sponsoring Organizations of the Treadway Commission (COSO, 1992). COSO was originally formed in 1985 to sponsor the National Commission on Fraudulent Financial Reporting, an independent private sector initiative, which studied the causal factors that can lead to fraudulent financial reporting and developed recommendations for public companies and their auditors, regulators such as the SEC, and educational institutions. The chairman of the National Commission was James C. Treadway, a former commissioner of the SEC.

sourcing of financial data, disclosure controls are concerned with the publication of mandatory information to investors. In particular, this type of control should "ensure that information (...) disclosed by the company (...) is (...) within (...) the Commission's rules and forms" (SEC, 2003a, p. 16). A company could create a disclosure committee to ensure accurate, timely, and complete disclosure as well as compliance with Section 302 (Vater, 2004).

Finally, the new law establishes the Public Company Accounting Oversight Board, which oversees the public accounting profession in order to assure high quality of external audits and further improve compliance with accounting rules in general and SOX in particular. Thus, SOX enhances corporate transparency considerably by improving the quality and the quantity of the information a company is obliged to communicate to its investors.

11.2.2 Effects of SOX on Companies in the United States

The effects of SOX on U.S. companies have been at the center of a few empirical studies. Bhattacharya, Groznik, and Haslem (2002) conduct an event study around the date when the first group of companies had to file according to SOX (August 14, 2002). While 96.5% of the 688 companies in the sample met the deadline, 15 created their own format of certification, and nine did not file anything. The study finds strong evidence that the market anticipated compliance with SOX and concludes that firms that did not file correctly may be in financial distress, may have agency problems related to relatively small institutional ownership stakes, or may have been audited by Arthur Andersen.

Rezaee and Jain (2003) study the market reaction to news related to SOX between February and July 2002 accounting for firm-specific levels of transparency and disclosure quality as measured by Standard and Poor's. They find positive (negative) abnormal returns for days where the likelihood of the passage of SOX increases (decreases). In addition, the market reaction is more positive for companies that scored higher on effective corporate governance, reliable financial reporting, and credible audit functions.

Jain, Kim, and Rezaee (2004) analyze market liquidity measures before and after the passage of SOX. Market liquidity and quality is assessed by quote and spread data as well as a measure of adverse selection. These variables uniformly indicate a drop in both market quality and liquidity following the accounting scandals that led to the passage of SOX. Subsequent to the passage of SOX and some SEC implementation rules, markets improved on these dimensions, an effect that was more pronounced for large firms.

The latest survey by Ernst & Young (2004b) shows that companies with a higher level of revenue need more time to comply with Section 404. Similar studies have been conducted three times between December 2003 and September 2004 (e.g., Ernst & Young, 2004a,b), which show that the effort necessary to implement Section 404 increased considerably over time. As compared to the first survey, 29% of the companies needed 50% more effort to comply with this rule, with another 23% of companies estimating the increase between 26% and 50%. The primary reason for this trend is identified to be the growing number of controls that have to be evaluated and tested. According to a research study by AMR, the total costs to U.S. companies grew from 2004 to 2005 by 10% to USD 6.1 billion.

Ge and McVay (2005) analyze a sample of 261 companies that reported a total of 493 deficiencies in their internal control systems between August 2002 and November 2004. In general, most of the weaknesses were related to accounting policies and to the segregation of duties. In particular, areas of financial accounting that caused the main difficulties were revenue recognition, account reconciliation, the treatment of the year-end reporting process, accrual accounts, derivatives' accounting, and income tax issues. It therefore seems that weaknesses in internal reporting are associated with the complexity of the accounts. By the same token, a higher level of organizational complexity (measured by, for instance, the number of reporting segments or the existence of foreign currency translation) seems to increase the difficulties to comply with Section 404. Finally, experience (expressed by a company's age and size) and profitability are associated with fewer weaknesses in internal control procedures, while being audited by one of the major accounting firms is positively associated with the disclosure thereof.

Engel, Hayes, and Wang (2004) analyze a sample of 353 U.S. firms that quit the equity markets and became private companies between January 1998 and January 2004. They find a modest but statistically significant increase in the rate of firms that went private after the enactment of SOX. They further find that abnormal returns associated with the introduction of SOX are positively related to firm size and turnover. Comparing the post- and pre-SOX period, companies that are smaller or have a larger level of inside ownership than average experience above-average returns when announcing their intention to become a private company.

Finally, Leuz et al. (2004) study companies that "go dark", i.e., they deregister — thus exiting the SEC reporting regime — but continue to trade in the OTC market. They find large negative abnormal returns at the announcement and filing of deregistration, which are more pronounced after the passage of SOX. They conclude that firms that deregister from the reporting requirements to the SEC are generally small (measured by total assets and market value of equity) and often distressed (indicated by higher leverage and a recent increase in short-term debt). The cost savings for these companies from being outside the SEC reporting regime are likely to exceed the benefits of continued reporting under the SEC regime. These benefits may stem, at least in part, from controlling shareholders in these companies protecting their private benefits of control and reducing their legal risks resulting from SOX with regard to the penalty for white-collar crime. In addition, Leuz et al. (2004) find that well-performing companies not only go dark but also leave the equity markets altogether by going private. Market reactions to the announcement of going private is significantly positive throughout their sample period particularly after the passage of SOX.

Thus, while SOX improved the quality of internal control mechanisms of financial reporting, markets appear to be able to differentiate between companies with sound accounting and governance practices even before these requirements became compulsory. Nevertheless, choosing a less transparent reporting environment, such as by going dark, seems to increase the costs of capital as Leuz et al. (2004) show. Therefore, whether costs of SOX outweigh its benefits, especially for foreign firms, is still an open question.

11.2.3 Implications of SOX for Foreign Companies

In addition to its effect on U.S. companies, SOX also has implications for all foreign companies that are listed on a U.S. stock exchange. Of the 3,617 companies listed on NYSE, 13% are from outside the UnitedStates. (NYSE as of June 30, 2005), most of which (86) are from Canada. As for Europe, the United Kingdom (64), the Netherlands (26), France (19), and Germany (16) account for the largest number of companies with NYSE listing (Table 11.1). These companies are not only subject to their national reporting rules but also have to comply with U.S. standards, such as SOX. In addition, even if a foreign issuer decides to delist, it still has to comply with U.S. reporting, disclosure, and governance standards unless it fully deregisters. Therefore, SOX likely has an impact on the cross-listing decision of foreign companies.

Companies listed in the United States compete in global capital markets with companies that are listed in their home jurisdiction only. Foreign companies are therefore likely to do a cost–benefit analysis on whether to voluntarily adopt U.S. corporate governance standards and/or to list on a U.S. stock exchange. The Swiss company SBB AG, for instance, has voluntarily adopted SOX to increase its transparency and therefore its attractiveness to international investors (Bigler, 2004). This is referred to as "bonding", which describes the phenomenon of companies opting into a more stringent corporate governance system of a foreign jurisdiction in order to send a credible signal to the capital market and the investment community (Reese & Weisbach, 2002). The benefits of bonding are mostly attributed to a lower cost of capital that results from a higher stock market valuation (Wòjcik, Clark, & Bauer, 2004).

Table 11.1: European companies listed on NYSE.

Country	Number of companies
United Kingdom	64
Netherlands	26
France	19
Germany	16
Switzerland	16
Italy	13
Spain	9
Russia	6
Finland	5
Norway	5
Greece	4
Ireland	3
Denmark	2
Luxembourg	2
Portugal	2
Austria	1
Turkey	1
Belgium	1
Guernsey	1
Hungary	1

Source: New York Stock Exchange (as of June 30, 2005).

Such a cost–benefit analysis will take into account the fact that stocks will trade at a discount if risks are not fully disclosed. Applying the "unraveling" theory (Milgrom, 1981; Jovanovic, 1982) to the situation at hand, a company with discretion regarding financial disclosure will choose to fully disclose the risks it faces only if it *ex ante* expects to benefit from this step, such as by lifting its own share price. Following this argument, foreign companies might choose to adopt more stringent U.S. disclosure standards to either increase their share price or to avoid the negative signal they would otherwise send to investors, which could depress the price of their shares. Therefore, foreign companies could "rent" the U.S. system by raising equity capital in the United States, which would make U.S. disclosure rules mandatory and their commitment to these standards credible. However, since the passage of SOX, the costs associated with being listed in the United States have increased dramatically (Ribstein, 2003).

Enforcement of SEC rules is generally considered as being fairly strong. While this is not questioned with regard to publicly listed U.S. companies, the same might not be the case for foreign firms. Siegel (2005) shows that in the years 1995 to mid-2002, the SEC took legal action against only 13 cross-listed foreign firms. This rather relaxed attitude is exemplified by a sample of cross-listed Mexican companies, where controlling shareholders were charged with embezzlement, effectively taking away assets from minority shareholders. All the SEC did was to delist six of these companies, while none of them has been charged of violating U.S. securities laws. This rather weak enforcement may limit the positive effect of bonding on the credibility of a company's published accounts.

Sutton, Lanoo, and Casey (2005) analyze foreign listing activity in the United States between the end of 2000 and 2003. They find that the number of foreign companies that listed on NYSE rose from 417 to 443, while the number of foreign issuers that listed on NASDAQ went down from 360 to 247 over the same time period. This reduction in NASDAQ listings relative to NYSE may be attributable to the burst of the technology bubble, which generally resulted in a decline of share issues by growth companies, rather than to SOX. These numbers alone therefore make it difficult to deduce whether SOX reduced the attractiveness of U.S. capital markets to foreign companies. Looking at Figure 11.1, which shows the number of new, rather than total, listings one can identify that foreign listing activity on NYSE declined steadily from 2000 onward, while the number of new U.S. companies listed on NYSE increased between 2000 and 2004. As a consequence, the proportion of foreign new listings decreased as well (Figure 11.2). This decline of new foreign listings relative to total new listings on NYSE might indicate

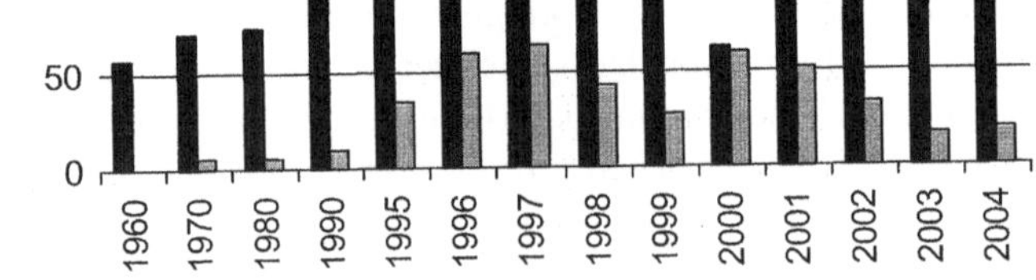

Figure 11.1: Number of new companies listings at NYSE (New York Stock Exchange, 2005).

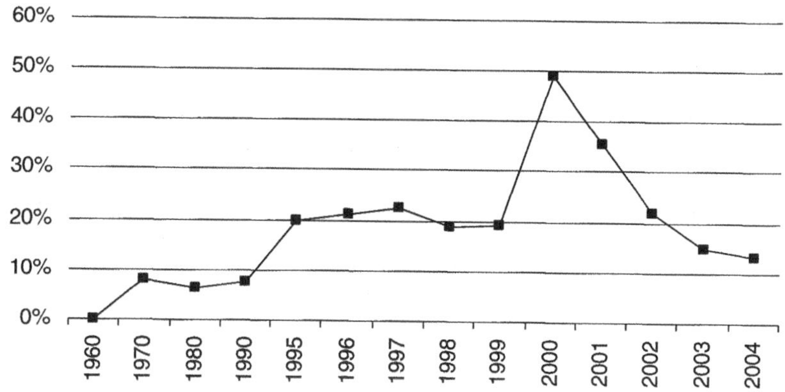

Figure 11.2: Share of foreign new listings to overall new listings (New York Stock Exchange, 2005).

that SOX has made the U.S. capital market less attractive to foreign companies and therefore indicates that the higher costs associated with cross-listing outweighs the benefits, such as the bonding effect described earlier.

A different interpretation of the relative decline in foreign listing activity is that the U.S. corporate governance system did not prevent corporate scandals and therefore does not seem to be superior compared to corporate governance rules of other industrialized countries. Moreover, the corporate scandals by themselves may have tainted the reputation of the U.S. system, which could have negatively influenced the decision to cross-list by foreign firms.

Witt (2003) suggests that shareholders, companies, and taxpayers may do a horse race of the different concepts of corporate governance legislation to decide which one is most advantageous and appropriate to their national circumstances. One of the dimensions along which a corporate governance concept is evaluated is complementary, which refers to the degree its different elements fit into each other (Schmidt & Weiß, 2003). Another dimension is consistency, which measures whether the individual elements of each corporate governance concept are complementary and reinforce each other. Inconsistent systems are considered economically inefficient even when single components are considered superior. New elements might be included in the existing system as a reaction to changes in foreign jurisdictions in order to be competitive.

Since the U.S. corporate governance system might serve as a blueprint for several other national corporate governance systems, changes in U.S. law are likely to lead to changes in other jurisdictions. As a consequence, even foreign companies that are not listed in the United States are (indirectly) affected by SOX. To illustrate, Peek, Blanco, and Roxas (2004) examine the effect of SOX on the oversight of audit companies in countries that are part of the North American Free Trade Area (NAFTA). It turns out that Canada brings its standards in line with SOX and that it joins Mexico to follow SOX regarding the structure and responsibilities of the audit committee and the accountability of the CEO and CFO, which are outlined above. In Europe, the commission of the European Union is considering incorporating a mandatory corporate governance statement in the 4th (78/660/EWG) and 7th (83/349/EWG) directive to inform investors about the quality of risk management and internal controls. The initiative is, however, opposed by the European parliament, which wants to avoid overregulation (Committee on Legal Affairs, 2005).

11.3 The Sarbanes-Oxley Act and German Cross-Listed Companies

11.3.1 The German Corporate Governance System

Germany's corporate governance system is generally considered a creditor-friendly stakeholder-oriented system, which means that it favors debt- over equity-holders and mandates the participation of employees in the oversight of a company. The legal foundations for listed companies are outlined in the joint stock companies' code (Atkiengesetz, AktG), which sets up a two-tier board system with a management board and a supervisory board. The German market for corporate control of public companies is considered to be underdeveloped relative to other industrialized countries as relatively few banks exercise control of the supervisory board through the pooling of shareholders' voting rights and the low market capitalization of most companies. As a reaction to corporate scandals around 1998, the focus of the German corporate governance legislation has been shifted to shareholders, whereby the consistency of the German corporate governance system, as defined earlier, has been maintained.[3]

Table 11.2 summarizes the main drivers of transparency within the German corporate governance system. With the enactment of KonTraG (Gesetz zur Kontrolle und Transparenz im Unternehmensbereich), for instance, a shift in the German

---

[3]See Schmidt and Spindler (2000) with regard to path dependency of the German corporate governance system. Schmidt and Weiß (2003) point out that KonTraG has contributed to a paradigm shift from insider to outsider control. See also Böcking (2003).

Table 11.2: Sources of transparency in the German corporate governance system.

	KonTraG	TransPuG	4th Financial-market support law	Cromme commission report	BilKoG	BilReG
Year of imple-mentation	1998	2002	2002	2003	2004	2004
Legal principle	Law	Law	Law	Comply or explain	Law	Law
Scope	All but focus on listed companies	All but focus on listed companies	All but focus on listed companies	Listed companies		
		Implementation of the German corporate governance code in the AktG	Supervision of share price manipulation	Shareholder interests Responsibility of supervisory and management board		
Focus	Obligation to implement risk management system	Risk management Accounting standards Risk management	Liability/responsibility of financial analysts Transparency of directors' dealing	Independence of auditors and supervisory boards Transparency of company management	Enforce-ment	Auditor independence Accounting standards

Note: BilReG refers to "Bilanzrechtsreformgesetz" (the law on international accounting and audit quality) (see also BilReG, 2004), KonTraG refers to "Gesetz zur Kontrolle und Transparenz im Unternehmensbereich" (law for control and transparency in the company), and TransPuG refers to "Transparenz und Publizitätsgesetz" (transparency and disclosure law).
Source: Deloitte & Touche (2003).

corporate governance system toward greater responsibility of management and the supervisory board coincides. First, it attempts to improve risk management practice and requires the introduction of a monitoring system that identifies risks that might affect the going concern of joint stock companies. The supervisory board has to verify the effective use of this system by management, which has to report any risk identified by the monitoring system to the supervisory board.[4] Second, as with SOX, the monitoring system is subject to a regular external audit.

According to Grewe (2000) and Scharpf (1999), risk identification is a continuous and systematic process. Addressing this latter point, a proper monitoring system can generally be subdivided into internal control, controlling, and early warning. The early warning system should be tied into the overall company strategy, and a risk strategy should be developed. As risks need to be identified on a continuous basis, this system should also ensure that the company could react to risks in a timely manner. Obviously, such a system will be a function of the complexity and the riskiness of the company's business. While the concept of "risk" is not clearly defined in the context of KonTraG, the German Institute of Chartered Accountants (IdW) suggests that risk can generally be considered to be "the possibility of disadvantageous future developments."[5] This definition applies to individual risks that affect the going concern but comprises risks that — although of minor importance when considered individually — potentially add up to major ones. Transactions that involve any of these risks need to be disclosed. Failure to report these in the annual report is considered a misstatement of the financial accounts and consequently an offense against legislation requiring a company to report its true and fair view.

Another example of the new German corporate governance regulation is BilReg, which requires companies to include a discussion of the business development in its financial report. Thereby, key financial performance indicators that can be traced to the financial statements should be used and explained. In addition, any foreseeable developments, their potential risks and rewards have to be explained and assumptions underlying the reported numbers have to be shown.[6] Finally, the new rules now make it mandatory to disclose financial risk management policies and details about specific methods and financial instruments used for that purpose.[7]

---

[4]This can be derived from § 111 I AktG, see Gruson and Kubicek (2003b, p. 395).

[5]See Grewe (2000). The Deutsches Rechnungslegung Standards Committee, DRSC (German Accountings Standards Committee) has released DRS 5 with regards to risk disclosure, but the risk definition is kept quite general.

[6]See § 289 I HGB Bundesgesetzblatt, 2004 I Nr. 65, whereby the term "risk" is not defined further.

[7]See § 289 II Nr. 2 HGB Bundesgesetzblatt, 2004 I Nr. 65.

An important event in the evolution of German corporate governance toward more transparency is the implementation of the German Corporate Governance Code. In essence, a company has either to follow its guidelines or explain its motivation for failing to do so (a principle called "comply or explain"). The intention is to single out companies that decide not to comply with its principles and rely on public pressure — rather than formal sanctions — to improve German corporate governance. Another important point is the establishment of expert committees within the supervisory board, which enhances the effectiveness of management supervision and helps controlling the risks a company faces. In particular, the code explicitly suggests establishing an audit committee that deals with accounting, risk management, and audit issues with the chairperson not having served as managing director. Table 11.3 shows how many German companies follow this suggestion and establish an audit committee. The adoption of audit committees is not uniformly implemented across German companies but seems to depend on company characteristics, such as company size and stock market segment.

The current rules and regulations in Germany leave considerable discretion with regard to the scope of risk management activities. Applying the argument of the unraveling theory mentioned earlier to the German situation, it seems likely that German companies make the amount of information reported on their risk management activities dependent on the expected reaction of current and future investors (Fischer & Vielmeyer, 2004).

Comparing risk management and disclosure under SOX to the German governance standards, the following important differences can be noted. Section 404

Table 11.3: Compliance with German corporate governance code.

	Establishment of an audit committee (%)
DAX	100.0
TecDAX	76.9
MDAX	81.8
SDAX	71.4
Prime	52.5
General	43.7
Total sample	63.2

Note: DAX, TecDAX, MDAX, SDAX, Prime, and General Standard are market segments of the Deutsche Boerse AG.
Source: von Werder, Talaulicar, and Kolat (2004).

refers to internal control systems of financial reporting mechanisms. The German laws and regulations on risk management refer only to risks that might affect the company as a going concern.[8] The crucial difference between both sets of rules is that disclosure requirements under Section 404 are not subject to management discretion and are therefore rather unbiased, which does not necessarily hold for the German case. In addition, the scope of disclosure as defined under Section 302 is much broader, as it refers to all financial information to be disclosed to the SEC and not only information pertaining to particular risks. Therefore, the establishment of a disclosure control system by the management board is an option that fits into the standards of the German joint stock companies' code (§76 AktG).[9] As mentioned above, following the suggestions of the German Corporate Governance Code, such as establishing an audit committee, is on a voluntary basis. This gives cross-listed companies enough flexibility to opt out of the German rules in case they conflict with SOX. In addition, Section 301 does not interfere with German law, as the supervisory board as a whole is regarded as the audit committee in case the German company does not establish one.[10]

To reduce the costs of compliance with SOX for cross-listed companies, several simplifications have been granted to German companies. For instance, SOX requires that the members of the audit committee are independent,[11] which means members of the audit committee are not allowed to receive any form of compensation from[12] or to be affiliated with the company.[13] This rule, however, is in conflict with the German Co-determination Act (Perino, 2003).[14] The SEC resolved this issue by considering the employee representatives on the supervisory board as independent.[15] In addition, the financial expert as a member of the audit committee required by Section 407 of a German issuer does not explicitly have to be US-GAAP literate, but a general understanding of the reconciliation from local GAAP to US-GAAP is considered sufficient (Gruson & Kubicek, 2003a). Therefore, given the flexible nature of both SOX and the German Corporate Governance Code, the rules

[8]See Menzies (2004, p. 39) and Gruson and Kubicek (2003b, p. 395).

[9]See Gruson and Kubicek (2003b, p. 395).

[10]See Gruson and Kubicek (2003a, p. 345), according to Section 205 SOX.

[11]See Section 301 SOX 3 (A), which amends Section 10 A of the Securities Exchange Act of 1934.

[12]See Section 301 SOX 3 (B) i.

[13]See Section 301 SOX 3 (B) ii.

[14]See § 7 MitbestG stating that four, six, or seven employees (depending on the size of the supervisory board) and two union members are members of the supervisory board. These members will receive the same remuneration as members of the supervisory board appointed in the general shareholders' meeting and will usually further receive their normal compensation, see Gruson and Kubicek (2003a, p. 350). See Ribstein (2003, pp. 10–12) for a detailed discussion.

[15]See SEC Rule 10 A-3 (b) (iv) (C) Exchange Act.

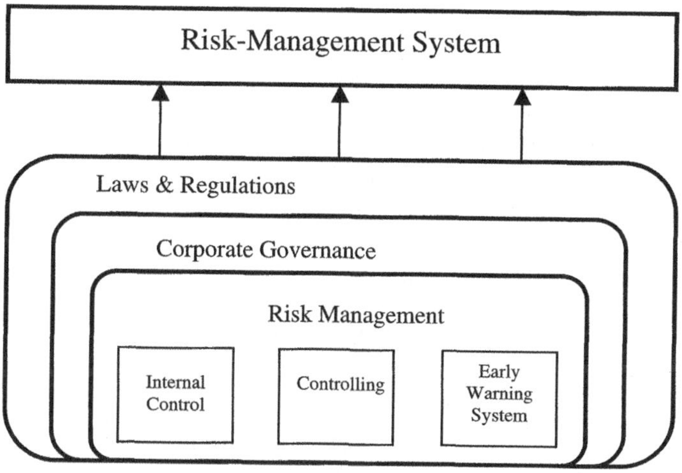

Figure 11.3: Internal control and risk management (van den Brink & Romeike, 2005).

affecting risk management of German foreign issuers in the United States are not in conflict with German corporate governance rules and regulation.

On the contrary, the U.S. rules are complementary to some of the elements of the German corporate governance system, which is facilitated by the developments in Germany from a stakeholder to a shareholder focused reporting and governance system. The emphasis of SOX is to increase the amount and quality of information disclosed and to use this information in combination with risk management measures to monitor and control managers.[16] As shown in Figure 11.3, internal control and risk management is interlinked. Therefore, the establishment of a system of internal control for risk management activities and the disclosure thereof is likely to be beneficial to a company in itself next to being just one of the additional reporting requirements introduced by SOX.

11.3.2 Questionnaire Design

To investigate the impact of SOX on German companies with listings in the United States, a survey was conducted based on a questionnaire (see Appendix 11.A.1). The survey covered issues pertaining to risk management and disclosure of risk within the German corporate governance system, changes of risk management and

[16]The interaction between internal control and risk management has also been stressed by COSO (2004).

disclosure in the context of SOX, synergies in the reporting required under German and U.S. laws, project management and costs of implementing SOX, and a cost/benefit analysis of the new regulation.

The questionnaire was sent to 18 German companies cross-listed in the United States, of which 16 replied. Table 11.4 summarizes the key characteristics of the sample firms. Most of these companies are large and operate on an international basis. DaimlerChrysler, for instance, experienced a stock price increase of 30%

Table 11.4: Sample of German companies cross-listed on NYSE.

Company	Industry	Stock type	Listing date	Issue type
Daimler Chrysler AG	Automobiles	Common stock	October 26, 1998	–
SGL Carbon AG	Industrial machinery	ADS common	June 5, 1996	ADR
Pfeiffer Vacuum TechnologyAG	Industrial machinery	ADS common	July 16, 1996	IPO, ADR
Fresenius	Health care providers	ADS common	September 17, 1996	ADR
		ADS preferred	November 25, 1996	
Deutsche Telekom AG	Fixed line telecommunications	ADS common	November 18, 1996	IPO, ADR
E.ON AG	Energy conglomerate	ADS common	October 8, 1997	ADR
SAP AG	Software	ADS common	August 3, 1998	ADR
Epcos AG	Electrical components and equipment	ADS common	October 15, 1999	IPO, ADR
Infineon Technologies AG	Semiconductors	ADS common	March 13, 2000	ADR
Schering AG	Pharmaceuticals	ADS common	October 12, 2000	ADR
Allianz AG	Full line insurance	ADS common	November 3, 2000	ADR

(Continued)

Table 11.4: (*Continued*).

Company	Industry	Stock type	Listing date	Issue type
Siemens AG	Electronic equipment	ADS common	March 12, 2001	ADR
Deutsche Bank AG	Banks	Common stock	October 3, 2001	–
Bayer AG	Specialty chemicals	ADS common	January 24, 2002	ADR
Altana AG	Pharmaceuticals	ADS common	May 22, 2002	ADR
BASF AG	Commodity chemicals	ADS common	June 7, 2002	ADR

Note: The listing date for DaimlerChrysler refers to the merged entity. Daimler-Benz, the German predecessor of DaimlerChrysler, was the first German company that cross-listed in the U.S. in 1993 (Oxelheim, Randoy, & Stonehill, 2001). In addition, the German companies Aixtron AG and GPC-Biotech AG are listed on the NASDAQ.
Source: New York Stock Exchange (as of June 30, 2005).
[http://www.nyse.com/international/nonuslisted/int_listed.html].

on the day the cross-listing decision was announced (Oxelheim, Randöy, & Stonehill, 2001). This considerable change in market value reflects the positive impact a cross-listing in the United States may have.

11.3.3 Results of the Survey

With regard to risk management and risk disclosure within the German corporate governance system, the survey results document that 81.2% of German companies cross-listed in the United States consider German laws on risk management and disclosure as adequate, while 25% regard them as being too imprecise. Thus, risk management and risk disclosure requirements are generally regarded as adequate, but laws and accounting standards need to be more precise. The principle "comply or explain" of the German Corporate Governance Code is widely accepted. Only 12.5% would prefer it to be mandatory, which is in line with the discussion in the previous section. These answers suggest that German companies prefer light regulation in the context of corporate transparency.

Regarding changes in risk management and disclosure caused by SOX, the survey suggests that the implementation of SOX has broadened the scope of risk management of German cross-listed companies considerably (68.8%). The changes are primarily around the integration of financial reporting within risk management activities and the extent of its documentation. New functions, such as monitoring and risk evaluation, have been established. The disclosure of sources of risk has been improved, but it is primarily restricted to U.S. reporting requirements (20-F). It therefore seems to have affected transparency in the statutory reporting required by U.S. law only, and did not generally improve the transparency of documents prepared by corporations for their German investors. Transparency in the statutory German risk disclosure improved for 50% of the companies. Thus, the effect of SOX primarily consists of broadening the risk management activities of the majority of cross-listed German companies.

SOX also had an impact on the supervisory board of German issuers. All respondents now have a financial expert as suggested by Section 407 as a member of their supervisory board. Companies put emphasis on the fact that the members of the audit committee are regarded independent as mandated by Section 301. Procedures for the contracting of audit and audit-related services and whistleblower guidelines have also been established.

The survey also inquired about potential synergies in the reporting required under German and U.S. laws. Only 25% of the sample firms consider the monitoring system required under German law as adequate for the implementation of Section 404. 62.5% of the companies questioned see overlaps between the monitoring systems required under KonTraG and Section 404. Despite this overlap, only 37.5% state that there are synergies between both systems. Consequently, only these companies are able to use results from the implementation of Section 404 in the statutory German risk disclosure, which implies that the implementation of Section 404 imposes considerable costs on the majority of firms. Thus, despite some perceived overlap between the German and the U.S. rules and regulations German cross-listed firms have to comply with, synergies between both systems appear to be limited.

A related point is the issue of costs of compliance with SOX, especially Section 404. 43.8% of the respondents state that the costs that have been incurred are high (more than EUR 5 million), 25% say they are medium (EUR 2.5–5 million), and 31.2% consider them as low (up to EUR 2.5 million). Future first-time compliance costs are said to be high for 50%, medium for 12.5%, and low for 37.5% of the respondents. The SEC extended the deadline for compliance with Section 404 for foreign companies, which 50% of the companies considered as necessary. The costs of compliance with SOX seem to arise primarily from addressing the requirements laid out in Section 404, but 81.3 % of the companies also incurred additional costs from establishing a disclosure committee and adjusting the structure of their audit committee in reaction to SOX.

As discussed, potential benefits from the compliance with SOX may arise from a strengthening of the system of internal controls of financial reporting, the identification of risks that might affect the company as a going concern, and/or lower cost of capital due to higher transparency. Within the sample, 31.3% see strengthening the system of internal controls of financial reporting as having a large impact, 43.8% say the impact is medium, and 25% perceive only a minor impact (Figure 11.4). The majority (81.3% of the sample firms) sees the identification of risks that might affect the company as a going concern as a minor issue, while 18.7% consider it to be of medium importance. Interestingly, 18.8% (81.2%) see a medium (minor) impact on the cost of capital. Hence, the effects of SOX on the identification of risks and the cost of capital overall appear minor, while a substantial number of firms identify benefits of SOX with respect to the functioning of their internal control systems.

Less than 50% of companies believe that it was an advantage being subject to the U.S. corporate governance prior to the SEC compliance date for Section 404. This means that the majority of the foreign companies do not see any benefits to comply with U.S. regulations prior to the compliance date. Table 11.5 summarizes effects on the bonding hypothesis from the questions on Section 404. In particular, 43.8% of the companies benefit from SOX 404 prior to the compliance date, but state that the extension is necessary. These companies generate benefits from the bonding under SOX even without complying with Section 404 yet.

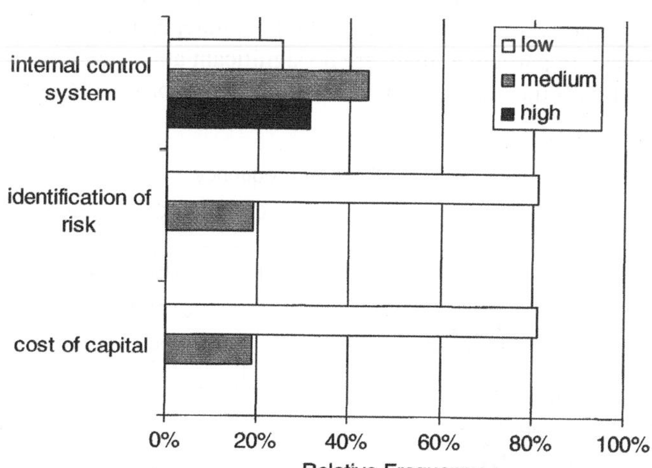

Figure 11.4: Benefits of the implementation of SOX.

Table 11.5: Evidence on the bonding hypothesis.

		Benefit prior to compliance date		
		Yes(%)	**No(%)**	**Total(%)**
Extension necessary	Yes	6.3	43.8	50.0
	No	37.5	12.5	50.0
	Total	43.8	56.3	100.0

With respect to the attractiveness of a U.S. listing, the sample firms perceive that SOX decreased the attractiveness significantly. As Figure 11.5 shows, more than 56.3% of the respondents consider their U.S. listing as less attractive than before the introduction of SOX. This result is even more pronounced with respect to potential foreign issuers without existing cross-listing. In particular, more than 87.5% of the respondents believe that SOX has made the U.S. capital market less attractive for potential foreign issuers. This result confirms and strengthens the empirical findings of Section 11.2.3, which has shown a decrease in new listing activity of foreign companies.

In order to verify the effects of the introduction of SOX on the sample of German firms with cross-listing in the United States, we study the abnormal returns of these companies to news during the year 2002 when details of SOX were discussed and agreed. The results show that market participants believe that the sample firms are hardly affected by SOX regulation, independent of the set of control variables used. In particular, there are no significant abnormal returns to these firms associated with the various steps of the legislative proceeding of SOX and

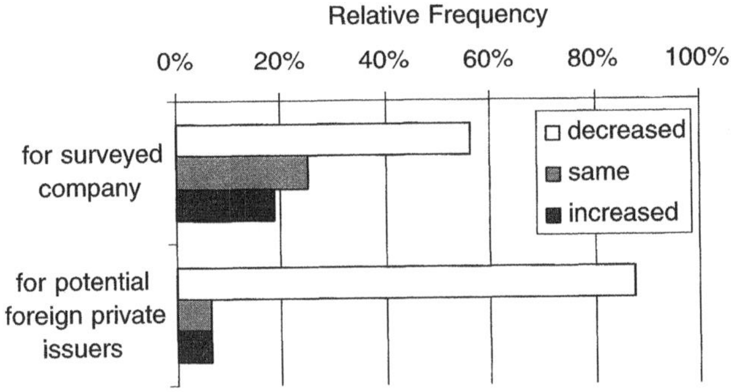

Figure 11.5: Attractiveness of a U.S. listing after SOX.

surrounding events, such as passing Congress (1/23/2002), the CEO significance order (7/3/2002), passing the Senate (7/15/2002), and the announcement of the SEC to post the names of CEOs/CFOs who fail to comply with the rule requiring certification of their companies' financial reports (7/29/2002). The requirement of CEO/CFO certification by the SEC is associated with marginally significant, positive abnormal returns, particularly for large firms. Only June 26, 2002, when the WorldCom fraud was announced, and July 30, 2002, when the President signed the law and SOX became effective, are associated with significant abnormal returns of −1.1% and −1.4%, respectively. Finally, August 14, 2002, when first CEO and CFO certifications of their companies' financial statements were due to be submitted to the SEC, is associated with small, marginally significant abnormal returns. Overall, these results corroborate the survey evidence that benefits in terms of greater transparency and costs in terms of increased disclosure requirements seem to balance for German firms with listing on NYSE.

11.4 Delisting and Deregistration

While SOX may have increased the costs to foreign companies that have their stock cross-listed on a U.S. exchange, it is important to note that companies still have to meet U.S. reporting requirements if they decide to delist from the U.S. stock exchange. This is one important aspect to be taken into account when considering bonding to U.S. securities laws. While debonding through deregistration from U.S. securities laws is subject to the conditions outlined below, delisting from a U.S. stock exchange may be achieved rather easily. For example, a company listed on NYSE may, according to Rule 806 of NYSE's listing manual, delist the day of its board approval, once NYSE received a certified copy of the delisting resolution. If NYSE issues a no-objection letter, the issuer may file a request for delisting with the SEC. The request is published in the U.S. federal gazette and is approved if no objection is filed within 21 days.

Contrary to a delisting, the process of deregistration is more elaborated. Companies with more (less) than USD 10 million of assets as of the end of the last fiscal year can deregister only if there exist less than 500 (300) U.S. shareholders. In determining the U.S. investor base, the principle of "look through" is applied. This means that every individual account by a U.S. customer that contains any of the stock in question is counted as one individual shareholder, even if several of these individual accounts are registered with the same financial intermediary. Therefore, it is almost impossible to deregister, and the apparent lack of cooperation by financial intermediaries renders deregistration even more difficult (Fischer zu Cramburg et al., 2004).

A company could successfully escape SEC reporting requirements either via a public tender offer to its U.S. shareholders or a merger with a company registered in the United States. The reporting requirements will be reinstated, however, if it exceeds the threshold of 500 (300) individual U.S. shareholders evaluated on a yearly basis (Fischer zu Cramburg et al., 2004). A study by the Deutsche Aktieninstitut (DAI) among German companies listed in the United States shows that companies believe the current deregistration practice to be inadequate (Fischer zu Cramburg et al., 2004). Considering the rules on deregistration, it seems to be safe to say that a company is almost irrevocably subject to U.S. standards once it is listed in the United States.[17] Given these difficulties, suggestions have been made to amend U.S. securities law to facilitate deregistration of foreign companies. Two of these suggestions, the Harvard Law School model and the European issuer model, are discussed below.

According to the Harvard Law School model developed by Pozen (2004), a company should be entitled to deregister if it offers to buy back shares held by U.S. investors. The price should be determined by an independent appraiser to obtain a "fair" price. The company would be allowed to deregister even if more than 300 U.S. shareholders remain after its offer has been made. The first step in the appraisal process would be a comparison of costs to U.S. investors of trading shares in the United States versus trading abroad. In a second step, disclosure requirements of the foreign issuers' home country have to be evaluated and compared to those required by U.S. rules and regulations. Finally, the appraiser would calculate incremental income taxes on dividends for the time before and after deregistration.

The European issuer model suggests several changes to U.S. securities law by granting several exceptions when the U.S. trading volume of a foreign issuer's stock is less than 5% of the worldwide trading volume of the most recent fiscal year. In addition, it is suggested that a company should have the right to terminate compliance with U.S. reporting requirements permanently if it has less than 300 U.S. shareholders for two years as of its last public offering or listing in the United States. The reports to be submitted to the SEC after being deregistered should be an English version of the financial report as required by the jurisdiction of its home country, if this report is in accordance with the standards of the International Organisation of Securities Commissions (IOSCO) and if the financial statements are prepared following IFRS. As its name suggests, this initiative is supported by several European institutions from different countries (AFEP, 2004).

---

[17]This may be beneficial for companies that want to overcome deficiencies in their home country law but may also deter companies from listing in the United States, see Ribstein (2003).

The European issuer model has been amended in a second letter to the Chairman of the SEC on March 18th, 2005 (see AFEP, 2005), continuing the dialog initiated in 2004 on the conditions for deregistration. The European argument is that companies whose securities are traded in a liquid, transparent, and well-regulated market should be granted more flexible rules of deregistration (AFEP, 2005). The suggestions made in 2005 include, next to the ones mentioned above, that all foreign issuers should be allowed to deregister if 10% or less of the respective securities are held in the United States or by U.S. residents or if their number is less than 3,000 (AFEP, 2005). As mentioned earlier, the deregistration requirements as defined by the Securities Exchange Act are complex and very difficult to fulfill for foreign issuers. The adoption of one of the models described above would ease these requirements and may have a positive impact on new foreign listings in the United States. This goal may be accomplished by a new initiative by the SEC scheduled for November 2005 (Schreiber & Grass, 2005).

In December 2005, the SEC (2005a, 2005b) published a new proposal to allow foreign private issuers to exit the Exchange Act reporting system. The new rules will ease the conditions with respect to a deregistration compared to the status quo. For example, the proposal foresees that in case that the issuer of equity securities is a well-known seasoned issuer, only one of the following criteria has to be met to qualify for a deregistration:

- the U.S. average daily trading volume of the subject class of securities has been no greater than 5 percent of the average daily trading volume of that class of securities in its primary trading market and U.S. residents held no more than 10 percent of the issuer's worldwide public float; or
- regardless of U.S. trading volume, U.S. residents held no more than 5 percent of the issuer's worldwide public float.

Hence the SEC proposal contains some criteria from the European issuer model. Since comments on this proposal can be submitted until February 28, 2006, we can not say until now whether the proposal will turn into law.

11.5 Conclusions

This chapter investigates the impact of the introduction of SOX on European companies listed in the United States. Since 2001, the share of new foreign firms listed on NYSE has declined, suggesting that SOX might have reduced the attractiveness of the U.S. capital market to foreign companies. Survey evidence of German firms suggests that only a minority of companies is able to generate synergies between the monitoring system under German law and the system of internal controls of financial reporting as mandated in the United States, although SOX appears in principle compatible with and complementary to the corporate governance system in Germany. The benefits associated with SOX compliance, such as statutory risk disclosure, increased transparency from statutory reporting, and bonding to the U.S. reporting regime, appear to be relevant only for few companies and do apparently not outweigh the incurred and future costs.

References

AFEP. (2004). Letter to the Chairman of the SEC — U.S. reporting obligations of foreign issuers. February 9, 2004. http://www.cbi.org.uk/ndbs/positiondoc.nsf/1f08ec61711f29768025672a0055f7a8/6D8B88C304A29C7B80256E5C004E437F/$file/caderegfinal.pdf

AFEP. (2005). Letter to the Chairman of the SEC — U.S. reporting obligations of foreign issuers. March 18, 2005. http://www.cbi.org.uk/ndbs/positiondoc.nsf/0/f58a575b6ab71edf80257015004b40ec/$FILE/secforeignissuersletter.pdf

Axarlis, C. (2004). Financial services policymaking in the United States: Theoretical foundations and practical implications, *Deutsche Bank Research*, EU-Monitor Nr. 16, July 19, 2004. http://www.dbresearch.de/PROD/DBR_INTERNET_EN-PROD/ PROD0000000000176653.pdf

Bhattacharya, U., Groznik, P., & Haslem, B. (2002). *Is CEO certification of earnings numbers value-relevant?* Working Paper. Kelley School of Business, Indiana University. http://ssrn.com/abstract=332621

Bigler, E. (2004). Umsetzung von Sarbanes Oxley auf freiwilliger Basis. *Der Schweizer Treuhänder, 12/2004,* pp. 1051–1056.

BilReG. (2004). Gesetz zur Einführung internationaler Rechnungslegungsstandards und zur Sicherung der Qualität der Abschlussprüfung (Bilanzrechtsreformgesetz — BilReg). *Bundesgesetzblatt 2004 Teil I, 65,* 9.

Böcking, H. (2003). Corporate governance und transparenz. In: A. Werder, & H. Wiedmann (Eds), *Internationalisierung der Rechnungslegung und Corporate Governance* (pp. 247–277). Stuttgart: Schaeffer Poeschel.

Committee on Legal Affairs. (2005). *Draft report: On the proposal for a directive of the European Parliament and of the Council Amending Council Directives 78/660/EEC and 83/349/EEC concerning the annual accounts of certain types of companies and consolidated accounts (COM(2004)0725 – C6-0164/2004 – 2004/0250(COD)).* http://www.europarl.eu.int/meetdocs/2004_2009/documents/PR/565/565714/565714en.pdf

COSO. (1992). Internal control-integrated framework — executive summary. http://www.coso.org/publications/executive_summary_integrated_framework.htm

COSO. (2004). Enterprise risk management — integrated framework — executive summary. http://www.coso.org/Publications/ERM/COSO_ERM_ExecutiveSummary.pdf

Deloitte & Touche. (2003). Corporate governance in Europe. Presentation Paper.

Engel, E., Hayes, R. M., & Wang, X. (2004). *The Sarbanes-Oxley Act and firms going private decisions.* SSRN Working Paper. http://ssrn.com/abstract=546626

Ernst & Young. (2004a). Emerging trends in internal control: Second Survey. May 2004. http://www.ey.com/global/content.nsf/US/AABS_-_Assurance_-_Internal_Controls_Summaries_Library

Ernst & Young. (2004b). Emerging trends in internal control: Third Survey. October 2004. http://www.ey.com/global/content.nsf/US/AABS_-_Assurance_-_Internal_Controls_Summaries_Library

Fischer, T. M., & Vielmeyer, U. (2004). Analyse von Risk Disclosure Scores: Risikoorientierte Unternehmenspublizität der DAX 100 Unternehmen. *Zeitschrift für kapitalmarktorientierte Rechnungslegung, 4*(11) 459–474.

Fischer zu Cramburg, R., Hannich, F. & Ziegert, N. (2004). Delisting und Deregistrierung deutscher Emittenten in den USA — Status Quo, Änderungsvorschläge und Ergebnisse einer Befragung US-notierter Unternehmen. *Studien des Deutschen Aktieninstituts, 28.* http://www.dai.de/internet/dai/dai-2-0.nsf/dai_publikationen.htm

Ge, W., & McVay, S. (2005). The disclosure of material weaknesses in internal control after the Sarbanes-Oxley Act. *Accounting Horizons,* (September), *19*(3), 137–158.

Grewe, W. (2000). Abschnitt P Ausgestaltung und Prüfung des Risikofrüherkennungssystems. In: Institut der Wirtschaftsprüfer (Eds), *WP Handbuch 2000* (pp. 1369–1400). Düsseldorf: IdW Verlag.

Gruson, M., & Kubicek, M. (2003a). Der Sarbanes-Oxley Act, Corporate Governance und das Deutsche Aktienrecht (Teil I). *Die Aktiengesellschaft, 48*(8), 337–352.

Gruson, M., & Kubicek, M. (2003b). Der Sarbanes-Oxley Act, Corporate Governance und das deutsche Aktienrecht (Teil II). *Die Aktiengesellschaft, 48*(8), 394–406.

Jain, P. K., Kim, J. -C. Rezaee, Z. (2004). *The effect of the Sarbanes-Oxley Act of 2002 on market liquidity.* SSRN Working Paper. http://papers.ssrn.com/sol3/papers.cfm?abstract_id=488142

Jovanovic, B. (1982). Truthful disclosure of information. *Bell Journal of Economics, 13,* 36–44.

Leuz, C., Triantis, A., & Wang, T. (2004). *Why do firms go dark? Causes and economic consequences of voluntary sec deregistrations.* SSRN-Working Paper. http://ssrn.com/abstract=592421

Menzies, C. (2004). *Sarbanes-Oxley Act, professionelles management interner kontrollen.* Stuttgart: Schaefer Poeschel.

Milgrom, P.R. (1981). Good news and bad news: Representation theorems and applications. *Bell Journal of Economics, 12,* 380–391.

Oxelheim, L., Randöy, T., & Stonehill, A. (2001). On the treatment of finance-specific factors within the OLI paradigm. *International Business Review, 10*(4), 381–398.

Peek, L., Blanco, H., & Roxas, M. (2004). *Sarbanes-Oxley Act of 2002: Corporate governance and public accounting firms oversight in NAFTA countries.* SSRN Working Paper. http://papers.ssrn.com/sol3/papers.cfm?abstract_id=489046

Perino, M. A. (2003). *American corporate reform abroad: Sarbanes-Oxley and the foreign private issuer.* SSRN Working Paper. http://ssrn.com/abstract=439501

Pozen, R. C. (2004). *Can European companies escape U.S. listings*? SSRN-Working Paper. http://ssrn.com/abstract=511942

Reese Jr., W. A., & Weisbach, M. S. (2002). Protection of minority shareholder interests, cross-listings in the United States, and subsequent equity offerings. *Journal of Financial Economics*, *66*, 65–104.

Rezaee, Z., & Jain, P. K. (2003). *The Sarbanes-Oxley Act of 2002 and security market behavior: Early evidence*. SSRN-Working Paper. http://ssrn.com/abstract=498083

Ribstein, L.E. (2003). International implications of Sarbanes-Oxley: Raising the rent on U.S. law. *Journal of Corporate Law Studies*, *3*(2), no pages. http://ssrn.com/abstract =401660

Scharpf, P. (1999). Risikomanagementsystem und Überwachungssystem. In: D. Dörner, D. Menold, & N. Pfitzer (Eds), *Reform des Aktienrechts, der Rechnungslegung und Prüfung* (August, pp. 177–202). Stuttgart: Schaeffer Poeschel.

Schmidt, R. H., & Spindler, G. (2000). *Path dependence, corporate governance and complementarity*. Johann Wolfgang Goethe Universität Frankfurt am Main: Finance & Accounting Working Paper Series, No. 27. http://www.wiwi.uni-frankfurt.de/schwerpunkte/finance/wp/408.pdf

Schmidt, R. H., & Weiß, M. (2003). Shareholder vs. stakeholder: Ökonomische Fragestellungen, In: P. Hommelhoff, K. Hopt, & A. von Werder (Eds), *Handbuch corporate governance* (pp. 107–127). Cologne: Schaeffer Poeschel.

Schreiber, M., & Grass, D. (2005). Emittenten überschätzen Zweitlistings im Ausland. *Financial Times Deutschland*, July 21, p. 19.

SEC. (2003a). *Final rule: Management's reports on internal control over financial reporting and certification of disclosure in Exchange Act periodic reports*. http://www.sec.gov/rules/final/33-8328.htm

SEC. (2003b). *Final rule: Disclosure required by Sections 406 and 407 of the Sarbanes Oxley Act of 2002*. http://www.sec.gov/rules/final/33-8177.htm

SEC. (2005a). *SEC votes to propose rules on foreign issuer deregistration. December 14, 2005*. http://www.sec.gov/news/press/2005-176.htm

SEC. (2005b). *Termination of a foreign private issuer's registration of a class of securities under Section 12(g) and duty to file reports under Section 15(d) of the Securities Exchange Act of 1934. December 23, 2005*. http://www.sec.gov/rules/proposed/34-53020.pdf

Siegel, J. (2005). Can foreign firms bond themselves effectively by renting U.S. securities laws? *Journal of Financial Economics*, *75*, 319–359.

Sutton, A., Lanoo, K., & Casey, J.P. (2005). *EU-financial regulation and supervision beyond 2005*. CEPS Task Force Report no. 54.

van den Brink, G. J., & Romeike, F. (2005). *Corporate governance und risikomanagement im Finanzdienstleistungsbereich*. Stuttgart: Schaeffer Poeschel.

Vater, H. (2004). Bedeutung, Funktion und Konzeption von Disclosure Committees nach den Vorgaben des Sarbanes-Oxley Act. *Zeitschrift für kapitalmarktorientierte Rechnungslegung*, *4*(4), 474–479.

von Werder, A., Talaulicar, T., & Kolat, G. (2004). Kodex report 2004: Die Akzeptanz der Empfehlungen des Deutschen Corporate Governance Kodex. *Der Betrieb*, *57*(26), 1377–1382.

Witt, P. (2003). *Corporate Governance-Systeme im Wettbewerb.* Wiesbaden: Gabler.
Wòjcik, D., Clark, G. L., & Bauer, R. (2004). *Corporate governance and cross-listing: Evidence from European companies.* SSRN Working Paper. http://ssrn.com/abstract=593364

Appendix 11.A.1 : Survey Questionnaire

I. Risk management and risk management disclosure in the German corporate governance system

(1) Current German laws and governance laws and regulations with regard to the establishment of a risk management system are: (a) sufficient and (b) concrete enough?
(2) Current German laws and governance regulations with regard to the disclosure of risks and risk management are: (a) sufficient and (b) concrete enough?
(3) The regulations of the German codex of corporate governance with regard to (a) the audit committee and (b) risk management should be binding?

II. Risk management and risk management disclosure in the context of the SOX

(4) The establishment of SOX in the United States impacted the scope of risk management for your company by (a) enlarging or (b) changing? Risk management. If answered by yes, please provide a brief description of these changes.
(5) The establishment of SOX in the United States impacted the scope of the disclosure of risk management for your company by (a) enlarging or (b) changing the disclosure of risk management? If yes, please provide a brief description of these changes.
(6) (a) The focus of Section 404 SOX is on internal controls over financial reporting. Is this appropriate to disclose risk management deficits?
 (b) Is there a direct impact of Sections 302 or 404 SOX on the organization of the risk management function in your company?
 (c) Is there a direct impact of Sections 302 or 404 SOX on the organization of disclosure on risk management in your company?

(7) Did you take an approach to integrate the implementation of Section 404 SOX in the enterprise risk management?
(8) Is the COSO framework, which is preferred by the SEC for the establishment of an internal control system, a useful linkage to risk management?
(9) Is a financial expert as defined by Section 407 SOX part of the audit committee of your company?
(10) Please provide a brief description of measures taken by your company to organize the audit committee to comply with SOX.
(11) The SEC has extended the compliance date with Section 404 SOX for foreign issuers for fiscal years ending on or after July 15, 2006. Is it beneficial today for your company to be bonded by U.S.-corporate governance laws?
(12) Is the extension necessary to be able to comply with SOX?
(13) Did your company establish a disclosure committee?

III. Links of German and U.S. corporate governance

(14) (a) Is the monitoring system to be established under KonTraG a starting point for the implementation of Section 404 SOX?
(b) Can results from the implementation of Section 404 SOX be used for the risk management disclosure in statutory reporting?
(c) The monitoring system as required under KonTraG makes reference only to such risks that might affect going concern. Section 404 makes reference only to internal control of financial reporting. Do you see overlaps of both requirements?
(d) Are there synergy effects from the monitoring system as required under KonTraG and the internal control of financial reporting as mandated by Section 404 SOX?
(15) Is an audit committee in compliance with German law able to fulfill the duties of an audit committee as mandated by SOX?

IV. General questions with regard to project management and implementation of SOX

(16) Is Section 404 SOX implemented by an internal project team? If yes, please note the departments which are part of the team.
(17) (a) Man hours used to date for the implementation of SOX are
low: up to 25,000 hours
medium: 25,001–50,000 hours

high: more than 50,000 hours.

Please include hours of an external consultant (public accounting firm).

(b) Man hours that will be needed in the future for the implementation of SOX are

low: up to 25,000 hours
medium: 25,001–50,000 hours
high: more than 50,000 hours.

Please include hours of an external consultant (public accounting firm).

(c) The Euro amount expensed to date for the implementation of SOX is

low: up to EUR 2.5 million
medium: EUR 2.5–5.0 million
high: more than EUR 5.0 million.

(d) The Euro amount needed in the future for the implementation of SOX is

low: up to EUR 2.5 million
medium: EUR 2.5–5.0 million
high: more than EUR 5.0 million.

V. Questions with regard to potential benefits of SOX

(18) The benefits of the implementation of SOX
- (a) with regard to the improvement of internal control of financial reporting is low, medium, or high.
- (b) with regard to the identification of risks that might affect going concern is low, medium, or high.
- (c) with regard to the cost of capital is low, medium, or high.

(19) Did SOX make the listing in the United States less attractive for your company?

(20) Did SOX make listings in the United States less attractive for potential new foreign issuers?

Chapter 12

Transparency and Capital Structure in Europe: Evidence of Firm, Industry, and National Institutional Influences

Raj Aggarwal and NyoNyo Aung Kyaw

12.1 Introduction

There is increasing interest in corporate transparency. In 2005, the European Commission adopted a directive covering minimum transparency and disclosure requirements for listed companies (Sheehan, 2005). This directive completes a package of financial services action plan adopted over the past two years. There is much interest globally in the possible impacts of these new transparency requirements, particularly in Europe. This chapter assesses how these new European transparency requirements may impact corporate capital structure, i.e., how they may influence the relative costs and attractiveness of debt versus equity. The study described in this chapter is the first to focus on the impact of transparency on corporate capital structures.

Since the time of Modigliani and Miller's (1958) irrelevance theory of capital structure, there have been numerous theoretical and empirical studies of corporate capital structure. According to modern theories of capital structure, corporate capital structure depends on firm and environmental characteristics that influence information asymmetry, manager–owner agency costs, financing costs, bankruptcy costs, and debt tax shields (Jensen & Meckling, 1976; Jensen, 1986; Myers & Majluf, 1984). As different countries have different legal systems, financial structures and institutions, levels of investor protections, and information disclosure

Corporate and Institutional Transparency for Economic Growth in Europe

ISBN: 0-08-044665-5

levels, the forces influencing corporate capital structure should be different across countries. Not only do legal and financial institutions differ internationally, but country-specific factors such as economic growth, inflation, interest rates, and regulatory regimes also differ across countries. Given these international institutional differences, it is fairly clear that financial contracting choices and therefore the optimal capital structure for firms will also differ internationally.

Indeed, the financing mix and leverage of firms in different countries have been shown to be different even for firms in the same industry. Early empirical studies suggest that a country's institutional features are responsible for this variation. Stonehill and Stitzel (1969) report the significant inter-country differences in debt ratios of firms in 11 countries. Aggarwal (1981, 1990) finds that country, industry, and size are all significant influences on capital structure among firms in Western Europe and Asia. Rajan and Zingales (1995), Demirgüc-Kunt and Maksimovic (1999), Wald (1999), Booth, Aivazian, Demirgüc-Kunt, and Maksimovic (2001), Chui, Lloyd, and Kwok (2002), and Song and Philippatos (2004) analyze capital structure choices of firms in different sets of countries. All of these studies provide evidence that international variations in various institutional factors are important in explaining international capital structure differences.

Corporate transparency reduces information asymmetry and can be defined to mean the extent to which outside investors can evaluate a firm's operations. Reduction of information asymmetry also reduces residual agency costs. The severity of agency costs and information asymmetry among managers, outside shareholders, and creditors determines firm access and cost of external capital and its choice of capital (debt or equity). The severity of information asymmetry and of these agency conflicts depends greatly on the information disclosure environment in a country. Since these levels of transparency differ internationally (Bushman et al., 2004b), we expect that firm capital structures in a cross-country sample will vary systematically with disclosure levels.

However, there does not seem to be any prior literature that examines the influence of international variations in transparency on corporate capital structure. While the prior studies on international capital structure cited above address the effect of firm characteristics and many country-level institutional factors on international variations in capital structure, they do not address the influence of transparency on corporate capital structure. This chapter fills that gap in the literature as it examines the influence of national transparency on the capital structures of firms in 14 European countries controlling for firm, industry, and country characteristics.

This chapter contributes to the overall theme of the book as expressed in Chapter 1—by focusing on how higher transparency levels can lead to lower costs of capital and higher levels of capital formation and economic growth rates. In particular, it also relates to Chapter 6 about the role of transparent bankruptcy laws in Europe, Chapter 10 about the adoption of new International Financial Reporting Standards (IFRS) in Europe, and Chapter 11 examining the impact of the Sarbanes-Oxley Act on European firms cross-listed in the US. This chapter also complements Chapter 9, which examines the legal determinants of the return on equity.

This study documents and re-confirms prior findings regarding the debt ratio influence of firm size (+), asset tangibility (+), profitability (−), business risk (−), growth opportunities (−), and industry average leverage (+). This study also documents the significant influence of a country's economic factors on capital structure, showing that capital structure depends on the levels of stock and bond market development, banking sector size, and the country's GDP growth rate.

More importantly, controlling for other variables previously known to influence corporate capital structure, this study documents that international variations in transparency levels significantly influence corporate capital structure levels. According to the pecking order theory of Myers and Majluf (1984), when firms consider outside financing, they prefer the issuance of debt before equity, as outside equity financing is more subject to information asymmetry problems. Transparency can also lead firms to pass up positive net present value (NPV) investments that require external financing (Almazan, Suarez, & Titman, 2003). Those firms tend to choose more conservative capital structures with lower debt ratios (i.e., with unused debt capacity in case future external financing is needed), leading to a negative relationship between information disclosure and debt ratios. We document that transparency that reduces owner–manager agency costs such as higher levels of accounting disclosures, financial governance, audit intensity, and enforcement of anti-insider trading laws is negatively associated with corporate debt levels.

In contrast, transparency that helps creditors control operating risks (and thus wealth transfers from creditors to owners), such as disclosure timeliness, institutional trading, and media coverage, is associated with higher debt levels. In addition to supporting the pecking order theory, our results are also consistent with the agency cost theory of capital structure. Our results have important public policy and managerial implications. For example, as there are differential impacts of transparency on debt or equity, public policy regarding transparency regulations and disclosure laws can be targeted to favor the development of equity or debt markets. Similarly, managers can focus on reducing the costs of external debt or external equity.

The next section reviews briefly the prior literature on transparency and capital structure determinants. Following that we describe the research design and the data. Finally, the results of the empirical estimates are discussed, followed by some conclusions.

12.2 Transparency and International Capital Structure Variations

12.2.1 Determinants of Capital Structure

While earlier empirical work has documented the stylized facts based on capital structure theories, in recent years theories of capital structure for international settings have been developed and tested.[1] Coates and Woolley (1975) and Borio (1990) show that a country's tax rates, inflation rates, and capital market characteristics are important determinants of international capital structure differences. The influence of these factors on capital structure is confirmed by Rajan and Zingales (1995) and McClure, Clayton, and Hofler (1999) who study the determinants of corporate capital structures in G7 countries; by Wald (1999) who examines the factors correlated with firm capital structures in France, Germany, Japan, the UK, and the US; and by Booth et al. (2001) who analyze capital structure choices of firms in 10 developing countries.

Song and Philippatos (2004) analyze the capital structure choices of firms in 16 OECD (Organisation for Economic Co-operation and Development) countries. They find that country characteristics explain deviations in international corporate capital structures after firm and industry factors are taken into account. Fan, Titman, and Twite (2003) study the capital structure and debt maturity choices of firms in a cross-section of 39 developed and developing countries and find that institutional factors, such as the tax system, the information environment, and the characteristics of suppliers of capital, affect capital structure choices of firms. Demirgüc-Kunt and Maksimovic (1999) examine the direct effects of institutional factors on debt and its maturity in 30 countries during the period 1980–1991. They find varying use of long- and short-term debt in countries depending on capital market development, banking development, institutional factors, and the firm size. Chui et al. (2002) investigate the effect of national characteristics on corporate capital structures across 22 countries for the year 1996. Controlling for economic development, financial structure, and firm variables in their analysis, they find that national characteristics significantly affect the corporate capital structures. As this brief review of capital structure

[1]See, for example, Stonehill and Stitzel (1969) and Aggarwal (1981, 1990).

studies indicates, international variations in firm characteristics and institutional factors are important factors in explaining international capital structure differences. However, no prior study has examined the impact of corporate transparency on capital structure. This chapter fills that important gap in the literature.

12.2.2 Role of Corporate Transparency

In an ideal, frictionless capital market, information is available without cost to all participants. In reality, information disclosure can be costly to interpret (for investors) and costly to disclose as firms incur both direct and indirect costs. Investment useful information is more easily available to some (e.g., insiders and managers) versus others (e.g., investors). Such information asymmetries cannot be eliminated without cost, as information is costly to generate, share, analyze, and assess. However, increased disclosure can lead to greater access and lower costs of capital. Yu (2005) documents how firm disclosure quality and transparency influence its credit spreads; Sengupta (1998) shows that the quality of a firm's disclosure policies influences its cost of debt; Bushee and Noe (2000) show that disclosure quality influences stock return volatility; and Lang and Lundholm (1993) show that firm disclosure policies impact analyst ratings of a firm. Thus, based on this admittedly indirect evidence, it seems that the nature and level of transparency is very likely to influence a firm's capital structure.

Further, Bushman et al. (2004a) posit that limited transparency of firms' operations for outside investors increases the moral hazard problem and thus demands a better corporate governance system. They document that corporate transparency differs internationally and reflects national institutional characteristics. Doidge, Karolyi, and Stulz (2004) develop and test a model of how country characteristics influence a firm's costs and benefits in implementing measures to improve their own governance and transparency. Further, Jaggi and Low (2000) document that national business environments impact levels of financial disclosure by firms in different countries. Thus, it seems clear that there are international differences in the nature and level of disclosure, differences that may also influence corporate capital structure.

Financial theory suggests that a major factor in a firm's choice of capital structure is the existence of asymmetric information and agency costs. The extent to which these costs can be controlled by appropriate financial contracts also depends on the level of asymmetric information and levels of disclosure. Providers of debt and equity capital to a firm, however, may not have the same reaction to higher levels of disclosure. Dominant and relationship-based lenders, such as main or controlling banks, may want lower levels of disclosure, while equity providers may like higher levels of disclosure to maximize firm value by reducing agency costs.

There may be different individual firm and socially optimal levels of disclosure.[2] Transparency can improve the allocation of capital in an economy and the availability of external financing to firms. However, transparency also affects the firm's relationships with its competitors and other non-investor stakeholders (e.g., employees, suppliers, and customers) and it can have a negative effect reducing firm value (Leuz & Verrecchia, 2000). High levels of transparency may make it easier for these non-financial stakeholders to press for and increase their claims on the firm's assets and earnings. For example, if a firm does well and is transparent about its good fortune, employees may extract higher wages, suppliers may extract higher prices, customers may extract lower prices, and governments and communities may extract higher taxes and other social expenditures. High levels of transparency also may discourage managers from seeking outside financing and, thus, use non-optimal and more conservative capital structures and forego investments in some positive NPV projects requiring outside financing (Almazan et al., 2003).

In addition, not all types of disclosure have the same impact on debt or equity holders. While owners are interested in reducing agency costs between managers and owners, debt holders may be more interested in preventing and controlling excessive risk-taking in a firm's operations — risk-taking that transfers wealth from debt holders to equity holders (debt holders bear the costs of failure, while equity holders benefit from the success of risky but potentially high-return projects). Thus, disclosure that reduces manager–owner agency costs or enhances equity holder rights is likely to increase the availability of and/or reduce the costs of equity leading at the margin to lower debt ratios. In contrast, disclosure that improves debt holder control of operating risks is likely to increase the availability of and/or reduce the cost of debt leading at the margin to higher debt ratios. Thus, we use a number of different measures of transparency (which are classified into two categories — those that are likely to have positive versus those that are likely to have negative associations with corporate debt levels).

In addition to the firm and national variables that influence capital structure, it is clear that transparency levels are also likely to be an important influence on capital structure. Further, since the level of corporate transparency differs inter-

---

[2]It has been noted that mandatory disclosure may be socially useful as it may force higher levels of disclosure and improve the allocation of capital. However, when disclosure rules apply to all firms, it may benefit firms with higher quality information more as non-disclosure may be interpreted as lack of good quality.

nationally (Alford, Jones, Leftwich, & Zmijewski, 1993; Bushman et al., 2004b), we expect that the observed financial structures in a cross-country sample should vary systematically across countries. In addition, some types of disclosure favor debt holders and thus higher corporate debt levels, while other aspects of disclosure favor equity providers and thus lower corporate debt levels. Therefore, our research design uses a number of measures of transparency. As shown in the next section, we test the impact of transparency on capital structure controlling for other relevant firm and country variables.

12.3 Variables, Research Design, and Data

12.3.1 Firm-Level Determinants of Capital Structure

In each country, differences in the capital structure choice of firms depend on the characteristics of such firms. In examining the impact of transparency on capital structure, it is important that we control for differences in firm characteristics. These characteristics are described below.

A firm's *level of fixed assets* (*tangibility*) should be associated with higher leverage as high levels of such assets can be used as loan collateral (Friend & Lang, 1988; Long & Malitz, 1985). Jensen, Solberg, and Zorn (1992) provide empirical evidence of the positive relation between tangibility and leverage. There are conflicting theoretical predictions about the effect of *profitability* on firm's level of leverage. The agency cost theory of Jensen (1986) suggests a positive relationship between profitability and debt level as the firm is committed to regular interest payments. However, the pecking order theory of Myers and Majluf (1984) predicts a negative relationship because firms prefer internal financing before raising new external capital such as debt.

There seems to be relatively clear evidence on the influence of *taxes* on capital structure. Debt has the advantage of providing an interest tax shield, while equity does not. The higher the tax rate, the greater will be the tax shield from interest expense. Hence, according to the trade-off theory, we expect higher debt level for firms with high tax rates. In contrast, less debt can be expected if the cost of bankruptcy is higher than the tax shield or other benefits of using debt. The trade-off theory, therefore, suggests a lower leverage for firms with high bankruptcy or financial distress probabilities. As in most prior literature, we use Altman's *Z*-score as a proxy for the firm's bankruptcy or distress risk (Graham, 2000; Frank & Goyal, 2003). A higher *Z*-score represents a lower bankruptcy risk.

Debt is often used to control agency costs in a firm. The agency cost model predicts that low-growth firms should hold more debt since debt service payments likely redirect resources that may be used for managerial perquisites. In contrast, for the firms with high growth opportunities, shareholders and managerial interests become more aligned and firms tend to have a lower optimal debt level. The complex version of the pecking order theory also predicts a negative relation between growth opportunities and leverage. However, the simple version of the pecking order theory predicts a positive relationship, as high growth would require the use of more external financing in the form of debt. *Dividends* can be an important determinant of leverage as dividends and debt are substitute mechanisms for controlling the agency costs of free cash flows.[3] However, the pecking order theory would forecast a positive association between debt and dividends (debt is needed to replace the cash flows lost to dividends).

The effect of firm *size* on leverage is well explored in the literature (e.g., Rajan & Zingales, 1995; Frank & Goyal, 2003), and larger firms tend to have higher debt capacity so that size has a positive relationship with debt ratios. However, large size can also be a proxy for less information asymmetry (Rajan & Zingales, 1995), increasing investors' preference for equity, and lowering debt ratios. We use the natural logarithm of sales revenue as a measure of firm *size*.

12.3.2 *Transparency and Institutional Determinants of Capital Structure*

12.3.2.1 Corporate transparency factors Measures of accounting transparency are from Bushman et al. (2004b), who define transparency as the availability of firm-specific information to those outside the firm. The framework used by Bushman et al. categorizes country measures of information disclosure under three headings: (1) the corporate reporting regime, including measures of intensity, measurement principles, timeliness, audit quality, and the intensity of governance disclosures (i.e., identity, remuneration, and shareholdings of officers and directors, and identity and holdings of other major shareholders); (2) the intensity of private information acquisition, including measures of analyst following, and the prevalence of pooled investment schemes and insider trading activities; and (3) information dissemination, including a measure of the extent of media penetration.

---

[3]See, for example, Jensen (1986). The relationship between debt and dividends has been tested in the empirical literature (Jensen et al., 1992). These studies find that debt and dividends are substitute mechanisms for monitoring and for controlling agency cost of free cash flows.

The direction of influence of these transparency variables on capital structure depends on how the resulting reduction in information asymmetry influences debt and equity investors' willingness to provide financing for a firm. As discussed earlier, disclosure that reduces manager–owner agency costs or enhances equity holder rights is likely to increase the availability of and/or reduce the costs of equity leading at the margin to lower debt ratios. In contrast, disclosure that improves debt holder control of operating risks is likely to increase the availability of and/or reduce the cost of debt, and is likely to be associated with higher debt ratios. Based on this analysis, for the eight specific transparency variables used in this study and described in Table 12.1, the expected relationships with corporate debt ratios are expected to be

Transparency measure	Debt relationship	Main reason
(1) Financial disclosure	–	Controls agency costs
(2) Governance disclosure	–	Controls agency costs
(3) Accounting disclosure	–	Controls agency costs
(4) Disclosure timeliness	+	Limits excessive operating risks
(5) Audit intensity	–	Controls agency costs
(6) Insider trading law enforcement[4]	–	Controls agency costs
(7) Institutional trading activity	+	Limits excessive operating risks
(8) Media coverage	+	Limits excessive operating risks

12.3.2.2 National financial structure and economic factors We might expect that the more developed and the more liquid the stock market, the less is the information asymmetry between management and shareholders and higher is the propensity for managers to issue equity leading to lower debt levels. *Stock market capitalization* and *stock market turnover* (Demirgüc-Kunt & Levine, 1996; Demirgüc-Kunt & Maksimovic, 1996, 1998) are used as measures for a country's stock market development. As higher development of debt markets would provide more flexibility for a firm's borrowing (LaPorta, Lopez-de-Silanes, Shleifer, & Vishny, 1997), we expect a positive relationship between bond market development and the level of leverage. However, this relationship can also be affected by the existence of spillover effects, such as those arising from the fact

[4]Note that for the measure of insider trading law enforcement, the lower the number, the higher is the enforcement quality of insider trading law (see Table 12.1).

Table 12.1: Data definitions, measurements, and sources.

Variable	Measurement/definition	Source
Firm-level variables		
Leverage	Long-term debt ratio = long-term debt/total assets, total debt ratio = (long-term debt + debt in current liabilities + accounts payables)/total assets	Global Vantage
Tangibility	Ratio of net fixed assets to total assets	Global Vantage
Profit ($t-1$)	Operating income on total assets lagged one period	Global Vantage
Size	Natural logarithm of total sales	Global Vantage
Tax rate	Income taxes paid/earnings before interest and tax	Global Vantage
Altman's Z-score	($3.3 \times$ pretax income + sales + $1.4 \times$ retained earnings + $1.2 \times$ (total current assets − total current liabilities))/total assets	Global Vantage
Growth opportunities	Market to book ratio	Global Vantage
Corporate transparency variables		
Financial disclosure	Disclosure concerning R&D expenses, capital expenditures, product and geographic segment data, subsidiary information, and accounting methods	Bushman et al. (2004b)
Governance disclosure	Disclosure related to identity of managers, identity of board members and their affiliations, remuneration of officers and directors, share ownership by directors and employees, identity of major shareholders, and the range of shareholdings	Bushman et al. (2004b)
Accounting disclosure	An attempt to capture cross-country differences in accounting principles used. The extent to which financial statements reflect subsidiaries on a consolidated basis and the general reserves are used — higher values associated with more informative financial statements	Bushman et al. (2004b)
Disclosure timeliness	Timeliness of disclosures, which increases with the frequency and comprehensiveness of interim reports	Bushman et al. (2004b)

Audit intensity	Measure of credibility of financial accounting disclosures, defined on the basis of the share of total value audited in a country represented by the Big 5 accounting firms—high value as an indication of high-quality audits	Bushman et al. (2004b)
Inside trading law enforcement	A dummy equal to 1 if the country enforced insider trading laws and 0 otherwise—a low value means more information acquisition by insiders	Bushman et al. (2004b)
Institutional trading activity	Private information collection, processing, and trading activities of institutional investors—proxied by the average ratio of the value of pooled investment schemes to GDP—high value means more information acquisition by institutional investors	Bushman et al. (2004b)
Media coverage	Penetration of the media channels measured by the average rank of countries' per capita number of newspapers and television	Bushman et al. (2004b)
Financial and economic variables		
Stock market capitalization	Stock market capitalization of listed companies/GDP	WDI, World Bank
Stock market turnover	Ratio of total value traded to total market capitalization	WDI, World Bank
Bond market capitalization	Bond market capitalization/GDP	World Federation Exchanges
Banking sector size	Domestic money bank domestic assets/GDP	IFS, IMF
GDP per capita growth	Growth rate of real per capita GDP	WDI, World Bank
Inflation	Rate of increase in GDP deflator	WDI, World Bank

that countries with better development of debt markets are also more likely to have better stock market development leading to higher equity ratio. *Bond market capitalization* is used as a measure for a country's development of debt market.[5] A country's emphasis on banks as a source of finance is an important factor in a firm's capital structure choice (Demirgüc-Kunt & Maksimovic, 1999). In addition to just providing loans, in some countries like Japan and Germany, banks play a significant role in information gathering and monitoring management (Bae, Kang, & Lim, 2002). Therefore, in bank-oriented countries with a highly developed banking sector, we expect a better access to external borrowing and, thus, higher debt levels. We use *banking sector size* as a measure of a country's bank orientation.[6]

Investors will be less willing to lend if they are not sure about the real returns on their loans, i.e., if they face higher inflationary risk. In addition, inflation uncertainty increases the firm's business risk through volatility in the firm's selling prices, costs, and the volume of sales. Therefore, in a highly inflationary country with high inflation uncertainty, firms will experience high business risk and will carry less debt in the capital structure. In addition, since inflation uncertainty raises the business risk, the tax shield benefits from debt become more uncertain and less valuable. In such an environment, where the tax shield benefit from debt is low, firms' propensity to use debt can be expected to be lower. Therefore, we expect a negative relation between inflation and leverage, especially long-term leverage (Hatzinikolaou, Katsimbris, & Noulas, 2002).[7] On the other hand, if interest rates do not adequately reflect the high inflation rate, inflation can be associated with higher debt level as the real repayment value of debt declines with inflation. *Inflation* is used as a measure of a country's inflationary risk. The strength of the economy is measured by the growth rate of real per capita GDP. As stated in Demirgüc-Kunt and Maksimovic (1999), the annual growth rate in national GDP is an indicator of the financing needs of firms. Therefore, we include annual *GDP per capita growth rate* as a control variable for overall financing needs of firms in our sample of countries.

---

[5]Debt market development in a country is measured by the total value of corporate and government bonds outstanding divided by GDP. As a rough proxy for bond market development, results should be viewed carefully.

[6]Demirgüc-Kunt and Maksimovic (1998, 1999), Chui et al. (2002), and Fan et al. (2003) also use this as a measure of a country's bank emphasis.

[7]Role of taxes and inflation in capital structure is also examined in Lee and Zechner (1984) and Auerbach and King (1983).

12.3.2.3 Research design: Capital structure model As described in the prior sections, leverage depends on a country's transparency, financial and economic variables, and firm-specific factors,[8] expressed as:

$$Leverage_{it} = \alpha_0 + \sum_j \alpha_j F_{jit} + \sum_k \alpha_k T_{kn} + \sum_l \alpha_l E_{lnt} + \alpha_q IndustryAvgLev_{qnt} + \varepsilon_{it} \quad (12.1)$$

where the dependent and independent variables are defined as follows:

(i) $Leverage_{it}$, leverage ratio of a given firm i at time t measured as either (1) total debt ratio or (2) long-term debt ratio.[9] Total debt is used especially to partially address the accounting differences between countries. We use book leverage instead of market leverage because market leverage is subject to market volatility.[10]

(ii) F_{jit}, a vector of firm-specific factors j for firm i at time t. Firm-specific determinants include tangibility (*Tangibility*), profitability ($Profit_{(t-1)}$), size (*Size*), tax rate (*TaxRate*), bankruptcy risk measure (*Z-score*), investment opportunities (*Growth*), and dividend paying dummy (*Dividend*).

(iii) T_{kn}, a vector of corporate transparency variables k for country n.[11] Corporate transparency variables are from Bushman et al. (2004b) and they include financial disclosure, governance disclosure, accounting disclosure, disclosure timeliness, audit intensity, inside trading law enforcement, institutional trading activity, and media coverage.

---

[8] As pointed out in prior literature on corporate transparency, the level of corporate transparency varies in different countries due to differences in the level of legal environment/enforcements and varying cultural values in those countries (Jaggi & Low, 2000). We also find that the corporate transparency variables are highly correlated with legal and cultural variables. Accordingly, we exclude legal and cultural variables in this analysis as we confirm that their influence on capital structure is captured by corporate transparency variables.

[9] Relative to total debt ratio, the long-term debt ratio is a more common measure of leverage in most capital structure research. However in some countries, especially in countries where the capital market is not well developed, long-term debt is not easily available. Thus, in these countries, many firms use large amount of permanent short-term funds. Consequently, for international comparisons, total debt ratio may be a better variable to study international capital structure. In addition, the distribution of total debt ratio is closer to normal than that of long-term debt ratio. Thus, from statistical point of view also, the total debt ratio is a better variable.

[10] Hovakimian, Opler, and Titman (2001, p. 5) find that the choice between book and market value does not influence empirical results significantly. Bowman (1980) also shows that the correlation between the book and market values of debt is very large. In addition, it should be noted that market values of traded equity often turns out to be excessively volatile, leading to severe measurement problems.

[11] As the transparency variables change very slowly (if at all) over time, it is assumed that they are time-invariant.

(iv) E_{lnt}, a vector of financial and economic factors l for country n at time t. Financial institution variables include stock market capitalization, stock market turnover, bond market capitalization, and banking sector size. The economic variables include annual GDP per capita growth and the level of inflation.

(v) *IndustryAvgLev*, average industry sector leverage for sector q in country n at time t to control for the industry sector effects. As suggested in Roberts (2002), firms may revert primarily to an industry average with only minor firm-specific deviations so that there should be a positive relationship between this variable and corporate leverage.

The regression for Eq. (12.1) is performed by using ordinary least squares (OLS) estimation with the robust Newey-West standard errors that allow for heteroscedasticity and autocorrelation.[12]

12.3.2.4 Data The primary data source for firm-level data is Standard and Poor's Global Vantage database. Global Vantage contains financial statement and stock price data for companies in many different countries in a comparable form. Therefore, it helps us to partially address the problem of the lack of consistent accounting and market information outside the United States (Rajan & Zingales, 1995). Data on country-level variables comes from the World Development Index (WDI) of the World Bank, International Financial Statistics (IFS) of the IMF, World Federation Exchanges (FIBV), and Bushman et al. (2004b).

As usual, we exclude financial and utility firms and firms in other highly regulated industries. We also exclude firms with missing observations that are required for analysis. Our sample covers 14 European countries in which there are at least 25 firms available. Our sample period is between 1990 and 2001. The countries in our sample are Austria, Belgium, Denmark, Finland, France, Germany, Ireland,

[12]Fixed-effect panel estimation is not used in this study due to the inclusion of time-invariant country factors, such as transparency variables. Use of fixed-effect model will eliminate those time-invariant variables, which are some of the main deterministic variables in the study. Another reason for not using the fixed-effect panel estimation procedure, especially for each country regressions in Tables 12.5 and 12.6, is due to the small number of observations for many countries in the data set and the use of the fixed-effect panel estimation is unable to produce reliable estimates. In addition, some forms of unobserved heterogeneity cannot be accounted for by means of fixed effects, but might be (partly) captured using the robust standard errors. Similarly, the country fixed effect or country dummies are also excluded to avoid redundancy as we have included country factors, such as transparency factors, economic and financial variables in the regressions.

Italy, Netherlands, Norway, Spain, Sweden, Switzerland, and the UK. This results in a final sample of 4437 firms and 27,078 firm-year observations in 14 countries, and sample coverage in each country is presented in Table 12.2.[13]

12.4 Empirical Results

12.4.1 Descriptive Statistics

Figures 12.1 and 12.2 present the country mean long-term and total debt ratios, while Table 12.2 presents the means and standard deviations of long-term and total debt ratios of our sample firms in 14 European countries. The highest country long-term debt ratio is found in Norway and the lowest in Germany. The highest country total debt ratio is found in France and the lowest in Germany. Comparing the countries with regard to their debt ratios, Belgium, France, Italy, Netherlands, Spain, and the UK seem to carry relatively higher levels of short-term debt, while Austria, Denmark, Finland, Ireland, Norway, Switzerland, and Sweden seem to carry relatively higher levels of long-term debt.

The means and standard deviations of firm-level variables, traditionally used as leverage determinants, are reported in Table 12.2. The data seem well behaved. We do not find much variation across countries in firm size, *Z*-scores, and growth. However, somewhat higher variation is found in profitability, tangibility, and tax rates across countries. The highest variation is found in firm profitability (with a coefficient of variation of 0.45) and the lowest variation is found in firm size (with a coefficient of variation of 0.06).

To gain a general idea about the distribution of country-level variables, we report the mean value of country-level variables for our sample of 14 European countries in Table 12.3. Interestingly, there is a wide variation in country-level variables, especially in the corporate transparency variables. Switzerland has the highest average stock market capitalization ratio and bank development, while it has very low GDP growth and inflation rates. Spain has the highest stock market turnover and inflation with very low bond market development. Denmark has the highest bond market development, while it is the least bank-oriented country. Ireland has the highest GDP growth rate, and Belgium has the lowest stock market development.

[13]As described later in the chapter, the results are very similar when the numbers of observations in all models are restricted to the observations available for the model with the highest need for information.

Table 12.2: Sample statistics.

Country	*N*-firms	*N*-obs	Long-term debt ratio		Total debt ratio		Tangibility		Profit		Size		TaxRate		*Z*-score		Growth	
			Mean	Std Dev	Mean	Std Dev	Mean	Std Dev	Mean	Std Dev	Mean	Std Dev	Mean	Std Dev	Mean	Std Dev	Mean	Std Dev
Austria	93	585	0.1245	0.1228	0.3385	0.1784	0.3536	0.1774	0.0255	0.065	5.3235	1.5405	0.2613	0.326	1.4664	0.6623	1.7834	2.1726
Belgium	85	549	0.1434	0.1194	0.3892	0.1702	0.2958	0.1882	0.0276	0.0803	5.8193	1.8367	0.2706	0.34	1.5922	0.9312	2.4965	2.6568
Denmark	144	985	0.156	0.1235	0.3605	0.1638	0.3452	0.1792	0.0365	0.0755	5.182	1.52	0.2702	0.2505	1.8805	0.8862	2.1237	2.5203
Finland	125	731	0.1942	0.143	0.3512	0.1763	0.3393	0.1986	0.0436	0.0799	5.8375	1.7581	0.2944	0.2678	1.8456	0.8247	2.2194	2.7062
France	698	3913	0.1344	0.1186	0.4007	0.1692	0.2064	0.1507	0.0298	0.0766	5.4705	1.9409	0.3459	0.3151	1.603	0.7886	2.5371	2.7758
Germany	720	4025	0.0956	0.1135	0.2943	0.1884	0.2611	0.1775	0.0013	0.1173	5.3859	1.9573	0.3812	0.3717	1.8285	1.0917	2.8281	3.0695
Ireland	62	478	0.1707	0.1456	0.3609	0.1784	0.4169	0.2441	0.041	0.0949	5.1899	1.7853	0.1822	0.2537	1.4978	1.3599	2.3109	2.1413
Italy	164	941	0.1173	0.1076	0.3939	0.159	0.2768	0.1824	0.026	0.053	6.0362	1.6301	0.3986	0.3221	1.2459	0.6117	2.0778	2.6097
Netherlands	210	1317	0.124	0.1206	0.3551	0.1824	0.3121	0.1888	0.0538	0.0802	5.9466	1.8621	0.267	0.2094	2.0679	1.1158	3.0205	3.3175
Norway	150	879	0.2495	0.1964	0.3785	0.193	0.3853	0.2643	0.0134	0.1171	4.9522	1.7434	0.2353	0.3166	1.4524	1.0023	2.2374	2.4607
Spain	133	932	0.1111	0.1137	0.368	0.1763	0.3962	0.2135	0.0399	0.0712	5.7098	1.4979	0.2481	0.2251	1.2298	0.7839	2.2342	2.5443
Sweden	294	1553	0.1535	0.1471	0.3051	0.1752	0.2797	0.2028	0.0122	0.1388	5.3488	2.0198	0.2491	0.2812	1.6984	1.1133	2.4887	2.5605
Switzerland	174	1238	0.1845	0.1396	0.3472	0.1618	0.3813	0.2076	0.0361	0.0768	5.9456	1.6196	0.2557	0.2687	1.6272	0.8163	2.3024	2.4587
UK	1385	8952	0.1069	0.119	0.3169	0.168	0.365	0.235	0.0359	0.1198	5.2295	1.8206	0.257	0.2423	1.9042	1.3345	2.8518	3.0648

Notes: This table provides the sample and descriptive statistics for 14 European countries used in this study for 1990–2001. Total debt ratio is measured by the ratio of total debt (total long-term debt + debt and current liabilities + accounts payables) to total asset. Long-term debt ratio is measured by the ratio of total long-term debt to total asset. Tangibility (TAN) is the ratio of net fixed assets to total assets, profitability (Profit) the ratio of operating income on total assets, size (Size) the natural logarithm of total sales, tax rate (Tax) the ratio of income taxes paid to earnings before interest and taxes, bankruptcy risk measure (Z-score) the Altman's Z-score, and investment opportunities (Growth) the firm's market-to-book ratio.

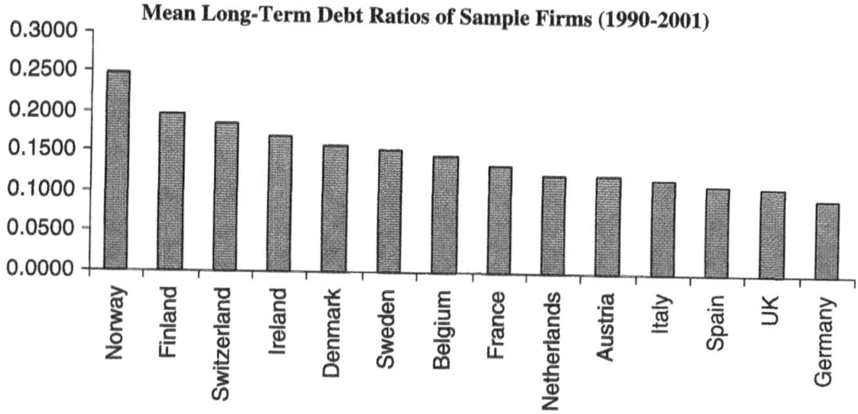

Figure 12.1: Mean total debt ratios of sample firms (1990–2001). *Notes*: This figure presents the mean total debt ratio of our sample firms in 14 European countries for the period 1990–2001. Total debt ratio is measured by the ratio of total debt (total long-term debt+debt and current liabilities+accounts payables) to total asset.

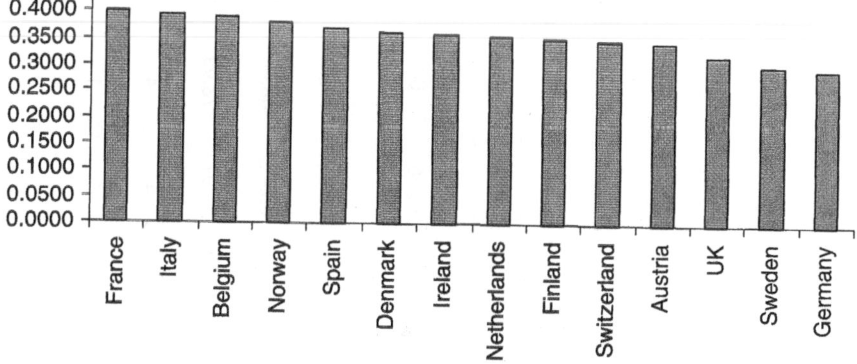

Figure 12.2: Mean long-term debt ratios of sample firms (1990–2001). *Notes*: This figure presents the mean long-term debt ratio of our sample firms in 14 European countries for the period 1990–2001. Long-term debt ratio is measured by the ratio of total long-term debt to total asset.

Table 12.3: Mean values of country-level variables for a sample of 14 European countries for the period 1990–2001.

Country	**Austria**	**Belgium**	**Denmark**	**Finland**	**France**	**Germany**	**Ireland**	**Italy**	**Netherlands**	**Norway**	**Spain**	**Sweden**	**Switzerland**	**UK**
Corporate transparency variables														
Financial disclosure	70.29	92.75	86.96	100	100	100	100	100	100	76.45	92.75	100	100	100
Governance disclosure	78.99	76.45	76.81	89.49	65.58	72.83	91.67	65.58	85.87	90.22	79.71	96.74	86.96	94.57
Accounting disclosure	68.48	39.13	68.48	68.48	70.65	39.13	100	68.48	46.74	68.48	100	39.13	68.48	100
Disclosure timeliness	68.12	63.04	73.91	78.99	78.26	68.12	69.57	86.96	78.26	94.20	89.13	86.23	73.91	86.96
Audit intensity	3	3	4	4	3	4	4	4	4	4	4	4	3	4
Inside trading law enforcement	0	1	0	1	1	1	0	0	1	1	0	1	1	1

Institutional trading activity	0.11	0.06	0.03	0.01	0.37	0.14	0.26	0.07	0.16	0.04	0.16	0.10	0.16	0.13
Media coverage	87.53	86.73	95.52	94.82	86.14	90.99	83.34	78.98	92.00	95.31	75.31	95.47	93.78	90.81
Financial and economic variables														
Stock market cap	0.15	0.09	0.46	1.03	0.58	0.39	0.64	0.35	1.05	0.32	0.51	0.89	1.88	1.38
Stock market turnover	0.51	0.23	0.60	0.53	0.78	1.33	0.57	0.73	1.02	0.73	1.53	0.74	0.85	0.57
Banking sector size	1.30	1.50	0.56	0.67	1.07	1.41	0.93	0.86	1.31	0.77	1.15	0.70	1.80	1.21
Bond market cap	0.53	0.91	1.78	0.31	0.54	0.91	0.29	0.82	0.76	0.34	0.10	0.68	0.92	0.84
GDP per capita growth	1.81	1.96	2.02	2.86	1.65	1.28	6.79	1.54	2.18	2.72	2.27	1.52	0.44	2.22
Inflation	1.77	1.85	2.19	1.99	1.42	1.79	3.43	3.66	2.31	3.36	3.77	2.40	1.25	2.96

Note: The definitions and sources of the variables are described in Table 12.1.

Table 12.4: Country and industry factors on capital structures.

	Long-term debt ratio			Total debt ratio		
	(1)	(2)	(3)	(1)	(2)	(3)
Intercept	0.0949***	0.1086***	0.1160***	0.3097***	0.3169***	0.3331***
	0.00	0.00	0.00	0.00	0.00	0.00
Austria	0.0186***	0.0152***		0.0219***	0.0216***	
	0.00	0.00		0.00	0.00	
Belgium	0.0389***	0.0370***		0.0722***	0.0722***	
	0.00	0.00		0.00	0.00	
Denmark	0.0491***	0.0484***		0.0433***	0.0436***	
	0.00	0.00		0.00	0.00	
Finland	0.0916***	0.0902***		0.0340***	0.0343***	
	0.00	0.00		0.00	0.00	
France	0.0272***	0.0272***		0.0834***	0.0837***	
	0.00	0.00		0.00	0.00	
Germany	−0.0107***	−0.0125***		−0.0227***	−0.0226***	
	0.00	0.00		0.00	0.00	
Ireland	0.0622***	0.0621***		0.0439***	0.0439***	
	0.00	0.00		0.00	0.00	
Italy	0.0122***	0.0092**		0.0770***	0.0769***	
	0.01	0.03		0.00	0.00	
Netherlands	0.0150***	0.0154***		0.0378***	0.0382***	
	0.00	0.00		0.00	0.00	
Norway	0.1425***	0.1409***		0.0622***	0.0616***	
	0.00	0.00		0.00	0.00	
Spain	0.0058	0.0033		0.0516***	0.0510***	
	0.18	0.45		0.00	0.00	
Sweden	0.0456***	0.0449***		−0.0119***	−0.0118***	
	0.00	0.00		0.01	0.01	
Switzerland	0.0806***	0.0782***		0.0303***	0.0303***	
	0.00	0.00		0.00	0.00	
Manufacturing	0.0181***		0.0168***	0.0103**		0.0122***
	0.00		0.00	0.02		0.01
Advanced manufacturing	0.0031		0.0039	0.0059		0.0051
	0.32		0.21	0.17		0.24
Services	0.0207***		0.0197***	0.0082**		0.0065
	0.00		0.00	0.05		0.13

(*Continued*)

Table 12.4: (*Continued*).

	Long-term debt ratio			Total debt ratio		
	(1)	(2)	(3)	(1)	(2)	(3)
F-value	136.00***	156.88***	32.81***	76.39***	93.52***	3.10**
Adj-R^2	0.0704	0.0664	0.0033	0.0426	0.0425	0.0002

Notes: This table presents regression of total and long-term debt ratios using country and industry dummies as sole explanatory variables. The excluded dummy is for the UK and primary industry. Total debt ratio is measured by the ratio of total debt (total long-term debt + debt and current liabilities + accounts payables) to total asset. Long-term debt ratio is measured by the ratio of total long-term debt to total asset. P-values are in the second row, below the coefficients. 28,503 and 27,078 observations are used for long-term debt and total debt ratios regressions, respectively. Number of observations for these two sets of regressions differs due to data availability. Primary industry: SIC code 0000-1999, agriculture, mining etc. Manufacturing industry: SIC code 2000-2999, food, textile etc. Advanced manufacturing industry: SIC code 3000-3999, machinery, electronics, etc. Services industry: SIC code 4000-9999, retailing, recreation, etc. (excludes finance, utilities, and regulated firms.)
***Significant at 1% level, **significant at 5% level, *significant at 10% level.

12.4.2 Country and Industry Influences

To assess the influence of country and industry effects on capital structure, we regress leverage only on country and industry dummies, and the results are reported in Table 12.4. We exclude the dummies for the UK and the primary industry sector for country and industry sector regressions, respectively, so that the coefficients should be interpreted as the significance of debt ratio differences relative to the UK and the primary industry sector. Regressions for long-term debt ratio are shown in columns 1–3, and regressions for total debt ratios in columns 4–6. Columns 1 and 4 of Table 12.4 present regressions with both country and industry sector dummies. Columns 2 and 5 show the regressions with only country dummies, and columns 3 and 6 show the regressions with only industry dummies.[14]

With very few exceptions, all estimated country and industry sector coefficients are significantly different from zero for both long-term debt ratio and total debt ratio regressions. We can explain 7.04 and 4.26 percent of the variability in long-term and total debt ratios, respectively, just by knowing the nationality and industry sector of a company. When the regressions are run with only country dummies, these R^2 decline slightly to 6.64 and 4.25 percent, respectively. However, with only industry sector dummies, the explanatory power declines to 0.33 and 0.02 percent

[14]Our industry sector groupings follow those in Chui et al. (2002). Each industry sector group, according to method used, can include both high- and low-leverage industries in the same sector, and more detailed industry grouping might be used to check the robustness of these results.

for long-term and total debt ratios, respectively, even though the joint significance of the coefficients (*F*-value) is still significant. These results indicate that while both country and industry sector effects are important, country factors (such as differences in financial and economic institutions) seem more important than industry factors in explaining variations in corporate debt ratios.[15]

12.4.3 Transparency and other Country Determinants of Debt Ratios

Table 12.5 reports the Newey-West estimations for the selected countries of firm-specific determinants of long-term debt ratios, while Table 12.6 reports similar results for the total debt ratios. These results show a positive relationship between tangibility and long-term debt ratio in all 14 European countries. Consistent with the pecking order theory, profitability is found to be negatively associated with the long-term debt ratio in the majority of countries (10 out of 14 countries with 6 of them significant). All of the significant relationships between size and long-term debt ratio are positive, indicating that the larger firms are better able to carry higher levels of long-term debt. Like the US evidence, the tax rate does not seem to influence the use of long-term debt in most European countries. Consistent with our conjecture, the Z-score is found to be highly significantly negatively related to long-term debt, indicating that firms with higher long-term debt are those with high probabilities of bankruptcy.[16] Dividend payment and the use of long-term debt are mostly found to be negatively related. We find mixed results regarding the effect of growth opportunities on firm leverage. The long-term debt ratio is found to be significantly positively related to growth opportunities for firms in Austria, Ireland, and Netherlands, while the relationship is significantly negative in Denmark, Norway, and Sweden.

Based on the results presented in Table 12.6, we find a significant positive relationship between tangibility and total debt ratio in eight out of nine countries, where the coefficients are significant. With no exception, profitability is always negatively and significantly related to the firm's total debt ratio, a finding consistent with the pecking order theory. There is a significant positive relationship (in 13 out of 14 countries) between size and total debt ratio indicating that the larger firms are more able to carry higher total debt. There is weak evidence (5 out of

[15]Regressions restricting the number of observations in all regressions to those used in the model with highest need for information are also estimated. The results for these regressions with restricted observations are very similar to the results reported in the chapter with no change in conclusions. These results are available from the authors.

[16]High Z-scores are an indication of low bankruptcy probability. It is true that there might be reverse causality with respect to tangibility and Z-score. Leaving them out does not change our main parameter estimates, the estimates for transparency variables, for total debt ratio regressions.

14 countries) of a negative relationship between the tax rate and the use of total debt. All significant relationships between the Z-score and the firm's total debt ratio are negative indicating that firms with higher total debt are those with high probability of bankruptcy. As with the results for the long-term debt ratio, the results regarding the effect of growth opportunities on total debt are also mixed. This ratio is found to be positively and significantly related to growth opportunities for firms in Austria, Ireland, and Italy, while the relationship is negative and significant in Belgium, Denmark, and Sweden. Overall, these results of country-wise regressions confirm the influence of firm characteristics on corporate capital structure and that this influence seems to vary internationally.

12.4.4 Pooled Transparency and other Determinants of Capital Structure

In Table 12.7 we report for our sample of 14 European countries the effects on long-term and total debt ratios of all three sets of variables: firm-level variables, corporate transparency variables, and national financial and economic variables. These pooled cross-country results for each set of determinants are described next.

12.4.4.1 Firm-level determinants of capital structure Consistent with the evidence reported in prior literature that tangible assets can be used as collateral for long-term debt (Friend & Lang, 1988; Long & Malitz, 1985), we find a positive and significant relationship between tangibility and long-term debt used by a firm. The coefficient for profitability is negative and always significant at less than 1 percent level for total debt ratio. This is consistent with the pecking order theory that firms with higher profitability would prefer internal resources to finance their investment opportunities before using external financing such as external debt. This result is also consistent with the findings of Rajan and Zingales (1995), Demirgüc-Kunt and Maksimovic (1999), Chui et al. (2002), and Fan et al. (2003).

Firm size is a positive influence on debt ratios and highly significant at the 1 percent level. One reason for this significant positive relationship may be that size may be an inverse proxy for the probability of bankruptcy (Rajan & Zingales, 1995). Our results indicate that the influence of tax rates on firm's long-term debt ratio is not significant. However, we surprisingly find a negative and significant relationship between the tax rate and the firm's total debt ratios.

Not surprisingly, firms with higher probability of financial distress, measured by lower Z-score, are those with high debt levels (significant at the 1 percent level). These results are consistent with the trade-off theory of capital structure. Surprisingly, for European firms we do not find any significant relationship between growth opportunities and long-term debt ratio, interestingly a finding

Table 12.5: Firm-level determinants of long-term debt ratio by country.

Country	**Intercept**	**Tangibility**	**Profit $(t-1)$**	**Size**	**TaxRate**	***Z*-score**	**Growth**	**Dividend**	**Industry Avg Lev**	***F*-value**	***N***
Austria	−0.0940**	0.1924***	−0.0077	0.0130***	−0.0008	−0.0286***	0.0118***	−0.0469***	1.0626***	6.22	433
	0.02	0.00	0.12	0.01	0.96	0.01	0.01	0.00	0.00	0.00	
Belgium	0.0363	0.2740***	−0.2584***	0.0005	0.0053	−0.0325***	0.0018	−0.0085	0.5615***	29.30	387
	0.15	0.00	0.00	0.90	0.66	0.00	0.48	0.43	0.00	0.00	
Denmark	−0.0155	0.2470***	−0.1520***	0.0125***	−0.0339*	−0.0311***	−0.0048**	−0.0116	0.7321***	25.65	655
	0.59	0.00	0.01	0.00	0.08	0.00	0.03	0.30	0.00	0.00	
Finland	0.0715*	0.3026***	−0.0189	0.0061	−0.0213	−0.0493***	−0.0006	−0.0367***	0.5591***	38.07	482
	0.09	0.00	0.83	0.12	0.24	0.00	0.82	0.01	0.00	0.00	
France	0.0277	0.2410***	−0.0969**	0.0035**	0.0063	−0.0477***	0.0006	0.0060	0.8028***	43.45	2610
	0.26	0.00	0.03	0.02	0.42	0.00	0.56	0.40	0.00	0.00	
Germany	0.0247*	0.2293***	0.0563***	−0.0012	−0.0048	−0.0182***	−0.0003	0.0151***	0.4443***	27.66	2807
	0.07	0.00	0.01	0.48	0.45	0.00	0.77	0.01	0.00	0.00	
Ireland	−0.1420***	0.1139**	0.0671	0.0446***	−0.0055	−0.0421***	0.0101***	−0.0004	0.4410***	17.89	324
	0.00	0.02	0.36	0.00	0.80	0.00	0.01	0.99	0.00	0.00	
Italy	−0.0857***	0.1457***	−0.2291**	0.0160***	0.0257	−0.0341***	0.0004	0.0081	0.8647***	13.39	630
	0.01	0.00	0.03	0.00	0.13	0.00	0.88	0.43	0.00	0.00	

Netherlands	−0.0983***	0.1636***	−0.0715	0.0210***	−0.0094	−0.0252***	0.0040***	−0.0200**	0.8382***	22.00	1017
	0.00	0.00	0.31	0.00	0.66	0.00	0.01	0.04	0.00	0.00	
Norway	0.0200	0.4733***	−0.0351	0.0087*	−0.0074	−0.0230**	−0.0076**	−0.0366**	0.3250***	48.18	563
	0.70	0.00	0.47	0.09	0.66	0.02	0.02	0.02	0.01	0.00	
Spain	−0.0139	0.1165***	−0.0643	0.0096**	−0.0145	−0.0388***	0.0004	−0.0175**	0.7247***	14.85	671
	0.67	0.00	0.54	0.03	0.47	0.00	0.86	0.05	0.00	0.00	
Sweden	0.0551**	0.2636***	0.0420	0.0076***	−0.0223	−0.0167***	−0.0050**	−0.0430***	0.3882***	18.85	939
	0.04	0.00	0.13	0.01	0.17	0.01	0.02	0.00	0.01	0.00	
Switzerland	0.0735*	0.2557***	−0.1441**	0.0044	−0.0002	−0.0419***	−0.0005	0.0056	0.3040**	22.79	930
	0.06	0.00	0.05	0.25	0.99	0.00	0.76	0.56	0.04	0.00	
UK	−0.0079	0.1145***	0.0127	0.0207***	0.0027	−0.0284***	0.0004	0.0065	0.0815***	102.47	7247
	0.35	0.00	0.56	0.00	0.66	0.00	0.54	0.37	0.00	0.00	

Notes: OLS regression estimates of $Leverage_{it} = \alpha_0 + \Sigma_j \alpha_j F_{jit} + \alpha_q \, IndustryAvgLev_{qnt} + \varepsilon_{it}$ with Newey-West standard errors considering heteroscedasticity and autocorrelation. $Leverage_{it}$, leverage ratio of a given firm i at time t measured as the ratio of long-term debt to total assets. F_{jit}, vector of firm-specific factors j for firm i at time t. Firm-specific determinants include *Tangibility*, $Profit_{(t-1)}$, *TaxRate*, *Z-score*, *Growth*, and *Dividend*. Average industry sector leverage for sector q for country n (*Industry Avg Lev*) at time t to control for the industry sector effects. The definitions and sources of the variables are described in Table 12.1. *P*-values are in the second row, below the coefficients.

***Significant at 1% level, **significant at 5% level, *significant at 10% level.

Table 12.6: Firm-level determinants of total debt ratio by country.

Country	Intercept	Tangibility	Profit ($t-1$)	Size	TaxRate	Z-score	Growth	Dividend	Industry Avg Lev	F-value	N
Austria	0.0763	−0.0874	−0.0228**	0.0230***	−0.0762**	−0.0521***	0.0108*	−0.0547***	0.8247***	7.71	440
	0.35	0.30	0.04	0.00	0.03	0.01	0.08	0.01	0.00	0.00	
Belgium	0.1498***	0.2590***	−0.6842***	0.0015	0.0077	0.0014	−0.0060*	−0.0486**	0.5116***	21.54	387
	0.00	0.00	0.00	0.80	0.72	0.91	0.10	0.02	0.00	0.00	
Denmark	0.0705	0.0339	−0.2878**	0.0247***	−0.0678**	−0.0388***	−0.0067**	−0.0454***	0.8097***	22.07	654
	0.29	0.48	0.04	0.00	0.02	0.00	0.04	0.01	0.00	0.00	
Finland	0.0824	0.2127***	−0.3909**	0.0165**	−0.0560*	−0.0268	−0.0019	−0.0504**	0.6491***	24.82	482
	0.32	0.00	0.03	0.02	0.06	0.17	0.68	0.02	0.00	0.00	
France	0.1112*	0.1631***	−0.3877***	0.0119***	−0.0180	−0.0049	−0.0008	−0.0163	0.5402***	16.18	2604
	0.09	0.00	0.00	0.00	0.12	0.55	0.63	0.19	0.00	0.00	
Germany	0.0697*	0.1851***	−0.0575	0.0105***	−0.0286**	−0.0167***	−0.0020	−0.0114	0.5764***	16.00	2807
	0.10	0.00	0.25	0.00	0.02	0.00	0.26	0.25	0.00	0.00	
Ireland	0.0056	0.0079	−0.1181	0.0407***	−0.0112	0.0117	0.0091*	0.0396	0.2139*	13.00	324
	0.92	0.88	0.14	0.00	0.67	0.21	0.08	0.23	0.08	0.00	

Italy	−0.1299**	0.0547	−0.6791***	0.0221***	−0.0209	−0.0010	0.0075**	−0.0009	0.9696***	17.33	630
	0.03	0.29	0.00	0.00	0.35	0.94	0.04	0.95	0.00	0.00	
Netherlands	−0.1805**	0.1544***	−0.4413**	0.0249***	0.0118	0.0130	0.0016	−0.0811***	1.0808***	15.21	1015
	0.02	0.00	0.03	0.00	0.68	0.18	0.55	0.00	0.00	0.00	
Norway	0.0288	0.3361***	−0.1582**	0.0195***	−0.0195	−0.0117	−0.0055	−0.0663***	0.5387***	26.56	563
	0.69	0.00	0.02	0.00	0.35	0.30	0.18	0.00	0.00	0.00	
Spain	0.2151***	−0.2161***	−0.3966***	0.0198***	−0.0221	−0.0459***	−0.0004	−0.0390***	0.5849***	15.19	671
	0.01	0.00	0.01	0.00	0.45	0.00	0.90	0.01	0.00	0.00	
Sweden	0.0750*	0.1618***	−0.0372	0.0263***	−0.0236	−0.0063	−0.0101***	−0.0567***	0.4061***	21.53	939
	0.10	0.00	0.50	0.00	0.20	0.50	0.00	0.00	0.01	0.00	
Switzerland	0.1919***	0.1631***	−0.2922***	0.0132***	0.0087	−0.0274***	−0.0010	−0.0121	0.2119	11.59	930
	0.00	0.00	0.00	0.00	0.64	0.01	0.69	0.32	0.24	0.00	
UK	0.1849***	0.0050	−0.0595**	0.0297***	−0.0346***	−0.0046*	−0.0012	−0.0374***	0.0751***	45.58	7214
	0.00	0.70	0.02	0.00	0.00	0.10	0.25	0.00	0.01	0.00	

Notes: OLS regression estimates of $Leverage_{it} = \alpha_0 + \Sigma_j \alpha_j F_{jit} + \alpha_q\ IndustryAvgLev_{qnt} + \varepsilon_{it}$ with Newey-West standard errors considering heteroscedasticity and autocorrelation. $Leverage_{it}$, leverage ratio of a given firm *i* at time *t* measured as the ratio of book value of total debt to total assets. F_{jit}, vector of firm-specific factors *j* for firm *i* at time *t*. Firm-specific determinants include *Tangibility*, $Profit_{(t-1)}$, *TaxRate*, *Z-score*, *Growth*, and *Dividend*. Average industry sector leverage for sector *q* for country *n* (*Industry Avg Lev*) at time *t* to control for the industry sector effects. The definitions and sources of the variables are described in Table 12.1. *P*-values are in the second row, below the coefficients.

***Significant at 1% level, **significant at 5% level, *significant at 10% level.

Table 12.7: Pooled firm and country-level determinants of long-term and total debt ratio.

	Long-term debt ratio			Total debt ratio		
	(1)	**(2)**	**(3)**	**(1)**	**(2)**	**(3)**
Intercept	0.0016	−0.3015***	−0.8534***	0.1110***	0.0438	−0.2273
	0.75	0.00	0.00	0.00	0.56	0.18
Firm-level variables						
Tangibility	0.1704***	0.1807***	0.1796***	0.0603***	0.0699***	0.0709***
	0.00	0.00	0.00	0.00	0.00	0.00
Profit ($t-1$)	0.0039	−0.0001	0.0012	−0.0777***	−0.0881***	−0.1015***
	0.69	0.99	0.94	0.00	0.00	0.00
Size	0.0139***	0.0134***	0.0152***	0.0232***	0.0225***	0.0242***
	0.00	0.00	0.00	0.00	0.00	0.00
TaxRate	0.0024	0.0013	0.0031	−0.0226***	−0.0256***	−0.0267***
	0.48	0.69	0.49	0.00	0.00	0.00
Z-score	−0.0290***	−0.0287***	−0.0305***	−0.0113***	−0.0096***	−0.0077***
	0.00	0.00	0.00	0.00	0.00	0.00
Growth (MV/BV)	−0.0004	0.0001	0.0004	−0.0022***	−0.0018***	−0.0013*
	0.39	0.81	0.44	0.00	0.01	0.09
Dividend	−0.0104***	−0.0044	−0.0013	−0.0434***	−0.0339***	−0.0313***
	0.00	0.13	0.73	0.00	0.00	0.00
Industry Avg Lev	0.3598***	0.2923***	0.1857***	0.3955***	0.3463***	0.2420***
	0.00	0.00	0.00	0.00	0.00	0.00

Corporate transparency variables					
Financial disclosure	−0.0007**	0.0008		−0.0007**	0.0000
	0.02	0.11		0.05	1.00
Governance disclosure	−0.0002	−0.0020***		−0.0006*	−0.0016***
	0.53	0.00		0.09	0.00
Accounting disclosure	−0.0006***	−0.0004**		−0.0002*	−0.0007***
	0.00	0.03		0.09	0.00
Disclosure timeliness	0.0018***	0.0036***		0.0015***	0.0044***
	0.00	0.00		0.00	0.00
Audit intensity	−0.0183***	−0.0348***		−0.0117*	−0.0339***
	0.00	0.00		0.09	0.00
Inside trading law enforcement	−0.0254***	−0.0479***		−0.0227***	−0.0325**
	0.00	0.00		0.01	0.02
Institutional trading activity	0.0829***	−0.0209		0.0975***	0.0693
	0.00	0.56		0.00	0.17
Media coverage	0.0041***	0.0094***		0.0015**	0.0030**
	0.00	0.00		0.02	0.03
Financial and economic variables					
Stock market capitalization		−0.0141***			−0.0134**
		0.01			0.04
Stock market turnover		−0.0067*			−0.0097*
		0.07			0.09
Banking sector size		0.0442***			0.0492***
		0.00			0.00

(Continued)

Table 12.7: (*Continued*).

	Long-term debt ratio			Total debt ratio		
	(1)	**(2)**	**(3)**	**(1)**	**(2)**	**(3)**
Bond market capitalization			-0.0349^{***}			0.0086
			0.00			0.50
GDP per capita growth			0.0098^{***}			0.0145^{***}
			0.00			0.00
Inflation			0.0034^{***}			0.0028^{**}
			0.00			0.02
F-value	280.95^{***}	163.45^{***}	88.74^{***}	170.44^{***}	88.79^{***}	44.51^{***}
	0.00	0.00	0.00	0.00	0.00	0.00

Notes: OLS regression estimates of $Leverage_{it} = \alpha_0 + \sum_j \alpha_j F_{jit} + \sum_k \alpha_k T_{kn} + \sum_l \alpha_l E_{lnt} + \alpha_q IndustryAvgLev_{qnt} + \varepsilon_{it}$ with Newey-West standard errors considering heteroscedasticity and autocorrelation. $Leverage_{it}$, leverage ratio of a given firm *i* at time *t* measured as the ratio of long-term debt to total assets. F_{jit}, vector of firm-specific factors *j* for firm *i* at time *t*. Firm-specific determinants include *Tangibility*, *Profit* $_{(t-1)}$, *TaxRate*, *Z-score*, *Growth*, and *Dividend*.T_{kn}, vector of corporate transparency variable *k* for country *n*. Corporate transparency variables are from Bushman et al. (2004b) and they include *financial disclosure*, *governance disclosure*, *accounting disclosure*, *disclosure timeliness*, *audit intensity*, *inside trading law enforcement*, *institutional trading activity*, and *media coverage*. E_{lnt}, vector of financial and economic factor *l* for country *n* at time *t*. Financial institution variables include *stock market cap*, *stock market turnover*, *bank emphasis*, *bond market cap*, *GDP per capital growth*, and *inflation*. Average industry sector leverage for sector *q* for country *n* (*IndustryAvgLev*) at time *t* to control for the industry sector effects. The definitions and sources of the variables are described in Table 12.1. *P*-values are in the second row, below the coefficients. 19,705 observations are used for models (1) and (2), and 12,199 observations are used for model (3) of long-term debt ratio regressions. 19,660 observations are used for models (1) and (2), and 12,174 observations are used for model (3) of total debt ratio regressions. Number of observations for these two sets of regressions has reduced compared to those in Table 12.6 due to data availability. Note also that Newey-West regressions do not report adjusted R^2 value.

***Significant at 1% level, **significant at 5% level, *significant at 10% level.

inconsistent with the US evidence where high growth firms have lower leverage. However, consistent with the pecking order theory, we find a negative and significant relationship between growth opportunities and the total debt ratio. Firms that pay dividends, indicated by a dummy variable, tend to use less debt—a result consistent with Frank and Goyal (2003). Consistent with the reversion to industry mean contention in Roberts (2002), we find that the coefficient of industry average leverage is positive and significant.

12.4.4.2 Transparency and national characteristics as capital structure determinants As seen in Table 12.7, in column 2 we add the corporate transparency variables to the firm-specific variables in the estimated model. Column 3 also includes financial and economic variables as determinants of corporate capital structure. While the financial disclosure levels in a country are generally negatively and significantly related to the firm's use of debt, only some of these relationships remain significant when we control for the other national financial and economic variables. There is a negative relationship between governance disclosure and firm debt ratios after controlling for national financial and economic variables. We also find significant negative relationships between accounting disclosure and total debt ratios even after controlling for financial and economic variables. We also find negative and significant relationships between long-term debt and audit intensity and insider trading law enforcement.[17] These findings confirm the contentions made earlier in this chapter. Of the owner–manager agency cost reducing transparency variables, we find that the governance disclosure and audit intensity have the highest influence on a firm's debt ratios. For example, one standard deviation increase in governance disclosure and audit intensity has approximately 3 percent reduction in the debt ratios as a fraction of total assets, while one standard deviation increase in financial disclosure, accounting disclosure, and anti-insider trading law enforcement leads to approximately 1.5 percent decrease in the debt ratios as a fraction of total assets.

Our contentions are also confirmed by the positive and significant relationships between institutional trading activity, media coverage, disclosure timeliness, and the firm's long-term debt ratio. The effect of these variables on total debt ratio is similar to that on the long-term debt ratio. Among the transparency variables that help creditors control operating risks (and thus wealth transfers from creditors to owners), disclosure timeliness has the highest level of influence on a firm's debt ratio with one standard deviation increase in disclosure timeliness

[17]Note that lower the insider trading law enforcement number, the higher is the enforcement quality (see Table 12.1).

leading to an average of 9 percent increase in debt ratios as a fraction of total assets. One standard deviation increase in media coverage leads to approximately a 7 percent increase in debt ratios as a fraction of total assets, while one standard deviation increase in institutional trading activities leads to about a 1 percent increase in debt ratios as a fraction of total assets.

12.4.4.3 Other country variables as determinants of capital structure The effects of national financial and economic variables are similar for the long-term debt or the total debt ratios. We find that high levels of stock market development and high stock market turnover are both significantly associated with lower debt ratios. We find a positive and significant relation between the relative sizes of a country's banking sector and total debt used by firms in that country. However, we find a significant negative relationship between a country's bond market development and the corporate use of long-term debt confirming the spillover effect of bond market development on a country's stock market development resulting in lower debt ratios. It is important to note that our measure of bond market value includes the value of government bonds.[18] As we can expect that there are some countries where the government is a major borrower and where the corporate bond market may still be relatively undeveloped, this variable might overestimate the actual bond market accessibility for business firms. Countries with higher economic growth rates are found to have a higher level of total debt. Higher levels of inflation are also associated with higher debt ratios because in such cases the real repayment value of debt possibly declines with inflation.[19]

12.5 Conclusions

European companies are scheduled to adopt international accounting standards and conform to higher levels of disclosure and transparency in 2005. There also continues to be much interest in the determinants of capital structure. Prior literature has examined the influence of firm-level variables and country characteristics on capital structure. While some studies have examined these determinants in

[18] FIBV — the source of our bond market data — reports the total market value of bonds outstanding, which includes the value of government bonds and does not provide data on private sector bonds.

[19] A set of regressions restricting the number of observations in all regressions to those available for the model with the highest need for information is also estimated. The results for these regressions with restricted observations are very similar to the results reported in the chapter, and our conclusions remain the same with either set of regressions. These results are available from the authors upon request.

various countries, others have done so across groups of countries. However, prior studies have not included transparency variables even though it is clear that transparency levels are related to contracting, agency, informational asymmetry, and other costs that determine the optimal proportions of debt and equity in a firm. This chapter fills an important gap in the literature as it examines for the first time the influence of international variations in corporate transparency on capital structure variations in 14 European countries (controlling for relevant firm-level and other country variables).

The results presented in this chapter document the significant influence of transparency and other national financial and economic institutional structures on international variations in corporate capital structure. While we document the influence of firm characteristics on corporate capital structure, more importantly this study documents that international variations in transparency levels significantly influence capital structure evels. We find that transparency variables that favor equity holder rights and reduce agency costs between owners and managers such as higher levels of financial, governance and accounting disclosures, audit intensity, and enforcement of anti-insider trading laws are all negatively associated with corporate debt levels. In contrast, transparency variables that help creditors control operating risks (thus transfers of wealth from creditors to owners) such as disclosure timeliness, institutional trading, and media coverage are associated with higher corporate debt levels. These results have important public policy and managerial implications. For example, these findings can influence policy regarding disclosure regulations, and managers can use disclosure to reduce the costs of external debt and equity.

Acknowledgment

The authors would like to thank M. Qi, J. Thornton, and X. Zhao, and other colleagues for useful comments on an earlier draft.

References

Aggarwal, R. (1981). International differences in capital structure norms: An empirical study of large European companies. *Management International Review, 1*, 75–88.

Aggarwal, R. (1990). Capital structure differences among large Asian companies. *ASEAN Economic Bulletin, 7*(1), 39–53.

Alford, A., Jones, J., Leftwich, R., & Zmijewski, M. (1993). The relative informativeness of accounting disclosures in different countries. *Journal of Accounting Research, 31*, 183–223.

Almazan, A., Suarez, J., & Titman, S. (2003). *Capital structure and transparency*. NBER Working Paper no. 10101, November.

Auerbach, A. J., & King, M. A. (1983). Taxation, portfolio choice, and debt-equity ratios: A general equilibrium model. *Quarterly Journal of Economics, 98*(4), 587–609.

Bae, K.-H., Kang, J.-K., & Lim, C.-W. (2002). The value of durable bank relationships: Evidence from Korean banking shocks. *Journal of Financial Economics, 64*(2), 181–214.

Booth, L., Aivazian, V., Demirgüc-Kunt, A., & Maksimovic, V. (2001). Capital structures in developing countries. *Journal of Finance, 56*(1), 87–130.

Borio, C. E. V. (1990). *Leverage and financing of non-financial companies: An international perspective*. BIS Economic Papers no. 27.

Bowman, R. G. (1980). The importance of a market value measurement of debt in assessing leverage. *Journal of Accounting Research, 18*, 242–254.

Bushee, B. J., & Noe, C. F. (2000). Corporate disclosure policies, institutional investors, and stock return volatility. *Journal of Accounting Research, 38*(2), 171–202.

Bushman, R., Chen, Q., Engel, E., & Smith, A. (2004a). Financial accounting information, organizational complexity and corporate governance systems. *Journal of Accounting and Economics, 37*, 167–201.

Bushman, R. M., Piotroski, J. D., & Smith, A. J. (2004b). What determines corporate transparency? *Journal of Accounting Research, 42*(2), 207–252.

Chui, A. C. W., Lloyd, A. E., & Kwok, C. C. Y. (2002). The determinants of capital structure: Is national culture a missing piece to the puzzle? *Journal of International Business Studies, 33*(1), 99–127.

Coates, J. H., & Woolley, P. K. (1975). Corporate gearing in the E.E.C. *Journal of Business Finance and Accounting, 2*(1), 1–18.

Demirgüc-Kunt, A., & Levine, R. (1996). Stock market development and financial intermediaries: Stylized facts. *World Bank Economic Review, 10*, 291–321.

Demirgüc-Kunt, A., & Maksimovic, V. (1996). Stock market development and firm financing choices. *World Bank Economic Review, 10*, 341–369.

Demirgüc-Kunt, A., & Maksimovic, V. (1998). Law, finance, and firm growth. *Journal of Finance, 53*(6), 2107–2137.

Demirgüc-Kunt, A., & Maksimovic, V. (1999). Institutions, financial markets, and firm debt maturity. *Journal of Financial Economics, 54*, 295–336.

Doidge, C., Karolyi, G. A., & Stulz, R. M. (2004). *Why do countries matter so much for corporate governance*? Working Paper no. 50/2004, ECGI Working Paper Series in Finance.

Fan, P. H. J., Titman, S., & Twite, G. (2003). *An international comparison of capital structure and debt maturity choices*. Working Paper.

Frank, M. Z., & Goyal, V. K. (2003). Testing the pecking order theory of capital structure. *Journal of Financial Economics, 67*(2), 217–248.

Friend, I., & Lang, L. (1988). An empirical test of the impact of managerial self-interest on corporate capital structure. *Journal of Finance, 43*, 271–281.

Graham, J. (2000). How big are the tax benefits of debt? *Journal of Finance, 55*(5), 1901–1941.

Hatzinikolaou, D., Katsimbris, G. M., & Noulas, A. G. (2002). Inflation uncertainty, and capital structure: Evidence from a pooled sample of Dow-Jones industrial firms. *International Review of Economics and Finance, 11*, 45–55.

Hovakimian, A., Opler, T., & Titman, S. (2001). The debt-equity choice. *Journal of Financial and Quantitative Analysis, 36*(1), 1–24.

Jaggi, B., & Low, P. Y. (2000). Impact of culture, market forces, and legal system on financial disclosures. *International Journal of Accounting, 35*(4), 495–519.

Jensen, M. (1986). The agency costs of free cash flow, corporate finance and takeovers. *American Economic Review, 76*, 323–329.

Jensen, M., & Meckling, W. (1976). Theory of the firm: Managerial behavior, agency costs and ownership structure. *Journal of Financial Economics, 3*, 305–360.

Jensen, G. R., Solberg, D. P., & Zorn, T. S. (1992). Simultaneous determination of insider ownership, debt, and dividend policies. *Journal of Financial and Quantitative Analysis, 27*(2), 247–263.

Lang, M., & Lundholm, R. (1993). Cross-sectional determinants of analyst ratings of corporate disclosures. *Journal of Accounting Research, 31*(2), 246–271.

LaPorta, R., Lopez-de-Silanes, F., Shleifer, A., & Vishny, R. W. (1997). Legal determinants of external finance. *Journal of Finance, 52*(3), 1131–1150.

Lee, M. H., & Zechner, J. (1984). Debt, taxes, and international equilibrium. *Journal of International Money and Finance, 3*(3), 343–353.

Leuz, C., & Verrecchia, R. E. (2000). The economic consequences of increased disclosure. *Journal of Accounting Research, 38*(Suppl.), 91–124.

Long, M. S., & Malitz, I. B. (1985). Investment patterns and financial leverage. In: B. M. Friedman (Ed.), *Corporate capital structures in the United States*. Chicago: The University of Chicago Press, NBER.

McClure, K. G., Clayton, R., & Hofler, R. A. (1999). International capital structure differences among the G7 nations: A current empirical view. *European Journal of Finance, 5*, 141–164.

Modigliani, F., & Miller, M. H. (1958). The cost of capital, corporation finance and the theory of investment. *American Economic Review, 48*, 261–297.

Myers, S. C. (1984). The capital structure puzzle. *Journal of Finance, 39*(3), 575–592.

Myers, S. C., & Majluf, N. (1984). Corporate financing and investment decisions when firms have information that investors do not have. *Journal of Financial Economics, 13*, 187–221.

Rajan, R. G., & Zingales, L. (1995). What do we know about capital structure? Some evidence from international data. *Journal of Finance, 50*(5), 1421–1460.

Roberts, M. (2002). *The dynamics of capital structure: An empirical analysis of a partially observable system*. Working Paper, Fuqua School of Business, Duke University.

Sengupta, P. (1998). Corporate disclosure policy and the cost of debt. *Accounting Review, 73*(3), 459–474.

Sheehan, B. (2005). Europe switches to US-style disclosure rules. *Global Finance*, March, 18–19.

Song, J. Y., & Philippatos, P. (2004). *Revisiting variations in international capital structure: Empirical evidence from 16 OECD countries*. Working Paper, University of Tennessee.

Stonehill, A., & Stitzel, T. (1969). Financial structure and multinational corporations. *California Management Review*, *12*(1), 91–96.

Wald, J. K. (1999). How firm characteristics affect capital structure: An international comparison. *Journal of Financial Research*, 22(2), 161–187.

Yu, F. (2005). Accounting transparency and the term structure of credit spreads. *Journal of Financial Economics*, *75*(1), 53–84.

Chapter 13

Multinational Enterprises and their Lobbying Activities in the European Union

Amjad Hadjikhani and Pervez N. Ghauri

13.1 Introduction

Most business research is based on the implicit assumption of corporate and political transparency and equal availability of information for all market participants (see, for example, Bernheim & Whinston, 1986; Kirchsteiger & Prat, 2001; Berton & Salanie, 2003). Many researchers, however, define transparency as an *ideal* condition far from political and business realities (see, for example, Bushee & Noe, 2000). They point out information specificity and asymmetry among market and political actors, for example, as key factors behind deviations from such ideal conditions (Johal & Ulph, 2002; Bushee & Noe, 2000). In this chapter we follow this line of thought, and argue that firms — because of the heterogeneity in capabilities and resources — do not have the same access to information. Moreover, for similar reasons, firms perceive and act differently towards the *same* information about government policies and market conditions.

A number of researchers in political science and management connect firms' lobbying behaviour to information asymmetry (Lagerlöf, 1997; Potters & Sloof, 1996). The early contribution of scholars like Truman (1951) and Dahl (1956) place these activities at the heart of the political process. This chapter conceives the above-mentioned view on lobbying and information asymmetry as an indispensable part of multinational enterprises (MNEs). Firms exploit information asymmetries to

Corporate and Institutional Transparency for Economic Growth in Europe

ISBN: 0-08-044665-5

gain some control of the political environment. They choose to lobby their political environment to gain specific support that others, not engaged in lobbying activities, cannot have. MNEs mobilise their resources and knowledge to interact with political groups and gain benefits that strengthen their competitive position in the international market. The fundamental research question for this chapter is to analyse and discuss how the lobbying activities of MNEs influence the overall transparency of markets. The overall contribution of the chapter, in terms of the analytical framework outlined in Chapter 1, is to show how lobbying affects the political decision-making process, and hence the political risk premium inherent in the cost of capital.

The political actions of MNEs have become more apparent during the last decade. The emergence of European Union (EU) has led to an increased lobbying activity in Europe. MNEs have developed centralised political units and use their specific information to direct their political actions. In order to gain access to an EU institution, business interests have to provide specific information and facts (basis) to the institutions that can assist them in their decision making. Here, we can distinguish two different effects as regards the resulting transparency. In case the action by a business interest is a joint effort to persuade politicians, then the lobbying activity may result in increased transparency, while if it is to the benefit of an individual firm only, the action will result in a decreased overall transparency. In the latter case, information asymmetry is used as a tool enabling firms to safeguard their own interest and to try to influence the decisions made by the institutions (Bouwen, 2002; John & Thomson, 2003; Damania, 2003). There are a number of middlemen and consultant firms that claim to assist both sides; firms as well as EU institutions, in this — sometimes — mutually beneficial activity. Table 13.1 presents the top 10 lobbying consultants in Europe.

The chapter aims to describe and discuss the lobbying behaviour of MNEs in relation to the EU, and in competition with other firms in a particular sector. While present research on international business explains the interplay by means of economic or institutional theories, this paper discusses the management of the political environment through behavioural theory (Cyert & March, 1963). The interaction with political actors is explained with business network theory (Johanson & Vahlne, 1990; Kooiman, 1993; Håkansson & Snehota, 1995). An integral part of this view is to focus on how the MNEs use their specific knowledge and resources to gain specific benefits not available to others. Lobbying behaviour is based on the ability of MNEs to use information asymmetry and resource heterogeneity for their own benefit. The main contribution of the chapter is that both sides, political and business actors are seen as being active in influencing each other, and also as being embedded in relationships with others.

Table 13.1: Top 10 lobbying consultancies in Europe.

Consultancy	Created	Staff	Parent company	Branches
Hill & Knowlton	1967	28	WPP, UK	Thirty cities in Europe, 35 worldwide
GPC Government Policy Consultants	1988	28	Omnicom, US	London, Edinburgh, associate agencies all over Europe except Luxembourg and Austria
Apco Europe	1995	20	Gray Advertising, US	(With GCI) All EU member states; Washington DC, Seattle, Sacramento, Beijing, Hong Kong, Moscow
Adamson Associates	1981	16	Independent, Belgium	Geneva, Strasbourg
European Public Policy Advisers	1987	16	Private shareholders international	Austria, Belgium, Czech Republic, Finland, France, Hungary, The Netherlands, Norway, Poland, Portugal, Russia, Spain, Sweden, UK, Germany, US (with International Trade Advisers), associated offices in Ireland, Denmark, Italy, Greece
European Strategy	1990	12	Grayling Group, UK	All EU countries (except Portugal, Greece, Austria); NY
Edelman Europe	1995	10	Edelman Public Relations Worldwide, US	Nine offices in Europe, 26 in the Americas and Asia/Pacific region
Robinson, Linton and Associates	1989	9	Burson–Marsteller, US	Uses the Burson–Marsteller network (most European countries, US and Russia)
Entente International Communication	1991	6	Private shareholders	All 15 EU member states, associated offices in other countries
Charles Barker BSMG	1990	3	BSMG, US	UK

Source: Ghauri and Cateora (2006, p. 222).

The chapter is organised as follows. In Section 13.2 we discuss lobbying activities in a corporate perspective. Section 13.3 deals with MNEs, their business network and lobbying behaviour. In Section 13.4 we discuss the data collection, whereas in Section 13.5 we present our four case companies and their lobbying activities. In Section 13.6 we then discuss the findings and Section 13.7 contains our conclusions.

13.2 Lobbying Activities of Firms

Most business researchers, when treating governments, assume a unidirectional influence of the political actors and that governments always aim for high transparency in releasing information. They also assume that all firms have access to the same political and legal information and adapt accordingly. While much attention is paid to firms and their business interaction with other business actors, the interdependencies between firms and political actors and the political activities of firms have attracted less research (Boddewyn, 1988; Ring, Lenway, & Govekar, 1990; Buckley & Ghauri, 1999a).

Studies focused on management of the political environment range from studies assuming that management is essentially a response to transparent information contained in governments' policies (Conner, 1991; Korbin, 1982; Kogut, 1991; Egelhoff, 1988) to studies aimed at formulating adequate strategies to deal with the political environment (Ring et al., 1990; Johnson, 1982). Research on, for example, coping strategies often approach the subject as an issue of risk management (Miller, 1992), of management of country risk (Cosset & Roy, 1991; Cavusgil, Ghauri, & Agarwal 2002), of firm–state interdependencies and industrial structures (Ring et al., 1990) and of firm–state interdependencies and corporate structures (Murtha, 1991; Lenway & Murtha, 1994). All have the presumption that transparency in market information enforces a homogeneous unidirectional relation with political actors. This chapter questions this view and argues that MNEs are active on the political scene. In Europe, for example, interest in these questions has increased during the last decade because of the success of the EU (Hooghe, 1995). In this context, lobbying activities are presumed not to necessarily aim to gain direct financial support but can strive to gain influence which will ultimately subsidise/support the firms' business activities (Alt & Chrystal, 1983; Boddewyn & Brewer, 1994), creating disadvantages for competing firms not involved in lobbying activities. Hence, in terms of corporate transparency this will increase uncertainty among competitors who are themselves not involved in approaching politicians.

Contrary to business studies, a number of researchers in political science have studied lobbying and information asymmetry in the market place (see, e.g., Johal & Ulph, 2002; Epstein & Hefeker, 2003; Potters & Sloof, 1996; Berton & Salanie, 2003; Fabella, 1991). Some researchers have approached the issue from the point of view of the state, in for example development economics (Maddison, 1991; Esping-Andersen, 1985) and/or regional economics (Hanf & Toonen, 1985; Nowtotny, Smith, & Trebling, 1989). The main actor in these studies is the government, and the issue of concern is the impact of government on firms. Some research on governance (see, e.g., Streeck, 1992; Fligstein, 1990) explains the failure of the political hierarchy in terms of non-transparency and information asymmetry. It introduces internal dynamics and differentiated social systems as factors that make centralised political control more difficult. These different strands of thought in political science are interesting since they, similar to this study, assume that MNEs are active when dealing with the political environment.

Here we argue that lobbying is related to exchange of information. For example, firm A may provide strategically important (macro) policy-relevant information to G (the government). G, through its policies, may then redistribute income and incentives between firms A and B by providing corporate policy relevant information to A and not to B (Lagerlöf, 1997). Hence, the interplay between G and firm A affects not only the behaviour of A and G, but also the behaviour of firm B and the market and political positions of A and B.

Lobbying is vital for the firms when exercising influence on political actors but it requires resource commitment and knowledge to achieve a better competitive position. Firm A organises its activities (commits resources and coordinates activities), collects information not only on G, but also on others with whom the government is interdependent. Firm A is also interdependent with those who are related to G. Firm A's knowledge about those that G is dependent upon can affect its persuasion power to convince G and to gain specific benefits. For example, as Rasmusen (1992) expresses, G always trades off the cost of acquiring and processing information against the benefit of being re-elected. Lobbying behaviour, as illustrated in Figure 13.1, is an outcome of information asymmetry in the market, and it reflects firms' resource commitment and knowledge.

The behavioural aspects permit us to understand how firms act to manage the non-transparent environment by lobbying. Lobbying behaviour is seen as a dependent variable which is determined by A's resources and knowledge, but also the resources and knowledge of B and G. We argue that the lobbying behaviour of firm A is rooted in a business network context in which A, B and G are embedded.

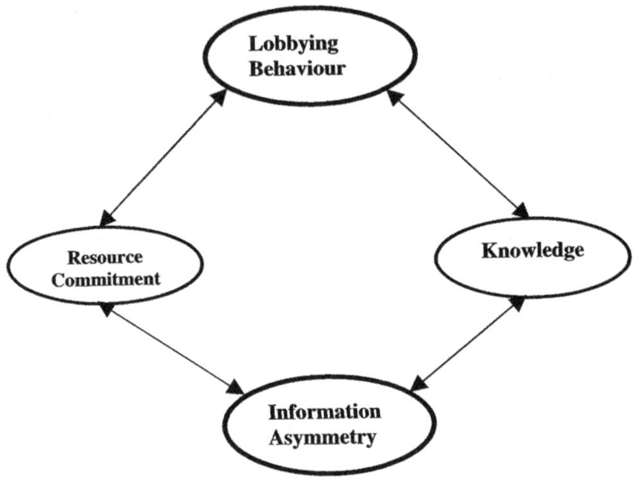

Figure 13.1: Lobbying behaviour and information asymmetry.

13.3 MNEs' Business Network and Lobbying Behaviour

The business network approach, which has its origin in social network and behavioural theory, has been extensively explored in international business studies (Buckley & Ghauri, 1999b, 2004; Forsgren, Hägg, Håkansson, Johanson, & Mattsson, 1995), however, it rarely touches the political relationships of the firms in their international market. We emphasise that MNEs are dependent on actors in their political environment, and that these actors are also dependent on the MNEs. The relationship may be particularly strong as firms make investments that affect groups like the media or others with whom politicians have interdependent relationships (Jacobson, Lenway, & Ring, 1993; Hadjikhani, 1996; Ghauri & Holstius, 1996; Damanian & Frederiksson, 2003). Political actors, in seeking legitimacy (Eliassen & Kooiman, 1993), incorporate values from these groups into their decisions. Thus, in this network, the business and political actors are interdependent, not only on one another but also on actors surrounding them as their activities influence all of them (Boddewyn, 1988; Boddewyn & Brewer, 1994; Georgiou & Roberts, 2004).

As argued by Keillor, Boller, and Ferrel (1997), a knowledge and resource commitment model can be explored for an analysis of the behaviour of firms in their political environment. In this model, the principal obstacles are discussed in terms of a resource commitment connected to learning about the foreign market.

By increasing political knowledge, the perceived risk of market investment declines and market business commitment increases. Commitment can be explained in terms of the size of investment towards the counterpart alone or by studying the links of tangible and intangible investments towards the partner and its network (Ghauri, 1999; Denekamp, 1995; Scott, 1994; Becker, 1961). Intangible commitment towards the network, referred to as 'idiosyncratic investment' (see Andersson & Weitz, 1992), reveals the fact that commitment in one relationship can spread to other relationships. Following this view, business actors in their interaction with political actors, gain experience and information about the values and activities of others in the network — such as certain interested parties or the media — and behave accordingly. This means that each business actor has a specific relationship with political actors that is dependent on the business actor's political commitment and knowledge. The relationship is not focal but includes all connected actors.

In this exchange relationship, MNEs require rules and supportive measures distributed by governments, and governments gain legitimacy as these enterprises satisfy the people and other groups to whom they are responsible. The interaction

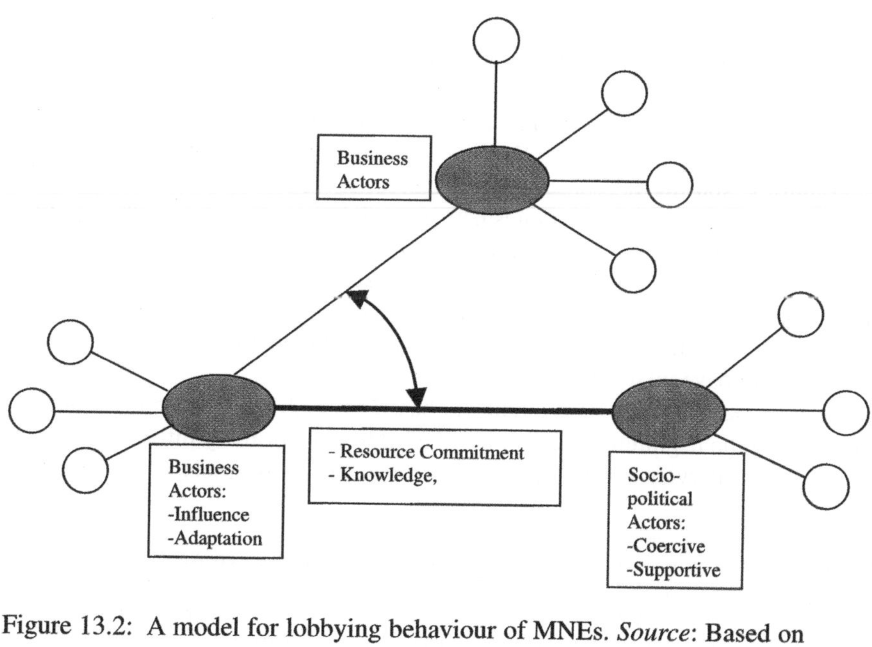

Figure 13.2: A model for lobbying behaviour of MNEs. *Source*: Based on Hadjikhani and Thilenius (2005).

between the two requires the adjudication of conflicting interests, but also provides the condition for exploring options and sharing common values (Hult & Walcott, 1990). As Figure 13.2 illustrates, the alternative behavioural options for the political actors are either coercive or supportive, and can contain general or specific influence (Boddewyn & Brewer, 1994; Kobrin, 1982; Hadjikhani & Ghauri, 2001).

Adaptation applies to the given political rules according to which enterprises adapt their behaviour (Miller, 1992; Makhija, 1993). Influence means negotiation and co-operation (Boddewyn & Brewer, 1994), where firms aim to gain support for their activities. By the development of knowledge and commitment, the process of change in political behaviour proceeds from adaptation to influence. Firms with a low level of knowledge and commitment rely on the first mode of political activity, which considers internal change in order to adapt business activities to the political rules. The alternative applies to the act of changing the counterpart's behaviour, namely, in overcoming the political rules which govern the enterprise's business activities. The final outcome of the management's decision becomes an antecedent to the firm's commitment and knowledge and the activities of political actors.

13.4 Method for Data Collection

In this section, we will discuss four case companies and their interaction with the EU political system. Our four MNEs have undertaken direct investment in several EU countries, starting decades ago.[1] The direct investments in more than 100 countries by our four case companies have forced them to be active in their political environments. The case companies consist of two Swedish MNEs, which are former state-owned companies and with an assumed close relationship to the political sphere (Telia and SAS) and two companies that are top global actors (ABB and Ericsson). All four companies are listed on the Stockholm Stock Exchange and have dual listings.

The information in the case studies is based on both primary and secondary sources from the beginning of 2000. For the MNEs, the primary information was collected via interviews with 11 Swedish managers in Brussels and with four

[1]We have chosen to focus on four case companies since prior research experience indicates that the subject "*the firms' lobbying with political actors*' is a sensitive area as many firms are unwilling to disclose information on this topic to outsiders. Firms which are successful in their lobbying activities tend to keep the relationship out of sight of public opinion, and those who are less successful are afraid of negative publicity.

bureaucrats in the Commission. Besides these, other interviews were conducted with managers in Sweden and also with Swedish representatives in the EU. Companies were asked specific questions about specific lobbying activities. The exploratory nature of the study demanded in-depth semi-structured interviews, which were all tape recorded and transcribed (Ghauri, 2004). The secondary data were collected from brochures and information released by these firms on their political operations in the EU, and also through published information provided by the EU.

13.5 Empirical Study: The Four Cases

13.5.1 Telia

Telia (Sonera) is a Swedish public company in the telecommunications industry with a turnover of more than 1 billion and 27,000 employees. More than 75% of the firm's total sale is raised in EU countries. Therefore, political decisions and co-operation with EU politicians are recognised as an important activity by the firm. After 1990, one vital issue that started to change the telecommunications market in Europe was the liberalisation of the market. Traditionally, the governments had a formal monopoly in the telecommunications market, but during the course of the 1990s, direct and indirect restrictions were torn down. The liberalisation process, which started around 1995–1996, practically started to function in 1998. Telia's manager argued that the processes of liberalisation and harmonisation had improved the technology and quality of the products and the service to customers. But, from their point of view, the technology and also the market are very complex and the handling of such issues by politicians may create complications.

According to Telia's managers this market cannot be handled without advanced knowledge and an appropriate strategy towards non-business groups. This is even more so now when the political decisions are delegated from the Swedish government to the EU. Abolishment of monopoly and increasing competition forced Telia's managers to develop new strategies and invest resources to manage political matters in the EU. In response to the perceived need to manage the relationship with the politicians, and also to handle the media and the political environment more generally within the EU, the company started a Market Development (MD) section with 10 people. This section has an important position in the firm as it is in charge of monitoring and influencing political decisions in the EU, and also customers in this market. The manager is to connect the section to other units within Telia (like technology development and production), to different units in the EU bureaucracy, and to other interest groups, such as, media.

For political lobbying they use a variety of contacts with lawyers, parliamentary staff, committees and commissions and Swedish representatives and ministers in the EU. To engage in the discussion platform within the Open Market Platform (OMP) committee, which deals with the telecommunication market, Telia's political group needs a wide and deep technological, market and legal information. Besides these, the manager emphasises the importance of social contacts. He explained that most of his time, more than 50%, was devoted to engaging in seminars, social gatherings and calls. The manager explained that the contact network is personal and it is always the personal chemistry that will govern the way it will function. Representatives can be changed and we, he explained, always follow the process and build a new contact net.

The manager explained that the task of the MD section eventually is mediation between different internal and external groups; i.e., to bridge a gap between the firm's competency and the needs of the groups in the environment. The most important task of the section, particularly for the manager, is to become connected to business and non-business groups, which have specifically to do with the telecommunications market. On the Commission level, DG 13, 4, 3 and 1 were useful for co-operation and exchange of information. Among other political groups, Telia also has a close relationship with the Swedish representatives both in the EU parliament and committees. Besides political actors, the non-business group to which Telia attached a particular importance for lobbying was the media. The media was used as an outlet for information — specifically to customers — about new products. The manager explained that the needs of and pressure from the customers usually affect the decisions of EU politicians.

There are more direct contacts with certain DGs dealing with the telecoms market. In the case of deregulation of the communication traffic in Europe, for example, a new directive proposal was needed. Since the telecoms market is complex and requires specific technological and market knowledge to understand, committees in the EU were obliged to cooperate with the MNEs. This was done using the OMP platform, with managers from Telia and a number of other telecoms operators playing a leading role. The OMP, as mentioned earlier, is the platform for sharing and discussing views within the industry in order to form *ad-hoc* committees that have information exchange with the Commission. Telia's approach was to show that the Swedish model was a well-functioning model. The manager's aim was to show that through private judicial agreements between the parties, the functioning of the telecoms market can be improved. By arguing that this 'agreement model' has worked well in Sweden, and using the Swedish telecoms company Tele2 as an example, the manager attempted in 1995 to persuade others to use this model as well. The Directive was discussed within the OMP-group and at the same time within the Commission. A new forum for these types of discussions has arisen, in the so-called European Interconnection Forum. The forum has a paid membership system for operators, and discussions are carried out similar to that of the OMP platform.

The parent company can, to a certain extent, affect the opinion *at home* and get support from the media and from politicians. The MD manager, on the other hand, typically deals with informing *European* media about the telecoms market. Media often visits the manager in order to get correct information. For representatives of the media, the telecoms sector is often perceived as difficult and complex. Similarly, it is vital for the politicians in the EU to have concrete technological and market information to make adequate political judgments. It is important to have knowledge of the distinctive characters/traditions within different countries, as well as of the products and the needs of customers.

13.5.2 SAS

Scandinavian Airline System (SAS) is the Scandinavian airline carrier with ownership stakes by the Danish, Norwegian and Swedish governments. In 1992, when the question of deregulation of the airline industry became a serious issue for EU politicians, SAS realised that there was a need to get closer to the decision makers. The head office decided to make investments in political lobbying and, among other activities, opened a political unit in Brussels. In total, the firm has engaged 14 people for this function, two of whom are located in Brussels, six in Sweden, and the rest in other European countries. The task of the unit in Sweden is to assist the unit in Brussels, for example by providing information or by negotiating with the Swedish politicians involved in the EU's political decisions. The political questions with which SAS is concerned cover areas such as the rules for flying time, consumer protection laws, taxes, competition law, pricing and environmental issues. Prior to Swedish entry into the EU, SAS already had experience in political questions like deregulation because — as mentioned above — the company is listed but still partially state-owned with ownership stakes by the governments of Denmark, Norway and Sweden, and thus has had to network with these three governments.

The main job of the unit in Brussels is to collect information and exercise influence on the rules before a proposal is sent to the Council of Ministers. To gain support for the suggestions, the unit first of all works with committees from the Commission and then with the Parliament. The unit also discusses the proposals with Swedish and Danish representatives in the EU. The manager explained that his duties are, among others, to engage in formal and informal meetings and to follow the media and the protocols.

More than 40% of the staff's time is spent in formal meetings, and 20% is devoted to informal activities like involvement in social arrangements (2–3 times a week). The remaining time is devoted to studying protocols, media, competition and consumers. One fundamental area mentioned by the manager is that of building and maintaining social relationships. The contacts are nurtured in social meetings aimed at assisting the co-operation. Engagement in informal clubs or parties is recognised as being an important part of the political process.

The acceptance of a proposal for discussion in a committee is related to how a proposal adopts the EU's political values. If a political question is not actualised by the EU or the media, the managers should collect enough technical and market information to convince the Commission that there is a need for a political decision in the interest of the consumers. The case of 'ground handling' is a typical example. The aim of SAS was the deregulation of ground handling for flight slots. SAS aimed at acquiring the freedom to be able to buy flight slots from different sellers. In London, for example, the airlines could choose from 7 to 8 alternatives. The SAS argument was based on the economic effect of deregulation. The decision could reduce the costs for the airline industry and subsequently reduce the prices and increase the quality of the service to the passengers.

The initiative was taken by SAS in 1992/1993, long before the issue was discussed in the media or in any political institution. The SAS manager realised that competitors like Lufthansa and KLM had a similar view and, accordingly, they decided to act together. They formed an *ad-hoc* group to put forward a suggestion to the DGVII and DGIV in the Commission. The committee involved in the question agreed and made the proposal to the Commission, since the proposal was in line with the consumer welfare policy. The proposal was sent to Parliament, but there, the Social Democrats and some other business groups resisted. The Social Democrats did this because they were against deregulation in general, while interest groups, like flying slots sellers, were against it because this type of deregulation would give more freedom to the airlines.

13.5.3 ABB

ABB is an amalgamation of a Swedish (Asea) and a Swiss (Brown Boveri) engineering companies. The manager of the political unit in Brussels explained that the relationship with political actors in the EU is one of the most important areas, especially for products such as the generation of power supplies. In 1993, ABB established a political unit engaging 15 people. Besides these people, five others in different European countries were taken on to deal with political matters. The main interest of the manager is to cover political issues like: (a) R&D and projects to develop new products; (b) deregulation and harmonisation of the market; (c) The White Paper—outlining the EU's energy policy for the year 2020; and (d) environmental questions like the reduction of chlorides in Central and Eastern Europe, the echo-audit, standardisation, EMAS (environmental certificate), and general social and economic questions like employment. The sections in the Commission, which deal with these issues, include DGIII for industry, DGXI for environment, DGXII for R&D, DGXVI for energy and DGXIV for public procurement.

In ABB's political unit, there are nine people whose main task is to collect the market, technological and political information needed to make proposals. The first important knowledge criterion mentioned by the manager is about the EU's bureaucratic function, i.e., the position of different people and the changes in their positions. He follows the daily news and incidents, since questions such as those involving chlorides or nuclear energy risks or alternative energy sources are usually also discussed in the media. The unit checks the public opinion in the media in order to give strength to the proposals passed on to the Commission. In addition to the influence that the unit aims to achieve in order to change the political rules, another primary goal is to obtain financial funds distributed by the EU for different projects.

The manager stated that one of the reasons for having a person responsible for political issues in Sweden is to maintain contact with the Swedish politicians active in the EU. Since the power of the EU Parliament is increasing, ABB's political unit is also working towards a close relationship with members of Parliament from 7 to 8 EU countries, which have mutual interests in questions like the energy policy and the environment. The task is to gain support not only in the Commission, but also in the European Parliament and the Council of Ministers. The effort is always accompanied by engagements in social meetings. According to the managers, this social investment is necessary in the periods both before and during negotiations. For an R&D project, for example, these contacts have both a continuous and a sporadic nature. They intensify when there is, or will be, a project.

ABB is a renowned international firm and one of the biggest companies in Europe. This facilitates social contacts and increases the credibility of the proposals. At the time of the interview, Percy Barnevik, the former Managing Director of ABB, was the chairman of the Competitive Advisory Group in the EU. This naturally facilitated the negotiation of ABB's proposals. The role of ABB, in the context of its high-tech products and declaration of social responsibility in terms of employment or environment and future vision, has strengthened

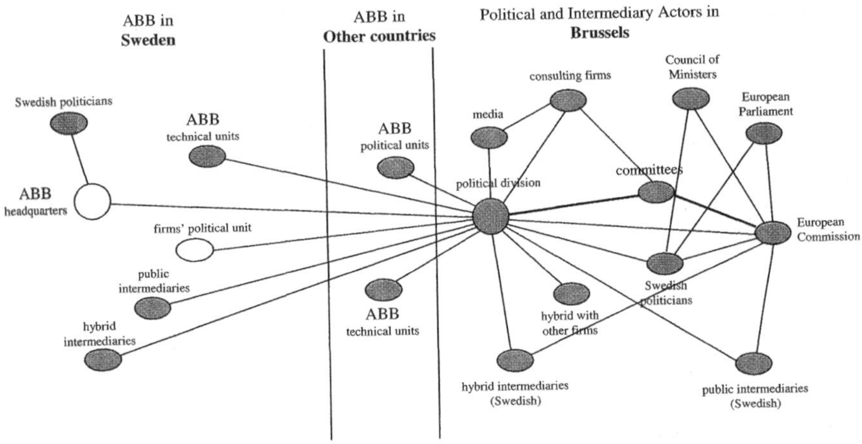

Figure 13.3: ABB's political network, as an example.

the position of the ABB's political unit. When a political issue has a general nature and is for the benefit of several competitors, then ABB acts as an industry group. For instance, all the competitors co-operate in Euroelectrics to propose future general plans for nuclear power.

The group in Brussels devotes 50% of its time to collecting information and informing groups and units related to the issues in question, and 50% of its time to external meetings and discussions. According to the manager, the relationships with these organisations and the social contacts with politicians are necessary, but it is the specific knowledge of the market, the industry and the technology that is the basis of affecting any political decision. One major task of the unit managers is to identify and explain the socio-political benefits of the proposals. In the case of 'Success story 95' for example, the technical solutions, along with the political and socio-economic applications of the proposal ensured that ABB succeeded in receiving SEK 15 billion from EU funds. The manager explained that it was because of these and the position of ABB's managing director in EU's political organisation that the firm received such a fund. Figure 13.3 explains the lobbying activities of ABB in the European Union.

13.5.4 Ericsson

Ericsson is a well-known telecoms firm that belongs to the global top five in its industry. At the end of 1990, due to the increasing political role of the EU in the telecommunications market, Ericsson decided to establish a unit in Brussels. The main task of the unit was to collect information and lobby on strategic issues like: (a) the liberalisation of the telecommunications market, which started at the end of 1980s; (b) the rules applying to mergers and acquisitions of telecoms companies; and (c) the harmonisation and mutual recognition of telecoms product standards (for example, if a product is tested in Sweden, it should also be accepted in other EU countries). One person with experience of foreign political affairs is responsible for the unit and he co-operates with 10–20 market co-ordinators/experts in Sweden. To develop a proposal, the manager involves those experts who possess the relevant technical and market knowledge. The manager's political task is: (a) creating and maintaining relationships with the EU's political units, i.e., contact with politicians, the treatment of political issues and the supervision of political decisions concerning the telecommunications market in countries like the United States; and (b) mobilising resources in Ericsson when a political proposal or decision is being processed.

On each issue, the manager deals mainly with the specific political section of the Commission. For technology and the treatment of product standards and the future telecommunications market, he deals with DGXIII; for the international markets with DGI; for industry in general with DGIII; for competition customs duties with DGIV and DGXXI. The political members of the committees lack detailed knowledge of the telecommunications market and technology, and thus depend on Ericsson and other companies in this field. Ericsson's technical knowledge of, for example, Intellectual Property Rights (IPR), compelled the Commission to ask the company to co-operate and to make technological suggestions.

The manager studies official journals, financial releases and cover reports on IT. This task takes up more than 15% of the manager's time. Some duties have a social nature, such as the engagement in formal social arrangements and meetings, specifically those which are arranged for people from the telecoms industry. But the manager explains that these contacts are mainly activated when a political issue is at stake, i.e., there is a problem of continuity in the contacts. The time spent in social and official meetings is 60%, including phone calls. The crucial factor is his and his colleagues' technological and market knowledge when explaining problems and suggesting solutions. Accordingly, the manager has to collect information about issues such as the customers' needs, the competitive rules, customs duties and new political suggestions and decisions.

The name of Ericsson as a big international firm, in conjunction with its established social contacts, facilitates the initiation of an issue. The GSM standard, which covers a large part of the telecoms market, and the technological development of the mobile phone, which has now become more adapted to the consumers' needs, are well known to the political members. These elements facilitate negotiations on issues such as standards for sub-contractors and the future development of products and the market. Since the committees may also involve competitors, the more technological and market knowledge a company can apply in order to convince the committees' political members, the more influence it can have on the content of the proposal suggested by the committees to the Commission and to the Parliament.

When a decision will produce benefits for several companies, they set up an *ad-hoc* group and involve industry groups in Brussels to reinforce the proposal. Competitors in the industry can, for example, co-operate temporarily on political questions like liberalisation and state subsidies. The ITA (Transatlantic Business Dialogue), for example, which aimed to eliminate the customs duties for IT products between the US and the EU, involved all the competitors in Europe working together to lobby politicians into drawing up new customs rules. A committee with 30 people from different countries was established. The committee engaged political groups, industry groups and experts from firms like Ericsson and Nokia. The result was presented by representatives from DGXIII and DGI to the Parliament and Council of Ministers, and finally led to the political decision between the US and the EU.

13.6 Discussion

These cases, despite their belonging to different industries and describing political actions in different years, have some crucial similarities. All firms acted to create and use information asymmetry to gain specific gains from the political actors. The information asymmetry was due to: (a) market imperfection, as all information and knowledge is not equally distributed among actors in the market; (b) firms committing different types of resources and building a variety of relationship networks. Asymmetry in knowledge and resource commitment created different types of relationships with the political actors. While firms in these cases benefited from their organisd resource commitment and specific knowledge, those of their competitors that were not involved in lobbying missed the privilege. All the case companies used their resources and knowledge in advance to exert influence before decisions were made. The specific support from the EU that these MNEs gained depended on the commitment and knowledge they expended on lobbying the bureaucrats and politicians in the EU. The presence of information asymmetries caused differences in firms' knowledge and resource commitment.

The cases reveal new facts, which enhance our understanding of lobbying in business networks, where information is not fully transparent. They further provide new knowledge on business networks comprising of both business and political actors. Below, the results will be discussed in more detail under three different headings: (1) horizontal and vertical relationships; (2) the political capability of the firms in terms of their commitment and knowledge; and (3) 'political agenda' and idea-generation.

13.6.1 Horizontal and Vertical Relationships

This study contributes to unlocking the lobbying black box and provides a framework for deeper study of the lobbying process. The cases of four MNEs manifest the complexity of the issues and also disclose how firms intentionally and openly aim to manage their political environment. In addition, the cases also reveal how lobbying interconnects the business and political markets with each other. Contrary to the earlier research, the chapter makes clear that firms in their lobbying activities are embedded in networks containing both political and business actors.

We adopt the view that business networks can be divided into a horizontal and a vertical dimension. While the vertical dimension refers to business actors, which have value-added business exchanges, the horizontal dimension refers to a non-exchange business relationship. Research on, for example, industrial networks (Hipple, 1988; Håkansson & Snehota, 1995), relationship marketing (Bitner, 1995; Sheth & Parvatyar, 1993), triadic relationships (Havila, 1996), and networks in the context of product and technology development (Håkansson, 1987) is limited to the study of vertical relationships. The four cases above, on the other hand, illustrate the importance of horizontal networks in firms' business relationships and as determinants of their competitive advantage. The four cases disclose how all the firms used their business and industrial competencies not only along the vertical dimension but also in their relationship to the political actors as well as to competitors along the horizontal dimension.

The cases also show that to study lobbying, the market must be divided into the two interconnected business and non-business markets. The inclusion of actors like the government into the network increases our understanding of how MNEs are embedded not only in business networks, but also in non-business networks. We argue that the study of lobbying enforces our view that business networks are composed of vertically and horizontally connected relationships. Thus, a network is a set of connected relationships that can support or hamper a focal relationship, depending on whether a dyadic relationship is affected by the wider relationships positively or negatively (Hart, 2004; Duck, 1993). One connected relationship can support, while another can hinder.

The cases above reveal that the degree and type of firms' lobbying actions depend on their political commitment and knowledge. As illustrated in Table 13.2, the firms acted at different times, with different purposes and used a variety of resources. The fundamental purpose of the firms was to influence and to avoid the costs of later adaptations. Firms with low commitment and knowledge have to incur both internal adaptation costs and the costs of a weakened competitive strength in the market. This is consistent with the view of an indirect interdependence between the political and business markets. The lobbying strengthens the firms' influence, co-operation and partnership (Boddewyn & Brewer, 1994; Coen, 1999; Damania, 2003), and commitment in social interactions with political actors (Hadjikhani & Ghauri, 2001).

13.6.2 Political Capability of the Firms

As illustrated in Table 13.2, all the investigated firms recognised political activities as a critical part of their market interaction. The four MNEs had several years of experience in political activity and had made significant organisational commitments. This commitment extended not only to Brussels, but also to other European countries. Telia, SAS and ABB, for example, had organised groups and people in several foreign countries to influence politicians. The cases illustrate how MNEs in their relationships with EU politicians mobilised both internal and external resources to influence political decisions.

In earlier studies, companies are generally seen as homogeneous units constrained by governments (see, e.g., Jansson, Dagib, & Sharma, 1995; Ghauri & Holstius, 1996; Bouwen, 2002). Our case studies present a completely different picture. The homogeneous behaviour can only be seen as referring to smaller firms as they all display rather defensive behaviour (Hadjikhani & Ghauri, 2001). The four MNEs, on the other hand, had an offensive proactive strategy. Their activity was geared towards influencing the decisions before they were actually made. Co-operation and negotiation tactics were used to obtain the desired results. The discussion of the cases also reveals the specificity of the managerial behaviour of the firms. Each of the four MNEs had specific agendas and the task was to gain specific political support (see below). The aspect of specificity is different to that proclaimed in studies of risk (Miller, 1992; Ting, 1988; Shubik, 1983) or on firm/state interdependence (Egelhoff, 1988; Porter, 1990; Ghauri & Buckley, 2002). While the main effort of the smaller firms is generally to gain information about political decisions affecting their export

Table 13.2: A summary for the firms' political activities.

	SAS	ABB	Ericsson	Telia
Major lobbying questions	Deregulation of flight industry, environment	Environment, R&D projects, deregulation, energy policy	Liberalisation and harmonisation, rules for merging	Liberalisation a and setting the standards
Organisational commitment	14 people, 2 in Brussels, 6 in Sweden, 6 in other European countries	15 people in Brussels, 5 people in other EU countries	1 person in Brussels, co-operating with 10–12 experts in Sweden and several people in other countries	10 people to deal with political and media business in Brussels. Top managers in Sweden
Information sources	Brussels, Nordic countries	Brussels, active in 8 EU countries for political questions	Mainly Brussels and Sweden and some other countries	Brussels and Sweden
Commitments year in Brussels	1992	1993	1990	1998 in Brussels
Forms of coalition for information and resource commitment	Alone, *ad-hoc* with competitors	Mainly alone	Alone, *ad-hoc*	Alone, *ad-hoc*
Network of interactions in EU	Committees in Commission and Parliament	Commission, the Council, parliament	Committees, Parliament and Commission	Committees and Parliament

activities (Hadjikhani & Ghauri, 2001), the MNEs in these cases made big commitments in several foreign countries to influence the political actors in Brussels.

13.6.3 Political Agenda for Lobbying

The notion of a 'political agenda' for lobbying has its origin in the recognition of a network arena for political activities. This is an arena in which business actors are related to non-business actors in the processing of political decisions, which impede or support the business activities. The notion is based on the network approach but is similar to Boddewyn and Brewer's (1994) view of a political market functioning parallel to the business market. However, applying the concept of a 'political agenda', the analysis of the four case studies shows that the relationships were issue related (as briefly mentioned above). For each political proposal, the political units needed information from experts and other interested parties in society. The relationships were activated to subject a specific political question for lobbying, and for new questions the MNEs activated another relationship. The fundamental task for all the MNE cases was to propose a technologically and socially appropriate agenda to the committees. The more genuine the idea of satisfying the EU's political units and their norms, the more specific the political support they gained. The lobbying agenda is also needed to satisfy social and economic groups connected to the political actors. Thus, they were to generate an idea and convince the EU politicians and their associated groups.

The firms lacking political commitment can become followers of the political rules. As the cases disclosed, the committees and Commission members had shortcomings in the technological knowledge required to generate ideas, which could reflect the needs of business and social groups. This made them dependent on the MNEs' and their specialists' having this competence. This means that firms that were not involved in lobbying or not encouraged to lobby were at a disadvantage.

As discussed above, the view of a political agenda basically divides the entire business activity into two different but interwoven areas (McLeay, Ordelheide, & Young, 2000; Boddewyn, 1988). One is the business arena, which considers the interaction with business actors, and the other is the political one, which involves the interaction of business and non-business actors. The political outcome is attractive to MNEs for several reasons (Etzioni, 1988). It creates winners and losers (Alt & Chrystal, 1983), and can reduce the organisational costs (Boddewyn, 1988). In case political actors are not transparent in their information, the firms involved in lobbying automatically achieve a better competitive position.

13.7 Concluding Remarks

This chapter studies lobbying from a network perspective. We argue that there are two types of networking activities: business and political networking. Lobbying is an essential, legitimate and distinguishable activity, which supplements business activities. To capture lobbying activities, the study introduced the concepts of commitment and knowledge. Firms' commitment and knowledge in both business and political markets are complementary and exist side by side. As an outcome of idiosyncratic relationships, the commitments in both areas diffuse and affect the relationships in each area. The higher the international business commitment, the greater the firm's legitimacy among people and political actors in the foreign markets, and the more influence the firm will gain. The greater the extent of lobbying, the more privileged the firm is in its business activities. Consequently, while some studies refer to the homogeneous (Miller, 1992) or unidirectional impact of government regulations (Hart, 2004; Kogut, 1991), and others adopt a dyadic view (Boddewyn, 1988, Ring et al., 1990; Jacobson et al., 1993), this study explores another dimension of business–political relationships. In accordance with the idea of the role of specificity in the network, we argue that the variation in managerial behaviour is explained by the differences in the firms' commitment and knowledge in the network, which in turn, to some extent, is based on the size and the resources of the firm. Table 13.3 explains the activities of MNEs in terms of these key variables.

Our case studies indicate the proclivity of MNEs to influence political decisions before they are made, and not after, which is contrary to studies performed by Boddewyn (1988) and Jansson et al. (1995). The act of exerting influence, either as a result of political actors' shortcomings or to acquire a competitive edge, is argued to be connected to the specificity in the relationships with the commercial and political actors. The more political knowledge and commitment an enterprise has, the more influence it gains and the more specific support it can receive. Consequently, it can be argued that a low level of political knowledge and commitment leads to low levels of influence and the enterprise will perceive the relationship with political actors as coercive. Furthermore, distinguishing the political network from the business network leads to another conclusion, which concerns the issue of the political agenda. In the process of gaining specific support from political actors, the function of the

Table 13.3: Political knowledge and commitment and variety of actions.

	MNEs
Commitment	High foreign political organisational and social commitment, idiosyncratic investment.
Knowledge	High previous political knowledge, high social and technical knowledge, high knowledge on institutions and high knowledge on specific questions. High knowledge of how the rules will affect the firm's business operation.
Political actions	The major activity is to influence. Political interactions with Swedish and foreign political actors in Brussels and other countries, interaction with other technical and legal units. Connecting the internal organisation capacity to the external needs.

business actors is typically to generate proposals, which can convince political actors. The success of this agenda depends on the management's ability to incorporate not only unique business resources and knowledge, but also the needs of the political actors and others on whom the political actors depend, such as consumers and media.

Contrary to an industrial network (Ford, 1990; Axelsson & Easton, 1992; Ghauri, 1999), the network in this study is contingent upon a situation, in which the position of political actors is not stable or transparent, and in which the values of the connected actors are changing. The network defined for this study comprises a set of actors—enterprises, media, governments, specialists, public opinion—linked to one another in various exchange relationships where their positions and relationships are dynamic. The interaction of these elements creates a loose network (Weick, 1979; Orton & Weick, 1990). More than 30% of the managers' time was devoted to finding out about the political actors' positions, about newcomers and new ideas released in the media and about the competitors' political activities. The commitment to new relationships, including social relationships, is one managerial device to keep networks alive. Lobbying is thus a legitimate process of relationship building among political and business actors and is no longer considered as covert activities or operations.

From our study of lobbying in this chapter follow several strategic managerial implications. First of all we can question the assumption of political actors as producers of given business rules. The view of unified and hierarchical power of political actors is true only for cases where a firm comes short in its political knowledge and commitment or disregards the benefit of managing the political environment. Firms that have a high level of commitment and knowledge also have the opportunity not only to manage but also to influence their political environment effectively. Our findings thus emphasise the importance of 'political competency'—the ability of the firms to mobilise and devote resources in dealing with political actors.

Another managerial implication relates to the influence on political decisions. Studies in international business typically largely disregard the lobbying activities of MNEs and stop at a discussion of the coerciveness of political actions. Adaptation strategies are presented as means to respond to the coercive actions of the political actors, and a large number of studies have presented a variety of ways to measure political risks. This study instead emphasises lobbying as a form of co-operation between the political and business actors. The co-operation between these actors is based on a mutually beneficial exchange. Political actors have shortcomings in, for example, market and technological knowledge and business actors need stability and rules supporting their business. Thus, the lobbying view illuminates the aspect of mutual gains and influence in co-operation between these two different types of actors. In case all actors in a particular market are involved, the transparency of markets will increase.

The third implication is the importance of a proactive strategy—to try to influence the political decisions before they are made. The identification of firms' activities as idea generation for a political agenda implies that management develops activities to convince the political actors. The purpose is to generate mutual benefits for the two parties and to gain a competitive advantage over competitors. Firms applying such influence aim to gain specific support and protect themselves from the cost of passive political adaptation. Knowledge about the political actors' needs and about other actors who become influenced by new political rules, can give a privileged position to the firms when managing their political relationships. The result of the lobbying activities of these firms is a lowered overall transparency of markets.

The final implication is related to the maintenance of a political network characterised by a loosely coupled structure. Lobbying activity extends beyond just relationship with political actors. It integrates other business and non-business actors that somehow contribute or hinder the business activities. This also means that firms in their international market, besides managing their business networks, also have to manage their political networks. These two networks are interwoven, but management of the political network subsidises the business activities, and the higher the political competence to manage the political network, the more specific will be the gain and competitive advantage. As a result the overall transparency of markets will decrease.

References

Alt, J. E., & Chrystal, K. A. (1983). *Political economics*. Berkeley: University of California Press.

Anderson, E., & Weitz, B. (1992). The use of pledge to build and sustain commitment in distribution channels. *Journal of Marketing Research, 19*(1), 18–34.

Axelsson, B., & Easton, G. (Eds). (1992). *Industrial networks: A new view of reality*. London: Routledge.

Becker, H. S. (1961). Notes on the commitment. *The American Journal of Sociology, 1*, 32–40.

Bern, T. (1994). *Lobbying in Europe "Lobbying i Europa."* Malmö: Nerenius & Santerus.

Bernheim, B. D., & Whinston, M. D. (1986). Menu auctions, resource allocation and economic influence. *Quarterly Journal of Economics, 101*, 1–31.

Berton, M. L., & Salanie, F. (2003). Lobbying under political uncertainty. *Journal of Public Economy, 87*, 2589–2610.

Bitner, M. J. (1995). Building service relationships: It's all about promises. *Journal of Academy of Marketing Science, 23*(4), 246–251.

Boddewyn, J. J. (1988). Political aspects of MNE theory. *Journal of International Business Studies, 14*(3), 341–362.

Boddewyn, J. J., & Brewer, T. L. (1994). International-business political behaviour: New theoretical directions. *Academy of Management Review, 19*(1), 119–143.

Bouwen, P. (2002). Corporate lobbying in the European Union: The logic of access. *Journal of European Public Policy, 9*, 365–390.

Buckley, P. J., & Ghauri, P. N. (1999a). *The global challenge for multinational enterprises*. Amsterdam, London: Elsevier.

Buckley, P. J., & Ghauri, P. N. (1999b). *The internationalisation of the firm: A reader*, (2nd ed.). London: ITB Press.

Buckley, P. J., & Ghauri, P. N. (2004). Globalisation, economic geography and the strategy of multinational enterprises. *Journal of International Business Studies, 35*(2), 81–98.

Bushee, B. J., & Noe, C. F. (2000). Corporate disclosure policies, institutional investors and stock return volatility. *Journal of Accounting Research, 38*(2), 171–202.

Cavusgil, S. T., Ghauri, P. N., & Agarwal, M. R. (2002). *Doing business in emerging markets*. Thousand Oaks: Sage.

Coen, D. (1999). The impact of U.S. lobbying practice on the European business-government relationship. *California Management Review, 41*(4), 27–44.

Conner, K. R. (1991). A historical comparison of resource-based theory and five schools of thoughts within industrial organization economics. *Journal of Management, 17*, 121–154.

Cosset, J. -C., & Roy, J. (1991). The determinants of country risk ratings. *Journal of International Business Studies, 22*(1), 135–142.

Cyert, R. M., & March, J. G. (1963). *A behavioral theory of the firm*. Englewood Cliffs: Prentice-Hall.

Dahl, R. A. (1956). *A preface to democratic theory*. Chicago, IL: University of Chicago.

Damania, R. (2003). Protectionist lobbying and strategic investment. *The Economic Record, 79*, 57–90.

Damania, R., & Frederiksson, P. G. (2003). Trade policy reform and endogenous lobbying group formation, and environmental policy. *Journal of Economic Behavior and Organization, 52*, 47–69.

Denekamp, J. (1995). Intangible assets, internationalization and foreign direct investment in manufacturing. *Journal of International Business Studies*, 26(3), 493–504.

Duck, S. (1993). *Individuals in relationships*. New York: Sage.

Egelhoff, W. G. (1988). Strategy and structure in multinational corporations: A revision of the Stopford and Wells model. *Strategic Management Journal, 9*, 1–14.

Eliassen, K. A., & Kooiman, J. (1993). *Managing public organizations, lessons from contemporary European experience*. London: Sage.

Epstein, G. S., & Hefeker, C. (2003). Lobbying contests with alternative instruments. *Economics of Governance, 4*, 81–89.

Esping-Andersen, G. (1985). *Politics against markets: The social democratic road to power*. New Jersey: Princeton University Press.

Etzioni, A. (1988). *The moral dimension: Toward a new economics*. New York: Free Press.

Fabella, P. V. (1991). The bias in favour of pro-tariff lobbies. *Journal of Public Economics, 44*, 87–93.

Fligstein, N. (1990). *The transformation of corporate control*. Cambridge, MA: Harvard University Press.

Ford, D. (Ed.). (1990). *Understanding business market: Interaction, relationships, networks*. London: Academic Press.

Forsgren, M., Hägg, I., Håkansson, H., Johanson, J., & Mattsson, L. -G. (1995). *Firms in networks, a new perspective on competitive power*. Acta Universitatis Upsaliensis, Vol. *38*, Stockholm: SNS Press.

Georgiou, G., & Roberts, C. B. (2004). Corporate lobbying in the U.K.: An analysis of attitudes towards the ASB's 1995 deferred taxation proposals. *The British Accounting Review, 36*, 441–453.

Ghauri, P. N. (Ed.). (1999). *Advances in international marketing: From mass marketing to relationships and networks*. Greenwich, CT: JAI Press.

Ghauri, P. N. (2004). Designing and conducting case studies in international business. In: R. Marchan-Piekkari, & C. Welch (Eds), *Handbook of qualitative research methods in international business* (pp. 109–124). Cheltenham: Edward Elgar.

Ghauri, P. N., & Buckley, P. J. (2002). Globalisation and the end of competition: A critical review of rent-seeking multinationals. In: V. Havila, M. Forsgren, & H. Håkansson (Eds), *Critical perspective on internationalisation* (pp. 7–28). Oxford: Elsevier.

Ghauri, P. N., & Cateora, P. R. (2005). *International marketing* (2nd ed.). London: McGraw-Hill.

Ghauri, P. N., & Holstius, K. (1996). The role of matching in the foreign market entry process in the Baltic States. *European Journal of Marketing, 30*(2), 75–88.

Hadjikhani, A. (1996). Sleeping relationship and discontinuity in project marketing. *International Business Review, 3*(5), 319–337.

Hadjikhani, A., & Ghauri, P. (2001). The internalization of the firm and political environment in the European Union. *Journal of Business Research, 52*(3), 263–275.

Hadjikhani A., & Thilenius, P. (2005). *Non-business actors a business network: The case of international firms in interaction with purchasers from a developing country.* London: Elsevier.

Håkansson, H. (Ed.). (1987). *Industrial technological development, adequate approach.* London: Croom Helm.

Håkansson, H., & Snehota, I. (1995). *Developing relationships in business networks.* London: Routledge.

Hanf, K., & Toonen, T. A. J. (Eds). (1985). *Policy making in federal and unitary systems.* Dordrecht: Kluwer.

Hart, D. M. (2004). Business is not an interest group: On the study of companies in American national politics. *Annual Review Political Science, 7*, 47–69.

Havila, V. (1996). *International business-relationship triads. A study of the changing role of the intermediating actor.* Doctoral thesis no. 64, Uppsala University.

Hooghe, L. (1995). Building a Europe with the regions: The politics of the commission bureaucracy under the structural funds. In: L. Hooghe (Ed.), *Cohesion policy. European community and substantial government.* Oxford: Oxford University Press.

Hult, K. M., & Walcott, C. (1990). *Governing public organisations: Politics, structure and institutional design.* Pacific Grove, CA: Books/Cole.

Jacobson, C. K., Lenway, S. L., & Ring, P. S. (1993). The political embeddedness of private economic transactions. *Journal of Management Studies, 30*(3), 453–478.

Jansson, H., Dagib, M., & Sharma, D. D. (1995). *The state and transitional corporations.* Cheltenham: Edward Elgar.

Johal, S., & Ulph, A. (2002). Globalization, lobbying and international environmental governance, review of international governance. *Review of International Economics, 10*, 387–403.

Johanson, J., & Vahlne, J. E. (1977). The internationalisation process of the firm—a model of knowledge development and increasing foreign market commitments. *Journal of International Business Studies, 8*(1), 23–32.

John, S., & Thomson, S. (2003). Lobbying in the 21st century: Lobbying in 2010. *Journal of Public Affairs, 3*, 9–13.

Johnson, C. (1982). *MITI and the Japanese miracle: The growth of industrial policy 1927–1975.* Stanford, CA: Stanford University Press.

Keillor, B. D., Boller, G. W., & Ferrel, O. C. (1997). Firm-level political behavior in the global market place. *Journal of Business Research, 40*, 113–126.

Kirchsteiger, G., & Prat, A. (2001). Inefficient equillibria in lobbying. *Journal of Public Economics, 82*, 349–375.

Kogut, B. (1991). Country capabilities and the permeability of borders. *Strategic Management Journal, 12*(Summer Special Issue), 33–48.

Kooiman, J. (1993). Socio-political governance. In: J. Kooiman (Ed.), *Modern governance—new government society interactions* (pp. 1–9). London: Sage.

Korbin, S. (1982). *Managing political risk assessment: Strategic responses to environmental changes*. Berkeley, CA: University of California Press.
Lagerlöf, J. (1997). Lobbying, information, and private and social welfare. *European Journal of Political Economy, 13*, 615–635.
Lenway, A., & Murtha, T. (1994). Country capabilities and the strategic state: How national political institutions affect multinational corporations' strategies. *Strategic Management Journal, 15*, 113–129.
Maddison, A. (1991). *Dynamic forces in capitalist development, a long-run comparative view*. Oxford: Oxford University.
Makhija, M. V. (1993). Government intervention in the Venezuelan petroleum industry: An empirical investigation of political risk. *Journal of International Business Studies, 24*(3), 531–555.
McLeay, S., Ordelheide, D., & Young, S. (2000). Constituant lobbying and its impact on the development of financial reporting regulations: Evidence from Germany. *Accounting, Organisations and Society, 25*, 79–98.
Miller, K. D. (1992). Industry and country effects on managers' perspective of environmental uncertainties. *Journal of International Business Studies, 24*(1), 693–714.
Murtha, T. P. (1991). Surviving industrial targeting: State credibility and public policy contingencies in multinational subcontracting. *Journal of Law, Economic and Organisation, 7*(1), 117–143.
Nowtotny, K., Smith, D. B., & Trebling, H. M. (Eds). (1989). *Public utility regulation: The economic and social control of industry*. Boston: Kluwer.
Orton, D., & Weick, K. E. (1990). Loosely coupled systems: A reconceptualization. *Academy of Management Review, 15*(2), 203–223.
Porter, M. E. (1990). *Competitive advantage*. New York: Free Press/Macmillan.
Potters, J., & Sloof, R. (1996). Interest groups: A survey of empirical models that try to assess their influence. *European Journal of Political Economy, 12*(3), 403–442.
Ring, P. S., Lenway, S. A., & Govekar, M. (1990). Management of the political imperative in international business. *Strategic Management Journal, 11*, 141–151.
Rose-Ackerman, S. (1978). *Corruption*. New York: Academic Press.
Scott, J. (1994)., *Social network analysis, a handbook*. London: Sage.
Sheth J. N., & Parvatiyar, A. (1993). The evolution of relationship marketing. Paper presented at the sixth conference on historical thoughts in marketing, May, Atlanta.
Shubik, M. (1983). Political risk, analysis, process and purpose. In: R. J. Herring (Ed.), *Managing international risk* (pp. 109–138). New York: Cambridge University Press.
Streeck, W. (1992). *Social institutions and economic performance: Studies of industrial relations in advanced capital economics*. London: Sage.
Ting, W. (1988). *Multinational risk assessment*. Westport, CT: Greenwood Press.
Truman, B. D. (1951). *The government process*. Knopf: New York.
Weick, K. E. (1979). *The social psychology of organising* (2nd ed.). Reading, MA: Addisson-Wesley.

Chapter 14

Corruption and Foreign Direct Investment: Japanese FDI Inflows into the European Union, 1996–2002[1]

Andrew Delios, Ram Mudambi and Pietro Navarra

14.1 Introduction

In this paper, we focus on a particular dimension of transparency: corruption. We raise the question: What is the nature of the link between corruption and foreign direct investment inflows? Prior research has pointed to both positive and negative influences of levels of corruption on levels of foreign direct investment (FDI) inflows. The basic idea behind much of the analyses is that corruption represents a cost: it increases the uncertainty associated with an investment opportunity, which in turn increases the cost of capital and hurdle rates of return for an investment. All other things equal, this increase in the cost of investing will result in lower levels of investment. At the same time corruption has been thought of as an opportunity, where a firm's managers can exploit weaknesses in a nation's institutional environment to gain advantages in competition.

Before addressing the issue of the net effects of corruption, it is important to recognize that corruption is just one dimension associated with the transparency of a nation's institutions. National institutional environments comprise the formal rules of a nation as defined by its political and legal institutions as well as the

[1]This research was supported by NUS Academic Research Grants (R-313000–052–112 and R-313-000-063–112).

Corporate and Institutional Transparency for Economic Growth in Europe

ISBN: 0-08-044665-5

informal rules, as they extend from the social and cultural dimensions of a country. Corruption is a key aspect of the transparency of a nation's political and legal institutions and therefore, has an impact on the level of political uncertainty and risk and the burden of regulation as it is related to the extent of market liberalization. Each of these dimensions in turn can influence the levels of FDI inflows, yet each of these dimensions is not separate from one another.

Indeed, corruption is often thought of as extending from, or being a consequence of, other dimensions of a nation's institutional environment. The role played by the regulatory state in the economy has been generally acknowledged as one of the major sources of corruption (Shleifer & Vishny, 1999; Rose-Ackerman, 1999). The political and bureaucratic allocation of scarce resources through an elaborate system of permits and licenses provides fertile ground for rent-seeking activities that in turn favor the emergence and development of illicit behavior. If excessive regulation stimulates corruption, then policy measures such as deregulation and privatization might reduce levels of corruption, through reductions in opportunities for private rent seeking by public officials (Rose-Ackerman, 1988; Bliss & Di Tella, 1997).

Corruption, in this line of reasoning, emanates from the interaction of corporate decision-makers on the one hand and politicians or regulators on the other. To the extent that politicians/regulators are able to extract legal rents or illicit payoffs from firms, this interaction has a direct bearing on the cost of capital and cash-flow forecasts (see Chapter 12). Pursuing this chain of reasoning, the burden of the regulatory state (of which corruption is a part) leads to a higher cost of capital, a lower incentive for firms to invest (see Chapter 9), and consequently, a lower economic growth rate (see Overview Figure, Chapter 1). In this chapter, we focus on the effects of corruption on investment decisions by foreign firms, i.e., on FDI.

Although, the intent of our study is not to investigate how corruption levels can be reduced by market liberalization reforms (when those reforms reduce the regulatory burden in an economy), these points do relate to the idea that corruption is not only just one dimension of a national environment, it is a dimension that could plausibly be a consequence of other dimensions. If this is the case, then it is possible that any observed relationship between corruption and FDI inflows might be spurious, or at least contingent on other dimensions of the environment. FDI inflows could possibly be influenced by a dimension that is correlated with corruption levels, or with a dimension that is thought to be a causal precursor to FDI inflows. We investigate this point in this study, both conceptually and empirically.

The chapter is organized as follows. In Section 14.2 we review the relevant background literature on corruption, domestic and foreign investment and economic growth. Then we move to a discussion of corruption and its correlates in national institutional environments, which is followed by our arguments about the expected relationships between corruption and FDI. In Section 14.3 we turn to an examination of these ideas using the empirical context of Japanese FDI into European countries. Both aggregate world FDI inflows and subsidiary establishments by Japanese firms are found to be insensitive to the level of corruption in a European economy. Instead, the level of government effectiveness is found to be the element of the institutional environment most closely tied to FDI inflows. In Section 14.4 we conclude that the influence of corruption on economic outcomes such as FDI inflows, needs to be considered in a broader context including a more comprehensive consideration of a nation's institutions. If this is not the case, the strength of inferences about the influence of corruption, will be less conclusive.

14.2 Literature Review

One of the most notable features about prior research on corruption is how it has been connected to the economic growth prospects, and the current economic states, of a nation. Much of the research arrives at the conclusion that corruption is negatively related to the level of economic activity and to the potential for future economic growth of a country.

The existing research, as coupled with anecdotal evidence, is conclusive on the point that corruption does matter. Corruption can exert its impact through its influence on individuals, corporations or the policy-making apparatus and administration of a nation. One of the leading sources for cross-national research on corruption raises the important point that when key decisions are determined by individuals that have little concern for the consequences of their decisions for the state and the wider community, the consequent political, economic and social costs are high (Transparency International, 2000). There is some evidence that a country's cultural roots affect individual decision-making in this regard (Robertson & Watson, 2004).

Corruption, when it emerges, can shift motivations of individuals from the state to those that are self-serving. Corruption has been stated to exert a negative influence on a state by compromising a nation's entire integrity system that includes the judiciary, as well as the legislative and executive branches of government (Pope, 2000). Individuals and the society in general, in countries characterized by having high levels of corruption can suffer the consequences of corruption in a variety of ways. If corruption is prevalent in an economy, capital that should go into social programs, or to either directly or indirectly aid individuals, can be funneled into the pockets of corrupt officials.

More specifically, corruption can have significant economic ramifications. Corruption can have a detrimental effect on a country's income distribution and in turn can worsen poverty (Gupta, 1998). Corruption has also been found to negatively influence capital accumulation. Further, it can decrease likelihoods of receiving capital from international agencies by threatening the efficacy of external stabilization programs (Asilis, 1994). In terms of business activity, Mauro (1995) found that corruption lowers private investment, which in turn, reduces economic growth.

Not all work on corruption reaches the conclusion that it impedes economic growth (Fitzpatrick & Kenison, 1999). Leff (1964) and Huntington (1968), raised the point that corruption serves as a facilitator that enables investors to avoid bureaucratic red tape and thus expedite the development of a project and thereby spur economic growth. Again, such a perspective concerns private domestic investment in a country, whereas the setting for our analysis is foreign direct investment.

14.2.1 FDI and Investment: An Overview

Domestic investment and foreign direct investment are important factors in economic growth. In the last decades of the 20th century, countries experienced increasingly greater reliance on FDI. Between 1973 and 1995, inward FDI grew from $25 billion to $315 billion (U.S.), which was faster than the growth of world trade of goods (Drabek & Payne, 2001). Further, developing and transition nations are particularly interested in attracting foreign capital since domestically sourced funds are often insufficient to finance their investment needs (Drabek & Payne, 2001).

Research from several theoretical perspectives has raised the point that transparent economic policies, free of corrupt activities, are vital for foreign investors, and for encouraging FDI inflows. Drabek and Payne (2001) outline several reasons why corruption can impede FDI inflows. Most of the arguments on the link between corruption and FDI focus on costs. Additional costs are incurred when firms are forced to contend with a lack of information that initially should have been fully available and disclosed to any potential investor. When bribery becomes a requirement for potential investors, risks increase and the costs of non-compliance increase (Drabek & Payne, 2001). Firms will only assume additional risks if the rewards are adequate. Additional costs due to corruption are likely to impede the flow of FDI into a country.

It has been pointed out that the 'cost' and 'risk' dimensions associated with corruption are distinct. If corruption only entails higher costs (e.g., bribery), this need not affect firm risk if the returns from engaging in corrupt practices are predictable. If this is true, corruption will only lead to higher prices, but have minimal effects on investment. However, if the returns from dealing with corrupt practices are unpredictable, the risk of doing business increases. There is evidence that it is the 'risk' or unpredictability aspect of corruption that affects investment levels (Campos, Lien, & Pradhan, 1999).

In response to the costs and risks of corruption, firms avoid conducting business in nations characterized by corruption. In emerging economies where the legal and regulatory framework does not sufficiently exist to prevent such corrupt activities, companies simply would not invest. Legal provisions against corruption and bribery in particular, can induce FDI flows (Drabek & Payne, 2001).

Conversely, corruption can reduce FDI inflows as multinational firms that seek to do business in an environment where corruption abounds are placed in a precarious position. They either accept the corruption as necessarily being the price of doing business and compromise ethical conduct, or they can be subjected to the ramifications of failure to partake in the corrupt necessities of a nation. Either way, corporate decision-makers face difficult choices, with the consequent choice often being that corruption impedes FDI inflows (Habib & Zurawicki, 2002).

14.2.2 Political Institutions and Economic Policies

In addressing the issue of whether and how corruption influences FDI, we begin by identifying the institutional context in which corruption and other elements of a national institutional environment are embedded. Work on national institutions makes the basic but important point that institutions regulate the process of decision-making at the national level, which in turn affects policy changes (McCubbins, Noll, & Weingast, 1989). These institutions represent the rules of the game in which public officials formulate their policy choices.

Over the last 10 years a new theoretical and empirical literature in economics has developed dealing with the analysis of the role played by political institutions in shaping economic policy (Mudambi, Navarra, & Sobbrio, 2001). In this intellectual endeavor political institutions are seen as the rules of the game that determine the incentives and constraints that policy-makers face when they interact in the creation of collective choices (Brennan & Buchanan, 1986). They are designed externally, made explicit by legislation and regulations and are formally enforced by an external authority such as the government or, more generally, the state. Examples of this type of institution are civil law, the form of government and the electoral system (North, 1990; Furubotn & Richter, 1998).

Several scholars, mostly from the field of economics, have analyzed the political micro foundations of economic policy focusing on the role played by electoral rules and regime types on the process of collective decision-making. In the main, they have focused on the effects of political institutions on macroeconomic policies such as taxes, public spending and income re-distribution (Austen-Smith, 2000; Milesi-Ferretti, Perotti & Rostagno, 2001; Persson & Tabellini, 2003). In contrast, international business scholars have focused on the effects of formal and informal institutions on international investment and trade. These studies have examined the effects of politico-economic institutional differences on a wide variety of international expansion strategies such as the choice of entry mode and the dynamic of entry strategies, the probability of survival and, most relevant to this study, the magnitude of investment in a nation (Henisz, 2000; Delios & Henisz, 2000).

With respect to the entry decision (FDI inflows), cross-national variation in the institutional environment adds uncertainty to new foreign operations that in turn raises the hurdle rate of return and discourages entry. Facing this situation, investors are more likely to enter countries where the future policy regime is relatively easy to predict (Loree & Guisinger, 1995; Gastanaga, Nugent, & Pashamova, 1998; Wei, 2000). Unstable policies lead to variability in the policy decision-making process. Such political instability produces uncertainty, both about the policy decisions taken by the outgoing government and about the policies likely to be initiated by the incoming government. Such political instability can exacerbate the effects of such well-known problems as the obsolescing bargain (Vernon, 1971; Ramamurti, 2000, 2003). This is because, a new government is even less likely to be bound by commitments made by a multinational enterprise (MNE) investor than a continuing one. Such turbulence on the political front has motivated researchers to take a close look at the impact of political instability on international business (Vernon, 1971; Mudambi & Navarra, 2003).

Consistent with the ideas we laid out in the introduction to this study, political instability is only one of the institutional characteristics influencing market strategies in international business. Another important determinant of firm behavior in international exchanges is the sensibility of a given country's political institutions to lobbying (see Chapter 13). Several scholars have suggested that in countries with more easily manipulated political regimes; the attainment of substantial economic returns depends more heavily on political activities (Dailami & Leipziger, 1998; Zelner & Henisz, 2000; Henisz & Zelner, 2001).

This brief overview highlights how the rules governing the process of public decision-making play a crucial role as they constrain the set of available policy choices and, thus, influence decisions taken by firms, including the foreign investment decision. As we discuss in the next section, related dimensions can influence levels of corruption in an economy.

14.2.3 Economic Regulation and Corruption

Economic regulation is one of the policy decisions that matters the most for the functioning of an economy. This issue concerns the extent of state intervention in the market economy and the degree of discretionary power of bureaucrats. According to the traditional public interest view (Pigou, 1947), economic regulation should be considered as the response to market failures ranging from monopoly power to externalities. These inefficiencies can be alleviated through benevolent governmental intervention. However, many scholars criticized this approach as unrealistic and questioned the appropriateness of assuming a government composed of selfless public servants (Stigler, 1971). This alternative view suggests that regulation is essentially a redistributive process influenced by self-interested individuals who want to gain specific benefits by means of governmental intervention.

This 'public choice' view of regulation sees it as a political process in which specific interest groups express their demands for political intervention as a way of redistributing rents to themselves. This theory predicts that different groups in the polity, according to their size, strength and organization, try to capture the regulatory agency to appropriate the rents generated by public intervention in the market (Tullock, 1967; Peltzman, 1976; Becker, 1983). According to this approach, the assignment of licenses for monopolies over new technology, quotas for imports of certain products or regulation that affects competition in a given industry, and lucrative public sector contracts typically involve both political and economic logic. As the role of politics in these assignments increases, substantial financial and managerial resources are diverted from economic activity to political rent-seeking (Bhagwati, 1982). This shift in resource allocation implies lower investment in tangible economic assets and greater investment in political assets. These political assets may even be used to protect illegitimate activities like grey and black-market operations.

Although with minor exceptions, it is widely recognized that well-established market institutions, characterized by clear and transparent rules, fully functioning checks and balances and a robust competitive environment reduce rent-seeking opportunities and, in turn, the incentives for corruption. Less competition leads to a situation in which firms enjoy higher rents so that bureaucracies with high control rights over them, such as tax inspectors or industry regulators, have greater incentives to engage in malfeasant behavior (Bliss & Di Tella, 1997). Ades and di Tella (1997, 1999) found that corruption is higher in countries where domestic firms are sheltered from foreign competition by natural or policy-induced barriers to trade, with economies dominated by a small number of firms with low levels of product market competition and where antitrust regulations are not effective in preventing anticompetitive practices.

As the preceding review has identified, corruption levels in a nation are connected to several other dimensions of the institutional environment. These dimensions can be thought of as precursors to corruption, or as dimensions that tend to be highly correlated with corruption levels. Our next section extends this point to examine how corruption might or might not be connected to FDI inflows based on the consideration of a separate institutional dimension as influence of FDI inflows.

14.2.4 Corruption and FDI

It has been suggested that MNEs cope with corruption by either avoiding locations where they encounter it or by adjusting their entry modes to reduce their exposure (Doh, Rodriguez, Uhlenbruck, Collins, & Eden, 2003). For the former case, avoidance would lead to lower FDI inflows, as if corruption pervasiveness grows, MNEs are more likely to choose arm's length entry strategies.

On the other hand, as the arbitrariness of corruption increases, MNEs are more likely to engage with local partners who bring an understanding of the corruption framework in which they expect to operate. Further, the MNE itself has a better understanding of the corruption framework in the host country when it is similar to that of its home country (Aharoni, 1966; Oliver, 1991). In both these cases, bringing knowledge of the local corruption environment reduces the risks associated with engaging with it.

Given this potential strategy for coping with corruption, does increasing corruption reduce the level of FDI? The evidence here is mixed. Several studies have failed to find a significant link between the extent of corruption and the level of FDI (Hines, 1995; Wheeler & Mody, 1992). However, more recent studies tend to find a consistent negative effect of corruption on FDI location decisions (Wei, 2000; Habib and Zurawicki, 2002). Hence, the first test we conduct in our analysis is to identify whether corruption is connected to FDI inflows into European countries.

The second test we conduct is to see if corruption is connected to FDI inflows, even when given the presence of a parallel but conceptually distinct dimension of the institutional environment. The additional dimension we consider is government effectiveness. As we have pointed out in our earlier review, corruption can be found in situations where regulation is burdensome and the government bureaucracy tends to be more ineffective in terms of increasing the costs of business, and reducing firm efficiency. In such a situation, the government can be thought of as being ineffective, or perhaps more clearly, corruption is just one indicator of government effectiveness, where government effectiveness has the more fundamental influence on FDI inflows.

14.3 Methods

14.3.1 Sample

Our sample comprises the entries of Japanese firms made into various European countries across two time periods. *Kaigai Shinshutsu Kigyou Souran-Kuni Betsu* (Japanese Overseas Investments—by Country), a publication of Toyo Keizai Inc., provided our data on FDI inflows. Japanese Overseas Investments enabled us to identify whether a Japanese firm established a subsidiary in a given country in a given year. To compile a list of aggregate Japanese FDI inflows into our sample countries year wise, we examined the list of Japanese foreign subsidiaries found in eight editions. Toyo Keizai compiled these data from information gathered in annual surveys of the overseas operations of listed and non-listed Japanese firms. We used the 1986, 1989, 1992, 1994, 1997, 1999, 2001 and 2003 editions to construct our longitudinal profile of Japanese FDI inflows by country.

After compiling our subsidiary-level data of Japanese FDI inflows, we drew data on regulatory environment from secondary sources. The data sources included the World Bank, UNCTAD, the United Nations Development Program (UNDP), and the European Union (EU). The complete list of variables and sources is provided in the Data Appendix. Using these sources, we were able to compile data on 43 European host countries, with the period of study being

Table 14.1: Summary statistics.

Variable	**Mean**	**S.D.**	***N***
	Endogenous Variables		
FDI (US$ million)	10240.2	23779.2	83
Japanese entries (number)	12.8256	26.649	86
	Exogenous Variables		
GDP (US$ billion)	226.728	431.904	85
Per capita GDP (US$ ‘000)	14.099	8.97406	85
EU member (dummy)	0.581395	0.496224	86
EU new member (dummy)	0.232558	0.424941	86
Government effectiveness	0.536047	0.975268	86
Control of corruption	0.609991	1.02256	86
English fluency	0.255814	0.438877	86
R&D expenditure (% of GDP)	1.32178	0.91607	73

1996–2002. In Table 14.1, we provide the summary statistics relating to all the variables used in this study.

14.3.2 Analysis and Results

Two levels of analysis were undertaken, related to the effects of political risk on inward FDI in Europe. The first (macro) level focused on aggregate FDI inflows into European economies. The second (micro) level focused on firm-level decisions on entry through setting up country subsidiaries. In order to isolate the effects of political risk, FDI and entry decisions were estimated first

Table 14.2: FDI inflows (Regressand: FDI).

Panel Estimates — Fixed Effects Model		
Regressor	**Parameter Estimates ('t' stat.)**	
	MODEL 1 Location variables only	MODEL 2 Location and institutional variables
GDP	23.13 (2.24)**	19.70 (1.98)**
Per capita GDP	9.72 (0.03)	−103.86 (0.11)
EU member	11555.21 (1.97)**	12169.06 (1.54)
EU new member	− 9019.55 (1.51)	−8619.14 (1.55)
R&D expenditure	3267.10 (1.42)	5448.45 (1.43)
Government effectiveness	–	19101.05 (2.08)**
Control of corruption	–	18203.38 (1.45)
English fluency	–	2045.68 (0.22)
Fixed effects:		
1997–1998	−10765.18 (1.88)*	−9889.25 (0.78)
2000–2001	403.27 (0.07)	−528.59 (0.04)
Diagnostics		
Adj. R^2	0.3596	0.3675
F stat.; (d.f.)	7.55 (6, 64)	5.52 (9, 61)
('p' value)	(0.0000)	(0.0000)
Log-L	−801.2716	−799.1252
Restricted Log-L	−820.2742	

Notes: Estimates significant at the 10 and 5% levels are marked with * and **, respectively.

with only location variables (Model 1) and then with location as well as institutional variables (Model 2). This procedure enables us to capture the net or marginal effect of political risk. A similar approach is adopted in Mudambi and Navarra (2003).

Institutional variables change relatively slowly. Hence, we collapsed our data into two panels, 1996–1999 and 2000–2002. These two periods also correspond relatively well to the business cycle that underlies the macroeconomic data in our sample countries. The Hausman test indicates that the fixed effects model is the preferred specification in all cases.

Estimates of macro FDI flows are presented in Table 14.2. Both models are significant overall as measured by the F statistic and R square indicates that the fit is good. Market size as measured by gross domestic product (GDP) emerges as a significant determinant of FDI inflows in both Model 1 and Model 2, but per capita GDP is insignificant. EU membership is significant and positive in Model 1, but this significance disappears in Model 2. In its place, government effectiveness appears significant, suggesting that EU countries may have more effective government services and policies than non-EU countries. The control of corruption has a positive effect, but it does not reach significance. English fluency is not significant.

Estimates of micro-level entry decisions are presented in Table 14.3. Again both Model 1 and Model 2 display overall significance and good fit to the data. In fact, the fit is considerably better than that of the macro FDI inflows. The estimates of Model 1 mirror those for the macro data. The estimates of Model 2 diverge in several ways. First, per capita GDP appears to be significant and *negative*. This may be capturing a wage effect, whereby countries with high levels of per capita GDP are also high-cost locations for conducting international operations. Second, the control of corruption is not close to significance and its sign is reversed. Third, English fluency is highly significant and positive, suggesting that an English fluent workforce is considered a positive factor by Japanese multinationals.

We note that entry decisions are bounded below by zero, i.e., the simple panel estimates are likely to exhibit truncation bias. As a robustness check, we present non-linear maximum likelihood Tobit estimates that incorporate a left truncation point at zero. These estimates are presented in Table 14.3 as Model 3. It will be seen that while the Tobit estimates suggest a significant truncation effect, the estimates with regard to all the key variables are very close to those of Model 2. The fact that the two estimation methodologies (least squares and maximum likelihood) provide us with comparable results, gives confidence in our findings.

Table 14.3: Japanese entries (Regressand: Japanese entries).

Regressor	Panel Model		**Tobit Model**
	MODEL 1 Location variables only	**MODEL 2 Location and institutional variables**	**MODEL 3 Location and institutional variables**
	Parameter Estimates ('t' stat.)		
GDP	0.05 (5.02)**	0.05 (9.55)***	0.05 (8.70)***
Per capita GDP	−0.10 (0.78)	−1.43 (2.34)**	−1.08 (1.65)*
EU member	5.02 (1.81)*	0.78 (0.13)	9.19 (1.25)
EU new member	1.70 (0.51)	0.76 (0.12)	−1.01 (0.14)
R&D expenditure	1.45 (0.84)	−0.44 (0.14)	0.95 (0.26)
Government effectiveness	—	18.29 (2.09)**	20.47 (2.05)**
Control of corruption	—	−6.35 (0.86)	−13.06 (1.51)
English fluency	—	14.27 (2.36)**	18.81 (2.62)**
Fixed effects:			
1997–1998	−1.80 (0.49)	12.42 (1.70)*	−0.16 (0.02)
2000–2001	−1.91 (0.50)	12.60 (1.77)*	−2.43 (0.52)
Sigma	—	—	16.78 (10.31)***
Diagnostics			
Adj.R^2	0.6501	0.7035	—
F stat.; (d.f.) ('*p*' value)	23.30 (6, 66) (0.0000)	19.99 (9, 63) (0.0000)	—
Iterations	—		4
Log-L.	−305.6840	−297.9396	−239.1198
Restricted Log-L.		−347.1918	

Notes: Estimates significant at the 10, 5% and 1% levels are marked with *, ** and ***, respectively.

Finally, we note that our sample includes a significant number of countries that were part of the former USSR. Systematically different levels of government effectiveness and corruption in these countries could drive our results. Hence, we re-estimated our models including a 'Soviet' dummy. None of our results were affected when this dummy was included in the specifications shown in Table 14.3. The 'Soviet' dummy itself was statistically insignificant, with the inclusion of this dummy not improving the overall fit of the models. Our results are hence robust to this specification change.

14.4 Conclusion

Our study examines a basic but fundamental aspect of transparency in the capital formation process, 'Does corruption influence the level of FDI inflows into European countries?' Our answer is that it does not. This answer aligns with part of the corruption–FDI literature, but it stands in contrast to the bulk of the work on corruption and FDI, that has found the extent of corruption to be negatively related to FDI inflows.

In contrast to this work, we find that FDI inflows tend to be strongly related to the level of government effectiveness in a nation. We observe this result for both dollar aggregate inflows of foreign direct investment as well as for counts of subsidiary establishments by Japanese investors in Europe. Given that we obtain results from two separate samples using different measures of FDI inflows, we take greater confidence in the robustness of the results.

Our work suggests that research on corruption and its influence on FDI inflows need to be staged in the broader context of the various related dimensions of the institutional environment in which corruption levels are ultimately determined. Doing so permits a better understanding to be developed of the influence of corruption on FDI inflows and other economic outcomes. The same research strategy also permits scholars to begin to disentangle the influences of individual dimensions of national institutional environments. Such an approach, when broadly applied, can perhaps yield better insight into what are the most fundamental determinants of economic activity, such as FDI, in individual countries.

This approach is particularly important when examining FDI inflows, or other outcomes, on a worldwide basis. Analyses of the relationship of FDI and corruption at a worldwide level have tended to find a strong negative influence of corruption on FDI inflows, yet in a European context, we have failed to find such a relationship. One reason for this could be the persistently low levels of FDI in numerous countries worldwide that have low GDP levels, low GDP growth, high political uncertainty, poor government transparency and effectiveness, and high corruption. Any of the aforementioned variables, aside from corruption, could lessen motivations for FDI, yet any empirical study that explores the link between corruption and FDI on a worldwide level will likely find a negative influence because of the persistence of low levels of FDI in sets of countries that have these characteristics.

The European setting provides a useful sampling alternative, as the economies we examine (as listed in the Data Appendix) do not have a large set of poor economic, political and legal infrastructure countries, which can drive empirical results in a worldwide sample. In this sense, we can obtain a better isolation of corruption's influence on FDI inflows by limiting our sample.

With our limited sample, and our observation of a null effect for corruption on FDI, can we conclude that corruption is neither good nor bad? We cannot interpret our results to such a qualitative appraisal of corruption. Instead, we interpret our results to indicate that corruption reflects other institutional dimensions of an economy that have a more fundamental influence on FDI inflows. Ultimately, as with all dimensions of an economy, and of a competitive environment, firms will develop strategies to contend with the costs and uncertainties created by those dimensions. Firms will have differential capabilities to accommodate these costs and uncertainties, which suggests that firms will respond in strategically different ways to these dimensions. A logical next step is to identify and analyze the characteristics of a firm that might align with an ability to effectively manage corruption levels in an environment, such that entry might be more feasible for one type of firm in a corrupt environment as compared to other types of firms.

An analysis that focuses on firm-level heterogeneity provides the firm-level counterpart to our investigation of country level determinants of FDI inflows. Aside from this potential avenue for future research, we must also note that our measure of corruption only picks up activities that are illegal under each country's system of laws. It is possible that by widening the definition of corruption to include rent-seeking activities that are technically legal, like various forms of lobbying, significant effects on FDI may be obtained. While such an exercise is fraught with measurement problems, it remains a fruitful avenue for research. Indeed, an attempt along these lines appears in Chapter 13 in this volume.

To conclude, we contend that simple corruption–FDI inflow investigations overlook the complexity of dimensions in an institutional environment that can have a contemporaneous influence on FDI inflows. As evidence in support of this idea, when even just one of these dimensions is considered, we find corruption to not have an observable influence on levels of FDI inflows into European countries.

A direct implication of this finding is that European countries oriented toward achieving economic growth at least partly through securing higher shares of FDI inflows need to work toward observable improvements in policy environments. Directives and actions aimed at ostensibly reducing the prevalence of corruption, at least as our analysis indicates, would likely be less effective than addressing institutional weaknesses that create opportunities for corruption. Actions addressed at improving government effectiveness, appear to have a strong effect at stimulating FDI inflows, or at least creating a more appealing environment in which to situate investment. Our analyses suggest that, common with popular press and anecdotal accounts, new EU members are the states that need to make the most progress on the effectiveness of their governments. A second set of actions, which states could address are the institutional antecedents to corruption. As institutions are strengthened and corruption is reduced, we will see reductions in uncertainty levels for foreign investors, a reduced capital cost of investing, and a consequent strong stimulus to foreign investment levels, which can themselves, be a positive influence on economic growth levels.

References

Ades, A., & di Tella, R. (1997). National champions and corruption: Some unpleasant interventionist arithmetic. *Economic Journal, 107*, 1023–1042.

Ades, A., & di Tella, R. (1999). Rents, competition and corruption. *American Economic Review, 89*(4), 982–993.

Aharoni, Y. (1966). *The foreign investment decision process. Division of Research.* Boston: Harvard Business School.

Asilis, C. (1994). *On corruption and capital accumulation*, Working Paper 36-94, International Monetary Fund, Washington D.C.

Austen-Smith, D. (2000). Redistributing income under proportional representation. *Journal of Political Economy, 108*, 1235–1269.

Becker, G. S. (1983). A theory of competition among pressure groups. *Quarterly Journal of Economics, 98*, 371–400.

Bhagwati, J. (1982). Directly unproductive profit-seeking (DUP) activities. *Journal of Political Economy, 90*(5), 988–1002.

Bliss, C., & Di Tella, R. (1997). Does competition kill corruption? *Journal of Political Economy, 105*, 1001–1023.

Brennan, G., & Buchanan, J. M. (1986). *The reason of rules: Constitutional political economy.* Cambridge: Cambridge University Press.

Campos, J. E., Lien, D., & Pradhan, S. (1999). The impact of corruption on investment: Predictability matters. *World Development, 27*(6), 1059–1067.

Dailami, M., & Leipziger, D. (1998). Infrastructure project finance and capital flows: A new perspective. *World Development, 26*, 1283–1298.

Delios, A., & Henisz, W. J. (2000). Japanese firms' investment strategies in emerging economies. *Academy Management Journal, 43*(3), 305–323.

Doh, J. P., Rodriguez, P., Uhlenbruck, K., Collins J., & Eden, L. (2003). Coping with corruption in foreign markets. *Academy of Management Executive, 17*(3), 114–127.

Drabek, Z., & Payne, W. (2001). *The impact of transparency on foreign direct investment*, Working Paper ERAD-99-02, World Trade Organization, Geneva, Switzerland.

Fitzpatrick, T. M., & Kenison, J. (1999). The impact of corruption on foreign direct investment: Corruption perceptions index and rates of foreign investment, Unpublished paper submitted to Transparency International, Berlin, Germany, August 8.

Furubotn, E., & Richter, R. (1998). *Institutions and economic theory: The contribution of the new institutional economics*. Ann Arbor: University of Michigan Press.

Gastanaga, V., Nugent, J. B., & Pashamova, B. (1998). Host county reforms and FDI inflows: How much difference do they make? *World Development, 26*, 1299–1314.

Gupta, S. (1998). *Does corruption impact income inequity and poverty?*, Working Paper 76–98, International Monetary Fund, Washington D.C.

Habib, M., & Zurawicki, P. G. (2002). Corruption and foreign direct investment. *Journal of International Business Studies, 33*(2), 291–307.

Henisz, W. J. (2000). The institutional environment for multinational investment. *Journal of Law, Economics and Organization, 16*, 334–364.

Henisz, W. J., & Zelner, B. A. (2001). The institutional environment for telecommunications investment. *Journal of Economics and Management Strategy, 10*(1), 123–147.

Hines, J. R. Jr. (1995). *Forbidden payments: Foreign bribery and American business after 1997*. NBER Working Paper 5266.

Huntington, S. (1968). *Political order in changing societies*. New Haven: Yale University Press.

Leff, N. (1964). Economic development through bureaucratic corruption. *American Behavioral Scientist, 8*(3), 8–14.

Loree, D. W., & Guisinger, S. (1995). Policy and non-policy determinants of US equity foreign direct investment. *Journal of International Business Studies, 26*, 281–299.

Mauro, P. (1995). Corruption and Growth. *Quarterly Journal of Economics, 110*(3), 681–713.

McCubbins, M. D., Noll, R. G., & Weingast, B. R. (1989). Structure and process, politics and policy: Administrative arrangements and the political control of agencies. *Virginia Law Review, 75*, 431–482.

Milesi-Ferretti, G. M., Perotti, R., & Rostagno, M. (2001). *Electoral rules and public spending*. Centre for Economic Policy & Research Discussion Paper 2742, The London School of Economics.

Mudambi, R., Navarra, P., & Sobbrio, G. (2001). Constitutional issues in modern democracies. In: R. Mudambi, P. Navarra, & G. Sobbrio, (Eds), *Rules and reason: Perspectives in constitutional political economy*. New York: Cambridge University Press.

Mudambi, R., & Navarra, P. (2003). Political tradition, political risk and foreign direct investment in Italy. *Management International Review, 43*(3), 247–265.

North, D. C. (1990). *Institutions, institutional change and economic performance*. New York: Cambridge University Press.

Oliver, C. (1991). Strategic responses to institutional processes. *Academy of Management Review, 16*(1), 145–179.

Peltzman, S. (1976). Toward a more general theory of regulation. *Journal of Law and Economics*, 19, 211–240.

Persson, T., & Tabellini, G. (2003). *The economic effect of constitutions*. Cambridge, MA: The MIT Press.

Pigou, A.C. (1947). *A study in public finance*. (3rd ed.), London: Macmillan.

Pope, J. (2000). Transparency International source book 2000, http://www.transparency.org/sourcebook/01.html

Ramamurti, R. (2000). A multilevel model of privatization in emerging economics. *Academy of Management Review*, *25*(3), 525–550.

Ramamurti, R. (2003). Can governments make credible promises? Insights from infrastructure projects in emerging economies. *Journal of International Management*, *9*(3), 253–249.

Robertson, C. J., & Watson, A. (2004). Corruption and change: The impact of foreign direct investment. *Strategic Management Journal*, *25*(4), 385–396.

Rose-Ackermam, S. (1988). Bribery. In: J. Eatwell, M. Milgate, & P. Newman, (Eds), *The new Palgrave dictionary of economic thought*. London: Macmillan.

Rose-Ackermam, S. (1999). *Corruption and government: Causes, consequences and reform*. New York: Cambridge University Press.

Shleifer, A., & Vishny, R. (1999). *The grabbing hand*. Cambridge, MA: Harvard University Press.

Stigler, G. (1971). The theory of economic regulation. *The Bell Journal of Economics*, *12*, 3–21.

Transparency International. (2000). Transparency International source book 2000, http://www.trans-parency.org/sourcebook/01.html

Tullock, G. (1967). The welfare costs of tariffs, monopolies and theft. *Western Economic Journal*, *5*, 224–232.

Vernon, R. (1971). *Sovereignty at bay: The multinational spread of US enterprises*. New York: Basic Books.

Wei, S. J. (2000). How taxing is corruption on international investors? *Review of Economics and Statistics*, *82*(1), 1–11.

Wheeler, M., & Mody, A. (1992). International investment location decisions: The case of U.S. firms. *Journal of International Economics*, *33*, 57–76.

Zelner, B. A., & Henisz, W. J. (2000). *Political institutions, political competition and infrastructure investment in electric utility industry*. Reginald H. Jones Center for Management Policy, Strategy and Organization Working Paper.

Data Appendix

European Economies

Countries in the data set: Albania, Austria, Belarus, Belgium, Bulgaria, Croatia, Cyprus, Czech Republic, Denmark, Estonia, Finland, France, Georgia, Germany, Greece, Hungary, Iceland, Ireland, Israel, Italy, Kazakhstan, Latvia, Lithuania, Luxembourg, Macedonia, Malta, Moldova, The Netherlands, Norway, Poland, Portugal, Romania, Russia, Slovakia, Slovenia, Spain, Sweden, Switzerland, Turkey, Ukraine, United Kingdom, Uzbekistan.

Variable	Definition	Source
	Endogenous Variables	
FDI	Foreign direct investment inflows (US$ m) Panel 1: 1997–1999; Panel 2: 2000–2002	World Investment Report, UNCTAD
Japanese entries	Number of Japanese FDI entries (Number) Panel 1: 1997–1999; Panel 2: 2000–2002	Delios database
	Exogenous Variables	
GDP	Real Gross Domestic Product (US$ billion) Panel 1: 1996; Panel 2: 2001	World Development Report, World Bank
Per capita GDP	Real GDP per capita (US$ '000) Panel 1: 1996; Panel 2: 2001	World Development Report, World Bank
EU member	1, if EU member; 0 otherwise	EU website
EU new member	1, if new EU member as of May, 2004; 0 otherwise	EU website
Government effectiveness	Composite measure, between −2.5 and +2.5, measuring the quality of government services and the policy environment Panel 1: 1996–1997; Panel 2: 2000–2001	The World Bank Institute, Global Governance Dept.*
Control of corruption	Composite measure, between −2.5 and +2.5, measuring the extent of corruption; higher values indicate better control of corruption Panel 1: 1996–1997; Panel 2: 2000–2001	The World Bank Institute, Global Governance Dept.*
English fluency	1, if country's English fluent population >80 percent; 0 otherwise	Human Development Report, UNDP
R&D expenditure (% of GDP)	R&D investment expenditures as a percentage of GDP, average Panel 1: 1992–1996; Panel 2: 1996–2000	Human Development Report, UNDP

* Kaufmann, Daniel, Aart Kraay and Pablo Zoido-Lobaton (2002). *Governance matters II: Updated indicators for 2000–2001*. World Bank Policy Research Department Working Paper. The indicators are composites of 250 individual measures, taken from 25 different sources, produced by 18 different organizations. Full details of the construction of these indices is provided in Appendices A and B of Kaufmann et al. (2002).

Author Index

Subject Index

Printed and bound by CPI Group (UK) Ltd, Croydon, CR0 4YY

16/09/2026

14963399-0006